Black

Black Hunger

Soul Food and America

DORIS WITT

University of Minnesota Press
Minneapolis • London

Excerpts from the prologue, chapter 2, and the epilogue originally appeared in
"In Search for Our Mothers' Cookbooks: Gathering African-American Culinary Traditions,"
in *Iris: A Journal about Women* 26 (Fall–Winter 1991): 22–27.

An earlier version of chapter 3 originally appeared as "Soul Food: Where the Chitterlings
Hit the (Primal) Pan," in *Eating Culture*, ed. Ron Scapp and Brian Seitz (Albany:
State University of New York Press, 1998), 258–87. Reprinted by permission.

Quotations from Arthur Schomburg's typescript proposal for a history of African American
cooking are reprinted in chapter 6 courtesy of the Arthur A. Schomburg Papers, Manuscripts,
Archives, and Rare Books Division, Schomburg Center for Research in Black Culture,
The New York Public Library, Astor, Lenox, and Tilden Foundation.

An earlier version of chapter 7 originally appeared as "What (N)ever Happened to Aunt Jemima:
Eating Disorders, Fetal Rights, and Black Female Appetite in Contemporary American Culture,"
in *Discourse: Journal for Theoretical Studies in Media and Culture* (Winter 1994–95): 98–122.

Published by the University of Minnesota Press
111 Third Avenue South, Suite 290
Minneapolis, MN 55401-2520
http://www.upress.umn.edu

Library of Congress Cataloging-in-Publication Data

Witt, Doris.
Black hunger : soul food and America / Doris Witt. —
1st University of Minnesota Press ed.
p.   cm.
Originally published: New York : Oxford University Press,
1999, in series: Race and American culture.
Includes bibliographical references and index.
ISBN 0-8166-4551-5 (pbk. : alk. paper)
1. African American women—Race identity.   2. African American
women—Ethnic identity.   3. African American women—Social conditions.
4. Food—Social aspects—United States—History—20th century.
5. Racism—United States—History—20th century. I. Title.
E185.86.W585 2004
305.896'073—dc22
2004012751

Printed in the United States of America on acid-free paper

The University of Minnesota is an equal-opportunity educator and employer.

12   11   10   09   08   07   06   05   04   10   9   8   7   6   5   4   3   2   1

For
Faye Smith, Eldon Smith,
and Bluford Adams

Contents

Acknowledgments

This project began many years ago as a dissertation in the Department of English at the University of Virginia. Shortly after I presented the initial prospectus to my advisor, Deborah McDowell, she cautioned me that "any book is a record of its exclusions." I cite this comment for two reasons. First, Debbie's belief from the outset that the dissertation would one day become a book gave me the confidence I needed to turn it into one. Second, I am now in a position to realize that any book is also a record of its debts, and mine are myriad.

For financial support during the research and writing of the dissertation, I am especially grateful to both the Commonwealth Center for Literary and Cultural Change and the Carter G. Woodson Institute for African-American and African Studies, both located at the University of Virginia. The staff and fellows at each provided a rich intellectual environment in which to work. An additional grant from the University of Iowa's Old Gold Summer Fellowship program enabled me to pursue further research necessary to transform the dissertation into a book.

During the early stages, the staff of the interlibrary loan office of the University of Virginia's Alderman Library retrieved literally dozens of cookbooks for me. Since then, the staffs of the interlibrary loan and special collections divisions of the University of Iowa's Main Library have provided equally courteous, efficient, and invaluable assistance. The Szathmary cookbook collection here at Iowa is a particularly welcome resource. For helping make research trips productive, I am likewise grateful to the staffs of Radcliffe's Arthur and Elizabeth Schlesinger Library on the History of Women in America, the New York Public Library and its Schomburg Center for Research in Black Culture, the New York Historical Society, and the Library of Congress.

Former Colorado State University librarian David Lupton shared his bibliography of cookbooks by African Americans at a pivotal moment during the early years of my research; this project would have been more arduous and less ambitious were it not for his largess. Others whose assistance has taken more specific form include Linda Brown-Byrne of the State Historical Society of Missouri; Victoria D. Swadley of the River Bluffs Regional Library of St. Joseph, Missouri; and Elizabeth Bramm Dunn of Duke University's Hartman Center for Sales, Advertising and Marketing History. Murry DePillars, Jeff Donaldson, and Faith Ringgold kindly granted me permission to include reproductions of their art, and Freida

High W. Tesfagiorgis took the time to correspond with me about hers. My work since coming to Iowa has been made easier by a series of industrious graduate research assistants. Special thanks to Elyse Myers for her diligence in pursuing Aunt Jemima leads, to Bidisha Banerjee for her assistance in retrieving materials I needed to complete revisions, and to Lori Muntz for her work on the index.

I have also benefited tremendously from the intellectual inspiration and personal generosity of many other people over the past few years. Had I not had the immense good fortune to get to know and learn from Deborah McDowell while I was a graduate student at Virginia, the dissertation from which this book is derived would never have been envisioned, much less written. Over the years, the example of her own impeccable scholarship and her probing responses to a constantly mutating manuscript challenged me not to take the easy way out. After all this time, I am happy to have a chance to offer this acknowledgment as a token of my affection, appreciation, and admiration. Like Debbie, Eric Lott and Susan Fraiman signed on to the dissertation committee without foreseeing how many years would pass before I would present them with a dotted line on which to sign off, but none ever complained. Eric stimulated my interest in cultural studies and provided trenchant critiques of my arguments while always cheering me on. Susan's incisive responses gave me focus while pushing me to rein in my more extravagant claims. This acknowledgment only hints at my indebtedness to both. Ann Lane later agreed to bring her historical expertise to the dissertation committee for the final go-around of the defense. Her perceptive reading of the project gave me added momentum to launch into the book.

The editorial staff at Oxford has been exemplary throughout. Liz Maguire went out of her way to speed me a contract before she left, and Susan Chang's patience and cheerful guidance ever since have made the whole endeavor a delight. Cynthia Garver and freelancer Carolyn Hassett were meticulous during the production process. Two anonymous readers for Oxford provided exceedingly helpful responses to the manuscript, and I appreciate their care. I was able to test claims on great audiences at the University of Virginia, Georgetown, the University of Iowa, Notre Dame, the University of Pittsburgh, and SUNY-Buffalo, and at the 1996 MLA convention in Washington, D.C. Others whose support has taken the form of soliciting portions of the manuscript for publication or responding to individual chapters include Kaki Dowling, Brian Seitz, Ron Scapp, Barbara Green, Alice Gambrell, Janet Lyon, Tania Modleski, and Jennifer DeVere Brody. Their confidence in my work has meant more than they know.

When I first began graduate studies at the University of Virginia, faculty members Karen Chase and Michael Levenson supplied me with the wherewithal to carry on, while Charles Rowell introduced me to black American writers. Members of various feminist reading and writing groups at Virginia reshaped my perception of what it means to be a scholar. Thanks go out especially to co-Jane-ites Audrey Bilger, Barbara Black, and Marla Weitzman. Kim Chambers Connor made me the beneficiary of one of the most selfless gestures I will ever witness; for that she continues to have my deepest gratitude and respect. I still miss the camaraderie of an incredible group of women at Charlottesville's SARA. Consummate scholar Jerry Ward always found time to talk with me about my cookbook "discoveries" during our shared tenure at the Commonwealth Center, and later Bill Jackson of the Woodson Institute offered just the right words of wisdom at just the right time.

Colleagues and students here at the University of Iowa and elsewhere have since provided a wonderful range of research tips, professional counsel, intellectual exchange, and personal support. Among them are Margaret Bass, Linda Bolton, Corey Creekmur, Ashley Dawson, Huston Diehl, Kathleen Diffley, Barbara Eckstein, Mary Lou Emery, Mel Friedling, Cheryl Herr, Sheila Hood, Kevin Kopelson, Martti Lahti, Teresa Mangum, Allison McCracken, Dee Morris, Judith Pascoe, Geoff Pope, John Raeburn, Maryann Rasmussen, Claire Sponsler, Tom Simmons, and Max Thomas. While Brooks Landon was showing me how to join the electronic information age, Jessica Renaud, finder of old-fashioned lost letters, delivered my Aunt Jemima chapter from certain ruin. Fred Moten inflated my ego with praise for what I was up to, while offering periodic reminders that I "really should take a look at" various blues or jazz recordings that spoke to food. Were I possessed of some minute portion of his vast stores of knowledge about music, I assuredly would have obliged. Just as my motivation was waning near the end, fellow foodies Rafia Zafar and Psyche Williams reinvigorated me with good e-mail vibrations from across the miles.

The thought of being able finally to thank friends and family in print has served as the stuff of daydreams for quite some time now. Philip Jefferson, Jamie Farquhar Mueller, Craig Mueller, and Mike Bennett have been valued intellectual comrades and cherished confidants over the years. Now that the book is done, I particularly look forward to taking advantage of the famed B&B hospitality. My dear friend Candace Caraco has selflessly shared her boundless knowledge, energy, and courage from the moment we first crossed paths; the narrative of our assorted escapades would itself fill a book, as would the account of all the ways I'm beholden to her. My sister and her family—Lida, Tim, Franklin, and Kyle Norris—make every visit home a pleasure. Throughout, I have been inspired by the memory and writings of my maternal grandfather, John Wheeler Witt.

My parents, Faye and Eldon Smith, taught me to believe that I could accomplish anything I set my mind to and have done everything in their power to bring my aspirations within reach. If terrific parents are ever cloned, mine should top the list. Last and most, Bluford Adams has devoted untold hours to responding to this book's various verbal and written incarnations, while providing (frequently wicked) comic interludes along the way. His intellect, generosity, and patience keep me going; his determination to act on his convictions serves as a constant challenge to be better than I am.

Black Hunger

Prologue

"Integration has its drawbacks," I said.

"It do," confirmed Simple. "You heard, didn't you, about that old colored lady in Washington who went downtown one day to a fine white restaurant to test out integration? Well, this old lady decided to see for herself if what she heard was true about these restaurants, and if white folks were really ready for democracy. So down on Pennsylvania Avenue she went and picked herself out this nice-looking used-to-be-all-white restaurant to go in and order herself a meal."

"Good for her," I said.

"But dig what happened when she set down," said Simple. "No trouble, everybody nice. When the white waiter come up to her table to take her order, the colored old lady says, 'Son, I'll have collard greens and ham hocks, if you please.'

"'Sorry,' says the waiter. 'We don't have that on the menu.'

"'Then how about black-eyed peas and pig tails?' says the old lady.

"'That we don't have on the menu either,' says the white waiter.

"'Then chitterlings,' says the old lady, 'just plain chitterlings.'

"The waiter said, 'Madam, I never heard of chitterlings.'

"'Son,' said the old lady, 'ain't you got no kind of soul food at all?'

"'Soul food? What is that?' asked the puzzled waiter.

"'I knowed you-all wasn't ready for integration,' sighed the old lady sadly as she rose and headed toward the door. 'I just knowed you white folks wasn't ready.'"

Langston Hughes, "Soul Food," 1965

April 1997 witnessed the victory of rookie golf professional Eldrick "Tiger" Woods at the U.S. Masters tournament in Augusta, Georgia. Even before Woods had a chance to accept the green jacket bestowed yearly upon the otherwise fortunate winner, veteran player Fuzzy Zoeller offered his sport's heir apparent some unsolicited advice about how to supervise the menu for the championship dinner: "That little boy is driving well. . . . You pat him on the back . . . and tell him not to serve fried chicken next year. Got it? . . . Or collard greens or whatever the hell

3

they serve." It took a couple of days for word to spread, but by the time the resulting scandal died down, Zoeller had lost an endorsement contract with Kmart and
Woods was himself in some hot water for cracking "off-the-record" jokes to a GQ
reporter about black penis size and lesbian sexual preferences (Pierce 199–200).

As these events unfolded, I was in the midst of completing this book, which
works from the premise that the connection between and frequent conflation of
African American women and food has functioned as a central structuring dynamic of twentieth-century U.S. psychic, cultural, sociopolitical, and economic
life. Everywhere assumed if rarely analyzed, this dynamic articulates (and is articulated by) relationships within and across boundaries of sexuality, gender, race,
ethnicity, class, religion, region, and nationality.[1] Since the production of white
and black masculinities was, perhaps paradoxically, already quite central to my
work on this topic, I followed with some interest the barrage of editorials seeking
to make sense of the latest example of ritual self-sacrifice by a white male sports
figure caught with fly closed but tongue wagging. Pretty much everyone understood why Zoeller's use of "boy" was racist, notwithstanding Woods's relative
youth. And, intuitively, we knew that the remarks about fried chicken and collard
greens were offensive too. We just could not quite agree on why. Some commentators—namely whites with southern roots—were inclined to point out that they
themselves certainly liked fried chicken and collard greens. In fact, their own
grandmothers had served them. Others, taking a cue from Woods himself, dwelled
on the young golf champion's multiethnic heritage. "He's only a quarter black—
and a quarter Thai, quarter Chinese, an eighth white and an eighth American Indian," explained a columnist in my local newspaper (C. Baldwin).

Albeit clichéd by now, the most famous dictum of French gastronome Jean Anthelme Brillat-Savarin still goes a long way toward explaining the widespread perception that Zoeller's remarks constituted a racist insult. "Tell me what you eat,
and I shall tell you what you are," Brillat-Savarin had memorably boasted (3).
Zoeller dispensed with his precursor's pretense of dialogism, but he surely had a
comparable aim in mind. Woods had the temerity to reign supreme at a sport
thought to be innately "white"—rewarding, as it does, slowness, deliberation, and
an affinity for polyester plaid. The situation demanded some form of redress, which
Zoeller took it upon himself to provide. Smart enough not to acknowledge directly
his apprehension that Woods's victory marked a significant incursion against the
faltering forces of white racial supremacy, Zoeller had recourse to chicken and
greens. The young champion's appetite would betray him in the end; at the dinner table the truth of his racial identity would inexorably come out. The ensuing
culinary panic might well have been exacerbated, moreover, by subliminal public
awareness of the even more symbolically charged foods that Zoeller had managed
to restrain himself from conjuring up: "just plain chitterlings," perhaps; watermelon, without a doubt.

To understand more fully what was at stake, though, we also need to attend to
the way that the popular press had been marketing Woods: not only as a symbol
of black/white racial progress, but also as the exception which proves the orthodox
wisdom that the residual race "problem" in the United States stems from a lack of
patriarchal presence in black America. The former endeavor was complicated by

the legacy of Nguyen Phong, the South Vietnamese soldier with whom Woods's father fought in Vietnam and after whom he nicknamed his son. "Tiger" thus encodes the potential for transnational solidarity among peoples of color that the U.S. national narrative of racial integration attempts mightily to repress.[2] At the same time, in an inversion of the usual scenario according to which black children are said to be tainted by their upbringing in "female-headed" households, the public was also treated to a barrage of articles on and photographs of the dynamic Woods duo of father and son. Only in passing was one likely to encounter references to the young golf star's Thai mother, Kultida, whom his father had also met while in Vietnam; occasionally reporters would allude to Earl's pre-Tida life as well, to the black wife and children he had earlier left behind. The implied moral of these stories, one rather suspects, is that black men, like their more recently dethroned angry white counterparts, can best assert their paternal authority by marrying women who know their places, women presumed culturally conditioned to make themselves invisible on demand. Putatively "submissive" Asian women fit the bill; "assertive" black women (and their white feminist imitators) most certainly do not.[3]

Zoeller's chicken-and-greens comment struck me as an aptly counterintuitive place with which to begin precisely because of this foundational elision of African American women—specifically of Earl Woods's first wife Barbara Hart—from the contextualizing story. What the subsequent hand-wringing clearly helped articulate was our collective recognition of just how precariously Tiger Woods is positioned within the prevailing binary racial logic of U.S. culture, with its fixation on the black "matriarchal" family's dysfunctional romance. In fact, after Woods described himself as "Cablinasian" during a post-Masters appearance on *The Oprah Winfrey Show*, he became fodder for a contemporaneous debate over whether the proposed addition of a "multiracial" category to U.S. Census Bureau forms would weaken institutionalized black political power.[4] Woods's explanation for avoiding the label "African American"—that he wishes to affirm his maternal as well as paternal heritage—was rendered ironic by his multimillion-dollar sponsorship deal with the Nike corporation, which is notorious for exploiting the labor of Asian women. Yet the explanation also offers an illuminating perspective on Fuzzy Zoeller's disdainful allusion to "whatever the hell they serve." Presumably the intended referent of "they" was African Americans, whose race Woods has been understood to represent. But my conjecture is that Zoeller's comment (and much of the fervored exegesis that it generated) betrayed nostalgic longing specifically for a black woman in the Woods family kitchen, a woman whose presence would have affirmed the continued relevance of our inherited conventions for ascertaining racial identity. The lingering question, after all, was "whatever the hell" would a Thai-Chinese-black-white-Amerindian U.S. Masters champion "serve"?

By referring to the connection between African American women and food as a central structuring dynamic of twentieth-century U.S. life, then, I do not aim to suggest that this book is strictly about either black women or food. It is, rather, about why the connection matters. In the chapters that follow I demonstrate how the linkage has operated, with politically mixed results, across a range of disparate domains—from (corporate) America's long-standing Aunt Jemima fixation; to activist Dick Gregory's fruitarianism and fasting; to a South Carolina hospital's institution of a drug-testing program for lower-class pregnant patients, the majority of whom just happen to be black. Yet since this study is informed by my belief that work on food requires detailed attention to historical context, in developing my claims I have chosen the late 1960s through the early 1970s as the focal point of discussions that otherwise range broadly from around 1889, when the Aunt Jemima trademark was appropriated from a vaudeville cakewalk tune for an expanding immigrant-labor-driven economy, until the mid-1990s, a few years after Quaker Oats "buppified" the breakfast-food icon in a centennial update.

As the object of denunciation, disavowal, or nostalgia, depending on one's age and political proclivities, the decade from approximately 1965 to 1975 is well suited to my topic. By now the narrative of the era's social upheavals is quite familiar; indeed, references to "1968" often stand alone.[5] In the United States, this period witnessed not only the escalation of a neocolonialist foreign policy that eventually made possible the birth of Tiger Woods, but also the emergence of the counterculture, with its interconnected calls for peace, racial justice, free speech, environmentalism, and the dismantling of the military-industrial complex; the partial relaxation of racially restrictive immigration policies enacted earlier in this century; the proliferation of demands for equality on the part of women, lesbians, gays, and other traditionally disempowered groups; the origins of a conservative backlash against all of these developments, which is still under way; and the beginnings of the transformation of the domestic economy away from manufacturing and production and toward low-paying service-related jobs. Despite the passage of legal and political measures aimed at ameliorating increasing frustration over discrimination against African Americans, the 1960s also marked the subordination of the integrationist Civil Rights movement to the overtly nationalist rhetoric of Black Power.[6]

This last development particularly interests me since it went hand in hand with the most sustained efforts by African Americans to critique and redeploy the racist iconography of the Aunt Jemima trademark. Even more important, the rise of Black Power also contributed to the celebration of foods previously stigmatized because of their association with the slave diet—fried chicken and collard greens certainly among them. "Soul food," as it came to be known, clearly exemplifies the cultural logic of black middle-class expansion after World War II. Under attack as assimilationists, many members of the black bourgeoisie were eager to assert their racial authenticity. But one of my aims throughout much of the book is to complicate this materialist narrative by exploring how the valorization of a primarily black (grand)mother-daughter practice, soul food cooking, was related to the concurrent vilification of African American women as castrating matriarchs. To this end, I locate the rise of soul food more specifically in the context of Black Power developments in women's reproductive and employment practices. Preexisting concerns regarding the birth control pill and racial genocide were intensified by, among other factors, the inclusion of "sex" as a protected category under the Civil Rights Act of 1964; the publication of the Moynihan Report and Lennart Nilsson's *Life* magazine photographs of the "Drama of Life before Birth" in 1965; and, in 1973, the Supreme Court decision granting women limited legal access to abortion. In this respect, I am arguing that the connection between black women and food, which culminated in the rise of "soul" during the late 1960s, underwrites on-going debates about the substance and boundaries of "American" personhood.

It will come as no surprise to observers of the contemporary cultural scene that this book began to take on its present configurations during the early 1990s. Not only was U.S. popular culture being inundated with narratives of beset black man-hood and nostalgia for the (seeming) solidarity of Black Power, but soul food itself was undergoing a revival. Manifestations of the latter trend included a line of canned soul food products marketed by famed Harlem chef Sylvia Woods; a chain of "chitlin drive-throughs" based in Atlanta; and a proliferation of upscale vege-tarian soul cafes in New York City, Washington, D.C., and other urban areas.[7] My attempt to rethink the 1960s and early 1970s from the perspective of the palate is primarily intended, however, as neither a vindication nor an outright dismissal of what were, at the time, prevailing discourses and practices of black nationalism—as exemplified by Elijah Muhammad's Nation of Islam, Amiri Baraka's Black Arts Repertory Theatre/School, and Ron Karenga's US Organization. Certainly I do hope to understand better the logic of conspicuous misogyny, homophobia, and anti-Judaism for many black nationalist ideologies of both then and now. But I am also quite interested in opening up alternate spaces for inquiry into the period that gave rise to the practice of what became known as "identity politics."

Early optimism over the political efficacy of speaking from and organizing around one's own experience of oppression has largely dissipated despite the con-tinuing visibility of debates over multiculturalism in the academy. Identity politics undoubtedly is problematic in its complicity with late-capitalist ideologies of bour-geois individualism, but in my opinion its proponents have nevertheless been quite right to reject narratives of domination and resistance that ignore funda-mental structures of oppression. Consequently, it seems useful at this juncture to revisit the sociocultural milieu which, by calling into question the values of white supremacist, heterosexist, capitalist imperialism, gave rise to a profusion of schol-arship on previously marginalized subjects, scholarship that has in turn provided the foundation for my own inquiries. Before offering a more detailed overview of my argument and further delineating my admittedly eclectic approach to work on food, then, I want first to explain how this book evolved out of what began as a thematic study of cooking and eating in the works of several African American women novelists.

In Search . . .

I became interested in African American culinary history while reading fiction, poetry, and essays by contemporary black women writers. Food, it seemed to me, was central to much of their work. Several characters in Toni Morrison's fiction labor as domestics or cooks: Pauline in *The Bluest Eye*, Ondine in *Tar Baby*, Sethe in *Beloved*. Key scenes in Morrison's fiction, moreover, revolve around food. When Pecola accidently splatters the fresh-baked blueberry cobbler, her mother Pauline comforts not Pecola but the child of her employer (*Bluest* 108–9). The protagonist of *Song of Solomon* suffers instead from too much maternal devotion, slowly realizing that he received his nickname because "my mother nursed me when I was old enough to talk, stand up, and wear knickers, and somebody saw it and laughed and—and that is why they call me Milkman" (78). Mother-child food relationships take on a quite different configuration in Dori Sanders's novel *Clover*. Precocious young narrator Clover Hill is suspicious of her white stepmother Sara Kate because the latter lacks familiarity with southern black foods, and her cooking, furthermore, is terrible: "The grits slid through my fork like water soup. If she cooks me grits again I will die, just plain die. 'Sara Kate,' I blurted out, 'you sure can't cook grits'" (64).

Other authors foreground the appetites of adult black women as consumers (rather than as providers or preparers) of food. In Alice Walker's *Meridian*, eponymous heroine Meridian Hill displays symptoms of anorexia that might be interpreted using recent feminist scholarship, such as Caroline Bynum's study of fasting among medieval women saints and Becky Thompson's work on "eating problems" among contemporary women of color. Gloria Naylor's *Linden Hills* explores similar themes. Aspiring buppie and late-night binge-eater Roxanne Tilson has "this real funny idea about a diet; you don't get fat if no one sees you eating" (152). Perhaps most memorable of all, Honey, the aptly named narrator of Carolyn Ferrell's "Eating Confessions," is an overweight woman who frequently socializes with her friend Rose at the "Monday Night Determination Diet Meeting" (453). There the latter admits to feeling remorse about her claims to be throwing a party when really she is "planning on eating that sweet potato pie by [her]self" (453). Their food-structured relationship is disrupted, however, when Rose meets a man and loses weight, and Honey uses food in an unsuccessful attempt to lure Rose away from him.

In *Bailey's Cafe*, Naylor appropriates for heterosexuality these incipiently lesbian inscriptions of the southern black diet, allowing the lower-class character Jesse Bell to describe how she seduced her upper-class husband with "slave food" such as cornbread and oxtail soup (124). "Husband," the otherwise unadorned Jesse Bell recounts having said, while gesturing toward a dessert item which she has wedged strategically between her legs, "this is sweet-potato pie" (124). "Didn't have a bit of trouble after that," she concludes (124). Similarly, in her poetry series *From Okra to Greens*, Ntozake Shange creates a love story in which the two main characters are the titular foods. The whimsical subtitles range from "okra's intellect addresses greens' mind" to "the night he went out with that hussy in red, rutabaga" (n. pag.). Alice Walker also transmutes characters into food in her short story "Olive Oil." Orelia and John consummate their love while cooking "a nice ratatouille, chopping and slicing eggplant, zucchini, and garlic" (35). As the story climaxes, they begin "oiling each other" and laugh "to think how like ratatouille and sautéed mushrooms they both tasted" (78).

For a variety of reasons, then, food struck me as pivotal in the work of many contemporary African American women writers. And, of course, the more I thought about it, the more I realized that food is simply central to African American literature. Folktales and slave narratives are often obsessively focused on this topic, as one would expect given the degredations of chattel slavery. Here I have in mind a tradition stretching from the exploits of Brer Fox and Brer Rabbit to the efforts of Charles Chesnutt's Uncle Julius to keep northern intruders John and Annie out of his grapevines, and from Frederick Douglass's memory of Colonel Lloyd's "excellent fruit," which "was quite a temptation to the hungry swarms of boys" (264), to Annie Louise Burton's recollection of having "nothing to eat" as a child (100), yet watching her newly freed mother share her family's "mouthful of bread" and "pea soup" with a white widow and her children (102). Long after the demise of legal slavery, furthermore, food has recurred as both a material and a metaphoric obsession throughout the emergent canon of African American literature. Examples range from Paul Laurence Dunbar's dialect poetry ("When De Co'n Pone's Hot") to Richard Wright's recollection of trying to emulate Gertrude Stein ("I would write: 'The soft melting hunk of butter trickled in gold down the stringy grooves of the split yam'" [267]); from Pauline Hopkins's portrayal of the delights of the fair dinner ("the knowing ones could trace the odor of a rare and tempting dainty—the opossum!" [212]) to Audre Lorde's memory of her father (who would give her "a morsel of meat or a taste of rice and gravy from his plate" [Zami 67]); from Zora Neale Hurston's description of Pheoby (who "switches a mean fanny round in a kitchen" [Their 15]) to Rita Dove's comically macabre "Why I Turned Vegetarian" ("Mister Minister, I found / the tip of your thumb / bit off a way back: / a neat cap").[8] And, were that not enough, where would black song lyrics—especially the blues—be without food?

Yet, despite the surfeit of source material, discussion of black culinary practices was largely absent from African American literary studies, including what were, at the time, two of the most highly acclaimed theories about African American literature: Houston Baker Jr.'s *Blues, Ideology, and Afro-American Literature* (1984) and Henry Louis Gates Jr.'s *The Signifying Monkey* (1988). Focused in what Gates viewed as a complementary fashion on blues and signifying (x), their works nonetheless appealed to me as offering possible paradigms for my own black-feminist-inspired approach to food—Baker's especially, because it develops a provocative materialist reading of African American literature based on black musical performance. Reversing, or dialectically transcending, his earlier belief that symbolic anthropology "offered avenues to the comprehension of Afro-American expressive culture in its plenitude" (1), Baker turns his attention in *Blues* to "the living and laboring conditions" of the masses of black people who created the vernacular "matrix" of the blues (3).

Of special interest to me was his inventive effort to locate the famous Trueblood episode from Ralph Ellison's *Invisible Man* in the context of the legacy of blackface minstrelsy:

As Ellison suggests, Afro-Americans, in their guise as entertainers, season the possum of black expressive culture to the taste of their Anglo-American audience, maintaining, in the process, their integrity as performers. But in private sessions—in the closed circle of their own community (such as that represented by store-porch inhabitants in Hurston's novel)—everybody knows that the punch line to the recipe and the proper response to the performer's constrictive dilemma is, "Damn the possum! That sho' is some good gravy!" It is just possible that the "gravy" is the inimitable technique of the Afro-American artist, a technique (derived from lived blues experience) as capable of "playing possum" as of presenting one. (194–95)

While I was fascinated by Baker's analysis, my own reading of African American literature finally led me to conclude that if this "gravy" were understood only as "inimitable technique," then the "lived blues experience" of hunger would, quite the contrary, surely derive from its lack. It seemed "just possible," in other words, that a materialist perspective ought to construe the "gravy" quite literally as gravy, food derived from the unremunerated labor of an African American *culinary* artist, usually (though by no means always) a woman. In turn, her lived blues experience would perhaps derive from the fact that she was at work in the kitchen with Hurston's Janie making gravy to cover the absence of meat while the men were out with Jody on the porch singing blues, playing possum—and awaiting dinner (*Their* 81 ff.). As Naylor says of one enterprising character in *Linden Hills*, if her husband "brought home air, Ruth would make gravy, pour it over it, and tell him not to bring so much the next time" (32).[9]

Accordingly, I began to speculate about how one might use food to develop a socialist-feminist theory for reading literature by African American women—both to supplement and to disrupt the closed dyad of blues and signifying propagated by Baker and Gates. Writing earlier in the 1980s, Angela Davis had opened her essay "The Approaching Obsolescence of Housework" (1981) by situating "cooking" alongside "washing dishes, doing laundry, making beds, sweeping, shopping, etc." as exploitative "women's work" (222). "Invisible, repetitive, exhausting, unproductive, uncreative—these are the adjectives which most perfectly capture the nature of housework," she wrote (222). Davis's call for the "abolition of housework as the private responsibility of individual women" still strikes me as valid (243). As a central component of both unpaid and paid domestic labor, food preparation is fundamental to the worldwide exploitation of women. Yet, though wanting to affirm this Marxian-derived perspective as an overriding framework for my inquiries, I was hesitant to label as simple "false consciousness" the (aesthetic) pleasure that housewives, servants, and others might understand themselves to derive from their labor in the kitchen. We need to be attuned, in other words, to the historical/cultural contexts and individual idiosyncrasies which render a standard materialist framework insufficient for thinking about the experiential dimension of food, cooking, and eating.[10]

In the process of trying to untangle these issues, I became increasingly fascinated by Ntozake Shange's contemporaneous *Sassafrass, Cypress & Indigo* (1982), a self-proclaimed "novel" that embeds recipes in the text as gifts of love handed down from mother to daughter. Indigo carries on Gullah traditions in Charleston, South Carolina; her older sisters, Sassafrass and Cypress, have moved to California and New York City, embracing Afrocentric and lesbian-separatist lifestyles, respectively. Meanwhile, their mother, Hilde Effania, maintains contact with her "wayward" daughters via letters. One that she sends to Sassafrass, for example, includes the following note: "Here is a recipe I want you to have, so there won't be too much heathen in your Christmas this year (I found a wonderful way to make a dressing for turkey with hot sausage, cornbread, and peanut butter that's supposed to be African but I know you don't eat pork)" (132). The recipe is named "Mama's Kwanza Recipe (for Sassafrass): Duck with Mixed Oyster Stuffing" (132). Through food, Hilde Effania tries to acknowledge Sassafrass's Afrocentric lifestyle while also reminding her of the traditions, such as eating pork at Christmas, which she is missing.

Shange's novel was published the same year as Alice Walker's much more widely acclaimed *The Color Purple*. Perhaps in part because of the attention paid to Walker's revision of the epistolary novel, Shange's formulation of what I like to term the "recipistolary" novel went relatively unheeded. Yet Shange, one might argue, has effected a more consequential appropriation of the genre of the novel than has Walker, for *Sassafrass, Cypress & Indigo* requires not simply to be read or spoken (or even viewed in a theater); it demands instead that we perform and consume it—that we cook and eat its recipes as an integral part of our experience of the work. Given the well-known history of black women's exploitation as domestic servants and given what I will describe in chapter 2 as the lesser known history of white appropriations of their recipes, the dual symbolic import of Shange's innovation should be evident. She takes on the role not of cook but of cookbook author, a role long denied to African Americans in a country where it was illegal for slaves to learn to read and write. By incorporating the performance of cooking into novelistic art, moreover, Shange insists that the forms of creative expression long attributed to African American women should be valued as highly as are the forms often reserved for whites and men. This, of course, was a central point of Alice Walker's germinal essay "In Search of Our Mothers' Gardens" (1974), which has long been an inspiration for my work.[11]

It took very little time before I shifted from trying to formulate a broader argument out of this notion of the "performative" novel to exploring cookbooks by African Americans. One catalyst for this inquiry was the publication in 1989 of an academic article analyzing two editions of *The Joy of Cooking* (1931, 1975) as literary texts. Susan Leonardi claimed that in the first edition of *The Joy of Cooking* "the establishment of a lively narrator with a circle of enthusiastic and helpful friends reproduces the social context of recipe sharing—a loose community of women that crosses the social barriers of class, race, and generation" (342). Working in African American feminist theory, I quickly recognized that Leonardi's vision was a lingering figment of the white feminist imagination. For those who have historically had few employment options besides underpaid, unorganized labor as domestic servants for white people, the "social context of recipe sharing" was, I assumed, not a "loose community" but more nearly a battleground where the social barriers of class, race, and generation (as well as ethnicity, sexuality, religion, and nationality) were not eradicated but more nearly constructed, maintained, and fortified.[12]

Consider, as an alternative perspective, a double anecdote recounted by African American actress-turned-cookbook-author Vertamae Smart Grosvenor in the 1986 edition of her underground classic *Vibration Cooking* (1970):

One day I was in line at the greengrocer. It was the morning of a very bad day for me. One child had a fever and the other had chills. I was on deadline, the typewriter was broken, the rent was overdue, it was raining, and the roof was leaking—you know the kind of day I'm talking about. On days like that I always make a mess of greens. Besides the curative properties, the ritual of fixing the greens—handling each green personally, folding leaf unto leaf, cutting them up, etc.—cools me out!

So there I was, in line, holding my collard greens. A white woman asked me, "How do you people fix those?"

Now, more than likely if I had not been in such a Purple Funk, I might have let the "you people" go by, but this particular morning I didn't. "Salad," I said.

"Salad?"

"Yeah, salad."

"But I was sure You People cooked them."

"No, never. . . . Salad."

"What kind of dressing?"

"Italian!"

A black woman overheard the exchange. She looked at me as if I had discredited the race. I have often wondered if that white woman went home and actually made a collard green salad with Italian dressing.

According to my mother, I did discredit the race when I cooked collard greens on TV. It was on the "Not For Women Only" Ethnic Week cooking series. I was the "soul food" chef, and I was in a dilemma.

I wanted to use the opportunity to prove that Afro-American cookery was more than chitlins and pigs' feet, and at the same time I wanted to acknowledge the traditional dishes.

I decided to go with a traditional "Soul Food" menu, but I'd prepare the dishes in a nontraditional way. For example, the collard greens: Instead of ham hocks, I would use a seasoning of peanut oil and bouillon cubes.

I figured that would take care of the Muslims and the vegetarians. I didn't even think about my mother. I had no idea of the embarrassment she would suffer.

It seems that some of her church sisters saw the show.

"Mrs. Smart's daughter was on coast-to-coast TV and cooked naked greens!"

"What did you say?"

"Umhuhm, yes she did!"

"Where you think she picked that up?"

"Maybe she was raised like that."

"Umhuh, uumm, umm-umm!"

"It's a shame before living justice, 'naked' greens."

"My, my, my . . ." (xvi–xvii)

Grosvenor develops a brilliantly nuanced analysis of the social "barriers" that come into play in the economy of recipe exchange, barriers that Leonardi had claimed are transcended. In the first anecdote, Grosvenor's desire to withhold the recipe from the intrusive white woman must contend with the pressure exerted by the neighboring black woman not to harm the reputation of African American cooking. The second anecdote implicitly critiques the racist tokenism of the "Not For Women Only" Ethnic Week in categorizing Grosvenor as a "soul food" chef, and it, too, shows how generational and communal pressure can be brought to bear to maintain culinary traditions, even as other pressures (i.e., the perception that pork is unhealthful) are a catalyst for alterations.[13]

Arjun Appadurai has argued that "[c]ookbooks appear in literate civilizations where the display of class hierarchies is essential to their maintenance, and where cooking is seen as a communicable variety of expert knowledge" (4). Many black cookbook authors have indeed used the act of writing as a way of establishing their "professional" credentials—and of contesting white racism in the process. By the time *Vibration Cooking* was published, however, a prevailing theme of African American cookbooks was the insistence that black cooking is improvisational, that it cannot be codified in writing. Grosvenor herself participated in the development of this culinary precept, which has operated not only as a strategy of resistance to white appropriations of black culture, but also as a means for upwardly mobile African Americans to affirm their racial authenticity.[14]

In an unpublished typescript prospectus for a book on "Negro" culinary practices, probably dating from the mid-1920s (Childs 88, n. 3), noted bibliophile Arthur Schomburg had actually anticipated these predominantly post–World War II claims that black cooking resists textualization. One of the most important aspects of African American culinary history, he asserted, is its perpetuation as living knowledge rather than static artifact. As John Brown Childs has observed, for Schomburg

> the boundary established by the black culinary arts was not merely a border. Its demarcation of something autonomous in Afro-American life arose from its integrity as a system of knowledge, a system known only to black people. The enclosed nature of this knowledge had to do with the very means of its transmission. Recipes were part of the "unwritten Negro cookbook." This unwritten book was partly an oral tradition. But, more strictly speaking, it resembled an underground form of written communication, a *samisdat*-type of sharing of information from hand to hand. . . . This culinary system was highly fluid and so required a social intimacy that could not be expressed on the printed page. (80)

I discuss the ideology of culinary improvisation at greater length in parts II and III of this book, and so for now I will note only that reading Schomburg's exuberant and literally un-"disciplined" proposal in the academic context of the early 1990s helped inspire me to reconceptualize the direction that my own project was taking.

By the time Gates's *The Signifying Monkey* appeared, "literary" studies in the United States were already being challenged by what is now ubiquitously known as "cultural studies," an interdisciplinary undertaking which at this point both needs no explication and surely cannot be adequately defined.[15] As the influence of Birmingham Centre scholarship began to grow stateside among academics working on race and postcolonialism, I became increasingly skeptical of my earlier aspirations to formulate a paradigm for reading African American women's literature.[16] Such an endeavor would force me prematurely to delimit the types of texts on which my study would focus. Why exclude song lyrics, or stand-up comedy, or religious instruction manuals, or, for that matter, cookbooks? Expanding my purview would, I also hoped, prevent me from begging the very questions I most needed to be asking—for instance, about how the concept of culinary authenticity operates in the construction of racialized subjectivities. Though most commonly claimed by anthropology, food is fascinating precisely because it transcends so many boundaries, disciplinary and otherwise. So also, I decided, should this book—even at the risk of exposing the limitations of my formal training as a literary critic, and even though the altered focus did not come without a cost.

How to Do Things with Food

The book I finally wrote is divided into three parts. The first, which coincidentally treats the paired breakfast breads of pancakes and beaten biscuits, aims primarily (but not exclusively) to understand how the mammy cook has been invoked to help constitute "whiteness," "masculinity," and "heterosexuality" as normatively unmarked, interarticulated identities. To this end, both chapters in this section link their investments in the post–World War II era to the sweeping social, cultural, political, and technological changes that characterized the United States at the turn of the century. Chapter 1 looks at perhaps the most famous mammy cook of all, Aunt Jemima. Drawing on my research into the trademark's origins, as well as recent work on blackface minstrelsy, I explore how the diverse narratives used to legitimate and critique Aunt Jemima over the past century have enabled both white and nonwhite Americans to formulate identities in a multiethnic national landscape. In chapter 2 I turn to a contemporary variant on the plantation school writer, former *New York Times* food critic and Mississippi-born gourmet Craig Claiborne. As a leading white aficionado of both French continental cuisine and soul food, Claiborne provides a useful entrée to the culinary milieu of the 1960s and 1970s. As a gay male food writer working in what had been a presumptively heterosexual female domain, Claiborne is also well positioned to expose many of the fault lines along which the era's social movements were divided. This chapter explores how the postbellum psychosexual narratives used to construct black women as dominatrixes of the kitchen have been continually recuperated to obscure not only the roles of capitalism and patriarchy in mistress-servant relationships, but also the disavowal of interracial homoerotic desire through which (southern) white manhood has historically been articulated.

Claiborne's writing exemplifies many of the tactics through which the contributions of African Americans to U.S. culinary history have been erased or distorted since the Reconstruction. Part II examines debates among black men over attempts to remedy these exclusions through the valorization of soul food. During the 1960s soul food emerged as a privileged signifier of white radical chic and black bourgeois authenticity. Concurrently, numerous black activists, including Elijah Muhammad and Dick Gregory, attempted to discredit soul food as an "unclean" practice of racial genocide. In chapter 3 I link soul food's fetishization of "hog bowels" to contemporaneous practices of black intraracial "othering," including the widespread equation of black women with "slave" mothers. I also interpret soul's putative "indefinability" in conjunction with the gender inscriptions of prevailing ideologies of improvisation associated with black music. Chapters 4 and 5 extrapolate from this analysis by construing the dietary stipulations of Muhammad and Gregory—particularly their efforts to purify their bodies of "filth"—as a function not just of their lower-class origins, but also of their differing attitudes about the historically precarious status of black masculinity in U.S. society. One of my main concerns in these chapters is the fact that Muhammad and Gregory used similar dietary obsessions to underwrite divergent sociopolitical agendas: whereas the former explicitly promoted black separatism, black patriarchy, and black capitalism, the latter allied himself with many contemporaneous movements for progressive political change.

Soul food might thus be said to contain, within its overt inscriptions of class and race, covert inscriptions of sexuality and gender. Part III considers the ramifications of this inscription for African American women who have participated, both intentionally and unwillingly, in the discourses of soul. I focus in chapter 6 on Vertamae Grosvenor. The "Geechee" cookbook author attempted to recontextualize the foods most commonly associated with slavery in order to negotiate a position between black nationalist and white feminist discourses. My discussion of her resulting formulation of a protodiasporic model of selfhood enables me to interrogate the ramifications for feminist scholarship on African American women of recent interest in black transatlantic cultural exchange. Chapter 7 reframes these issues by exploring soul's inscription of the dietary practices of African American women as either natural or pathological. I cross-map the construction of black female appetite in discourses of eating disorders and fetal harm and then bring to bear upon this discussion Black Power's common representation of African American women's wombs as a site of black male imprisonment. This analysis allows me to demonstrate how the connection between black women and food has been implicated in contemporary fascination with white fetal "innocence" and black male "criminality" alike.

In developing this project, I have remained aware of Arthur Schomburg's belief that textual analysis has its limitations for work on food, as it does for the study of many other cultural products, such as music. Something inevitably gets lost in "translation." Similarly, my lived experience as a white woman has profoundly shaped my interpretive point of view, opening up some ways of knowing but foreclosing others, doubtless to the detriment of aspects of this book. Yet, though I am not overly immersed in continental philosophy, Jacques Derrida's cautionary critique of Western culture's privileging of orality—his interrogation of the desire for "presence," in short—has informed my belief that writing a book that understands food to be always already embedded in texts was a thing worth trying to do.[17] My focus here, in fact, is on discourses about food and identity that were very much intended for public consumption—with all the concerns about co-optation and inauthenticity that an orientation toward popular culture inevitably entails. My aim is to understand how and why discussions of putatively private practices such as cooking and eating have been mobilized for political ends.

Accordingly, I do not attempt to locate myself within the well-elaborated disciplinary matrix of anthropology, since to do so would be to offer a misleading representation of my primary intellectual influences and orientation.[18] But this study is informed by an engagement with the writings of Mary Douglas, especially her analysis of pollution rituals in *Purity and Danger* (1966).[19] My reading of Douglas led me, in turn, away from anthropology and toward Julia Kristeva, whose psychoanalytic reinterpretation of Douglas's claims has been pivotal for my thinking. I draw heavily on the concept of "abjection" as delineated by Kristeva in *Powers of Horror* (1980), as shown to be a normative operation of the bourgeois imagination by Peter Stallybrass and Allon White, as incisively critiqued and then (queerly) politicized by Judith Butler, as put in service of progressive philosophical inquiry by Iris Marion Young, and as brilliantly reconfigured for postcolonial theory by Anne McClintock.[20] A result of the inevitable failure of the processes of othering through which the distinction between self and not-self is inaugurated, abjection, in Kristeva's view, is the fleeting recognition that the threat (and temptation) of self-dissolution is harbored within.

McClintock's work is particularly valuable in that it explicates "the paradox of abjection as a formative aspect of modern industrial imperialism" (72). In the process of making this analysis, she draws helpful distinctions among abject objects, states, and zones; between agents of abjection and abjected groups; and between psychic and political processes of abjection (72–73).[21] These distinctions enable McClintock to move beyond Kristeva's political conservatism by putting psychoanalysis in service of a critique of the intertwined global forces of capitalism and imperialism. In fact, she makes a compelling argument for her belief that "the disciplinary cordon sanitaire between psychoanalysis and history is itself a product of abjection" (72). McClintock's work has helped me understand that one of my main goals all along, had I only realized it, was to formulate "a *situated psychoanalysis*—a culturally contextualized psychoanalysis that is simultaneously a psychoanalytically informed history" (72). Since food is fundamental not only to the global economy but also to Kristeva's initial theorization of abjection, it offers a particularly apt vehicle for exploring these mutual exclusions of psychoanalysis and Marxist political economy alike.

I had already been guided in this effort by Hortense Spillers and Deborah McDowell, both of whom have interrogated the value of psychoanalytic models for African American feminist theory. In her well-known 1987 essay "Mama's Baby, Papa's Maybe," Spillers explored the centrality of the myth of black matriarchy for U.S. cultural and sociopolitical life. She argued that African Americans cannot be construed within the traditional symbolics of gendered identity. The historical exclusion of African American men from the Law of the Father has led, she further claimed, to a hyperbolized fixation on black mothers. It was Spillers's theoretical innovations that initially encouraged me to explore the relationship between, on the one hand, representations of the black female body as a site of sustenance/pollution and, on the other, the disproportionate burden of social regulation historically borne by African American women.[22] McDowell's work, by contrast, helped me understand why claims that psychoanalysis is simply irrelevant to black culture can function as a strategy for delegitimating inquiry into intraracial power imbalances, particularly those inhering in black private life. In this respect, her 1989 essay "Reading Family Matters" has provided a valuable template for my thinking in its attention to how psychoanalytically inflected narratives of family were being deployed throughout the late 1970s and early 1980s in order to justify African American cultural and political conservatism. Commercially successful black women writers such as Ntozake Shange and Alice Walker were prime targets of the attacks.

Of course, by the time "Reading Family Matters" was published, we were already beginning to witness the mass-marketed return of the "endangered" black man to which I earlier alluded. The spate of "'hood" films which began with Spike Lee's Do the Right Thing (1989) remained strong during the early 1990s.[23] By the mid-1990s, the trade and academic publishing industry had also begun to focus attention on black manhood.[24] Much of this latter work has been indebted, in turn, to the evolution of gender and queer theory out of women's and lesbian/gay studies. It was only after I had drafted substantial portions of this argument that I realized how thoroughly my work participated in this trend, as well as in the more recent fascination with "whiteness."[25] Yet even as I have incorporated discussion of masculinity and whiteness alongside that of black women's self-representations, I am admittedly still wary of the ease with which one can slip from investigating hegemonic subject positions to perpetuating their continued dominance. As Robin D. G. Kelley has wryly observed of the rise of black masculinity studies, "while black feminists were the wedge that opened up discussions of diversity within black communities, they were eased on out real quick" (9). Hence my efforts to keep a variety of voices in dialogue in this book, to benefit from the insights of emergent fields of inquiry while keeping an eye on the ramifications of the way I am framing my questions.

Mass-culture artifacts such as Do the Right Thing obviously speak to the withdrawal of public and private funds from urban America throughout the 1980s. But as Spillers, McDowell, Paul Gilroy, Angela Davis ("Black"), Michael Awkward, Kendall Thomas, Phillip Brian Harper, Elizabeth Alexander ("We're"), and others have demonstrated, it is entirely problematic for conservative social, political, and economic policies that perpetuate far-ranging injustices around the world to be represented in narrowly nationalistic terms as a "crisis of black masculinity" (Gilroy, "It's" 313).[26] Chandra Mohanty has argued that "Western feminist scholarship cannot avoid the challenge of situating itself and examining its role in . . . a global economic and political framework" ("Under" 54). Her cautionary warning is clearly germane to work on U.S. black nationalisms as well. For this reason I, like many scholars of race during the 1990s, have been challenged by Paul Gilroy's efforts in The Black Atlantic (1993) to formulate an alternative vision of black culture as a syncretic process which emerged out of an enforced diaspora, but which has subsequently been elaborated via voluntary transatlantic interchange. What Gilroy offers, in short, is a model for progressive black internationalism.

Though this book remains focused on a U.S. context, I have set out to demonstrate that work on food can help us make sense of how we come to understand ourselves as individual and collective subjects, and therefore also how we come to ally ourselves with and against the prevailing social order. In keeping with my founding debts to African American feminist theory, moreover, I have tried never to lose sight of the agenda concisely articulated by the Combahee River Collective in 1977. "The most general statement of our politics at the present time," they famously write, "would be that we are actively committed to struggling against racial, sexual, heterosexual, and class oppression and see as our particular task the development of integrated analysis and practice based upon the fact that the major systems of oppression are interlocking" (13). The challenge I set for myself has been to think about food using just such a model—one which takes as a given the complexity of our articulation as human subjects and which affirms that progressive academic analysis should be motivated by a desire for social justice.

PART I

SERVANT PROBLEMS

ONE

"Look Ma, the Real Aunt Jemima!"
Consuming Identities under Capitalism

Filene's department store
near nineteen-fifty-three:
An Aunt Jemima floor
display. Red bandanna,

apron holding white rolls
of black fat fast against
the bubbling pancakes, bowls
and bowls of pale batter.

This is what Donna sees
across the "Cookwares" floor,
and hears "Donessa?" *Please,
this can not be my aunt.*

Father's long-gone sister,
nineteen-fifty-three. "Girl?"
Had they lost her, missed her?
This is not the question.

This must not be my aunt.
Jemima? Pays the rent.
Family mirrors haunt
their own reflections.

Ladders. Sisters. Nieces.
As soon a live Jemima
as a buck-eyed rhesus
monkey. Girl? Answer me.

Elizabeth Alexander, "Ladders," 1990

On 27 April 1989, the Chicago-based Quaker Oats Company announced plans to update its Aunt Jemima trademark for the 1990s. The two-page news release begins as follows:

> Aunt Jemima, one of America's oldest packaged food trademarks and a symbol of quality breakfast products for 100 years, will be given a new look this year. The facial appearance is unchanged. Noticeably different, however, is a new, stylish, grey-streaked hairdo, and her headband has been removed. Other changes include cosmetic touches such as a different style of collar and the addition of earrings.
>
> "We wanted to present Aunt Jemima in a more contemporary light, while preserving the important attributes of warmth, quality, good taste, heritage and reliability," said Barbara R. Allen, Vice President-Marketing for Quaker Oats Company's Convenience Foods Division, makers of Aunt Jemima products. "Based on the results of consumer research over a five-month period, we think the new design does that." ("Aunt Jemima Trademark" 1)

This preemptive strike was intended to fortify the corporate line on the trademark's symbolic meaning several weeks before the altered image was itself actually "released" into the U.S. marketplace—or into an ideological battleground, to be more precise, where efforts to "preserve" and valorize the iconography of slavery are fiercely contested. Given the context, the public relations staff at Quaker Oats was obviously not about to comment on why the company "wanted" to update the trademark image in the first place.

The *Chicago Tribune* obliged them by publishing the story for mass consumption in its Business section the following day in an article headlined "At Age 100, a New Aunt Jemima." Reporter Janet Key incorporated substantial portions of the Quaker Oats news release, including the prepackaged quotation by Barbara Allen, without acknowledging her written source. Key's article transmitted precisely the propaganda Quaker Oats had provided, though she did at least contact one of the two persons the release listed as having further information. In response to her inquiries as to why "the name won't be changed," Key was informed by Quaker Oats spokesperson Ron Bottrell: "That kind of familiarity and recognition is an invaluable asset" (6).

What are we to make of the longevity of the Aunt Jemima trademark and of the ambiguity of the symbolic attributes that Quaker Oats wants to preserve by keeping it? After all, "warmth" is surely a characteristic of Aunt Jemima as cook; "good taste," of Aunt Jemima food products. "Quality," "heritage," and "reliability" could refer to either. One might infer from this symbolic slippage that the trademark is intended to signify both cook and food. Like her precursors, the big-breasted mammies of post–Civil War lore, Aunt Jemima *prepares* and *is* food; she/it is the ever-smiling source of sustenance for infants and adults. Yet one obstacle faced by Quaker Oats in trying to maintain this dual symbolic meaning while presenting the visual image of Aunt Jemima in a more "contemporary" light is that the new picture could be said to represent not so much a servant-producer as a middle-class consumer. Ex cathedra pronouncements of Barbara Allen and Ron Bottrell notwithstanding, the 1990s' Jemima looks more like a "Mrs." than an "Aunt." And viewed from this perspective, "good taste" should be her attribute as a discriminating shopper, not as a stack of pancakes.[1]

Of course, one assumption I am begging here is that a middle-class black matron has a "look" which we all readily recognize. This is a problem that Jean-Christophe Agnew neatly skirts. Midway through a December 1989 *Village Voice* review of Susan Strasser's *Satisfaction Guaranteed*, Agnew pauses momentarily in an attempt to resolve the contradictions posed by the upscale Aunt Jemima:

> For instance, what are we now to make of a figure like Aunt Jemima, whose 100-year-old kerchief was finally removed from her head during her most recent makeover last July? Now she is said to look like Oprah Winfrey. But then again, Oprah's face and body have themselves been inducted into the *Wiz's* vast warehouse of interchangeable cultural signifiers. (30)[2]

By invoking the instability of Winfrey as a referent, Agnew dismisses the possibility of making meaning of Aunt Jemima at all ("looks like" ad infinitum). In particular, he would appear to be alluding to the highly publicized sixty-seven-pound weight loss in 1988 of the popular talk show host and television producer, and perhaps also to tabloid allegations that an August 1989 *TV Guide* cover picture of the newly slim Winfrey depicted her face atop Ann-Margret's body.[3]

Simply put, Allen, Agnew, and I are on the verge of a three-way interpretive collision. Allen stops at a symbolic red light that has not changed since 1889; for Quaker Oats, the trademark symbolizes "warmth, quality, good taste, heritage and reliability." I pause in the intersection at a 1989 semiotic yellow, unsure what meaning to make of Jemima's new depiction as a buppie slave. Agnew speeds toward 2089 at the glimmer of a poststructuralist green; in his view, the trademark can be endlessly deconstructed, its meaning finally indeterminate. I use this specter—of hermeneutic chaos at the site of the trademark's centennial makeover—as a way of foregrounding from the outset some of the contradictions and discontinuities that underwrite my work on food, African American women, and U.S. racial identities.[4]

What ever happened to Aunt Jemima? Nothing and everything. On the one hand, the trademark is where it has been for the last century, on grocery store shelves, and the same conflicted fears and desires that gave rise to it in 1889 surely enabled its retention in 1989. Yet, without going so far as to label Aunt Jemima and Oprah Winfrey interchangeable, one might well conclude, on the other hand, that the updated trademark needs also to be interpreted in new ways. Neither the cultural work performed by representations of black women nor the manner in which black women are interpellated as subjects is today precisely what it was a century ago.[5] For if Aunt Jemima foregrounds one axis of U.S. desire for African American women to be the ever-smiling producers of food, to be nurturers who themselves have no appetite and make no demands, then Oprah Winfrey surely also foregrounds another axis, one that has been latent in the popular fascination with the Aunt Jemima trademark from its inception: U.S. fear of what black women consume or, perhaps more precisely, U.S. obsession with black female appetites.

This concern has played itself out on numerous levels, from gastronomic to sexual to economic. The foreclosed question "What does Aunt Jemima eat?" quickly mutates to encompass other aspects of black female consumption, including access to the wealth and power that can satisfy desire. Certainly one suspects that popular interest in Winfrey's eating habits during the late 1980s and early 1990s was in no small part a function of her enormous wealth: even the notorious *TV Guide* body-switch cover was accompanied by a story entitled "The Richest Woman on TV? Oprah!" (Feinberg).[6] Similarly, though *Saturday Night Live* producer Lorne Michaels failed in his attempt to have guest-host Winfrey impersonate Aunt Jemima in a 1986 skit, it is noteworthy that in the sketch the trademark was to have been a target of downsizing at Quaker Oats (A. Edwards 215–17). Granted, such popular interest in Winfrey has generally operated at the benign end of the spectrum; the state-sponsored hysteria over "welfare queens," "quota queens," and "condom queens" thus better illustrates the invidious underpinnings of this concern with black female power.[7] Meanwhile, the majority of African American women—neither multimillionaires nor recipients of public assistance—are rendered invisible.

This book is centrally concerned with the tension between these two poles, with how the binary through which black women have been designated as both provider/producer and castrator/consumer has structured U.S. culture. It is concerned with the disjunction between the minimal power that African American women have wielded in the United States and the often exaggerated perceptions of their power. Much fine work has been done on this "Mammy/Sapphire" dichotomy, primarily by black feminist scholars from the humanities and social sciences.[8] My own contribution differs, however, in its focus on food. I take dietary practices to be fundamental to the myriad ways we come to understand ourselves as embodied subjects. I take the association of African American women with food, moreover, to be fundamental to the ongoing production of U.S. subjectivities and U.S. national culture.

In this chapter I begin laying the groundwork for this argument by looking in greater detail at the multiple narratives that have been generated over the past century either to legitimate or to discredit the Aunt Jemima icon in a multiethnic, patriarchal, class-stratified country, including, in the last section of the chapter, the copious responses of black Americans. My research into the trademark's history has suggested that Aunt Jemima has functioned as a pivotal trope for African American women precisely because "she" has enabled members of so many other demographic groups to forge an identity for themselves in the United States. Yet even though much of the debate over the trademark has quite rightly revolved around the iconography of race and racial masquerade in U.S. culture, we should still bear in mind that Aunt Jemima is also a mass-produced commodity, and as such, "it" has all too successfully distracted our attention from the exploitative underpinnings of the economic system through which commodities are created and circulated.

In Search, Redux

> Everybody's looking for Big Mama,
> spatula in hand and ample

table set for all of master's children,
serving generous portions
of forgiving love with open
gold-tooth smile.

Everybody needs to nestle in
her warm, full bosom, hear again
that throaty voice belt out
deep-valleyed lullabies of blackness
(shouting hosannas or moaning
blues for good man gone).

Where did Aunt Jemima go? And when
will she return to reassure us
that her delicious laughter
was innocent and wholesome to partake of
and no more subtle
and no more dangerous
than her pancakes?

Naomi Long Madgett, "In Search of
Aunt Jemima (Alias Big Mama)," 1978

Perhaps one sign of the timeliness of my hypothesis is the fact that by the early 1990s Aunt Jemima had become something of a cottage industry in the academy, with scholars regularly publishing new work on topics ranging from blacks in advertising and black collectibles to the influence of black stereotypes on U.S. social policy.[9] A few of these scholars, such as Marilyn Kern-Foxworth and Megan Granda, have undertaken important new research into the history of the Quaker Oats trademark; others invoke Aunt Jemima mainly as a widely recognizable trope. These textual explorations have been complemented in recent years by several museum exhibits and television specials on representations of African Americans in popular culture. There is, as a result, a seeming surfeit of information available about the trademark icon, as well as about the cultural construction of "mammy." Still, in part because Quaker Oats has rarely allowed academic researchers access to its archives, taken collectively what these studies offer is many now-familiar anecdotes and largely inadequate documentation of sources.[10] Narratives spun in one text are recycled in the next, with acknowledgment but only sporadic fact-checking in several of the scholarly works, and with neither acknowledgment nor fact-checking in the works intended for general readers.

Whether cited or not, at-hand or at-second-remove, one book seems to have functioned as the "ur" text for most of the post–1960s accounts of Aunt Jemima: Arthur Marquette's *Brands, Trademarks and Good Will: The Story of the Quaker Oats Company* (1967). Writing as the integrationist civil rights agenda was giving way to the more uncompromising politics of Black Power, Marquette pretty clearly aimed to position the Aunt Jemima trademark as a legitimate inheritor of white global capitalism and black folk culture alike. In fact, the book reads as though it were commissioned by the merchandising department of Quaker Oats, which it almost certainly was. Although information and language from his chapter on Aunt

Jemima ("The First Ready-Mix") are frequently reproduced in academic as well as nonacademic discourse, it is important to recognize that *Brands, Trademarks and Good Will* contains neither footnotes nor a bibliography. Much of what the author has to say about the (early) history of Aunt Jemima cannot be documented through any publicly available records; some of what he has to say surely cannot be documented at all. In what follows, consequently, I would like to try to understand better the implications of this process whereby an intentionally fabricated "legend" has been taken up as (semi-) scholarly fact.

The basic outline of the narrative Marquette offers is as follows. The Aunt Jemima trademark originated not in the antebellum South but rather in the Gilded Age Midwest. In 1888 Missouri journalist Chris Rutt bought a flour mill with Charles G. Underwood, a friend who already had connections to the milling industry. Faced with a glutted market, the two decided to retail the surplus flour as a ready-made pancake mix. Initially sold in plain paper sacks, the mix was without a trade name until the fall of 1889, when Rutt attended a performance by the blackface team of Baker and Farrell at a local vaudeville house. One act was "a jazzy, rhythmic New Orleans style cakewalk to a tune called 'Aunt Jemima' which Baker performed in the apron and red-bandanna headband of the traditional southern cook" (Marquette 143). Hoping to associate his product with what was rapidly becoming a widespread postbellum celebration of antebellum plantation cooking, Rutt appropriated both the name and the image for his pancake mix.

In 1890 Rutt and his partner sold the mix to the R. T. Davis Milling Company. Marquette claims that it was Davis who then "envisioned a living Aunt Jemima to advertise his wares. . . . Here was a new advertising concept: to bring a trademark to life" (144). The first woman Davis hired, former slave Nancy Green, made her debut as Aunt Jemima at the Chicago World's Columbian Exposition of 1893. Outside a booth built to resemble a giant flour barrel, she cooked pancakes, sang, and told stories. Describing Green as "utterly unself-conscious" (145), Marquette avers that she "loved crowds and loved to talk about her own slave days, her stories no doubt partly apocryphal but nonetheless entertaining. . . . From this complicated patter emerged the image of a wise old cook from the Deep South of Civil War times, who had brought her secret pancake recipe to a benighted northland through the courtesy of the R. T. Davis Milling Company" (145–46).

In addition to distributing a button for the fair with a drawing of Aunt Jemima (a standard mammy caricature) and the caption "I'se in Town, Honey," the company subsequently published a souvenir booklet titled "The Life of Aunt Jemima, the Most Famous Colored Woman in the World" (Marquette 146–47). The booklet included anecdotes told by Green about her life in the antebellum South, "factual" material about her work at the World's Fair, and fictive tales about Aunt Jemima and her "employer" in Louisiana, Colonel Higbee (147). One story, for example, has the Union troops about to tear out the colonel's mustache by the roots when Aunt Jemima serves them her pancakes and saves both Higbee and his mustache. Green subsequently traveled around the country performing cooking demonstrations in a variety of venues, including grocery stores and other expositions. Meanwhile, the "I'se in Town, Honey" slogan was used in nationally distributed magazine advertisements and on billboards.

In 1919 Aunt Jemima Mills (the R. T. Davis Milling Company having been renamed in 1914) attempted to bolster sagging sales by hiring the J. Walter Thompson advertising agency to initiate a campaign for the pancake mix. Created by James Webb Young, the campaign was eventually dubbed "the legend of Aunt Jemima." Seven years later Quaker Oats acquired the trademark, but sales quickly plummeted during the Depression. In order to try to reinterest the public in a non-necessity item, Quaker Oats advertisers decided to hire someone to portray Aunt Jemima once again, Nancy Green having been killed in an automobile accident in 1923. Open auditions in Chicago resulted in the discovery of Anna Robinson, whose appearance more nearly approximated the "mammy" stereotype than had that of the slender Nancy Green. After describing Robinson as "a massive woman with the face of an angel," Marquette reminisces: "Never to be forgotten was the day they loaded 350 pounds of Anna Robinson on the Twentieth Century Limited and sent her to New York in the custody of Lord and Thomas advertising agency people to pose for pictures" (154). Her first appearance as Aunt Jemima was at the Chicago Century of Progress Exposition in 1933, and subsequently the Aunt Jemima package was redesigned around her likeness.

During the mid-century decades of Robinson's iconographic reign, Quaker Oats employed many other African American women to perform the role of Aunt Jemima, including prominent singer Edith Wilson. The company also attempted to diversify its marketing strategies for Aunt Jemima products but met with little success. The main exception was the Aunt Jemima Kitchen (or Aunt Jemima's Pancake House), which opened in 1955 as part of the original Disneyland theme park in California. Two years later the attraction began featuring actor Aylene Lewis as yet another "real" Aunt Jemima, and it became so popular, Marquette reports in concluding his chapter, that by 1962 a larger building was necessary.

Because of his lack of documentation, it is exceedingly difficult to determine the accuracy of Marquette's account of the trademark's history. One can, for example, locate early Aunt Jemima advertisements (c. 1896) using the caption "I'se in Town, Honey" and directing the reader to "Send 4c. in stamps for Life History of 'Aunt Jemima' and her Pickaninny dolls," thus corroborating the existence of the World's Fair souvenir booklet to which he alludes.[11] Similarly, full-page "plantation school" advertisements for Aunt Jemima mix, with drawings signed by N. C. Wyeth and text setting forth what became the "legend" of Aunt Jemima, did begin appearing in the *Saturday Evening Post* by 1920. One from May 1920 is captioned "The Cook Whose Cabin Became More Famous Than Uncle Tom's"; by September the reader indeed learns of "How Aunt Jemima Saved the Colonel's Mustache and His Reputation as a Host." Another from January 1921 is headlined "Aunt Jemima Bids Goodbye to the Old Plantation"; an installment from the following month claims that "At the World's Fair in '93 Aunt Jemima Was a Sensation." This last informs the reader that "*everybody* at the Fair wanted to taste those golden-brown cakes; time after time the Columbian Guards had to come and keep the crowd moving, since it blocked almost completely that part of the great Agricultural Hall" (figure 1-1).[12]

Other of Marquette's "facts" in circulation about the trademark's history are, by contrast, less readily verifiable through primary sources, if not flatly contradicted

FIGURE 1.1 Detail from "At the World's Fair in '93 Aunt Jemima Was a Sensation," *Saturday Evening Post*, 1921. Photograph by the University of Iowa Audiovisual Center Photo Service.

by them. For instance, he gives the date of Nancy Green's death quite specifically as 24 September 1923 (146), but the accident was actually reported in the 31 August 1923 edition of the *Chicago Daily Tribune* ("3").[13] More tellingly, neither this story nor Green's obituary listing, published in the *Tribune* on the same day, mentions her profession ("Green"). Perhaps Green was as widely beloved for her portrayal of Aunt Jemima as Marquette would like us to think, but evidence is not forthcoming from the *Tribune*. It may be no coincidence that the *Tribune* had also mentioned nothing in its coverage of the World's Fair of 1893 which might substantiate Marquette's claim that "[s]pecial police had to be recruited to monitor" the R. T. Davis exhibit because Nancy Green was so popular (146)—a claim that obviously echoes the "World's Fair" installment of Young and Wyeth's "legend of Aunt Jemima" campaign. Obscuring the boundary between fantasy and fact even further, the same advertisement informed readers that at the World's Fair Aunt Jemima pancake flour had received "the highest Medal and the Diploma of Excellence" ("At"). The *Tribune's* coverage at the time does include a fine-print listing for the R. T. Davis award; it also reveals that such prizes were anything but hard to come by at the fair, with at least two hundred "Bronze Medals" having gone to flour manufacturers alone ("Awards"). Nor, for that matter, do contemporaneous books on the fair appear to have considered the Aunt Jemima booth at all worthy of being singled out from among the thousands of competing exhibits.[14]

Marquette's no less frequently cited claim that Rutt conceived the Aunt Jemima trademark after seeing a vaudeville performance by "Baker and Farrell" poses even greater mysteries. The *New York Clipper*, the newspaper of record for nineteenth-century U.S. theatre, includes no reference to a Baker and Farrell among its listings for vaudeville acts appearing in St. Joseph, Missouri, in the fall of 1889. A 23 November 1889 issue does, however, announce that the solo act of "P. F. Baker" had been expected at the Grand Opera House in St. Joseph on the 17th of that month (617). St. Joseph area newspapers—including the *Daily Herald*, the *Daily Gazette*, and the *Daily News*—all publicized Baker's eagerly anticipated appearance in a comedy called "The Emigrant."[15] Most notable for our purposes here was a *Herald* preview describing Baker as a "well known German Comedian" who had

> formerly appeared in St. Joseph, in connection with Mr. Farron, in "Chris and Lena." "The Emigrant" is a pleasing comedy, and in the hands of "Pete" Baker and his support it is put on in a manner that at once charms and amuses. Baker himself as *Emigrant* and *Aunt Jeremiah*, is simply immense, and brings down the house every time. . . . The company is a first-class one, the play nice and clean, and deserves to meet with success. (14 Nov. 1889: 4)

Morning-after reviews of Baker's actual St. Joseph performance mention nothing of "Aunt Jeremiah," but the *Herald*'s account of the sold-out show was certainly no less effusive in its praise, observing that "Mr. Baker never appeared to a better advantage than last evening, and as *Ludwig*, the emigrant, won new admirers. His songs were repeatedly encored and it seemed as if the audience could not hear too many" (18 Nov. 1889: 4). Noticeably more grudging, a *News* reviewer reported: "There is nothing to the comedy drama but what has been seen many times before, but it is decidedly amusing and apparently satisfying to the audience" (18 Nov. 1889: 2). Less a play than an assemblage of skits and songs, "The Emigrant" was evidently well received at least in part because Baker was already "one of the best known character comedians in the country" (*News*, 15 Nov. 1889: 2).[16]

The questions raised by this information are readily apparent. Should "Baker and Farrell" be redesignated an inaccurate recollection (or transcription) of "Baker and Farron"? Was "Aunt Jeremiah" one of Baker's variations on "Aunt Jemima"— or perhaps simply an overworked reviewer's misapprehension of the name? In his vast *Annals of the New York Stage*, theatre historian George Odell sheds some light on these questions. Therein he lists numerous performances of Baker and Farron, and he reports that as early as 25 April 1881 the team had put on "a piece called The Emigrants, with P. F. Baker as Ludwig Vinkelsteinhausenblauser and Aunt Jemima, T. J. Farron as Dennis McGraw and Christina Waldhauser" (XI: 387). Evidently Baker and Farron's style was not to the liking of the highbrow Odell, who had earlier referred to them as "that team in comedy not so very refined" (XI: 281). But he also allows that by 1882 they were considered a "rising" act (XI: 478). The two men continued to perform "Chris and Lena," "The Emigrants," and other plays for the next few years. By no later than 1886, however, they had gone separate ways.[17] According to Douglas Gilbert, Baker eventually moved on to the "legit stage," where he became one of several "pronounced favorites" (39). Gilbert refers in this same passage to "Tony Farrell" as another vaudevillian who later gained success in more elite theatrical venues (39); this information may shed some light on the origin of the "Baker and Farrell" story.

Granted, new evidence could turn up to prove me wrong. But taking into account the other inaccuracies in Marquette's text, it seems likely that the man Rutt is alleged to have seen perform "Aunt Jemima" was Pete F. Baker, working alone. Then again, as my phrase "alleged to have seen" ought to remind us, since we still have no absolute proof that Rutt ever actually witnessed anyone's blackface performance of "Aunt Jemima"—or, for that matter, of "Aunt Jeremiah"—this speculation about Baker's identity should be taken not as a gesture toward closure, but rather as a catalyst for further interrogation. My own contribution in the next section will be to look in greater detail at some variations in the narratives used to legitimate Aunt Jemima. My goal is to remind us of a point that too often seems forgotten in work on the trademark: the semiotic production and consumption of Aunt Jemima iconography was inextricably linked to the material production and consumption of Aunt Jemima pancake mix in a rapidly expanding commodity system, a system that itself relied on an influx of exploitable labor and the development of new markets to achieve its profits.

The (Other) Emigrants

> This is for Hattie McDaniels, Butterfly McQueen, Ethel Waters
> Saphire
> Saphronia
> Ruby Begonia
> Aunt Jemima
> Aunt Jemima on the Pancake Box
> Aunt Jemima on the Pancake Box?
> AuntJemimaonthepancakebox?
> auntjemimaonthepancakebox?
> Ainchamamaonthepancakebox?
> Ain't chure Mama on the pancake box?
>
> Mama Mama
> Get offa that damn box
> And come home to me
>
> And my Mama leaps offa that box
> She swoops down in her nurse's cape
> Which she wears on Sunday
> And on Wednesday night prayer meeting
> And she wipes my forehead
> And she fans my face for me
> And she makes me a cup o' tea
> And it don't do a thing for my real pain
> Except she is my Mama
> Mama Mommy Mommy Mammy Mammy
> Mam-mee Mam-mee
> I'd Walk a mill-yon miles
> For one o' your smiles
>
> Donna Kate Rushin,
> "The Black Back-Ups," 1983

Thus far we have been able to locate evidence corroborating the claim that Aunt Jemima "started out as a white man in drag," to cite one of the more recent recyclings of Marquette's narrative (Hine 91). In keeping with the conventions of nineteenth-century minstrelsy and vaudeville, the *Gazette's* description of Pete Baker as a "German Comedian" very likely referred to his stage impersonation of the emigrant Ludwig, not necessarily to his own ethnic heritage. Yet it is also quite possible that Baker's audience perceived him, at some level, as an actual German. Either way, one should bear in mind that in 1889 the vaudeville stage was actually dominated by Irish performers (Snyder 48). Baker, moreover, would have been working in the wake of a long history in which popular respect for German immigrants was mirrored by contempt for Irish ones, contempt comparable in some quarters to that manifested toward African Americans.[18] As further evidence is located, it will be worth speculating whether a "German" comedian's performance of a black female role could have been perceived as less "natural," and therefore more transgressive, than would a comparable performance by an "Irish" comedian.

Subsequently, and still according to Marquette, ex-slave and excellent cook Nancy Green was the first of many "real" black women hired to enact Aunt Jemima once the stage role had become a trademark for pancake mix. As a copy of a parody of a slave cook, Green, paradoxically, would have been simultaneously less original and more authentic than Baker. Yet even this already unstable story of origins must be further complicated by other extant narratives. In *Blacking Up*, Robert Toll points out that the popular postbellum black minstrel Billy Kersands was most famous for performing the song "Old Aunt Jemima." In fact, it was a song which "by 1876–77 Kersands had reportedly already performed 2–3,000 times" and which remained his signature "throughout his long career" (259). Granting the accuracy of Toll's information, Green's performance at the Chicago World's Columbian Exposition of 1893 would have been even more complicated than I just suggested. To be precise, one might construe it as a black female ex-slave's adaptation of a white male businessman's appropriation of a "German" male vaudevillian's imitation of a black male minstrel's parody of an imaginary black female slave cook.

Recent work on blackface minstrelsy can help us make some sense of this convoluted narrative of origin. In *Love and Theft*, Eric Lott explores the ambivalent racial tendencies underwriting the antebellum minstrel show. For him, the black female roles (performed, at the time, solely by white men) can be understood as

> a cover for black maleness. Her typically jutting protuberances and general phallic suggestiveness bear all the marks of the white-fantasized black men who loomed so large in racialized phallic scenarios. It makes perfect sense that castration anxieties in blackface would conjoin the black penis and the woman. . . . Another referent for whites of Lacan's threatening (m)Other, Franz Fanon argued, is precisely the black male. (152)

Lott reads the portrayal of black women in early blackface minstrelsy, in other words, primarily as a way of coding both castration anxiety and interracial homoerotic desire. If his interpretation is correct, and I think it is, then the "primal scene" that Marquette details of Aunt Jemima's "conception" in the post-Reconstruction years might well lend itself to an analogous reading. "Here was the image Rutt sought!" Marquette almost giddily proclaims of Rutt's beholding of Baker in black mammy drag (143). The added emphasis of the exclamation point is perhaps suggestive of Marquette's, if not Rutt's, psychic investment in Baker's Aunt Jemima performance, a sighting which, we should bear in mind, may have taken place only in Marquette's overactive imagination.

This argument for locating in the trademark inscriptions of postbellum (and, no doubt, Black Power–era) interracial male homoerotic desire finds support as well in the lyrics to at least one version of "Old Aunt Jemima." Ubiquitous minstrel entrepreneur J. H. Haverly claims that the following verses were "[o]riginally sung by Billy Kersands" (13):

> The monkey dressed in soldier clothes,
>   Old Aunt Jemima, oh! oh! oh!
>   [repeat after each line]
> Went out in the woods for to drill some crows,
> The jay bird hung on the swinging limb,
> I up with a stone and hit him on the shin,
>   Oh! Carline, etc.

> The bullfrog married the tadpole's sister,
> He smacked his lips and then he kissed her,
> She says, if you love me as I love you,
> No knife can cut our love in two,
>   Oh! Carline, etc.
>   (13)

Preceded by a fairly innocuous opening stanza in which the singer pokes fun at the dull worship style of white churches (Toll 259–60), the second and third stanzas quoted here gravitate toward the more explicitly politicized territory of black union soldiers and, perhaps, the emergence of lynching as a practice of racial repression. Considering the tendency of minstrel humor to dwell on alleged black male sexual prowess and white male inadequacy, this interpretation of the "jay bird hung on the swinging limb" is supported by the third verse, with its hint of death-defying miscegenation between the lip-smacking, phallic bullfrog and the sister of the effeminate tadpole. This version of "Old Aunt Jemima" might, then, have been understood by Kersands's audiences to allegorize anxieties about the fragility of postbellum racial boundaries, namely their transgression by black men and white women. It seems not impossible, moreover, that the lyrics could also have created space for subconscious homoerotic pleasure in the imagining of virile yet vulnerable black male bodies. In Robyn Wiegman's account, "the central figuration of the white woman's sexuality in the rape mythos must be understood as a displacement of the deeper and more culturally complex relation between black and white men" (97), a relation in which black men are metonymized by their genitals.[19]

At the same time, one of the risks Lott takes in construing early minstrelsy's "black women," as surrogates for black men is that in such a reading the phallus is reinscribed as a privileged signifier, fundamental to the articulation of social categories such as gender, class, and race. Even while allowing for veiled anxieties about castration and male homosocial desire, it seems important not to lose sight of the strong probability that the white (and later black) male performance of black femininity also registers anxieties about black women. Certainly this would have been the case in the context of the postbellum years that I, unlike Lott, am considering, when discussions of women's rights and racial uplift positioned black women at the (precariously repressed) intersection of at least two highly contentious national debates. Furthermore, Aunt Jemima's creation also coincides with Ida B. Wells's early crusades against lynching, as well as with her efforts to contest the exclusion of African Americans from the World's Fair of 1893.[20] In fact, Wells's pamphlet *The Reason Why the Colored American Is Not in the World's Columbian Exposition* (1893) would have posed a striking ideological challenge to R. T. Davis's "The Life of Aunt Jemima."[21] As Patricia Turner succinctly observes, "Aunt Jemima's was the kind of face people wanted to remember; Ida B. Wells's was the kind they wanted to forget. And that is exactly what happened" (50).

In short, we need to supplement awareness of the possible homoerotics of Aunt Jemima's "origins" among male performers on the minstrel and vaudeville stage with other modes of analyzing the investments of various social groups, including women, in Aunt Jemima iconography. With this concern in mind, Michael Rogin's work on Jewish immigrants and the Hollywood film industry offers an even more compelling model for understanding the trademark's function in the early decades of this century, and perhaps for explaining its longevity as well. Focusing in *Blackface, White Noise* on a pairing he refers to as "Uncle Sammy and My Mammy" (the title of his first chapter), Rogin returns repeatedly to the famous image of a blacked-up Al Jolson (as Jack Robin, né Jakie Rabinowitz) singing "My Mammy" to his Jewish mother at the end of *The Jazz Singer* (1927). "Blackface is grounded in mammy," according to Rogin, "since the nurturing figure that deprived black men and women of adult authority and sexuality gave white boys permission to play with their identities, to fool around" (13). Although Rogin, like Lott, is most centrally concerned with the investments of white (this time, immigrant Jewish) men in blackface, his analysis also offers some useful pointers for thinking about the motivations of women from non-WASP ethnic backgrounds in portraying, literally or figuratively, Aunt Jemima. Consider, for example, the trademark's import for two well-known women of the post–World War I period: Italian vaudevillian Tess Gardella and Jewish novelist Fannie Hurst.

Gardella performed in blackface under the stage name "Aunt Jemima." She most famously appeared as "Queenie" in the 1927 production of *Show Boat* but was also known for her rendition of "Carolina Mammy," which not surprisingly was one of Al Jolson's signature tunes (J. Young 123). As vaudeville historian Anthony Slide has observed, "Today Aunt Jemima is a familiar name on pancake syrup, but fifty years ago Aunt Jemima meant a plump, jovial Italian woman in blackface, whose real name was Tess Gardella" (*Vaudevillians* 3; see also Ibee; Sobel 153). Slide further hypothesizes that "the secret of [Gardella's] success lay in her being the black mammy of the Ethel Waters type in A Member of the Wedding, in whose arms everyone wished to be held and loved. Aunt Jemima represented warmth and joy, and the fact that she was really white doubtless helped to win over those with racial antagonisms" (Encyclopedia 16).

Writing in 1994, Slide may have viewed Gardella as "really white," but I would stress that Italian women were among the prospective immigrants denied admittance to the United States according to restrictive legislation passed in 1924 to stave off the "rising tide of color" (in Lothrop Stoddard's noxious phrase), at the same time Gardella was achieving fame as "Aunt Jemima." Jews in particular were targeted by this law (Takaki 307). It seems likely, therefore, that Gardella's success was owing not to her perceived "whiteness" but instead to her ethnic positioning between white and black. Like both Jewish and African American women, Italian women have historically been portrayed as matriarchal nurturers—domineering precisely in their excessive capacity for affection—and so Gardella could be hailed as a natural delineator of black womanhood, while allowing the audience a comfortable distance from actual African American and Jewish women alike.[22]

Slide, furthermore, has not been the only post–World War II commentator to offer a misleading representation of Gardella's ethnicity. Twenty years before Slide characterized Gardella as "really white," Toni Morrison oversaw production of The Black Book (1974), a "scrapbook" on African American history. Among the numerous photographs the book features is one of the face and shoulders of a heavyset, broadly smiling woman wearing a head-rag. Confusing the story of Aunt Jemima's lineage even more, if possible, the caption on the photograph reads "Lois Gardella, the original Aunt Jemima, 1933" (Harris 179). A contemporaneous review of The Black Book published in Ms. magazine includes only this photograph out of the dozens of available options, and reviewer Dorothy Robinson has this to say about it: "One of my favorite pieces of folklore was the discovery of Lois Gardella, the original Aunt Jemima (1933), a beautiful woman!" (41). One can only infer that Robinson, following the compilers of The Black Book, mistook not just Gardella's first name but also her racial identity. Yet such an error can hardly come as a surprise, since by the 1920s and 1930s blacking up had become primarily the province of African American stage performers (Watkins, On 104–80).

The elision of Gardella's "Italian-ness" in these more recent accounts lends further credence to Rogin's claim that blackface has enabled the demographic diversity of the United States to be rescripted in key cultural sites into a black/white binary, a binary through which non-Anglo immigrants attempted to remake themselves as legitimate white Americans. Fannie Hurst actually thematizes this process in her hugely popular novel Imitation of Life. Published in 1933, its narrative recounts the successful efforts of a young Jewish widow, Bea Pullman, to create a business empire by appropriating the candy and waffle recipes and cooking skills of her African American maid, Delilah Johnson. In developing her story, Hurst almost certainly drew upon contemporaneous advertising campaigns by the Quaker Oats Company on behalf of its acquired product: Delilah Johnson becomes "Aunt Delilah," and her recipes become "Delilah's Delights." (John Stahl's 1934 film version goes even further, substituting pancakes for waffles and depicting the face of the Johnson character, played by Louise Beavers, on pancake-mix boxes and billboards.) A main subplot of the novel requires Delilah to suffer the rejection of her daughter, Peola, a "tragic mulatta" who is passing for white.

Rogin points out that Hurst, "who herself passed as gentile, doubled her Jewish family drama" by using *Imitation of Life* to turn "the American family romance (as the wish through passing to replace the parents of one's birth) into melodrama" (123–24). Though I concur with this analysis, I would also follow Lauren Berlant by pointing out that the novel's racial doubling and psychic projection take on a fundamentally gendered dimension: Hurst rarely mentions Delilah without making some reference to her size, weight, and appetite.[23] We are told, for example, that Delilah was "a buxom negro woman who, with the best intentions in the world, swelled the food budget so considerably" (100) and that "[s]eeing Delilah faint was the equivalent to beholding a great building slump to its side of earthquake" (316).

Hurst's timely deployment of a corpulent mammy character—contemporaneous, as it was, not just with Gardella's success, but also with the alleged debut of the rotund Anna Robinson as Aunt Jemima at the Chicago Century of Progress Exposition—becomes even more intriguing if one reads it together with a brief autobiographical narrative she published two years later entitled *No Food with My Meals*.[24] Therein Hurst describes her obsession with the slimming craze, which she says began to overcome her just as she was writing *Imitation of Life*. "Some women are born frail," she announces, with characteristic aplomb. "Some have frailty thrust upon them. Still others achieve it, and at what price glory!" (2). Hurst then details her efforts to achieve frailty and therefore glory, admitting, "There was to come a time, fallen so low had I, when to stand with my nose plastered against the plate-glass windows of lunchroom emporiums, where flapjacks, later to be smothered under melting butter and golden syrup[,] were being juggled, became one of my favorite outdoor sports" (27). Having passed through the stage when she "pitied obesity in others, and did all in [her] power to either induce or encourage it" (33), Hurst reports that her current wish is to be freed from her obsession with food and dieting—though she fears that she is "too infected with this slimming phobia to hope for complete redemption" (52).

Hurst concludes *No Food with My Meals* with a list of "acknowledgments" (55), including ones "[t]o a cook who learned to defile her art in order to brew me dishes unwanted and unsavory," "[t]o the books written during this period which abound perhaps unduly in foods coveted by their author," and "[t]o myself for finally realizing that I am funnier than any character I have ever succeeded in depicting in fiction" (56). Though she never directly mentions *Imitation of Life*, she seems to be acknowledging that her own desire for and fear of food (and one of its potential bodily corollaries, fat) resulted in her having projected onto the character Delilah a psychology untouched by the slimming fad. Delilah, in other words, functions as a dual mode of novelistic wish fulfillment: she is both the object of Hurst's derision, that which Hurst loathes in herself, and what Hurst wishes she could be—able to experience and satisfy her appetite "naturally." The distinctions Hurst draws among types of "frailty"—born with, thrust upon, and achieved—might even be construed as coding her relationship to white Protestant identity. Clearly viewing herself as an outsider to prevailing standards of female beauty, as a Jewish woman for whom "achieved" frailty was fraudulent, Hurst needed to create Delilah and Peola in order to deflect attention from the fact that she herself was only passing as a gentile. "There was," as she writes, "no suppressing the enormity that was Delilah, nor was there desire to suppress it" (*Imitation* 103).

Surely a no less significant point to be made here, though, is that Hurst's obsession with "suppressing" her appetite bore a complicated relationship to the socioeconomic context of the early 1930s. Exploring the popularity starting around 1933 of the "industrial toxin" dinitrophenol as a reducing drug, Hillel Schwartz has argued: "Rather than curtailing dieting, the Depression decisively shifted the emphasis in dieting from production to consumption, from metabolism to appetite, from glands to calories" (191–92). Far more successfully than did Anna Robinson, Hurst's fictive Delilah Johnson cathected this ever-evolving U.S. cultural obsession with eating. Yet Schwartz makes clear that the language of reducing "referred to salaries, dividends, wages, budgets, credit and the gold content of the dollar as well as to weight" (192). As Hurst herself certainly knew, in the United States of 1933, a substantial percentage of the population was eating little or no food with its meals out of financial necessity. Bearing such seeming contradictions in mind should allow us to resist the temptation to analyze the history of Aunt Jemima solely on the level of iconography and impersonation. Women, especially immigrants, have been far more likely to work as factory producers of commodities such as Aunt Jemima pancake mix than as either vaudeville performers or literary delineators of Aunt Jemima—at least when the factory jobs have been available. What we need to understand, consequently, is how the trademark's deployment in early twentieth-century U.S. popular culture was related to its ability to legitimize contemporaneous developments in U.S. capitalism.

As we have seen, Aunt Jemima products had initially been marketed in an expanding consumer system via an appropriation of the iconography of slavery. The trademark thus participated in widespread debates over the role of the post-Reconstruction South in the formation of U.S. national culture. Robert Rydell has suggested that segregated World's Fair exhibits such as those involving Aunt Jemima generally served to justify U.S. racism at home and imperialism abroad.[25] While promoting the immediate gratification and standardization of mass-produced food products, the millers also constructed a romanticized past, when food was prepared by hand as an act of black female familial devotion. Aunt Jemima was situated between two worlds: capitalism and slavery, technology and art, standardization and improvisation, money and love. As Marquette put it, in a fashion that exemplifies perfectly the mystifications of commodity fetishism, "Aunt Jemima's pancakes weren't just pancakes. They had personality, and that personality was in great measure attributable to the imaginative Nancy Green" (138).

By representing the product as the extension of a slave woman, the makers of Aunt Jemima pancake mix not only contributed to the widespread naturalization of black women's culinary abilities, in effect denying that their cooking as slaves and domestic servants was a form of expropriated labor, but they also enabled the product's purchasers to disavow knowledge of the labor that actually went into the creation of Aunt Jemima mix—that of an emergent class of factory food workers,

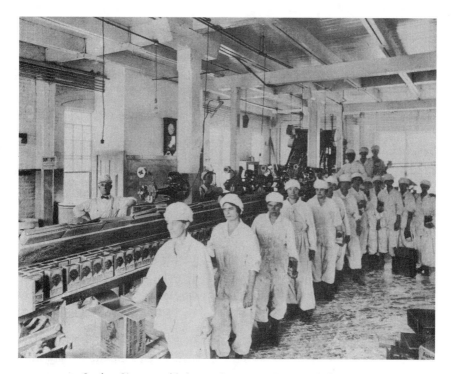

FIGURE 1.2 Quaker Oats assembly line, c. late 1920s. From Arthur F. Marquette's *Brands, Trademarks and Good Will*, 1967. Photograph by the University of Iowa Audiovisual Center Photo Service.

many of them immigrant women. As Megan Granda has observed, plantation school advertisements such as the "legend of Aunt Jemima" series served up "a nostalgic image that hardly corresponded to what an increasing number of Euro-Americans saw as the frightening reality of a rising Black and immigrant proletariat" (29). Yet it was precisely black and immigrant women's common preference for factory work over domestic labor that fueled what became known by the late nineteenth century as the "servant problem." Because they offered alternative employment opportunities to working-class women who might otherwise have hired themselves out as domestic servants, consumer-staples manufacturers such as the owners of Aunt Jemima helped to create precisely the demand which their new "convenience" products aimed to supply.[26]

One photograph Marquette includes in *Brands, Trademarks and Good Will* reveals just these repressions in his history of the Quaker Oats mix (figure 1-2). Probably taken in the late 1920s, the photograph is of a group of assembly-line workers at a plant in St. Joseph, Missouri. After purchasing the Aunt Jemima trademark in 1926, Quaker Oats had, the caption tells us, "streamlined production" at the factory (n. pag.). In the photograph a group of gaunt "white" women, all dressed identically in white coveralls and caps, are shown standing in line next to a conveyor belt laden with boxes of Aunt Jemima pancake mix. On the far side of the belt are at least two white foremen, presumably charged with overseeing the women employees. These uniformly grim-faced women are a telling counterpoint not just to the multiple images of Aunt Jemima that smile forth from box after box of pancake mix on the assembly-line belt, but to the depictions of happy homemakers that smiled forth from the pages of Aunt Jemima advertisements in *Ladies' Home Journal, Good Housekeeping,* and other magazines aimed at middle-class white women. Whereas the originators of Aunt Jemima directly celebrated the subordination of African American women in marketing the mix, subsequent owners of the trademark such as Quaker Oats clearly depended on the cheap factory labor of, among others, those women whose class, country of origin, or ethnicity made them ineligible for participation in the group that the product purported to benefit.

A 1911 *Good Housekeeping* article called "Philanthropic Food Factories" offers a good example of the way the mainstream white press had attempted to alleviate lingering concerns about exploitative labor practices and, no less importantly, about the sanitariness of store-bought foods. The article offered photographs of female factory workers receiving manicures (553), toiling to the accompaniment of "popular and classic airs" (556), and otherwise enjoying the luxuries of life on the assembly line. But even in the process of trying to demonstrate that factory-produced food is more trustworthy than its home-cooked equivalents, the Quaker Oats photograph still manages to foreground precisely the anxieties about "dirty" (immigrant) workers which it aimed to foreclose: a sign containing the warning "Don't Spit" is visible on the left side of the frame. It was understood that disgruntled slaves had had at their disposal numerous modes of retaliation against masters and mistresses—serving up tainted food products certainly among them. For this reason, the "Don't Spit" sign can be seen to reveal, however inadvertently, the failure of capitalism to quell the fears of worker rebellion that had constantly structured life for the white elite in the slaveholding South.

In her study of the role of immigration in the expansion of consumer capitalism at the turn of the century, historian Elizabeth Ewen explains:

> The new standard of living to which the upper and middle classes was becoming accustomed [by 1900] was, in fact, a double standard. If middle-class families were now able to consume what they had once produced, immigrant working-class families produced—although no longer at home—what they could not consume. . . . The tenement line divided not simply rich from poor, but those who had access to new products and new technology from those who did not. (23)

One of Aunt Jemima's more important historical functions has surely been to obscure just such ideological contradictions stemming from the exploitation of assembly-line labor in the development of U.S. consumer capitalism—the exploitation, moreover, of a heavily immigrant female labor pool whose boundaries were policed through the continual renegotiation of the color line.[27] In this context, it can only be seen as historically fitting that the "German" comedian Pete Baker had portrayed Aunt Jemima as part of a play called "The Emigrant." As overdetermined chance would have it, furthermore, during the late nineteenth century an actual German immigrant, Ferdinand Schumacher, had helped found the company that eventually purchased and became known for the pancake mix trademark: Quaker Oats (Marquette 10–77).

Treating the practice of blacking up as an important "rite of passage from immigrant to American," Michael Rogin argues that we should

> condens[e] into a single figure the structures of white supremacist racial integration that built the United States: black labor in the realm of production, interracial nurture and sex (the latter as both a private practice and a unifying public prohibition) in the realm of reproduction, and blackface minstrelsy in the realm of culture. (5)

I would go one step further to point out that Aunt Jemima already condenses these structures into a single, literally realized, figure. A product of the dialectic between commodity capitalism and popular culture, Aunt Jemima was created to suture contradictions in ideologies of racial, ethnic, gender, and class difference in an economy increasingly dependent upon mass production and exploitable labor. Although the trademark is generally construed as a symptom of a racially bifurcated country, it would be more accurate to say that it has historically marked a space where members of a heterogeneous population could, through the production, performance, and/or purchase of black womanhood, "play with their identities" (albeit in unequally empowered ways) and navigate the changes wrought since the late nineteenth century by immigration, urbanization, industrialization, and imperialism.

As this chapter's concluding section will attempt, in part, to demonstrate, locating Aunt Jemima in this more comprehensive framework should enable us to rethink the relationship of African American women to Aunt Jemima. In a 1972 "rap" on domestic service called *Thursdays and Every Other Sunday Off*, Vertamae Grosvenor described a trip she once made to a grocery store in a white New York City neighborhood. Midway through her shopping, Grosvenor had paused to take stock of her purchases: "Now it turned out that I stopped right by the Aunt Jemima shelf. A white lady with a baby was passing. The baby looked at me, looked at the pancake boxes on the shelf, looked back at me and said, 'Look Ma, the real Aunt Jemima!'" (70). Read as a critique of the way the trademark has colonized the identities of African American women, the anecdote works quite admirably. Yet even the incomplete history I have discussed suggests that, far from operating exclusively in a black/white binary as a lingering racist icon of slavery, Aunt Jemima is better understood as a site where the statuses of many other demographic groups in addition to African American women were altered according to the needs of an ever-changing country. The compulsion to repeat an undocumented narrative about Aunt Jemima can thus be understood, perhaps, as a parable about the ongoing creation of "America." The harder we try to get at the truth of our history, the more inextricably entangled we end up in that history's self-legitimating "legends."

Free at Last

> Does anybody know what ever happened to
> Aunt Jemima on the pancake box?

Rumor has it that she just up and disappeared.
     Well, I know the real story
You see I ran into Aunt Jemima one day.
     She told me she got tired of wearing that rag
          wrapped around her head.
And she got tired of making pancakes and waffles for
          other people to eat while she couldn't sit
               down at the table.
     She told me that Lincoln emancipated the slaves
But she freed her own damn self.
     You know
The last time I saw Aunt Jemima
     She was driving a Mercedes-Benz
     with a bumper sticker on back that said
"Free at last, free at last,
     Thank God all mighty
     I am free at last."

          Sylvia Dunnavant, "Aunt Jemima," 1983

In fall of 1994 Quaker Oats announced that singer Gladys Knight had agreed to represent Aunt Jemima products in television advertisements. Faced with accusations that she was perpetuating a derogatory image of black women, Knight was quick to formulate an important distinction: "I'm not Aunt Jemima. I'm only a spokesperson. . . . What matters to me is what's inside the box" (quoted in Waldron 59). Three years earlier the company had launched a community partnership program with the National Council of Negro Women (NCNW), an organization of racial "uplift" founded by Mary McLeod Bethune in 1935. Also greeted with skepticism by many African Americans, "The program included a contest in seven cities with NCNW community-based sections that encouraged individuals to nominate the black, female leader who best exemplified community service, church activism, family ideals, and career development" (Kern-Foxworth, *Aunt* 104). Whether praised or condemned, both ventures might be understood as a continuation of a long-standing tradition whereby black resistance to the Quaker Oats trademark has gone hand in hand with complicity in its perpetuation. What this complicated situation suggests is that Aunt Jemima should not be read simply as a site of white male corporate appropriation of African American women's bodies and histories, though as Sylvia Dunnavant's poem implies, that is a valid and necessary interpretation. Rather, one direction I have been heading is to construe the trademark as a site where such individual and collective boundaries have been mutually, albeit by no means equivalently, constructed and contested.[28]

    In the remainder of this chapter I will pursue this issue by looking more carefully at some of the diverse strategies of appropriation, mimicry, parody, and critique that African Americans have brought to their engagements with Aunt Jemima. I aim, then, to follow scholars such as Marilyn Kern-Foxworth in restoring a sense of African American agency to our understanding of the trademark's history. My analysis in this section is indebted to Homi Bhabha's theorization of stereotypes as a site of colonial ambivalence and therefore potentially also of anticolonial resistance (see "Other" and "Signs"). Yet, while pursuing this line of thought, I will heed Catherine Cole's critique of strains of formalism in postcolonial theory. As she persuasively argues, "scholars must place 'wonders' from the postcolonial world in a richly detailed historical and social context before declaring all hybrid cultural phenomena to be subversive signs" (215). African American recastings of the trademark which contest the semiotic system of white racial supremacy while naturalizing other modes of social inequality will thus by no means necessarily function in a purely "subversive" fashion. No matter how psychically satisfying, after all, a revenge fantasy that has Aunt Jemima engaging in hyperconspicuous consumption (i.e., "driving a Mercedes-Benz") surely has its limitations as a template for progressive social action.

This complicated interplay between collusion and opposition in African American deployments of the trademark can be seen as early as the simultaneous appearance of Nancy Green and Ida B. Wells at the 1893 World's Columbian Exposition in Chicago. Marquette, as we have seen, claimed that Green's stories about her own days in slavery were incorporated into the Aunt Jemima legend. Of most interest to me is the narrative attributing Aunt Jemima's origins to Colonel Higbee's "Deep South" Louisiana plantation. Thus far my research has turned up no evidence confirming that this narrative was in (wide) circulation prior to the publication of the "legend of Aunt Jemima" advertising series around 1920. But even if Green did not help create this fiction at her 1893 World's Fair debut, one should still be aware that Louisiana has long functioned as the epicenter of the United States for the racially ambiguous figure of the creole, a figure that has historically destabilized ideologies of black/white racial difference.

As Barbara Ladd has explained, in the years following the Louisiana Purchase in 1803, the definition of "creole" became a locus of contestation (527–32). To avoid being deprived of legal rights according to the "one drop" rule prevalent in the upper South, many creoles began to insist on the white racial purity of their Spanish and French heritage, purity which they signified by capitalizing "Creole," even as "the association of 'creole' with suggestions of colonialist race mixing persisted" (Ladd 529). By the 1880s, as the South was dismantling the tiny gains of Reconstruction and the rest of the country was being urged to support U.S. imperialism abroad, the Creole had again emerged in popular fiction and entertainments as a site of anxiety over the threat of miscegenation.[29] Lacking further evidence about precisely when and how the connection between Aunt Jemima and Louisiana emerged, I can only speculate for now about the extent to which Nancy Green might have helped implicate the Aunt Jemima trademark in the turn-of-the-century fixation on the prospective creolization of the United States.[30] But even if Marquette's attribution of the story to Green is incorrect, the participation of numerous African American women has still clearly been fundamental to the product's success over the years, and the result has been just such dialogizations of Aunt Jemima.[31]

At times, moreover, the black media has been more willing to acknowledge such complicity than has the white media. For example, whereas the *Chicago Daily Tribune* did not find Nancy Green's death particularly noteworthy, the *Chicago Defender* gave the 1923 accident front-page coverage under the headline "Aged

Woman Killed When Autos Crash." After offering details of the accident and the ongoing investigation, the paper observed, albeit in transparently restrained tones:

> In the death of Mrs. Green Chicagoans recall the history of an interesting figure. She was the original "Aunt Jemima" of pancake fame, and because of her native ability to make "flapjacks to the queen's taste" was selected by a milling company to travel the country as demonstrator and introduce their wheat cake brand wherever she went. She did this work for 20 years and attended all the world's fair expositions since 1893, with the exception of the Paris exposition, when she refused to cross the water.[32]

Taking into account the *Defender*'s frequent attacks on white dominance else-where in its news coverage, the last sentence could be understood to attribute to Green a hint of defiance in the role of Aunt Jemima which she might otherwise have been understood to lack.[33] Furthermore, contrary to Marquette's insistence on her "loyalty" to her white employer, Green's ultimate political aim of black em-powerment seems fairly clear from the activities of her private life: when not im-personating Aunt Jemima, she is reputed to have helped raise up to $3 million for the black community in her adopted home of Rockford, Illinois (C. Campbell 45).[34]

If we can generalize from a 1932 study of how southern urban blacks responded to selected national advertising campaigns, the *Defender*'s evident lack of enthusi-asm for Nancy Green's official profession must have reflected widespread contempt for the Aunt Jemima trademark among African Americans in the early decades of this century (P. Edwards 197–253). Asked to rate two different advertisements for the pancake mix—the first of which prominently featured the character of Aunt Jemima and the second of which did not—male and female laborers and profes-sionals alike condemned the first one: "Don't like reference in reading matter to Aunt Jemima's master" (242); "I have never bought Aunt Jemima flour, because it pertains to a slavery type of Negro" (243); "Don't like head rag and bandanna. Colored people don't wear them now. Don't see why they keep such pictures be-fore the public" (243); "I am prejudiced intensely against any picture of former slave mammy" (244); "I positively *hate* this illustration" (245).

Kern-Foxworth reproduces the complete results of this study and takes note of an important irony. Though they uniformly disliked the trademark's allusion to slavery and often refused to purchase Aunt Jemima products as a result, "the ad-vertisement where Aunt Jemima dominated the picture did capture the attention of the respondents more quickly than the one where her presence was minuscule" (*Aunt* 84). As it turns out, moreover, the advertisement foregrounding Aunt Jemima was among the more innocuous of available examples, its caption reading simply: "She Mixed Four Different Flours in a Special Way" (Edwards 227).[35] One can only speculate as to the nature of their commentary had the respondents been presented with some of Quaker Oats' less cautious appeals to the latent discon-tents of white domesticity. "Buckwheats with the 'Tang' Men Hanker For," blared a contemporaneous caption from the January 1927 issue of *Ladies' Home Journal*, thus positioning black women as guarantors of white male sexual, as well as gastro-nomic, satisfaction. Two years later, however, readers of the *Journal* would have encountered a much tamer subcaption: "Buckwheats with the Taste Men Hanker For" ("Surprise"). Perhaps the company had received complaints.

By the late 1930s, then-Communist-sympathizer Langston Hughes had joined this anonymous chorus of African American voices expressing disgruntled fascination with Aunt Jemima. He targeted both Hurst's *Imitation of Life* and Stahl's film version of the book in a short skit called "Limitations of Life." Set in Harlem and performed in 1938 at his Harlem Suitcase Theatre, the skit has three main characters, whose names parody those of the actors in Stahl's film. Audette Aubert (after Claudette Colbert) is a *"pretty blond maid"*; Mammy Weavers (after Louise Beavers) is *"a colored lady, in trailing evening gown, with tiara and large Metropolitan Opera program, speaking perfect English with Oxford accent"*; and Ed Starks (after Ned Sparks) is *"a sleek-headed jigaboo in evening clothes"* (656). In addition to reversing the racial identities of the actors, Hughes mocks corporate America's iconography of servitude. His directions for the stage set include the following notation: *"At right, electric stove, griddle, pancake turner, box of pancake flour (only Aunt Jemima's picture is white)"* (656). When Mammy Weavers suggests to Audette that she might like a day off, the servile maid responds, *"(flipping a pancake)* Not even a day off, Mammy Weavers! Ah wouldn't know what to do with it" (657). After Audette exits the stage, Ed remarks in exasperation: "Once a pancake, always a pancake! *(picks up Jemima box with white auntie on it, and shakes his head)"* (657).

As Jane Caputi has noted, the line "once a pancake" originated in Hurst's novel, and Sterling Brown had also appropriated it for the title of his blistering 1935 review of the novel and film in *Opportunity* magazine. Similarly, in her "Glossary of Harlem Slang," Hurst's former secretary Zora Neale Hurston had targeted the character of Delilah by pointedly defining "pancake" as "a humble type of Negro" (94). Yet, in their private correspondence with Hurst, neither Hurston nor Hughes offered anything but praise for *Imitation of Life*. Caputi contends that because Hurst was a well-known patron of black writers, both Hurston and Hughes chose to communicate through their art the criticism that they felt unable to offer her directly (701–2). But, arguably, they both also chose the more effective, because public, strategy of resistance. "Limitations of Life" is said to have been a great success among the African Americans in the audience, though most of the white patrons, Arnold Rampersad wryly observes, "were less amused" (*I, Too* 365).[36]

Meanwhile, black actors such as Hattie McDaniel and Louise Beavers continued to portray versions of the Aunt Jemima stereotype on-screen, despite criticism from black civil rights organizations and the black press. *Ebony*, which was begun after World War II as a literal imitation of *Life* magazine, had by 1948 begun castigating Hollywood for "sticking to the same old stereotypes of moon-faced maids and groveling menials, zoot entertainers and bug-eyed Stepin Fetchits in casting Negroes" in a series of newly released films ("Movie" 56). The same article carefully points out that Beavers "personally hates cooking and housework. When she was called upon to flip griddle cakes in *Imitation of Life*, a cook had to give her lessons in the art" (57). While Beavers made sure that the roles she played on-screen were contradicted by her private persona, McDaniel was more defiant in countering criticism of her willingness to conform to Hollywood expectations, responding that she would "play maid's roles as long as Negroes in real life work as menials" (57). Of course, another of her rejoinders to the same reproach is deservedly more legendary: "Why should I complain about making seven thousand dollars a week playing a maid? If I didn't, I'd be making seven dollars a week actually being one!" (quoted in Bogle 82). Though their weekly earnings were surely far less than McDaniel's, the hundreds of working-class African American women who over the years enacted Aunt Jemima in less prestigious venues than Hollywood—like the disavowed aunt of Elizabeth Alexander's poem "Ladders"—might well have justified their decisions in a similar fashion.

In this contradictory context of black defiance of and compliance with the popular equation of black women with domestic servitude, Quaker Oats managed to retain the image of a grinning, obese Aunt Jemima during the two decades following World War II, James Baldwin's 1951 pronouncement that "Aunt Jemima and Uncle Tom are dead" notwithstanding ("Many" 27). As the integrationist Civil Rights movement transformed during the subsequent decade into a nationalist drive for Black Power, however, African American male activists, writers, and artists intensified their attacks on the trademark. Malcolm X and Eldridge Cleaver both weighed in, but the most memorable appropriations stemmed from visual artists.[37] Jeff Donaldson's *Aunt Jemima (and the Pillsbury Dough Boy) '64* (1963–64), Joe Overstreet's *New Jemima* (1964), and Murry DePillars's *Aunt Jemima* (1968) all moved beyond ridiculing the trademark as a demeaning continuation of slave iconography to appropriate it as a symbol of the necessity of physical resistance to white domination.[38]

Paradoxically recuperating the trademark's origins among female impersonators in blackface minstrelsy, these artists tend to depict a phallicized Aunt Jemima in combat. Overstreet offers up a barefoot, bandanna-wearing, heavy-breasted black woman, more nearly a "Jezebel" than a "mammy" in her insistent sexuality (figure 1-3). Yet this Pop-art "New Jemima" is armed with an automatic rifle that is positioned at her waist as a symbolic erection. More tellingly, the woman's smiling gaze is directed at the viewer, while her rifle appears to be firing of its own accord in another direction entirely—a sign, according to Megan Granda, of the futility of modern technology and the failure of even this reincarnated Jemima to wield authentic black power (60). Donaldson and DePillars instead appropriate the trademark for the tradition of socialist realism with which Granda suggests their work has affinities (54–57). In their renderings, Jemima is a brawny proletarian. DePillars shows a bare-breasted, domineering, and obviously angry black woman bursting forth from a box of pancake mix, spatula raised in preparation for using it as, one surmises, a weapon (figure 1-4). Far from sexualizing her, the protruding breasts of this Jemima appear to be her most threatening feature. Whereas DePillars incorporates references in his drawing to the Chicago police force and to sites of numerous race riots, Donaldson is the only one of the three artists to depict an actual enemy (figure 1-5). His painting portrays an unarmed but decidedly masculine-visaged black woman defending herself from the raised billy club of a pot-bellied white police officer.

Despite important differences in their appropriations of Aunt Jemima, then,

FIGURE 1.3 Joe Overstreet, *The New Jemima* (102⅛" × 60¾"), 1964, 1970. Acrylic on fabric over plywood construction. Courtesy of The Menil Collection, Houston. Photograph by Houston Hickey-Robertson.

Overstreet, Donaldson, and DePillars all seem to be suggesting that the Quaker Oats trademark can be taken as an efficacious and/or representative comrade in the struggle against (bourgeois) white oppression only to the extent that "she" can be iconographically revisioned as a "he" and symbolically returned to the male-dominated minstrel/vaudeville stage. Considered from this perspective, all three works reveal marked concern with the role of black women in a so-called black man's revolution.

Currently unobtainable documents relating to Quaker Oats' advertising campaigns may eventually surface to prove the following speculation wrong, but it

FIGURE 1.4 Murry N. DePillars, *Aunt Jemima* (17¾" × 15"), 1968.
Ink on paper. Courtesy of the artist.

seems to me that the company's accommodationist update of the trademark in
1968 is best understood as an attempt to contain such militant redeployments of
Aunt Jemima. After all, during an historical era in which African Americans were
widely valorizing blackness in the form of dark skin and Afros, the company offered up a lighter, slimmer Aunt Jemima, her neatly straightened hair tucked
under a headband. The official post-1968 Jemima would have appeared diametrically opposed to the political radicalism symbolized by someone like, for example,
Angela Davis. Yet to the extent that this company-sanctioned drawing of the
trademark has since lent itself to descriptions highlighting its racial hybridity—
e.g., "Afro-Asiatic" and "Creole"—one should also be aware that Quaker Oats' response to its black male critics may well have opened up avenues for counterhegemonic readings that the critics themselves did not foresee.[39]

Most notably, in his 1970 poem "Aunt Jemima of the Ocean Waves," Robert
Hayden avoided the revolutionary and nationalistic orientation of the male visual
artists. Instead he explored the legacy of minstrelsy for private interactions among
black Americans, namely by depicting an encounter between an African Ameri-

FIGURE 1.5 Jeff Donaldson, *Aunt Jemima (and the Pillsbury Dough Boy)* '64 (48" × 48"), 1963–64, oil on linen. Courtesy of the artist.

can male carnival patron (one infers) and a sideshow Aunt Jemima impersonator. As the poem begins, the patron is meditating on the connection between this performer and the "freak show" into which she is attempting to lure the crowd:

> Enacting someone's notion of themselves
> (and me), The One And Only Aunt Jemima
> and Kokimo The Dixie Dancing Fool
> do a bally for the freak show.
>
> I watch a moment, then move on,
> pondering the logic that makes of them
> (and me) confederates
> of The Spider Girl, The Snake-skinned Man. (18)

Appalled by what he has seen, the narrator quickly decides to absolve the performers of blame for their collusion with white racism, concluding that the "[p]oor devils have to live somehow" (18).

Shortly thereafter he is lying on a nearby beach when the Aunt Jemima delineator accosts him: "Trouble you for a light?" (19). Immediately the patron betrays his inability to assess accurately the woman's intentions: his description of her as "[u]nmindful (perhaps) / of my embarrassment" acknowledges that he cannot inhabit her point of view (19). The performer's motivations in conversing with the man thus left open to question, much of the rest of the poem is given over to her narration of her past, including her travels abroad "as the Sepia High Stepper" (19) and as "Mysteria From / The Mystic East—veils and beads / and telling suckers how to get / stolen rings and sweethearts back" (20). The woman concludes this narrative of her life with a caustic summation: "So here I am, so here I am, / fake mammy to God's mistakes. / And that's the beauty part, / I mean, ain't that the beauty part" (20). Her listener observes that the woman enjoys her joke but acknowledges, "I do not, knowing what / her laughter shields. And mocks" (21).

The "beauty part" of the woman's situation seems evident: as "fake mammy to God's mistakes," she is being held responsible for creating the sideshow "freaks," which inevitably calls into question her own humanity as a black woman. Presumably the narrator does not join in her amusement because he knows that the woman's "laughter shields" her anger at the racism of the dominant white society. But one cannot help wondering if he also perceives her laughter to "mock" him, along with her white creators and audience. The woman could well be contemptuous of him for having paused to view her performance in the first place, for having succumbed to an unexplained desire to gaze upon a pivotal emblem of black oppression, indeed for having been complicit in the interracial cultural dynamic through which the Aunt Jemima stereotype is sustained. In this fashion, the poem intimates that even members of a colonized group cannot always distinguish between authentic and inauthentic cultural practices. The narrator wants to believe that the woman is sincere in making him a "confederate" to her deconstruction of her stage personas, but he cannot quite rid himself of the belief that she is still wearing the mask. The poignancy of the poem thus derives, at least in part, from his perception not only that the joke might finally be on him, but that he will never even know for sure whether it is or not.

Meanwhile, as the various epigraphs to this chapter are intended to demonstrate, it did not take long for African American women activists, writers, and artists to emerge as leaders in challenging Quaker Oats' refusal to retire the trademark. In *Thursdays and Every Other Sunday Off*, Grosvenor prefaced her grocery store anecdote with the information that "Aunt Jemima is younger, lighter, and slimmer these days. And her head rag is not a rag anymore. It's a headband, and if you look closely you will see a bit of straight dark brown hair showing. But Quaker Oats blew it, cause on the syrup (next to the pancake) she is shown with the original head rag. Check it out" (69). What is particularly noteworthy, however, is that Grosvenor used her discussion of the trademark to critique not primarily corporate capitalism, but far more centrally the racism of the white women's liberation movement: "While Ms. Anne is out solving the feminine mystique, who is cleaning the house?" (65). By treating Aunt Jemima as a symbol for black women—a "she" rather than an "it"—Grosvenor not only neglects to interrogate the ways in which men benefit from the ideological construction of domestic labor as a privatized relationship between white mistress and black servant, but she also obfuscates the fact that the labor of most immediate concern to Quaker Oats is that of factory employees rather than domestic servants.

FIGURE 1.6 Betye Saar, *The Liberation of Aunt Jemima* (11 ¾" × 8" × 2 ¾"), mixed media, 1972. Courtesy of the University of California, Berkeley Art Museum; purchased with the aid of funds from the National Endowment for the Arts.

The same year, visual artist Betye Saar likewise appropriated these periodic corporate makeovers of Aunt Jemima as a strategy of resistance to white racism—and perhaps, like Grosvenor, to racist white "women's libbers" as well. In *The Liberation of Aunt Jemima* (1972), Saar juxtaposes multiple images of the trademark as it appeared after the 1968 update against a mammy figure evocative of the Aunt Jemima cookie jars sold in the first half of this century: very dark, very heavy, eyes bulging, teeth bared in a grin (figure 1-6).[40] Providing a useful reminder that it was not just African American men who advocated militarized resistance during the Black Power era, this cookie-jar Jemima holds "a gun instead of a rolling pin," and a fist positioned as a Black Power salute rises up from the bottom of the frame (Saar, quoted in Andrews). Unlike the phallic protagonists in the works by Overstreet, Donaldson, and DePillars, however, Saar's mammies are not masculinized. Dick Gregory had insisted in a 1971 *Ebony* article that the continued representation of Aunt Jemima as "fat" and "out-of-shape" was a form of psychic abuse in-flicted upon black people by white racism ("My" 72). But in Saar's work the polit-ical threat emerges precisely because her armed Aunt Jemima is otherwise identi-cal to the cookie jars created by white America: obese, black, and smiling. The potential for rebellion, her portrayal might suggest, is already contained within the stereotype and simply awaits activation under the right historical circumstances.

If Saar both embraced and distanced herself from the masculinist posturing of prevailing Black Power ideologies, by the early 1980s other African American women artists, such as Freida High W. Tesfagiorgis and Faith Ringgold, had begun appropriating the Aunt Jemima trademark for overtly black feminist politics. Whereas Tesfagiorgis's distinctive pastel painting *Aunt Jemima's Matrilineage* (1982) deploys Afrocentric feminism to intimate that the Aunt Jemima trademark has re-pressed origins in West African cultures, Ringgold's story quilt *Who's Afraid of Aunt Jemima* (1983) offers a still more elaborate deconstruction of the famous mammy cook stereotype in that it dialogizes not just the visual trademark but also the so-called legend of Aunt Jemima (figure 1-7).[41] The quilt intersperses visual iconography with written prose narrating the history of Ringgold's protagonist, now called Jemima Blakey. We learn of Blakey's birth to free parents in Louisiana; of her decision to defy their wishes in eloping to Florida with a preacher's son; of her inheritance of an employer's wealth and subsequent move to New York; of her successful career as a restaurant owner and caterer; of her relationship with her son and daughter; of her return to New Orleans to open a new restaurant; even of her death in, surely not coincidentally, a car accident (text reproduced in Granda 71–75, n. 12).[42]

The significance of this artistic strategy, according to Megan Granda, is that in Ringgold's quilt Aunt Jemima ceases to be a stereotype because "[s]he no longer signifies a collective identity" (62). As had the originators of the "legend of Aunt Jemima" campaign, "the artist creates a historical character by presenting the viewer with 'episodes' of her life" (62). Whereas Marquette claimed that James Webb Young drew on Nancy Green's griotic skills in creating his famed advertising series, Ringgold reverses this process of appropriation (yet again). She reinvents the Aunt Jemima legend so as to refute the trademark's hegemonic portrayal of a surnameless and contentedly subservient mammy.[43] Her critique is further ironized, according to Eleanor Munro, by the fact that it is "delivered in the ma-terial terms of a household item under which one might be expected to take a comfortable nap" (*Faith* 21).

Yet what perhaps most interests me about the quilt is Ringgold's success in ex-posing the repressions in the presentation of Aunt Jemima's racial identity. Earlier I explained how the narrative associating Aunt Jemima with Louisiana might have implicated the trademark in anxieties about the racial instabilities of the Cre-ole. In her quilt, Ringgold foregrounds these syncretic aspects of African Ameri-can identity in a variety of ways. For instance, we learn that Jemima's mother "was half Indian. A real beauty in her youth, she was coal black with long braids and keen features" (quoted in Granda 74). Jemima's daughter Georgia is described, by contrast, as "high yaller liken her Pa," with "green eyes and long straight hair she could sit on" (quoted in Granda 73). Meanwhile, Jemima's son Lil Rufus has three

FIGURE 1.7 Faith Ringgold, *Who's Afraid of Aunt Jemima* (90" × 80"), painted and pieced fabric, 1983. Private collection. © 1983 Faith Ringgold Inc. Courtesy of the artist.

daughters with his white wife Margo, who is, aptly enough, German; despite this Caucasian ancestry, all three girls are dark-skinned like their grandmother Jemima (Granda 73).

After Jemima and Big Rufus are killed in the car accident, they are given "an African funeral—Praise God! Dressed Jemima in an African gown and braided her hair with cowry shells. Put Big Rufus in a gold dashiki" (quoted in Granda 75). One might argue that Ringgold uses this ending to subsume the racial and ethnic "impurities" acknowledged earlier in the quilt narrative into an essentialized African identity. But I would suggest instead that her depiction of the funeral actually serves to undermine Afrocentric models to the extent that they can tend to elide or delegitimate the non-African constituents of black American culture. In other words, the African funeral can be understood as a failure of imagination on the part of Jemima and Rufus's children. Caught up in a black nationalist rebellion that downplayed the political militancy of preceding generations, they were unable to recognize that their parents had already formulated strategies of resistance to white domination—albeit thoroughly compromised strategies that emerged in the wake of postdiasporic cultural exchange. Among other things, Jemima had inherited a white man's money, and she and her husband went to their graves as wealthy capitalist entrepreneurs. As I have already indicated, I do not think black resistance should be uncritically equated with black capitalism. Nevertheless, it is important to recognize that, since the quilt was produced in the context of Reagan-era attacks on black "welfare queens," the success of Ringgold's Jemima as a restaurant owner provides a salient counternarrative to pejorative representations of African American women as lacking a sufficient work ethic.[44]

In her contemporaneous poem "The Black Back-Ups," Donna Kate Rushin might also be construed as critiquing this neoconservative political discourse of the early 1980s. The poem is dedicated to the women of color whose expropriated and largely invisible labor has kept American society functioning: the launderers for college students, the back-up singers to stars such as Elvis Presley and James Taylor, the actors who have been confined to roles as asexual domestic servants in Hollywood films. Granted, Rushin tends to obscure the important distinction which Hattie McDaniel herself had drawn between relatively well-paid actors who portray domestic servants and usually underpaid workers who perform domestic labor. Yet, by incorporating the common childhood dozens chant "Ain't chure Mama on the pancake box" into her poem (63), Rushin does effectively turn the reader's attention to the toll exacted by black women's work as domestic servants on the black children who, left alone, are forced to "mother" themselves.[45] Intriguingly, moreover, though she portrays the poem's child-speaker as indulging in a fantasy segment in which her or his mother resists the hegemonic Quaker Oats narrative ("And my Mama leaps offa that box"), Rushin refuses to allow this dream sequence to sustain itself: "Mama Mommy Mommy Mammy Mammy / Mam-mee Mam-mee / I'd Walk a mill-yon miles / For one o' your smiles" (63). "The Black Back-Ups" thus demonstrates how the legacy of blackface minstrelsy has inflected even the most intimate of African American relationships. Crying for her or his mother, the child is transformed into none other than Al Jolson serenading his mother in *The Jazz Singer*.

Published seven years later, Elizabeth Alexander's poem "Ladders" explores terrain hauntingly similar to that of both Rushin and Robert Hayden, while offering the reader a somewhat less ambiguous set of expectations for action. By juxtaposing the "white rolls / of black fat" against the "bowls / and bowls of pale batter," Alexander evokes the mammy's historical transfiguration from flesh into food. Donna, meanwhile, initially "sees" not her own aunt—but rather the emblem of decades of degradation, a specter to be disavowed. Through her call to "Donessa," the aunt attempts to relocate herself and her "audience" in an actual familial relationship. The failure of her attempt forces us as readers to admit to the silent niece's complicity in the making of Aunt Jemima. A nod from Donessa would expose her aunt as a simulacrum, a model "of a real without origin or reality: a hyperreal" (Baudrillard 166). In depicting the anguished (and angry) aunt's unceasing demands for recognition, the poem challenges the reader not to disavow the "long-gone sister," not to dismiss her as "Jemima?" or a "buck-eyed rhesus /

monkey." "Ladders" dares us, moreover, to accept the aunt's decision to put on the mask in the first place, for when all is said and done, helping to create the reality-effect of Aunt Jemima "[p]ays the rent." My study of the sometimes liberatory and sometimes politically compromised association between African American women and food might be construed as an extended response to the imperative "Answer me."

two

Biscuits Are Being Beaten

Craig Claiborne and the Epistemology
of the Kitchen Dominatrix

Of course I'll gladly give de rule
    I meks beat biscuit by,
Dough I ain't sure dat you will mek
    Dat bread de same as I.

'Case cookin's like religion is—
    Some's 'lected, an' some ain't,
An' rules don't no more mek a cook
    Den sermons mek a Saint.

Well, 'bout de 'grediances required
    I needn't mention dem,
Of course you knows of flour and things,
    How much to put, an' when;

But soon as you is got dat dough
    Mixed up all smoove an' neat,
Den's when your genius gwine to show,
    To get dem biscuit beat!

Two hundred licks is what I gives
    For home-folks, never fewer,
An' if I'm 'spectin' company in,
    I gives five hundred sure!

        (Miss) Howard Weeden,
        "Beaten Biscuit," 1899

"**B**eaten Biscuit" appears in a volume of plantation school poems by the discreetly credited (Miss) Weeden. Introduced to the public by Joel Chandler Harris, *Bandanna Ballads* is "[d]edicated to the memory of all the faithful mammies who ever sung southern babes to rest" (n. pag.). Like other works from this tradition, the poems hearken to a romanticized or, more accurately, fictionalized antebellum past, a period when "the old-time quality negro" (x), as Harris puts it, was "quaint and gentle . . . tender-hearted and devoted" (xi). The speaker is clearly intended to be a slave woman; the implied listener, probably her mistress.

Weeden's poem encapsulates many of the issues that drew me to the topic of African American women and food in the first place. In particular, it dramatizes what one might risk terming a "primal scene" of recipe exchange, in the kitchen, between women: a primal pre-textual scene because the transmission is oral, not written; a primal precapitalist scene because no money changes hands; a primal southern scene because the giver of the recipe is black and the receiver is white; a primal plantation school scene, finally, because the exchange, for reasons the slave and the mistress would doubtless construe quite differently, fails to take place.[1] No rules are communicated. This transaction thus differs in several important respects from the narrative that was used to explain R. T. Davis's acquisition of a slave woman's "secret" pancake recipe. As one of the Young/Wyeth advertisements from 1921 put it, Aunt Jemima "had sold to a big milling company in the North the pancake recipe that had made her famous, the recipe that no other mammy cook could equal" ("Aunt"). Both men and money intrude into this scene of exchange, which was for obvious reasons represented as having been an unmitigated success.

In addition to providing an intriguing counterpoint to the "legend of Aunt Jemima" campaign, "Beaten Biscuit" fascinates me because it was published in the same year that the domestic science movement held the first in a series of national conferences through which it began to be institutionalized in the academy in departments of home economics (Shapiro 7). Three years earlier Fannie Farmer had published The Boston Cooking-School Cook Book, a text largely responsible for standardizing the format of the recipe and cookbook as we know them today: ingredients listed in columns in the order of use; succinct, depersonalized instructions for making the dish. Known as "The Mother of Level Measurements" (Shapiro 106), Farmer would have been scandalized by the assumption that knowledge of "how much to put and when" could be taken for granted. "Correct measurements," she insists, "are absolutely necessary to insure the best results," and "the majority need definite guides" (27).

Clearly Weeden is setting up the "mammy" cook in opposition to the "scientific" cooks from New England who had begun to infiltrate the South by 1900.[2] As culinary historian Laura Shapiro explains:

> Domestic scientists were inspired by the nutritive properties of food, by its ability to promote physical, social, and, they believed, moral growth. The flavors of food were of slight, somewhat anthropological interest. They did understand very well that many people enjoyed eating; this presented still another challenge. Food was powerful, it could draw forth cravings and greedy desires which had to be met with a firm hand. . . . Containing and controlling food, draining it of taste and texture, packaging it . . . decorating it—these were some of the major culinary themes of the domestic-science movement. (6–7)

The cuisine these women created was, as one might imagine, far from manna to the white southern palate accustomed to biscuits given two-hundred to five-hundred licks, and the figure of the mammy cook was increasingly invoked among southern whites as the rapidly vanishing source of epicurean delights. This trend was sufficiently widespread that by 1905 William Lloyd Garrison's grandson Oswald Garrison Villard was moved to comment, in bemusement: "To hear people talk in Georgia or Virginia we might easily think that every slave was a Chesterfieldian butler or a mistress of the art of old-time cooking" (quoted in Katzman 192).[3] Within six years, a "Black Mammy Memorial Institute" had been founded in Athens, Georgia, to replicate "the special training given the negroes of the old régime, by the best class of Southern slaveholders" (Berry 563) and, consequently, "to fill a crying need" (Berry 562). So powerful was this fantasy that decades later southern cookbooks still abounded with references to the "wizard of the kitchen" (Colquitt xvi, n. 1) or the "beaming, be-turbaned darkies" (Ott 9) who were unable to articulate how they created their culinary masterpieces.[4]

Yet the mythologizing component of their vision is easily seen if one takes into account the fact that perhaps nowhere in the South was this philosophy of domestic science practiced with more fervor than at newly established black colleges such as Hampton and Tuskegee. In her memoir in the 1905 volume *Tuskegee and Its People*, for example, Mary L. Dotson tells how during her first years at Tuskegee she "knew nothing of the science of foods; nothing at all, at that time, of anything that indicated that cooking is a real science. . . . I began to study chemistry in the academic department, and when it was applied in my cooking lessons my eyes were opened. I now saw much that I had not dreamed of" (203–4). In a testimony of scientific revelation which might well be set to the tune of "Amazing Grace," Dotson admits that she once was blind, but now, Fannie Farmer be praised, she sees.

Systematically coerced into domestic service, as they have been since the Civil War, many black women were in fact sympathetic to this modernist religion of science and technology, a religion that aimed to elevate the status of household labor, to turn the kitchen into a laboratory and the home into an efficiently run factory. Not that their strategy necessarily worked. As David Katzman has argued, despite the concerted efforts of reformers, "The presence of servants permitted traditionalism to dominate in the organization of the household; modernization, the 'industrial revolution' in the home, accompanied the reduction in numbers of or the disappearance of servants" (ix).[5] Southerners, in particular, were ambivalent about whether their kitchens should be allowed to succumb to historical change.

"Beaten Biscuit" thus situates us once again—but from a different vantage point—in the era that gave rise to Aunt Jemima, an important transitional era when cooking, eating habits, and cookbooks, like many other aspects of U.S. culture, became increasingly standardized, scientized, and commodified; an era when the slave-labor-intensive lineage of southern cuisine began to be displaced by modern technology and consumer capitalism.[6] Yet, as we have seen, the numerous anxieties which accompanied these changes went well beyond what the South labeled not the "servant problem" but rather the "'trouble with Negroes'—Negroes and servants being synonymous terms in the average [white] Southerner's vocabulary" (Langhorne 108). For middle- and upper-class white southerners, complaints about the unavailability or unreliability of servants and nostalgia for dying dietary practices surely also served to express individual and collective fears about threats to white patriarchal power in a volatile social order. I am interested less in how these plantation school narratives functioned at the turn of the century, however, than in why they have been continually recuperated up to the present, especially in the years following the demise of Black Power.

If Michael Rogin is right to argue that the blackface mammy role has historically given "white boys permission to play with their identities, to fool around" (13), then in this chapter I will focus primarily on well-known food critic Craig Claiborne to pursue the question of how the mammy cook has functioned in the bourgeois white male imagination so as to allow this free play of identity, not to mention why white boys have wanted or needed thus to "fool around" in the first place. Though my discussion of numerous cookbooks by white women will acknowledge the salience of the "between women" scenario such as that represented by "Beaten Biscuit," I aim finally to destabilize commonplace representations of (southern) domestic labor in which white men and white male power have been largely invisible.[7] My working hypothesis will be that these discourses about dominating domestics and endangered diets are useful because they enable the negotiation of fissures, or contradictions, in the psychic as well as socioeconomic structures through which hegemonic identities (such as white masculinity) have been produced in the United States, including the simultaneous necessity for and foreclosure of cross-racial, homoerotic desire. The metaphor of the "closet," which Eve Sedgwick has brilliantly located as the nucleus of Western constructions of male sexuality, might from this perspective find a more racially nuanced counterpart in the "kitchen."[8]

"To Create or Have Created"

> Although many people who have an intense interest in French cooking would sooner eat TV dinners than use the word "gourmet," I could tell that the guests . . . were gourmets from the way they referred to the prominent figures of American *haute cuisine* by their first names. . . . "I got that recipe from Julia," one of them might say, or "Craig said it was superb."
>
> Calvin Trillin, *American Fried,* 1974

Now retired, Craig Claiborne was a food and restaurant critic for the *New York Times* from 1957 until 1972, and again from 1974 until 1988.[9] The first man to be named food editor of a major metropolitan newspaper, Claiborne published hundreds of columns during his thirty-year tenure and authored or coauthored over twenty cookbooks. He achieved a measure of fame, as well as some notoriety, in the process.[10] Trained at L'École Hôtelière, L'École Professionnelle de la Société Suisse des Hôteliers (the Professional School of the Swiss Hotel Keepers Association), Claiborne has, not coincidentally, been an unabashed Francophile in his culinary allegiances (*Feast* 92). He is one of a group of food writers and chefs whom John Hess and Karen Hess labeled "The Gourmet Plague" in their dyspeptic history of American cooking, *The Taste of America* (1977). According to Hess and Hess, the professional epicures who dominated the American culinary scene after World War II disdained fresh, high-quality food, plainly prepared:

> But take the breast of an American chicken (the most tasteless and cottony part of a tasteless and cottony bird), blanket it with a pasty white sauce (calling it *velouté* makes it so very French, *n'est-ce pas?*), arrange it prettily on a bed of spinach (frozen, chopped, and bound with that same horrid sauce.—you may now call it *à la Florentine*), strew slivered almonds or grated cheese about, glaze it, and you have a gourmet masterpiece. (153)

Claiborne is singled out for disapprobation, but Hess and Hess also target Julia Child, Simone Beck, James Beard, Jacques Pépin, and Claiborne's frequent collaborator, Pierre Franey. In their penchant for flour-laden sauces and canned or frozen foods, in their "use of costly ingredients *because* they are costly" (155), all are responsible for propagating what Hess and Hess view as woefully bowdlerized French cooking that does a disservice to France and the United States alike.

Though a self-professed "snob" (*Feast* 23), especially in his continental-oriented culinary philosophies, Claiborne has never been reticent about his roots in the U.S. South. He discusses his Mississippi childhood and youth in his 1982 autobiography *A Feast Made for Laughter* and again in his 1987 cookbook *Craig Claiborne's Southern Cooking* (hereafter *Southern*). Claiborne describes the southern cooking on which he was raised as falling "into three categories—soul food, which is a blend of African and American Indian; creole cookery, which is a marriage of innocent Spanish and bastardized French; and pure French, desserts mostly, from the first edition of *The Boston Cooking-School Cook Book*" (*Feast* 31). Whereas Hess and Hess contend that Fannie Farmer "embodied . . . all the major ills of twentieth-century culinary teaching" (113–14), Claiborne considers her *Boston Cooking-School Cook Book* to be, "in its original concept, the first great cookbook in America" (*Feast* 31).

Even as he remained loyal to the most influential of the domestic scientists, Claiborne's ideologically loaded references to the "blend" which gave rise to soul food and the "marriage" which resulted in creole cookery are a suggestive reminder that he was writing in the wake of the social movements of the 1960s and 1970s. One of soul food's more prominent white popularizers by 1969, he was clearly paying lip service to efforts to recognize the diversity of American culture, including its culinary heritage.[11] Then again, if we take into account my discussion in the preceding chapter of the racial anxieties that could have been associated with Aunt Jemima's Louisiana origins, it is also worth noting that Claiborne effectively elides African American contributions to creole cookery in his determination to formulate distinct "categories" of culinary identity.

Given this somewhat cagey obscuration of the fact that gastronomic miscegenation accompanied human miscegenation in the South, it should come as no surprise that Claiborne's recollections of his upbringing often sound as though they were written in the 1880s rather than in the 1980s. Born in 1920 to a downwardly mobile upper-class family, his earliest memories revolve no less around the family's African American servants than around his parents and two older siblings.

While the Claibornes occupied a "fairly handsome and solidly built" house with "a fireplace in almost all the bedrooms" (*Feast* 3), the servants lived in "two well-kept wooden shacks or shanties that were referred to as 'nigger cabins'" (*Feast* 5). The walls of these "drafty" shacks "were covered with full-sized pages of the Sunday rotogravure sections of the Memphis *Commercial Appeal*" (*Feast* 5), presumably because Claiborne's "black friends" (*Feast* 6) did not find the Mississippi climate as "temperate" as he did (*Feast* 3). "In the very beginning," he further recalls, "I had a black nurse named Aunt Catherine who was, in fact, my surrogate mother. For better or worse, Southern-style in those unreconstructed days, I never knew or wondered about her last name" (*Southern* xiv). By referring to his 1920s childhood as though it had taken place prior to the Reconstruction—if not outside postbellum U.S. history entirely—Claiborne is better able to naturalize and disclaim his class, race, and gender privilege over the person whose job it was to take care of him. His ambivalent "for better or worse" trumpets his "unreconstructed" desire to believe that his childhood perceptions of his black nurse are not wholly fictive, that the woman he called "Aunt Catherine" thought of herself as his "surrogate mother."

Having located himself squarely in the tradition of plantation school writers, Claiborne explains that his father lost his wealth in the early 1920s, when Claiborne was still an infant, and moved the family to a nearby town. Subsequently, his mother decided to open their home as a boardinghouse, this being "one of the few paths a properly brought up and aristocratic young southern woman could follow while holding her chin and prestige up" (*Feast* 13). Claiborne describes his mother as "a fantastic and 'born' cook" (*Feast* 25) who "could dine in New Orleans and come back to reproduce on her own table the likes of oysters Rockefeller, oysters Bienville, the creole version (so different from the original French) of rémoulade sauce with shrimp" (*Feast* 31). But he also admits that "she was not alone in her efforts" (*Feast* 25). Despite the collapse of his father's investments, the Claibornes were able to retain hired help:

> Although our finances had reached a nadir, we still had numerous servants in the kitchen, all of them black. And that kitchen is where I spent my childhood. The servants—Joe and Blanche and Sally and Hugh—were my friends and playmates.
> Blanche was the chief cook and she made the best fried chicken in the world. (*Southern* xvi)

Claiborne's willingness to pay homage to the culinary talents of these employees is compromised by the fact that the acknowledgments page of *Southern Cooking* mentions no one named Joe or Blanche or Sally or Hugh, whose last names Claiborne evidently never bothered to learn either. Under "chicken" in the index, he offers several dishes called "My mother's" so and so (351–52), but the fried chicken recipe does not mention Blanche.

These discrepancies in Claiborne's attribution of culinary credit are most clearly illustrated in his account of his relationship with Blanche's chief assistant, Joe. Claiborne describes Joe as "a buffoon. A short man with close-cropped hair, there was something about him that looked just a bit oriental" (*Feast* 28). Having defused the threat Joe posed as a culinary rival by quite literally Orientalizing him,

Claiborne then allows that he was a "magnificent cook" who "made the best lemon meringue and custard pies in the world" (*Feast* 28). Joe, moreover, was essential to Claiborne's own first endeavors in the kitchen:

> When I was about twelve or thirteen years old I *conceived* my first "*original*" dish. For some reason unfathomable to me, I decided I would like to sample creamed chicken livers, and I mentioned this to Joe, the second in command of that boardinghouse kitchen. And *prepare* it he did to my great delight. It consisted simply of sautéed chicken livers served in a light cream sauce, heavily spiced with black pepper.
>
> Another of my youthful *inventions* in that kitchen was a dish that (long before I became a professional food writer) stood me in good stead, Sunday after Sunday, when I entertained at lunch in my bachelor quarters in Chicago. My mother would, at times, *serve* eggs Benedict (a distinctly Yankee creation) for special occasions. I decided *to create or have created* my own version of that dish. I asked Joe to *make* me sliced ham on toast triangles with a poached egg and a cheese sauce spooned on top. He did, and it was a great success. (emphasis added; *Southern* xvii)

Claiborne, it would appear, is torn between two narratives. In his idealized fantasy world he is indeed the originating genius. Asking Joe to "prepare" the food does not undermine the myth of Claiborne the "creator." But, of course, conception cannot so easily be separated from preparation; "to create" and to "have created" are not the same thing. This method of appropriating culinary credit is quite typical not just among southern cookbook writers, but also in U.S. culinary history as a whole. Repeatedly one finds that the highly acclaimed cookbook writer, eminent host, or renowned chef is white and that the unnamed servants and (line) cooks are all persons of color.[12]

This use of the creation/preparation distinction to deny credit to African American cooks is perhaps most memorably exemplified among Claiborne's predecessors by cookbook author Marion Cabell Tyree. She explicitly situates her *Housekeeping in Old Virginia* (1879) as a response to changes wrought on upper-class white households by the Civil War.[13] When discussing the physical labor involved in making bread, for instance, Tyree draws a noteworthy distinction between the "theory" and the "practice" of bread-making:

> Resolve that you *will* have good bread, and never cease striving after this result till you have effected it. If persons without brains can accomplish this, why cannot you? I would recommend that the housekeeper acquire the practice as well as the theory of bread-making. In this way, she will be able to give more exact directions to her cook and to more readily detect and rectify any blemish in the bread. Besides, if circumstances should throw her out of a cook for a short time, she is then prepared for the emergency. In this country fortunes are so rapidly made and lost, the vicissitudes of life are so sudden, that we know not what a day may bring forth. It is not uncommon to see elegant and refined women brought suddenly face to face with emergencies which their practical knowledge of household economy and their brave hearts enable them to firmly meet and overcome. (19)

The binary opposition Tyree sets up between "theory" and "practice" anticipates in many ways the writings of Claiborne over a century later. Here the mistress functions as the "brains" in the domestic operation, the learned authority who

must oversee and instruct the witless cook. White theory gives rise to black practice. At the same time, in granting that it is possible to know the theory and not
the practice—indeed in granting that during "emergencies" theory is finally su-
perseded in importance by practice—Tyree undermines her own narrative fiction. This is not to suggest that black practice gave rise to white theory; such a
claim would reify the stereotypical association of blacks with the work of the
body and of whites with the life of the mind. It is rather to point out that the entire theory/practice dichotomy has functioned to help distinguish the roles of
mistress (or master) and servant at times when those boundaries were in flux. In
the years following not just the Civil War and Great Migration, but also the Civil
Rights and Black Power movements, writing cookbooks and talking about servants became a way of "performing" white (southern) identity, perhaps most especially by those who perceived their privileged social and economic position to
be at risk.[14]

Claiborne is thus by no means a pioneer in his distorted representation of
African Americans in U.S. culinary history. Nor was he alone in continuing this
plantation school legacy in the 1980s. Some of the best known contemporary
southern food writers, including Nathalie Dupree and Camille Glenn, adopt
strategies similar to Claiborne's in reconciling their status as well-off whites with
an altered sociopolitical terrain which, on the whole, allows less candor in celebrations of white supremacy than had previous eras.[15] In choosing to foreground
the former *New York Times* food critic, then, I do not mean to suggest that he has
been the only cookbook author in recent years to propagate plantation school ideology or that he is more deserving of disapprobation than are the others. And in
critiquing the racism of much southern white culinary history, I also do not mean
to err in the opposite direction by attributing culinary ability solely to African
Americans. In this sense, Claiborne's belief "that given the proper training in the
kitchen of a great French restaurant, any American black with cooking in his or
her soul, would be outstanding" is a reductive racist bromide in the guise of a com-
pliment (*Feast* 31).

As John Egerton cautions in *Southern Food,* "Not all blacks have been great
cooks, of course, and not all great cooks have been black" (16). But such stereotypes "die hard," he continues, "whether they are positive or negative—and both
extremes tend to be far removed from the truth. It is worth remembering that most
Southern whites did not own slaves in the colonial and antebellum periods and
did not have black servants after the Civil War" (16). Though Egerton is surely
underestimating the extent to which even lower-class white southerners relied on
the domestic labor of African Americans both before and after the Civil War, it
does seem evident that the widely shared desire to maintain boundaries between
servant and served is insufficient to explain the force, as it were, with which the
figure of the mammy cook is embedded in the white southern psyche—not to
mention in the national consciousness more broadly construed.[16] Accordingly, in
the next section I want to think further about the role of the black female kitchen
dominatrix in the construction of white American subjectivities by analyzing the
postbellum fascination with a much-touted southern breakfast bread: not commodified Aunt Jemima pancakes, but rather mammy-beaten biscuits.

To Beat or to Be Beaten

> Gone are the splendid brave old days
>   When cooking was a feat,
> When it stirred one's blood like victory
>   Just to hear the biscuit beat!
>
> Now the stately kitchens stand
>   Forsaken and forlorn,
> And now life's but a cowardly affair
>   Since all the cooks are gone!
>
> (Miss) Howard Weeden,
> "The Old Biscuit Block," 1904

Weeden clearly missed beaten biscuits. As in her earlier poem, she fixates in "The Old Biscuit Block" on the labor involved in their creation. But whereas "Beaten Biscuit" foregrounded a "private" exchange between cook and mistress, this poem explicitly expresses nostalgia for the relations of production that gave rise to the biscuits—chattel slavery. Indeed, for Weeden they seem to have borne the metonymic burden of slavery. Yet, in militarizing her recollection of hearing "the biscuit beat," she also locates the memory specifically in time, giving it, in effect, a history. Beaten biscuits signify not the Old South but the destruction of that South in the Civil War. For whites such as Weeden, they signify not victory but defeat. To the extent beaten biscuits mark the demise of the antebellum South, they are what I will term, following Slavoj Žižek, a "symptom" of the transition from a quasi-feudal system of slavery to capitalism. They operate at the intersection of the Marxian commodity and the Freudian/Lacanian fantasy, revealing both "the positive network of social relations" in capitalism and "the lack ('castration') around which the symbolic network is articulated" (Žižek 49). As such, beaten biscuits offer a useful perspective on the psychic investments of white Americans in maintaining the myth of mammy.[17]

Because the process of baking bread entails knowledge, experience, and strenuous physical labor, it has long been a topic of great concern to the writers of domestic manuals. Catharine Beecher and Harriet Beecher Stowe, for instance, viewed bread-making as the test of a good cook. "There are," they warned, "fifty ways to spoil good bread; there are a hundred little things to be considered and allowed for, that require accurate observation and experience" (315). Differences in the moisture content of the flour, in climate and altitude, in oven temperature— all these variables could affect the outcome dramatically. Bread not only frustrated their attempts to forge a science of domesticity, but it also took on a larger social significance. As Pierre Bourdieu has observed, "the taste for particular dishes . . . is associated, through preparation and cooking, with a whole conception of the domestic economy and of the division of labour between the sexes"; labor-intensive dishes are "linked to a traditional conception of woman's role" (185). The ability to recognize and "serve" good bread thus became for Beecher and Stowe a marker of what Bourdieu calls "distinction," signifying one's rank in the social hierarchy, for when allowed to rise unkneaded, "the bread is as inferior in delicacy and nicety to that which is well kneaded as a raw servant to a perfectly educated and refined lady" (Beecher and Stowe 174).

Like Beecher and Stowe, southern food writers also focused extensively on bread when discussing the demise of culinary traditions in the South. It is no coincidence that Tyree used bread in making the theory/practice distinction I discussed in the preceding section: after Emancipation, inexperienced cooks found bread-making to be a particularly daunting task. As had Tyree, *Virginia Cookery-Book* (1885) author Mary Stuart Smith expresses considerable consternation that persons she considers her racial, social, and (therefore) intellectual inferiors are able to make high-quality bread. She advises readers to take "comfort in reflecting that such stupid people have acquired the art that no one need despair, if she have only a willing mind" (4). At the same time, Smith also suggests that "a willing mind" alone will not suffice: "But I must say that the *best* bread-makers whom I know knead for at least an hour, and with all their might. Even then there is a magic in the touch of certain gifted ones that all cannot hope to acquire" (3). As was Tyree, Smith is caught here between competing ideologies. To suggest that it took only physical labor to make good bread would devalue work that she aimed to elevate. To acknowledge that it took more than physical labor to make good bread would be to attribute intelligence to black cooks, which she did not want to do. Thus her contradictory assertions: when African American cooks succeed in bread-making, they are "stupid people" who have a "magic in the touch"; when white cooks want to "learn" bread-making, they need have only a "willing mind."

But if upper-class southern whites found bread in general difficult to replace when "all the cooks were gone," their strongest psychic investments seem to have been in the most slave-labor-intensive of all southern breads: beaten biscuits. Certainly Weeden was not the only one to wax nostalgic about hearing "the biscuit beat." Smith also reminisces about how, in "the Virginia of olden time," beaten biscuits were considered "indispensable" to the "properly furnished" breakfast table: "Let one spend the night at some gentleman-farmer's home, and the first sound heard in the morning, after the crowing of the cock, was the heavy, regular fall of the cook's axe, as she beat and beat her biscuit-dough. Grown familiar, how appetizing the sound, as the gauge of good things to follow soon!" (7). The intensity of the memory would suggest that, like Weeden, Smith derived as much pleasure from listening to the cook "beat and beat her biscuit-dough" as she did from partaking of the finished product. Each day the second "sound heard in the morning" reassured her that all was well for privileged whites in the antebellum South. Another day of slavery had dawned.

Yet it turns out that for Smith, again as for Weeden, the biscuits actually signify not slavery but the demise of slavery: "Nowadays beaten biscuits are a rarity found here and there, but soda and modern institutions have caused them to be sadly out of vogue" (7). Whereas kneading or beating the dough by hand altered the texture of the wheat gluten and created air pockets that enabled the bread to rise, soda could be used to leaven it chemically—though the resulting bread differed markedly. And other "difficulties," Smith continues, also stood "in the way" (7):

In the first place, there must be a biscuit-block, usually the trunk of some solid oak or chestnut tree, felled and sawed off to a convenient height, when, of course, it must be planed smooth, and set up in some accessible place in or near the kitchen. Any ordinary table would soon be knocked to pieces, if used for this service. A machine may be obtained that answers the purpose admirably, but it is rare. We have only seen one specimen in use. Then an axe, with a short, stout handle, must hang ever ready to be applied to this use, and this alone is a condition hard to comply with in a Southern kitchen, where servants are careless, as a rule. Lastly, most servants object nowadays to the trouble of preparing this bread. But the house-keeper who has the energy to surmount these difficulties, and essays her skill in following the recipe here given, may be assured that she will be rewarded for her pains. (7–8)[18]

Smith's comments should remind us that the postbellum fascination with beaten biscuits was actually fueled not just by the demise of slavery and the emergence of the servant problem, but also by the advent of labor-saving devices, including bread-making machines. After the Civil War a number of such machines were created to assist "the work" of beating the biscuit dough; the first patent was awarded in 1877 to Evelyn L. Edwards of Vineland, New Jersey. According to John Egerton, Edwards's machine was operated by a hand crank that was used to turn two rollers, through which the dough was passed repeatedly. "Like the cotton gin," he reports, "this Yankee invention swept through the South, and for another half-century or more, it not only saved beaten biscuits from extinction but actually made them smoother, prettier, and more popular than before" (219).[19]

References to these machines turn up regularly in latter-day plantation school cookbooks, and usually they are accompanied by some version of "old biscuit block" nostalgia. For instance, in *Mammy Lou's Cook Book* (1931), Betty Benton Patterson prefaces her recipe for "Beaten Biscuits Nashobia" with this comment: "We admit that there seems little reason in this recipe but the result is perfect—if beaten to blisters. An electric machine does the work, but somehow we feel disloyal to Mammy and her rolling pin in admitting the truth" (166). By implying that black women slave cooks preferred the more labor-intensive mode of making the biscuits, Patterson denies her own complicity in the exploitation of their labor.

Also writing in 1931, and capitalizing on the resurgent popularity of blackface entertainment during this era, *Miss Minerva's Cook Book* author Emma Speed Sampson attributes the following commentary on beaten biscuits to the malapropism-inclined cook who serves as her narrator:

Moughty few homes air lef' whar the fust thing in the mawnin' you kin hear the blim! blim! bang! bang! er biscuit gettin' beat. In the ol' days that was as regular a soun' as the ol' dominicker a-crowin'. Nowadays beaten biscuit air mos' ginerally either done without or they air boughten at the sto'. The boughten ones air right down tasty, them what air made by some lady what turned her gumption ter account.

Co'se they ain't nothin' quite so good as beaten biscuit made fraish an' et hot the minute you draw 'em outer the oven. The rules fer beaten biscuit air many an' various. Some uses butter fer lard an' some uses water fer milk but they air one thing that all agrees on an' that air elbow grease. Beaten biscuit ain't no lazy cook's vacation. Beatin' the dough till it blisters air the maindes' thing. (149–50)

Sampson differs from Patterson in acknowledging that store-bought biscuits were still the product of human exertion, though she does imply that the "lady" who made them is simply working off surplus energy rather than exchanging her time and labor for money. She also has the narrator point out that "[i]f you use the brake you mus' run yo' dough under it some hun'erd times," before allowing that "a pint er flour air moughty little ter expen' so much animation on so's it would be better ter double the rule" (150). Even with the aid of a machine, the process of making beaten biscuits was labor-intensive.

It was, then, as emerging technologies began to transform "happy eaters" of mammy-made delicacies into often dissatisfied consumers of culinary commodities (including, no doubt, Aunt Jemima products) that many southerners and non-southerners alike started viewing beaten biscuits with fetishistic fascination.[20] Of course, unlike the commodity form, beaten biscuits foreground the labor through which they are created and thus the relations of domination between mistress or master and slave.[21] Yet, far from acknowledging their own dominant position, these southerners attributed to the black women who had usually made the biscuits power, which in actuality they utterly lacked. Consequently, their fixation seems less compatible with a Marxian than a Freudian definition of fetishization: "Mammy" could be seen to possess the phallus in the form of a powerful rolling pin. But as I have already suggested, we can more readily historicize their psychic investment in beaten biscuits by understanding it as a "symptom" of the South's transition from slavery to capitalism. "With the establishment of bourgeois society," Žižek has argued,

> the relations of domination and servitude are *repressed*: formally, we are apparently concerned with free subjects whose interpersonal relations are discharged of all fetishism; the repressed truth—that of the persistence of domination and servitude—emerges in a symptom which subverts the ideological appearance of equality, freedom, and so on. (26)

Their very name valorizing the exploitation of slave labor, beaten biscuits—or, more accurately, the fascination therewith—can be understood as a symptom that foregrounded the "persistence of domination and servitude" in relations between white and black Americans after the demise of legal slavery. In need of further explication, however, is why the fantasy of "Mammy and her rolling pin" in particular has provided such a unique and lasting cathexis. Through my continued focus on Craig Claiborne, I hope to demonstrate how the psychic formation of white southern men—already legendary for their angst-ridden negotiations of position in a racially bifurcated "family romance"—might have served as a prototype for the reconfiguration of middle-class white manhood in the wake of the liberatory social movements of the 1960s and 1970s.[22]

In the excerpt quoted earlier, Mary Stuart Smith made quite explicit what would appear to be the simultaneously masochistic and sadistic tendencies embedded in her recollections of hearing the "biscuit beat," claiming that while the servant goes to the "trouble of preparing" beaten biscuits, the housekeeper is the one who "will be rewarded for her pains." Memorably ambiguous, "her pains" is almost certainly intended as a reference to the psychic sufferings of the supervising mistress (i.e., Smith herself), but one might easily construe it as an inadvertent ac-knowledgment of the physical labors of the servant as well.

Similarly, when discussing beaten biscuits, Claiborne fixates on the "beating" as much as on the biscuits—so much so that anyone familiar with Freud's work on the etiology of childhood flagellation fantasies should find his recollections in-triguing:

> My mother, a Southern belle if ever there was one, loved beaten biscuits and served them often when she had friends over for afternoon coffee or "tea." Beaten biscuits, as any Southerner knows, are one of the most arduously made of all foods known to man. You combine flour with butter or butter and lard plus cold water and possibly milk to make a dough. You knead this well, turn it out onto a solid surface, and beat it by hand with a mallet or rolling pin for twenty minutes or longer until the dough "blisters." It is then rolled out, cut into small rounds, and baked until crisp without browning. Mother always served them split in half and with thin slices of Smithfield ham sandwiched between.
>
> Outside the room in which I slept there was the sawed-off, wide circular stump of a walnut tree, and it was there, early in the morning, that I could hear the beating of that biscuit dough, whack after whack after whack. (*Southern* xv)

Even more richly detailed than was Smith's rendition, Claiborne's account of beaten biscuits moves from third person ("Mother served") to second person ("You combine" and "You knead") to the elision of agency entirely ("It is then rolled"). The displacements, reversals, and negations are actually quite evocative of the three developmental stages of childhood flagellation fantasies that Freud identi-fies in "A Child Is Being Beaten." Therein he argues that such fantasies should be interpreted as the conscious manifestation of repressed infantile sexual desires.

Beating fantasies, in other words, enable the child to resolve her or his posi-tioning in the triangulated family romance. The imagined beating functions in Freud's interpretation as a form of punishment for the repressed incestuous desire for one's parent. That Claiborne himself identified with the participants in the scene of flagellation is perhaps suggested by his discussion of beaten biscuits in *Southern Cooking*. Echoing Freud's comment that "in the third phase it is almost invariably only boys who are being beaten" (196), Claiborne observes that one cookbook with which he is familiar "instructs the cook to 'use boys to do it'" (254)—a particularly telling phrase since, not unlike Smith's invocation of "her pains," it ambiguously situates the "boys" as both objects and agents of action. Claiborne's earlier reference to "the sawed-off, wide circular stump of a walnut tree" would tend to suggest, furthermore, that he harbored vivid castration anxi-eties as well. Yet, whereas in the classic Oedipal triangle the punitive figure is the father, Claiborne consciously identifies his mother as the most powerful and threatening figure in his life.

As we have already seen, after Claiborne's father lost his wealth, his mother opened a boardinghouse and became the family "breadwinner." Claiborne notes that his parents had traded normative gender roles, his mother becoming the head of the household and his father retreating into financial dependency. Claiborne's early narrative is filled, furthermore, with references to the strong will of his mother. Though he claims at the outset to admire her, as the autobiography progresses he increasingly depicts her as domineering, controlling, and overly invested in himself, her youngest son. In fact, Claiborne's discussion of his mother culminates in a baroque description of his decision never to speak with or see her again:

> By far the most turbulent, inundating, tormenting, and tumultuous incident of my adult life was my *final* and *total* estrangement from my mother. In any summation of my life as it had thus far been lived, it looms so large as to be impossible to ignore. Whether good or bad, for better or worse, I am at peace with myself, the cause and effect of my separation from her.
>
> Prior to that separation I lived in an atmosphere of total suffocation as—it seems to me—only a mother's love can suffocate. I felt emasculated in her presence. And even in the presence of her letters. I was inundated with her letters, which served as a giant-sized umbilical cord wrapped unceremoniously and noose-like around my neck. (*Feast* 103–4)

Claiborne's representation of the mother-son relationship is reminiscent of Kristeva's conceptualization of abjection as "a desire for separation, for becoming autonomous and also the feeling of an impossibility of doing so—whence the element of crisis which the notion of abjection carries within it" (quoted in Baruch and Serrano 136). The prototypical instance of abjection is birth, and indeed Claiborne's early references to being "suffocated" and "inundated" by his mother become direct references to her womb by the end of the passage. Yet one should note that Claiborne conflates his fear of being strangled by the umbilical cord with "emasculation." To separate himself from his mother is to achieve not personhood but manhood. His mother thus supersedes his father as the source of castration anxiety.

Claiborne proceeds to describe the night of their "awful confrontation, the most powerful and poignant moment of " his adult life (*Feast* 104). After an evening out at the theatre, during which he and his mother had quarreled, Claiborne recalls that he "was depositing her at the hotel as all good southern sons and lovers must do, at her 'doorstep'" (*Feast* 105):

> On that evening I had felt her physical presence more closely than usual. She sat too close to me for filial comfort. It was an annoyance I could never have spelled out to her, nor hinted at.
>
> In her hotel room before I kissed her good night, I was angry and somehow I must have expressed this.
>
> "Sometimes," she said, "you really drive me to the point of exasperation." She placed her tiny, lace-edged, embroidered handkerchief onto her mouth and turned her head away from me. "I'm your mother and that's all I've ever wanted to be."
>
> "But, Mother," I said, the word coming out as reflexively as breath or an inadvertent yell, "that's what I mean!" . . .
>
> I never saw her again. (*Feast* 105–6)

The easy slippage from "sons" to "lovers" would suggest that Claiborne wants us to condemn his mother for encouraging him to violate the Law of the Father—namely, the prohibition of mother-son incest. Such an interpretation is surely supported by his earlier allusion to marital vows, "for better or worse," in describing his decision to "separate" from her. Claiborne's fascination with the beaten biscuits that his mother "served" would, in this scenario, be interpreted from a Freudian perspective as the conscious manifestation of his need to punish himself for having desired his mother sexually. The "whack after whack after whack" to which he awoke would have functioned as a continual flagellatory penance for his incestuous fantasies of the day and night before.

The problem with this interpretation is that the narratives that Freud and Claiborne spin are not, finally, about heterosexual incest at all. Freud says that, for the boy, the "phantasy which has as its content being beaten by the mother, and which is conscious or can become so, is not a primary one. It possesses a preceding stage which is invariably unconscious and has as its content: 'I am being beaten by my father'" (198). This primary and unconscious fantasy has the meaning "'I am loved by my father'" (198). In other words, it turns out that for both boys and girls "the beating-phantasy has its origin in an incestuous attachment to the father" (198). Freud, however, not only believes that such father-son incestuous attachments are imagined, but as Judith Butler has demonstrated, he also effectively heterosexualizes childhood homosexual desire (Gender 57–65). Thus, for example, he claims: "The boy, who has tried to escape from a homosexual object-choice, and who has not changed his sex, nevertheless feels like a woman in his conscious phantasies, and endows the women who are beating him with masculine attributes and characteristics" (200).

Claiborne, by contrast, relates in elaborate detail memories that he presents as (and I take to be) actual childhood sexual encounters with his father, encounters that he vividly describes in terms of same-sex desire:[23]

> Because of our financial status, it was necessary that every available bed in our home be filled, mostly with paying guests. I do not know when or how the decision was made that I would occupy the same bed as my father. I slept next to him, spoon-fashion, my slender upper arm securely holding him around his chest. That happened at the time when I had just achieved the capacity of seminal flow.
>   . . . In the beginning, my going to bed with him was a casual, unplanned affair. Until one winter evening when I put my arm around him and onto his left arm. I followed that arm onto the hand and discovered his fingers enfolded around the throttle of his lust, the object that best reflects the strength and status of a man's desire.
>   In the years that followed I was to relive—in my cultivated daydreams—the enormity of that experience in my mind and I tried many times to describe the ecstasy of it, to come to grips with it by putting it into understanding. I have compared it to an electric shock applied with thundering haste to all of my existence. There was an all-engulfing gushing of adrenalin[e], the likes of which I have never known before or since. It was as though all of my being were inundated with warm waves of ecstasy, the sensation of drowning and awakening shaken but on a safe but hitherto unexplored island.
>   To say that it altered my approach and outlook on life, particularly where sex is concerned, is to put it mildly. (Feast 20)

Though their "affair was never consummated," Claiborne continued to sleep in the same bed with his father and often engaged in what he terms "an exploration" of his father's body (Feast 20). He uses similar imagery and even precisely the same language as he had when describing his desire for separation from his mother. Whereas before Claiborne felt "suffocated" by her devotion, here the "sensation of drowning" and "all-engulfing gushing of adrenalin[e]" lead to an experience of "ecstasy." "Inundation" is now "safe." To the extent his father too becomes the "abject"—possessed of both penis and womb—he is not repulsive but seductive.

Acceptance of his homosexual desires did not come easily. In fact, Claiborne never directly acknowledges his sexual orientation toward men in the autobiography but instead refers obliquely to nights spent in a drunken "stupor, touring the streets, dangerously roaming in search of sexual gratification" from "uniformed objects of desire" (*Feast* 107). He also allows that, prior to embarking on a lengthy course of "psychotherapy" (which he pointedly describes as "less weighty" than "psychoanalysis"), he suffered from feelings of "self-detestation" and was prone to "self-destruction" (*Feast* 108). Through therapy, Claiborne was able "to emerge from the straightjacket of [his] childhood" (*Feast* 108)—tied, he claims, by his mother—and come to terms with his "desire to possess" his father sexually (*Feast* 109). "My God," he writes, "what forgotten truths and happenings the mind can dredge up, what horrors lie buried under layer after layer of fantasy and wishful and unwished-for hope and self-hatred" (*Feast* 108). Claiborne and his father had violated what Butler calls (after Michel Foucault) the productive function of Phallic Law, which implicitly stipulates that incestuous desire will be hetero- rather than homosexual, and so the encounter had to be repressed. His lingering flagellatory fantasies can thus perhaps be read as "*not only the punishment for the forbidden genital relation, but also the regressive substitute for that relation*" (189). The "whack after whack after whack" would have offered Claiborne not just punishment for his taboo relationship with his father, but also a surrogate masochistic pleasure.[24]

Freud, of course, quite problematically associates masochism with passivity and femininity, and he also treats sadism and masochism as having reversible etiologies. Gilles Deleuze has argued instead that "sadism and masochism . . . are not respectively made up of partial impulses, but each is complete in itself " (67). The two inclinations should be understood to stem, in other words, from entirely distinct psychic causes. As a result,

> there is between sadism and masochism an irreducible dissymmetry: sadism stands for the active negation of the mother and the inflation of the father (who is placed above the law); masochism proceeds by a twofold disavowal, a positive, idealizing disavowal of the mother (who is identified with the law) and an invalidating disavowal of the father (who is expelled from the symbolic order). (68)

Or, as Tania Modleski has succinctly rephrased Deleuze's claims, in masochism "the male child allies himself with the mother against the law of the father, which it is the function of the mother to beat out of the son, whereas sadism involves an alliance with the father against the mother" (*Feminism* 69). If we extrapolate from Deleuze's revisionary reading of Freud to construe Phallic Law as foreclosing the possibility of homosexual incestuous desire (the boy "nevertheless feels like a woman in his conscious phantasies"), it seems clear that Claiborne does identify his mother with the law, and he wants the reader to blame her for imposing it on him. It is not Claiborne's father but his mother who, by insinuating "her physical presence more closely than usual" and consequently presuming that her son would play his predetermined role in the heterosexual family romance, enforces this (never spoken) taboo against homosexual incest. Hence Claiborne's seemingly inexplicable anger at her on the night of their estrangement: "It was an annoyance I could never have spelled out to her, nor hinted at."

The Epistemology of the Kitchen

> In most accounts of domestic service written by servants, the male figures were generally distant, shadowy figures. They seemed to intrude into the household rather than to be an actual part of it. Or they seemed to be relatively powerless in the household.
>
> David Katzman, Seven Days a Week, 1978

However tidy this summation may seem, there remain some lacunae both in Claiborne's narrative and in my own interpretation as presented thus far, constitutive breaches which Peter Stallybrass and Allon White offer useful guidance for addressing. In The Politics and Poetics of Transgression, they mount a compelling case in support of their claim that that which was socially marginalized in early modern bourgeois culture—e.g., the lower classes, servants, carnival, bowels, excrement, pigs, sewers, filth—was symbolically central to early modern self-representations (5). Extending Jane Gallop's argument that "[o]ne of psychoanalysis's consistent errors is to reduce everything to a family paradigm" (144), Stallybrass and White attempt to rethink Freud's theorization of the family romance so as to demonstrate the symbolic centrality of the socially marginalized servant class.

Freud, they concede, "brilliantly imagines the splitting of the subject, but then he proceeds to suppress the social terrain through which that splitting is articulated. The drama is played out in an imagined household where servants bear a symbolic part mainly as displacements of the biological parents" (153). In their opinion, his strategy can be understood as an effort "to rewrite unconscious desires in closer conformity to the endogamous rules of the bourgeoisie. Paradoxically, to desire one's mother, despite the incestuous implications, is more acceptable than to desire a hired help" (159). Incest, in effect, was more acceptable to Freud than was slumming. By denying the centrality of servants to the bourgeois child's psychic development, indeed by denying that frequently the parents might have functioned as a displacement of the servants, he was enabled to claim that "[t]he symbolic order of the family romance was . . . inscribed biologically" and therefore to be "placed in the immutable world of nature, not in the historical work of social struggle" (Stallybrass and White 163–64).

Perhaps as a result of his years spent in psychotherapy, Claiborne encourages readers of his autobiography to replicate this highly significant repression. He quite consciously invokes Freudian paradigms, in other words, to construct his personal history in terms of a doubly forbidden, because queer and actually realized, family romance. Though he does try at one point to suggest that his sexual relationship with his father was a result of economic depression in the South and his family's subsequent financial decline—the father and son having had no choice but to violate normative codes of bourgeois domesticity and occupy the same bed (*Feast* 20)—he more frequently describes his upbringing in terms of innate biological compulsions.

His father, Claiborne reflects, was "not responsible for his actions, an unwitting victim of circumstance" (*Feast* 109). At the same time, he was also "a supernatural innocent with an unswerving belief in the goodness of man and life on earth and an eternal belief in the goodness of God" (*Feast* 109). His mother likewise

> was a victim of culture, of her time and place. The ultimate southern belle. An aristocrat living in her illusory spiritual (and at times actual) garden of magnolia and Cape jasmine. She was uniquely born into a southern world in which the family was not composed of individuals but the body entire, one bond, one blood.
>
> Thus, in that mystic land, known as the South, as the mother's heart pumped blood through her own veins and arteries, thus it courses—or so she believed—through the body of her children, rhythmically and in time, heartbeat for heartbeat, even though those children had emerged from the womb days, months, years, even decades earlier.
>
> And if any member of the family wandered away from the heart and hearth it was an amputation, pure and simple, the deprivation of a limb. (*Feast* 109)

This time figuring "the woman from whose womb [he] had emerged" as both abject and castrated mother (108–9), Claiborne shifts away from the initial historically specific invocations of "circumstance," "time," and "place" to represent the South as a mythical site immune to the incursions of political struggle and social change, a "mystic land" ruled by devouring white women obsessed with the bonds of blood.

Given his overdetermined investment in the family romance topos, it comes as no surprise that left insufficiently accounted for in Claiborne's painstaking exploration of his psychosexual development is the role of the numerous servants who populated the Claiborne household, including his beloved Aunt Catherine and "chief cook" Blanche. At the outset of "A Child Is Being Beaten," Freud actually refers to Harriet Beecher Stowe's novel *Uncle Tom's Cabin* as a common "stimulus to the beating-phantasies" of children (180). Consequently, one can only presume that at some level he understood race to be no less constitutive of the need for (imagined) punishment than are other determinants of identity such as gender and sexuality. Thereafter, however, questions of racial difference do not enter into his analysis.

Similarly, at the outset of his autobiography, Claiborne makes it clear that he came into consciousness as a privileged white male in no small part by defining himself in relation to, and against, the subordinated black servants. Only as he progresses into the discussion of his emergent sexuality does he elide the function of these employees in his psychic formation. What I want to suggest, however, is not that Claiborne's obviously charged relationship with his parents should be construed simply as a displacement of a more "primal" attachment to one or more of the servants, although to a certain extent this may have been the case. Rather, it seems to me that only by using the servants to create a "shadow" family romance was Claiborne able to resolve the contradictions among his parents' deviation from socially sanctioned gender roles, his own illicit sexual relationship with his

father, and the presumptively heterosexual, patriarchal structure of the white nuclear family.[25] In particular, I would hypothesize that the conscious figuration of a
powerful black woman in the kitchen was necessary to enable the young, queer
misfit "Craig" to establish a coherent identity as "Mr. Claiborne." As Hortense
Spillers has observed of African American women: "My country needs me, and
if I were not here, I would have to be invented" ("Mama's" 65). For upper-class
white southerners such as Claiborne, actual memories of black domestics made the
invention seem all the more real.

As we have seen, Claiborne's fondest memories are of his Aunt Catherine. "I
adored her above all creatures, including my mother," he announces, with characteristic hyperbole, in the early pages of his autobiography (6). "I adored my mother
on isolated occasions; Aunt Catherine was ever present, watching over me, holding me close, tending my fevers and shielding me from harm of any sort night and
day" (*Feast* 6). In keeping with Stallybrass and White's reminder that servants,
rather than mothers, were most often charged with the regulation of the child's
bodily functions in the bourgeois household (155), Claiborne revels in the memories of his Aunt Catherine's "touch" and "smell" (*Feast* 8), and of being fed by her
"three times a day with my sterling silver baby spoon" (*Feast* 6). He claims,
though, to "have no recollection whatsoever of her ever cooking a single dish," insisting: "What she did do, and what is forever engraved on my soul, is churn clab-
ber, a thickened sour milk, which she made on the back porch with butter and
buttermilk" (*Feast* 6). Claiborne ate this concoction while "sitting in Aunt Catherine's lap, rocked back and forth in her solid brown rocker" (*Feast* 8).

As his "surrogate mother," not only did Aunt Catherine manage his bodily
functions, but Claiborne specifically associates her with milk and even goes out of
his way to point out that "she had suckled my brother when he was a newborn"
(*Feast* 11). It seems likely that only by (retrospectively) projecting all threats to
his bodily integrity onto his biological mother is Claiborne able to represent Aunt
Catherine as a principle of pure, unconditional, and unmenacing nurture. Unlike
his gender-bending parents, moreover, she conformed, if only in Claiborne's imagination, to prevailing ideologies of gender, race, and class.

Because of their financial difficulties, the Claibornes moved to another small
Mississippi town in 1924, leaving this idealized nurse behind (*Feast* 8–11). Claiborne claims that his childhood affinity for the kitchen in his new home stemmed
in part from his discomfort with prescribed practices of white masculinity as he
was growing up:

> In the town where I lived, it was expected that all young boys would participate in
> the local school's athletic program. You played football, baseball, or basketball and,
> preferably, all three. In this respect I was a pariah and, as a consequence, there were
> very few white children I wanted to associate with or, perhaps, more to the point,
> who wanted to associate with me.
>
> So Blanche's kitchen became my playground. Blanche was the chief cook and
> therefore it was *her* kitchen. She was tall, amply shaped, dark-skinned, and her
> straight black hair was pulled back into a bun. On those rare occasions when she
> would sit on the kitchen stool, she would grab me in her arms. Her bosom was a mar-
> velous thing to lean against. (*Feast* 29)

Perceiving himself as a "pariah" on the public playground because of his lack of athletic prowess, the young boy retreats to the black female–ruled world of the kitchen, a haven where he is protected from the taunts of his hostile white peers.[26] In "Blanche's kitchen" white patriarchal dynamics are, if only temporarily, displaced. Providing nurture on "rare occasions" and representing reassuringly circumscribed authority, the "chief cook" becomes a combined mother and father, one who neither forces Claiborne to enact stereotypical straight white masculine behavior, nor threatens him with inundation/castration for his queer, incestuous desires. In the kitchen, through Blanche, the prepubescent Claiborne is able to "fool around" with his identity so as both to shirk the gender role expectations of the dominant white society and to reconfigure the triangulated conflicts of his interactions with his parents.

But this sanctuary, too, was lost to the young Claiborne. The second formative trauma in his interactions with the servants occurred when he was "thirteen or fourteen years old" (Feast 29), this being also, surely not coincidentally, the age at which he dates the start of his sexual liaison with his father.[27] "And that was my world," Claiborne recalls, "which, one bright morning, casually and without forethought shattered" (Feast 29). On the morning in question he was reclining on a living room chair, reading a book. Hugh, whom Claiborne tellingly (because superfluously) describes as "a touch effeminate," began vacuuming the room (Feast 30). When the servant started to clean the area near Claiborne's chair, he addressed his employers' son in familiar terms, as was the accepted practice between them: "Craig, lift your foot" (Feast 30). Feeling what he describes as "the old stirrings of a crude southern maleness in my blood," Claiborne instructed Hugh henceforth to address him as "Mr. Claiborne" (Feast 30). Hugh responded by looking briefly at Claiborne, unplugging the vacuum, wrapping the cord carefully, and exiting the room. "I was petrified, stunned at my behavior," Claiborne recollects. "There seemed no place to turn and no place to hide" (Feast 30).

Again invoking biological determinism, this time to explain his own conduct rather than that of his parents, Claiborne asks us to believe that his assertion of white male social privilege was an unwonted manifestation of (blue) blood. But given his contemporaneous recognition of his erotic investment in men and his coding of Hugh as gay (in addition to being "a touch effeminate," Hugh was at the time engaged in a type of domestic labor stereotypically allocated to women), we might also read this scene as one of "homosexual panic," a moment of recognition which Claiborne immediately disavowed (Sedgwick, Epistemology 19). Validating Eve Sedgwick's insistence upon the centrality of the closet to Western constructions of heterosexuality, Claiborne, having effectively declared himself straight, was left with no choice but to look for a "place to hide."[28] The import of what I am suggesting is that Claiborne responded to Hugh's request as though it were an assertion not simply of racial equality but, more threateningly, of sexual equivalence. Black male assertions of racial equality were, after all, necessary to the maintenance of (southern) white male dominance; the more public the challenge, in fact, the better. An "effeminate" black male assertion of sexual equivalence would have functioned, by contrast, as a return of the repressed in the constitution of (southern) white manhood: its homoerotic investment in black male bodies.

In her work on such interracial male frisson, including its terroristic expression via the practice of lynching, Robyn Wiegman has explained how during the nineteenth century the black/white racial binary began to be articulated in the United States through discourses of sexuality and sexual difference (44). Appropriating Foucault's claim that the category of "man" is only a relatively recent invention in Western history, she argues that "the specification of difference functions to allay the deeply threatening potential of human sameness: of a cosmic order in which the ascendancy of the white masculine is no longer universalized, but reduced to its own corporeal particularities" (48).[29] Thus, for example, in nineteenth-century racial science, blackness was "feminized and the African(-American) male was disaffiliated from the masculine itself" (54). Through this disaffiliation not only were many of the psychological, social, and economic challenges posed by black male enfranchisement contained, but "the competing and complementary relations of patriarchy and white supremacy were finally adjudicated to the overarching privileges of white men" in a rapidly expanding capitalist economy (61).

Given the ongoing reverberations of this inscription, Claiborne's perception of a black male domestic as "effeminate" was surely overdetermined under the prevailing racial ideologies of both the early 1930s (when the encounter occurred) and the mid-1980s (when the encounter was recollected).[30] His demand to be called "Mr. Claiborne" can be understood as asserting a "correspondence between penis and phallus—between the masculine body and its potential for a dis-corporated power"—while also necessarily exposing the phallus as a function of "the materialist determinations of white racial supremacy" (Wiegman 89). Hugh, after all, could not be allowed to claim the same correspondence.

This line of thought can help us make some sense of Claiborne's narrative regarding the consequences of his repudiation of the black male servant. Displacing the sexually vulnerable white female body from this primal southern scene of interracial confrontation between men, Claiborne instead invokes an asexually invulnerable black woman. His racist and homophobic disavowal of Hugh in the living room is reconfigured as Blanche's traumatic expulsion of him from the kitchen:

> An hour must have passed before I summoned the courage to push open the door of that kitchen. When I did enter, it was precisely as I had feared. Hugh was not there. Blanche was at the sink, her back to the room. Sally was wiping a kitchen counter. Neither of them spoke. I walked through the kitchen and out the back door.
>
> Blanche never held me again. And ever after I was Mr. Claiborne. *Persona non grata* in the world of my childhood, the place where I once had been hugged and loved. Even, perhaps, needed. (*Feast* 30)

Because unwitnessed and therefore unnecessary, Claiborne's assertion of racial privilege and sexual dissimilarity in a casual encounter with Hugh had effectively signaled the servant community that the employers' son could no longer be trusted: he had begun to believe in the fictions through which white masculinity is equated with disembodied authority. Having thus violated what he would only belatedly recognize as the Law of the Kitchen, Claiborne was exiled from a comforting world of semiotic flux into an alien one of symbolic differentiation, cast out of his childhood closet by his surrogate family. Yet far from being sexually "outed,"

Claiborne was instead denied all possibility of being racially "in." He had acted straight; now he must play it white. And it was the black woman responsible for "the beating of that biscuit dough" who, by pretending henceforth that he really did possess the phallus, had the power to force him to live with the ramifications of his unconsidered assertion of straight white masculine privilege. Unwillingly, or so he would have us believe, "Craig" became "Mr. Claiborne."

But, of course, his representation of Blanche as the dominatrix of the kitchen surely also stems from his need to disavow not just his social dominance over the black servants, but also his own will to that power. Only when he "*misnames* the power of the female*" in the servant community is he able finally to sublimate his own "effeminate" distance from the Law of the Father and assume the mantle of "Mr. Claiborne" (Spillers, "Mama's" 80). Only by imputing the "real" phallus to Blanche is he enabled to claim for himself the illusory correspondence between penis and phallus which a white male supremacist social order has denied to black men. It is Blanche who is positioned to bear the blame for imposing upon Claiborne the necessity for masculine charade that she has withheld from the hapless Hugh. It is Blanche who is understood to have foreclosed future possibilities for interracial male solidarity, forcing the black boy to admit he is powerless and the white boy to pretend he is not. Thus banished by a domineering black woman from the kitchen of his childhood, Claiborne was left holding (what else but?) the rolling pin as an adult.

Writing in the 1980s, Claiborne was certainly aware of the import of movements for African American, women's, and lesbian/gay liberation for a memoir about growing up white and gay in the segregated South and taking up a traditionally "female" career. "This was an age long before the time of the black revolution in this country," he says at one point, before allowing that his mother "treated her servants like children" (*Feast* 25). And in describing how he embarked upon his career as a food critic, Claiborne remarks that, at the time, "there was not a male food editor on a single metropolitan paper" in the entire country (*Feast* 121). One way to read his autobiographical writing, consequently, is as an allegory about the impact of the social flux of the 1960s and 1970s on the psychic formation of white men. By 1970 the tenuous interracial (male) solidarity of civil rights activism had given way to the proliferation of movements organized around the politics of identity. If the traditional American family romance looked hopelessly defunct to many social observers, Claiborne could (and, in a sense, did) offer his narrative as evidence that the rest of the country was now following in the footsteps of the South—where homoeroticized bonds between white and black men had long been regulated and disrupted by devouring white mothers and dominating black mammies alike.

Put another way, in the post-Stonewall era, gay men such as Claiborne emerged as the return of the sublimated in the construction of heterosexual (white) manhood. And far from being rendered atypical by his sexual deviation from normative masculinity, Claiborne's positioning among the social divisions that emerged in the late 1960s actually allows him to serve as a model for understanding the psychic processes through which white men stave off challenges to their authority by casting themselves, and allowing themselves to be cast, as disempowered. One white female reviewer of A Feast Made for Laughter noted that Claiborne was "the first male food editor in a journalistic world dominated by women" (Fussell 12), thus presenting his elevation to that post at the most prestigious newspaper in the country as a marker of social progress rather than a continuation of white patriarchal privilege. After all, the question is why the dozens of women who had more experience and better qualifications than Claiborne did not get the job. This is not to deny that as a gay man in a heterosexist society Claiborne was denied access to many benefits of patriarchy, particularly those which accrue to white men of the middle class. Yet he surely achieved success in his field because, as well as in spite, of his status as a gay white male. Operating both inside and outside hegemonic ideologies of gender and sexuality, Claiborne could symbolize white male desire for authority over women in the home without also denaturalizing belief in "separate spheres" for women and "real" (i.e., straight) men.[31]

Part II will continue this discussion of the causes and implications of the historical "misnaming" of black female power—including Hortense Spillers's influential assertion that African American women stand "out of the traditional symbolics of female gender" and should consequently be understood as a "different social subject" entirely, one unaccounted for in psychoanalytic theory ("Mama's" 80). My focus, though, will be on anxieties about the precarious status of black masculinity in U.S. culture. When black nationalists such as Amiri Baraka began claiming in the 1960s that "[m]ost American white men are trained to be fags" ("American" 216), such homophobic slurs said little about either straight or gay white men but much about the psychic disavowals required of those who wished to inhabit the hyperbolized black male subjectivities being celebrated during the Black Power era.[32] Since one of the things they had to disavow was black femininity, food, I argue, became a particular concern.

PART II

SOUL FOOD
AND BLACK MASCULINITY

three

"Eating Chitterlings Is Like Going Slumming"
Soul Food and Its Discontents

> "Yessuh," he said, handing over the yams, "I can see you one of these old-fashioned yam eaters."
> "They're my birthmark," I said. "I yam what I am!"
>
> Ralph Ellison, *Invisible Man*, 1952

Readers of Tom Wolfe's *Radical Chic and Mau-Mauing the Flak Catchers* (1970) will perhaps recall that the March 1970 issue of *Vogue* magazine carried a column by Gene Baro on "Soul Food." Published four years after chants of "black and white together" had given way to demands for "Black Power" (Sitkoff 199), and two years after the Black Panthers unveiled the slogan "Off the Pigs" at Huey Newton's trial (Heath 64–66), the column begins with a quasi-religious fantasy of interracial gastronomy:

> The cult of Soul Food is a form of Black self-awareness and, to a lesser degree, of white sympathy for the Black drive to self-reliance. It is as if those who ate the beans and greens of necessity in the cabin doorways were brought into communion with those who, not having to, eat those foods voluntarily now as a sacrament. The present struggle is emphasized in the act of breaking traditional bread. (Baro 80; see also Wolfe 31)

This short-lived outbreak of "*nostalgie de la boue*, or romanticizing of primitive souls," as Wolfe puts it (32), is not without intrinsic interest as an episode in the ongoing narrative comprising white patronage of (white productions of) black culture. Often functioning, according to Marianna Torgovnick, as a surrogate mode of articulating the West's fears and obsessions about itself (18), fascination with the primitive might also be interpreted following Stuart Hall's model for racism. Hall has argued that racism is best understood not "as a simple process, structured around fixed 'selves,'" in which blacks are positioned "as the inferior species," but instead as a far more intricate dynamic of attraction and repulsion, of "inexpressible envy and desire" ("New" 28). Imbricated in both the production of the psyche and the relations of production, the food practices of radical chic offer an ideal site to investigate the complicated processes of othering and identification that have helped constitute certain strains of both white racism and white radicalism in America. As Kobena Mercer tersely inquires of Norman Mailer's White Negro: *"What is it about whiteness that made them want to be black?"* ("1968" 432).[1]

But while acknowledging that too often the status of "whiteness" has been assumed rather than interrogated, it is also imperative to recognize the heterogeneous constitution of "blackness." Within African American culture, one readily encounters a multiplicity of competing discourses about what had come by the early 1960s to be called "soul food." These discourses span historically far-ranging social and political positions that have been obscured because discussions of "soul" tend to rely on simplistic, often insufficiently historicized dichotomies of master versus slave, white versus black, and especially black bourgeoisie versus ghettoite. With this concern in mind, in part II of this book I will take a closer look at the ideological contestation among black men over the emergence of soul food during the 1960s and early 1970s. My aim is to foreground some of the subtleties which are lost when soul is either uncritically embraced as the essence of blackness or else dismissed as an inauthentic, blackface product of white radical chic or black bourgeois "slumming." In the process, I also hope to make some sense of soul food's complicity with certain pivotal, powerful, and enduring stereotypes of blackness. We need to understand, in other words, not just why soul food is more complicated than we have thought, but also why it has been so easy to think that it is less complicated than it is.

Soul food is generally subsumed under the 1960s rubric "soul," a term often defined as "indefinable" and discussed with reference primarily to men and music. These obfuscations and elisions deserve scrutiny.[2] At the same time, the emergence of soul food should be construed not just synchronically but also diachronically, as part of an ongoing debate among African Americans over the appropriate food "practices" of blackness.[3] This debate became particularly fraught in the wake of a resurgent struggle for the rights of U.S. citizenship after World War II. During this period, numerous individuals and organizations were attempting to formulate, enact, or critique a paradigmatic black identity based on what I will term, borrowing from critical legal theory, the "juridical fiction" of the Western humanistic subject: rational, autonomous, self-interested, heterosexual, white, male.[4] It was in this sociopolitical context that proponents of soul food such as LeRoi Jones (prior to his reincarnation as Black Arts guru Amiri Baraka) began valorizing it as an expression of pride in the cultural forms created from and articulated through a history of black oppression. In this same context, detractors such as Elijah Muhammad and, subsequently, Dick Gregory condemned the "slave" diet as an unclean and/or unhealthful practice of racial genocide.

Yet it is intriguing that aficionados and abstainers alike often betrayed a profound and seemingly unconscious ambivalence toward the cuisine that they associated with black slavery, black poverty, and black Christianity. This ambivalence is surely not unrelated to Hall's model for racism. It might be more accurately interpreted, however, as a dynamic of intraracial identification and othering, a dynamic whose instabilities can be probed to expose fissures in the construction of black American subjectivities. My discussion will foreground this dynamic to scrutinize the dialectic between soul food and selfhood. It will try to understand the passionate intensity of the debate by asking whether or to what extent certain key ontologies of blackness—particularly those in which blackness is stigmatized as "filthy," "polluted," or "dangerous"—have been thought to reside not in black bodies but instead in foods said to nourish those bodies. I pose this surely unanswerable question as a way of thinking about why a reference to chitterlings, to allude to the obvious titular example from Eldridge Cleaver (40), can elicit the sort of response usually reserved for the word "nigger."

Roger Abrahams has claimed that on a "superficial level, we see similar stereotyping mechanisms [result] in social distancing in the discussions of chittlin'-eating Blacks, tamale-eating Mexicans, potato-eating Irish, and most repulsive to some, the frog-eating Frenchman and the dog-eating Chinese" (22).[5] While keeping such parallels in mind, it also seems important to pay attention to the dissimilarities in how food operates in the construction of divergent ethnic identities. Hence my specific focus on soul food here, as a gesture toward future comparative work on cross-cultural practices of culinary othering. The challenge, as I see it, is not just to posit a structuralist, metonymic relationship leading from soul food to chitterlings to blackness to filth; it is also to understand how and why the metonymy was operating as it did for specific persons at a specific historical moment. My argument is that the debate over soul food was constituted by, and in turn helped constitute, many of the contradictions inherent in post–World War II attempts to revalue or reconstruct black manhood, especially Black Power efforts to control, contain, and abject the often fungible category of the "feminine."

"Relishing Hog Bowels"

> What constitutes through division the "inner" and "outer" worlds of the subject is a border and boundary tenuously maintained for the purposes of social regulation and control. The boundary between the inner and outer is confounded by those excremental passages in which the inner effectively becomes outer, and this excreting function becomes, as it were, the model by which other forms of identity-differentiation are accomplished. In effect, this is the mode by which Others become shit.
>
> Judith Butler, *Gender Trouble*, 1990

Craig Claiborne published an essay called "Cooking with Soul" in the 3 November 1968 issue of the *New York Times Magazine*. Though not destined to go down in radical-chic infamy, his essay is more suggestive than Baro's *Vogue* column of the motivation subtending white male fascination with soul food:

> One of the complaints among soul-food devotees in New York—and they are predominantly displaced Southerners—is that the food in most soul-food restaurants is more Southern than soul. The menus mostly feature such typical Southern dishes as fried chicken, spareribs, candied yams and mustard or collard greens. One rarely finds trotters, neckbones, pigs' tails and chitterlings. (109)

To understand the import of Claiborne's desire to separate the southern from the authentically soul, we might do well to recall here that in 1962 Amiri Baraka had written an essay called "Soul Food." Published in his collection *Home* in 1966, the essay presaged the late 1960s' fascination with and commodification of the purported food practices of slavery. This interracial embrace of black culture was evidenced, among other ways, by a proliferation of restaurants, college cafeteria menus, newspaper columns, magazine articles, and cookbooks, all devoted to soul food.[6] In clear contradiction to Claiborne, however, Baraka celebrated as no less soul than southern many foods that he claimed the "ofays seldom get to peck" (102): these foods included not only chitterlings and neckbones but also maws, knuckles, pork chops, fatback, fried porgies, potlikker, turnips, kale, watermelon, black-eyed peas, grits, gravy, hoppin' john, hushpuppies, hoecake, buttermilk biscuits, pancakes, dumplings, okra, and (intriguingly) the Nation of Islam's bean pies—as well as what Claiborne would term the "Southern dishes" of fried chicken, barbecue, sweet potato pies, and mustard and collard greens.

Given this mutability in the perception of soul food's ingredients, one might surmise that what was at stake for many patrons of African American cooking was not an accurate rendition of culinary history. Indeed, had accuracy been at issue, at least some minimal notions of historical development and regional variation would have had to displace soul's reification into the monolithic sign "Slavery" of the diverse practices which, over time, actually constituted American chattel slavery. The lines of culinary demarcation would, by and large, have been drawn around class and geographic location within the South at least as much as around race; the divergent contributions of rural and urban black women and men to the creation and execution of these culinary traditions would have been systematically analyzed.[7]

Rather, soul food circulated relatively unheeded by whites through a variety of discursive contexts until the mid-1960s. But in the wake of the rise of Black Power it became a site of interracial struggle over the regulation of (what many perceived as an unregulated explosion of) blackness. This bears out Eric Lott's claim that precisely "when the lines of 'race' appear both intractable and obstructive . . . there emerges a collective desire (conscious or not) to bridge a gulf that is, however, perceived to separate the races absolutely" ("White" 475). Feelings of "sympathy for the Black drive to self-reliance" notwithstanding, white purveyors of soul food such as Claiborne and Baro were surely also attempting to negotiate and/or contain, via their representations of African American culinary traditions, the volatile racial and sexual politics of the late 1960s. And for reasons that should become increasingly clear as we progress, the food fetishes that emerged as an expression of this desire were not the "beans and greens of necessity" but instead the entrails and extremities of hogs—intestines in particular. As a *Time* magazine writer opined for the uninitiated in a 1969 article titled "Eating Like Soul Brothers": "Today, as 200 years ago, the true 'stone soul' dish is chitterlings, pronounced 'chitlins.'" The elided syllable evidently distinguished genuine "insiders" to black culture from less sedulous fellow travelers.

Yet if white patrons of soul food were engaged in what Lott has described, in a related context, as "a simultaneous drawing up and crossing of racial boundaries"

(*Love* 6), their efforts to play auteur of African American culinary practices need to be situated, as I have suggested, in the context of ongoing intraracial practices of culinary regulation. These practices have also revolved around the drawing up and crossing of boundaries—racial and "Otherwise"—via chitterlings. In order to explicate some of the theoretical issues underlying this latter debate, I will take as my focal point for the remainder of this section Ralph Ellison's *Invisible Man*, a novel that predates but still anticipates the hierarchical inversions of the Black Power era. Surely the most famous post–World War II literary expression of the contradictory quest for a paradigm of black male identity, *Invisible Man* provides a valuable site for exploring the triangulated relationships among blackness, food, and filth prior to the valorization of soul food.

The narrator/protagonist of *Invisible Man* has been educated at a black southern college generally understood to have been modeled after Ellison's own alma mater, Tuskegee. The college is led by Dr. Bledsoe, who is clearly cut from the same mold as Tuskegee's "Founder," Booker T. Washington (Sundquist 33–35). Cynical yet naive, the Invisible Man has grown to despise Dr. Bledsoe as a fraudulent "race-man" who truly believes "white is right," a "Tom" who teaches the students to aspire to be accepted by whites while simultaneously staying in a subordinate place as blacks. After leaving the college and going north to New York, the narrator vacillates between embracing his racial identity, including the foods eaten by poor southern blacks, and rejecting this identity in an effort to gain acceptance, which in the terms of the novel translates into "visibility," among whites.

Almost midway through the novel, just after he succumbs to the lures of the yam vendor, the Invisible Man fantasizes about exposing Dr. Bledsoe as an impostor:

> And I saw myself advancing upon Bledsoe, standing bare of his false humility in the crowded lobby of Men's House, and seeing him there and him seeing me and ignoring me and me enraged and suddenly whipping out a foot or two of chitterlings, raw, uncleaned and dripping sticky circles on the floor as I shake them in his face, shouting:
>   "Bledsoe, you're a shameless chitterling eater! I accuse you of relishing hog bowels! Ha! And not only do you eat them, you sneak and eat them in *private* when you think you're unobserved! You're a sneaking chitterling lover! I accuse you of indulging in a filthy habit, Bledsoe! Lug them out of there, Bledsoe! Lug them out so we can see! I accuse you before the eyes of the world!" And he lugs them out, yards of them, with mustard greens, and racks of pigs' ears, and pork chops and black-eyed peas with dull accusing eyes. (265)

From a post-*OutWeek* vantage point, it is tempting to argue that the "truth" of this famous scene of "outing" is not racial but sexual in nature, that Bledsoe is being exposed (to put it in the crude terms implicit in the Invisible Man's accusation) not as a nigger but a faggot. Certainly the markers of both a gay sexual encounter and a gay outing are present. One man confronts another, "standing bare," in a public place; the former possesses knowledge of the latter's secret. The accuser "whips" out a "foot or two of chitterlings" in the way he might whip out his penis, and the chitterlings drip "sticky circles on the floor" evocative of semen. The accused is charged with indulging, in "private," in a "filthy" habit, which in another context might refer to masturbation, but here would surely suggest gay male anal sex as well.[8] The accuser fantasizes, moreover, that after the climactic confrontation the accused "would disintegrate, disinflate!" (265). Contemporary queer theory aside, however, if we recall that by the late 1940s lesbians and gays had already become a main target of anti-Communist hysteria, the scene is no less reminiscent of Joe McCarthy than Michelangelo Signorile, and thus one might surmise that the charged double entendre of this de-closeting would have been as apparent in 1952, when Invisible Man was published, as it is currently.[9]

The possibility that chitterlings can code male homosocial or homosexual desire, as well as what Baraka later called "Negro-ness" (Blues 219), may help explain why they became the most fetishized of soul foods by the late 1960s—among not just black men but also aspiring white "soul brothers" such as Craig Claiborne.[10] But it seems to me that we would be mistaken to conclude that this scene from Invisible Man is really a scene about sexuality "passing" for one about race.[11] I would focus rather on an ambiguity in the epistemological framework of the Invisible Man's accusations, an ambiguity which discourses of race and sexuality have had in common: "You're a sneaking chitterling lover! I accuse you of indulging in a filthy habit, Bledsoe!" There is a slight discrepancy here. The first charge implies a culinary ontology. Bledsoe does not simply eat chitterlings; he is "a sneaking chitterling lover," and to be a sneaking chitterling lover is to be a particular sort of person, a "filthy" person. The second accusation, that Bledsoe indulges "in a filthy habit," is, by contrast, not necessarily a statement about the sort of being he is. Eating chitterlings does not necessarily a "chitterling lover" make. Elsewhere in Invisible Man the narrator equivocates between the two epistemologies of gastronomy, opting for the former in the renowned yam scene. The choice to eat or not to eat a yam is so fraught because it entails not merely a discrete act of eating but a revelation about the sort of being the Invisible Man is, an admission of the ontological inescapability of, presumably, his blackness.[12]

Historians of sexuality have made analogous distinctions with respect to homosexuality. Most obviously and controversially, Michel Foucault has argued that the category of the homosexual is not a stable transhistorical identity but instead a creation of the late nineteenth century (History 43). Whereas previously a person might have been said to engage in (deviant) sexual acts with members of the same sex, in late Victorian society the homosexual emerged as a deviant, as someone whose sexual desires set him or her apart, ontologically, from the heterosexual. Homosexuality began to refer to a category not of deeds but of persons, not to what one did but to what one was.[13] I draw this analogy—which otherwise has its limits—to remind us that, like libidinal desires, food and hunger are used to legitimate contradictory claims about the ontological status of race and sexuality. Consequently, to understand the complicated evolution of soul food during the civil rights and Black Power eras, one must pay attention not just to the ambiguous, protean relationship between what a black self is or desires and what a black self eats, not just to how various participants in the debate over soul food attempted to manipulate this ambiguity, but also to the latent potential for the slippage of "filth" among discourses of race and sexuality, as well as among ethnicity, class, gender, and nationality. More specifically, one must understand how the slippage can operate via food.

Structural anthropologists argue, of course, that "filth" is a relational category, one that has no absolute existence, no universal definition; filth is simply that which remains outside a given system of order, matter (or actions) out of place. This line of thought is most famously explicated by Mary Douglas in *Purity and Danger*. She observes that "ideas about separating, purifying, demarcating and punishing transgressions have as their main function to impose system on an inherently untidy experience. It is only by exaggerating the difference between within and without, above and below, male and female, with and against, that a semblance of order is created" (4). Douglas's claims have been particularly influential in their insistence that what is excluded from the social order is, in fact, constitutive of that order. But having recognized the foundational function of such exclusions, we are still left with the question of what sort of relationship, if any, obtains between social categories and individual subjectivity. This is precisely the sort of question that structural anthropology cannot, at least in Julia Kristeva's opinion, confront.

Accordingly, in *Powers of Horror* Kristeva draws on her own previous work in psychoanalysis to reinterpret Douglas's study of pollution rituals. Her goal is to locate a correspondence between social structures such as the classification of pure/impure and the structures of subjectivity. "Why that system of classification and not another?" she asks. "What social, subjective, and socio-subjectively interacting needs does it fulfill?" (92). More to the point here, "Why does *corporeal waste*, menstrual blood and excrement, or everything that is assimilated to them . . . represent—like a metaphor that would have become incarnate—the objective frailty of the symbolic order?" (70). It is in the process of answering these questions that Kristeva develops her theory of abjection. She has described it as "an extremely strong feeling which is at once somatic and symbolic, and which is above all a revolt of the person against an external menace from which one wants to keep oneself at a distance, but of which one has the impression that it is not only an external menace but that it may menace us from the inside" (quoted in Baruch and Serrano 135–36). According to Kelly Oliver, the abject "is neither good nor evil, subject nor object, ego nor unconscious, nature nor culture, but something that threatens the distinctions themselves" ("Nourishing" 70–71).[14]

Judith Butler has quite rightly critiqued Kristeva's willingness to render heterosexual reproductivity normative by construing abjection as an irruption of the realm of the maternal Semiotic into the patriarchal logic of the Symbolic order (*Gender* 79–93). But since one of my aims in this chapter is to explicate soul food's figuration of black women as slave mothers, Kristeva's work on abjection still has resonance for understanding the fascination and disgust with which Ellison's fictive Invisible Man accuses Bledsoe of "relishing hog bowels" because she argues that "[f]ood loathing is perhaps the most elementary and most archaic form of abjection" (2). As Oliver has explained: "It is food, what is taken into the body, along with excrement, what is expelled from the body, which calls into question the borders of the body" ("Nourishing" 71). Kristeva's concern with maternity leads her to privilege breast milk in her analysis because it confounds the separation between mother and infant. But though she never mentions the sausage known in her adopted country as "andouille," it seems to me that her theory might help us account for why chitterlings—rather than, say, "black-eyed peas with dull accusing eyes"—have borne the metonymic burden as the "stone" soul food. Consequently, it can help us explain the twinned responses of attraction and repulsion that a mention of soul food often seems to arouse. As the organ of a hog through which food becomes excrement, and accordingly through which hog and not-hog are negotiated, bowels point to the fragility of the boundary dividing self from other. In Ellison's scenario, clearly phallic as well as anal, hog bowels might be construed as the "in-between, the ambiguous, the composite," signifying simultaneously order and disorder (Kristeva 4). In effect doubly disorderly, they can be interrogated to reveal connections between food taboos and the social prohibitions upon which "America" has been founded.

That is, in the U.S. social order hog bowels are overdetermined to be both fetishized and abjected—an object of cathexis and catharsis, of desire and disavowal. They have multiple metonymic possibilities because they encode America's twinned fascination with gay sexuality and with blackness, obsessions displayed after World War II most obviously among the Beats.[15] As that which transgresses the boundaries between food and excrement, phallus and anus, origin and decay, chitterlings point to the fragility of the system through which privileged identities such as whiteness, masculinity, and heterosexuality are maintained as what Kristeva calls corps propre, and blackness, femininity, and homosexuality, as unclean and improper (see Roudiez viii). Chitterlings remind us that these othered identities are "filthy" not because they are an "external menace" to the social order but because, like our own bowels and excretions, they "may menace us from inside."[16]

The implications for Black Power racial ideologies of such internalizations of the Other were perhaps most succinctly expressed by a closing refrain of Melvin Van Peebles's popular blaxploitation film Sweet Sweetback's Baadasssss Song (1971): "Chicken ain't nothing but a bird / White man ain't nothing but a turd / Nigger ain't shit." Invoking the conflation of blackness and shit only to repudiate it, the aphorism suggests that shit is instead a (prosaic) turd menacing the white man from inside, whereas blackness is something else entirely, something simultaneously less valued than shit yet potentially even more transgressive, something that draws us "toward the place where meaning collapses" (Kristeva 2) or where . . .

"The Walls Come Tumbling Down"

They will shout loudly about soul because they will have lost it.

Ishmael Reed, Mumbo Jumbo, 1972

Having set forth a psychoanalytically informed model for interpreting the late 1960s' male fascination with hog bowels, and having speculated that this fascination was at least partially underwritten by the era's homoerotic investments in black male bodies, I want now to return to my assertion in the introduction to this chapter that soul food has been understood (and dismissed) as a phenomenon of black bourgeois "slumming." In their study of transgression, Peter Stallybrass and

Allon White attempt to delineate the dynamic process through which the European middle class came into existence via the continuous construction of boundaries between itself and the lower classes, boundaries which only unsuccessfully disguised the constitutive function of the exclusion. In their widely cited words,

> the 'top' attempts to reject and eliminate the 'bottom' for reasons of prestige and status, only to discover, not only that it is in some way frequently dependent upon that low-Other . . . but also that the top *includes* that low symbolically, as a primary eroticized constituent of its own fantasy life. The result is a mobile, conflictual fusion of power, fear and desire in the construction of subjectivity: a psychological dependence upon precisely those Others which are being rigorously opposed and excluded at the social level. It is for this reason that what is *socially* peripheral is so frequently *symbolically* central. (5)

We can see this process operate by tracing how the symbolic domains of "the human body, psychic forms, geographical space and the social formation are all constructed within interrelating and dependent hierarchies of high and low" (Stallybrass and White 2). The transgression of hierarchy in one domain will disrupt or destabilize—but by no means necessarily overturn—hierarchies in each of the others. Their perspective is thus at odds with Mikhail Bakhtin's utopian tendency to equate carnival with social revolution (e.g., *Rabelais* 7).

In the course of developing this thesis, Stallybrass and White look briefly at the relationship between class formation and dietary practices, including widespread cross-class preoccupation with the pig. They point out that though as a general rule cultures "are frequently identified and stigmatized through culinary habits which infract the taboos and culinary habits of the identifying group," carnival celebrations among the lower classes in Europe frequently associated pigs with Jews in "a grotesque hybridization of terms expressly antithetical to each other according to the dietary rules of their victims" (53). The pig, for them, can be understood as both a target and a means of "displaced abjection," which Stallybrass and White define as a "process whereby 'low' social groups turn their figurative and actual power, *not* against those in authority, but against those who are even 'lower' (women, Jews, animals, particularly cats and pigs)" (53). Their arguments provide a valuable model for helping us historicize U.S. interracial fixation on hog bowels in the context of the expansion and consolidation of the African American middle class after World War II.

Consider, for example, a sardonic comment made by future Black Panther Information Minister Eldridge Cleaver in his prison manifesto *Soul on Ice* (1968). Lending credence to the arguments of Stallybrass and White, Cleaver foregrounds class as an axis of culinary analysis, insisting that the soul food fad was propelled by middle-class blacks:

> You hear a lot of jazz about Soul Food. Take chitterlings: the ghetto blacks eat them from necessity while the black bourgeoisie has turned it into a mocking slogan. Eating chitterlings is like going slumming to them. Now that they have the price of a steak, here they come prattling about Soul Food. The people in the ghetto want steaks. *Beef Steaks.* I wish I had the power to see to it that the bourgeoisie really *did* have to make it on Soul Food.

The emphasis on Soul Food is counter-revolutionary black bourgeois ideology. The main reason Elijah Muhammad outlawed pork for Negroes had nothing to do with dietary laws. The point is that when you get all those blacks cooped up in the ghetto with beef steaks on their minds—with the weight of religious fervor behind the desire to chuck—then something's got to give. The system has made allowances for the ghettoites to obtain a little pig, *but there are no provisions for the elite to give up any beef!* The walls come tumbling down. (40)

Writing in 1965, Cleaver insinuates that members of the black bourgeoisie were engaged, through dietary discourses and practices, in a hypocritical attempt to embrace their racial identity by othering it onto the black working class and poor. If Stallybrass and White are correct in their claims, this process of discovering one's "own pleasures and desires under the sign of the Other" would surely be fundamental to the establishment of middle-class black, as well as middle-class white, identity (201). Such an argument seems particularly apt, too, if one recalls that soul food emerged in the years following the publication of sociologist E. Franklin Frazier's unflattering *Black Bourgeoisie* (1957)—a study which not only questioned the racial authenticity of middle-class African Americans, but which memorably labeled their social life "The Gaudy Carnival" (200).

Certainly the Invisible Man's desire to "out" Bledsoe is also implicitly a fantasy about class. The former's deployment of ontologizing discourses of race ("You're a sneaking chitterling lover!") can be understood to code resentment of the latter's bourgeois satisfactions.[17] And certainly this slippage of "filth" between race and class is evident in the essay valorizing "Soul Food" by the Rutgers- and Howard-educated Amiri Baraka, who made a point of parading his origins in a "*lower* middle-class Negro family" (emphasis added; *Black* 222). Displaying the *nostalgie de la boue* which Cleaver would later dismiss as "counter-revolutionary," Baraka dwells on soul food as the food of poverty and necessity, observing, for example: "People kill chickens all over the world, but chasing them through the dark on somebody else's property would probably insure, once they went in the big bag, that you'd find some really beautiful way to eat them. I mean, after all the risk involved" ("Soul" 102–3). Inasmuch as Hettie Jones has since observed of her ex-husband Baraka that "[h]e was the middle-class one—everything he liked to blame on me!" (104), one can only be skeptical of his celebratory treatment of black poverty. Yet, even as Baraka's brief discussion of African American culinary traditions lends credence to Cleaver's indictment of soul food as a practice of middle-class black slumming, we should also note that his contemporaneous writings about music do offer a more complex, if still symptomatic, understanding of the ideology of soul.

For example, in a 1963 discussion of the evolution of black musical traditions, Baraka had seemed quite a bit more ambivalent in his evaluation of soul. He claims in a passage from *Blues People* that the emergence of soul might be understood as "an attempt to reverse the social roles within the society by redefining the canons of value. . . . White is then not 'right,' as the old blues had it, but a liability, since the culture of white precludes the possession of the Negro 'soul'" (219). Though he generally finds the "social aggression" of soul to be laudable (219), Baraka does still reveal a distrust of its authenticity, admitting: "Many times this re-evaluation proved as affected and as emotionally arid as would a move in the opposite direction" (218). Owning up to the nostalgic underpinnings of his own fascination with black music, he critiques in particular "the spectacle of an urban, college-trained Negro musician pretending, perhaps in all sincerity, that he has the same field of emotional reference as his greatgrandfather, the Mississippi slave" (218). Such a display, Baraka concludes, "seems to me merely burlesque, or cruder, a kind of modern minstrelsy" (218).

The problem, however, is that even as he distances himself from soul's commercialized association with the black middle class, Baraka fails to question the prevailing doctrine that in the discourses of soul, the "smell" of Negro-ness becomes "valuable" (219). Put into the theoretical terms I have been using, he insinuates that soul does not entail (displaced) abjection at all:

> Even the adjective *funky*, which once meant to many Negroes merely a stink (usually associated with sex), was used to qualify [soul] music as meaningful. . . . The social implication, then, was that even the old stereotype of a distinctive Negro smell that white America subscribed to could be turned against white America. For this smell now, real or not, was made a valuable characteristic of "Negro-ness." And "Negro-ness," by the fifties, for many Negroes (and whites) was the only strength left to American culture. (*Blues* 219–20)

An anecdote related by Mel Watkins in a 1971 essay on "The Lyrics of James Brown" amply illustrates the significance of this sort of claim for Black Power attitudes toward food. Watkins writes of a teenager who, upon leaving the Apollo after a concert by the self-styled Godfather of Soul, affirmed, "The dude is as down as a chitlin'" (22). Two decades after the Invisible Man had "outed" Bledsoe for his "filthy habit," chitterlings were no longer a "private" passion to be indulged in (middle-class) shame. "Negro-ness" no longer required closeting. "Say it loud," as Brown himself famously commanded, "I'm black and I'm proud."

What I want to suggest instead is that if we construe Baraka's "Negro smell" to be not a racialized state of being but rather one name for the psychic residue of the processes of othering through which hegemonic American identities have emerged, then it is surely no more possible for the black proletariat actually to embody Negro-ness than it is for the black bourgeoisie, indeed no more possible for African Americans as a group actually to embody Negro-ness than it is for Caucasians. Baraka's "real or not" implicitly acknowledges this important distinction. This is by no means to downplay the lived reality of racialized subjectivities and racial oppression or the acute awareness of being othered which W. E. B. Du Bois famously termed "double-consciousness" (8). The implication of my argument is rather that the construction of coherent selfhood is not possible even for subordinated groups without unconscious and therefore unavoidable processes of abjection.

Working from this perspective, one cannot help but dwell on Baraka's argument that soul can be understood as an embrace of a black "stink." The problematically *gendered* as well as classed underpinnings of such a fantasy were surely exposed by the frequently apologetic references in African American cookbooks of the subsequent decade—and particularly in cookbooks written by black women—to the *smell* of chitterlings while they are cooking. "The very idea of chitlings turns up many a nose," entertainer Pearl Bailey observes in *Pearl's Kitchen* (1973), just before acknowledging, "I don't care too much for that odor myself" (11).[18] Inasmuch as Bailey also includes the minutiae of her household cleaning practices in her cookbook ("do you realize how dusty and dirty the cushions on the furniture can get?" [93]), we might well infer that even while taking pride in foods associated with the traditional southern black diet, she still felt it necessary to disassociate herself from soul's (metaphorical) black stink. Having herself grown up among the black working class, Bailey's disavowal can easily be read as a critique of both white radical chic and black bourgeois slumming, and, to an extent, it probably was. However, I would suggest that the complexity of her motivations is even more intelligible if we recognize that Black Power's fascination with soul food was constituted by yet another mode of displaced abjection, a mode that paradoxically both necessitated and transcended divisions of class among blacks. As Baraka's parenthetical conflation of "stink" with "sex" might be interpreted to suggest, the discourses of soul associated the filth of black selfhood generally with femininity and specifically with lower-class black maternity.

"It Always Starts with Mama"

Hell, Mary
Bell Jones,
full of groans
the slum lord
is on you
Cursed are you
among women
and cursed is
the fruit of
your womb,
Willie Lee,
as it was
in 1619
is now
and ever
shall be
SHIT
without end
Amen

Jon Eckels, "Hell, Mary," 1971

Journalist Lerone Bennett Jr. had memorably registered the close association between soul and black maternity shortly after Baraka published *Blues People*. In a 1964 essay called "Ethos: Voices from the Cave" from *The Negro Mood*, Bennett located soul in opposition to white U.S. values which he, like Baraka, construed as overly technologized and therefore dehumanizing. Insisting that soul deconstructs (rather than simply inverts) the "Platonic-Puritan dichotomies of good-bad, white-black, God-devil, body-mind" (85), Bennett develops the "cave" analogy in greater detail. He conjures up the spectacle of "Negroes who have been, to borrow Plato's image, sitting chained for four hundred years in a cave with their backs to the sun. White men told them for four hundred years that they were the shadows they saw on the wall. The Negro is breaking his chains now and is turning around to face the fire of the sun" (94).

Bennett specifically deploys the metaphor of maternity in his analysis of soul by referring to the "protracted pains" of the Negro's birth in a racist country (84) and to "the womb of this non-Puritan, nonmachine, nonexploitative tradition" (89). But even while invoking pregnancy and parturition, he effectively subsumes the specter of sexual difference into a totalizing and explicitly masculinist narrative of racial domination and rebellion. The "voices" speaking forth from this cave are all male—which comes as no surprise given Margaret Homans's demonstration of how the Platonic topos of the cave works to elide the role of women in human reproduction ("Woman"). Yet when Bennett claims that the Negro "fleshes out, in his androgyny, the hoped-for synthesis" of white and black (90), the repressed female Other returns to haunt the essay. Despite his tenuous effort to use "androgyny" as a signifier of biracial identity, the word surely anticipates the Black Power era's widespread obsession with purifying black manhood of the taint of femininity.

But to understand the ramifications for black culinary history of soul's imbrication in discourses of black maternity, we need first to contextualize soul's emergence more broadly in relation to Black Arts and Black Power practices of displaced abjection. Replete with language of misogyny, homophobia, and anti-Judaism, the literature of these movements is well known to provide a veritable case study thereof.[19] Numerous poets, for example, conjure the specter of enemies within and without who must be conquered by the ever-vigilant black man: "mulatto bitches" and "Stinking/Whores!" (Baraka, "Black" 223); "faggot[s]" (D. Lee, "Re-Act") and "konk-haired blood suckin punks" (W. Smith 283); and, to speculate about one probable referent of the Jon Eckels poem quoted above, "slum lord" Jews.[20] Phillip Brian Harper has persuasively argued "that the response of Black Arts nationalism to social division within the black populace is not to strive to overcome it, but rather repeatedly to articulate it in the name of black consciousness" (44). He also explains that the cultural workers in the Black Arts movement who used such language were responding in part to accusations that poetry and other artistic practices were bourgeois and therefore effeminate (51). Since many of them also associated this intellectual work with both gay and Jewish subcultures—witness Baraka's close ties to Beat figures such as Allen Ginsberg during the late 1950s—the repeated attacks on "owner-jews" might perhaps be read as one of many strategies through which middle-class black male artists adopted proletarian personas (Baraka, "Black" 223). In other words, they articulated concerns about "inappropriate" intellectual influences via the more overtly masculinized arena of economics.

These interlocking discourses of displaced abjection might also be understood to manifest what was, at the time, a widespread structure of African American male feeling: black nationalist homosexual panic.[21] This structure is particularly well evidenced in the prison memoirs, in which constant allusions to "shit" and other bodily detritus reflect not only oppressive living conditions and class/race resentment, but also preoccupation with the homoerotics of prison life and the ever-present threat of rape.[22] David Flournoy writes in "Testament" (1968), for example, of his preconceptions of prison, allowing that he "had made up my mind that the first time some guy approached me about sex that I was going to get me another life sentence. I saw no other way. I mean, I couldn't go running to the officials 'cause in a way it's better to be a punk than a rat when you got to live in this joint for years and years" (30–31). Even in the process of proclaiming his determination to kill before submitting to rape, Flournoy betrays the fact that he has already fantasized himself a "punk." In this fashion, discourses about prison rape are inscribed by the larger society's prohibition of same-sex desire.[23]

Eldridge Cleaver likewise closes his notoriously homophobic attack on James Baldwin in *Soul on Ice* with the apocalyptic prediction that "'There's a shit-storm coming'" (107). Intriguingly, though, his strategy for expressing the threat posed by male homoeroticism is to draw an analogy between black gay men and black mothers: he claims that "many Negro homosexuals . . . are outraged and frustrated because in their sickness they are unable to have a baby by a white man" (100). Only by conjuring the historical transgression committed by and upon black women—that they have "allowed" white men to father their children—is Cleaver able to articulate the nature of Baldwin's "sickness." Black male homosexuality is thus stigmatized by being equated with miscegenational black motherhood, and both are seen as a pathological distortion of black culture resulting from white domination.[24] In this context, it is relevant to note the implicit accusation underlying Jon Eckels's condemnation of his fictive character "Mary Bell Jones": at issue is not just the fact that she engages in sex with the slum lord, but that her "groans" might signify pleasure rather than repulsion in the act.

Cleaver was not alone in displacing his anxieties about the status of black masculinity onto the scene of reproduction. Perhaps nowhere is the apprehension expressed with more rhetorical flair than in the writings of George Jackson, who begins *Soledad Brother* (1970) by conflating his imprisonment with chattel slavery and symbolizing both via reference to the womb:

> It always starts with Mama, mine loved me. As testimony of her love, and her fear for the fate of the manchild all slave mothers hold, she attempted to press, hide, push, capture me in the womb. The conflicts and contradictions that will follow me to the tomb started right there in the womb. The feeling of being captured . . . this slave can never adjust to it, it's a thing that I just don't favor, then, now, never. (9–10)

As I have already indicated, Hortense Spillers's "Mama's Baby, Papa's Maybe" works to explicate the relationship between this ambivalent fixation on the legacy of slavery and the pervasive belief in U.S. society that black men have been "captured" by black women. Her inquiry might thus be construed as an alternative psychoanalytic theory of abjection, one expressly geared to the contingencies of African American history.

Spillers explores the significance of the fact that, whereas the dominant white society has traditionally privileged the role and name of the father in maintaining "legitimate" generational continuity, according to the codes of slavery, black children would follow the condition of the mother. Through this strategy, the legal system "removed the African-American male not so much from sight as from *mimetic* view as a partner in the prevailing social fiction of the Father's name, the Father's law" (80). One important consequence of this removal, Spillers contends, is that the black female "breaks in upon the imagination with a forcefulness that marks both a denial and an 'illegitimacy.' Because of this peculiar American denial, the black American male embodies the *only* American community of males which has had the specific occasion to learn *who* the female is within itself " (80). Working from the perspective provided by Spillers but giving it a slight causal twist, we might understand Jackson and Eckels's anachronistic equation of black women with "slave" mothers as a tactic that enabled them to deny the politically conservative implications of their social vision. In their usage, slavery was emptied of its historical reference to a socioeconomic system which denied the humanity of black women as well as men, and it was reinscribed as a familial trope which justified an ongoing power struggle between heterosexist black male nationalists and practically everyone else. The discourse of psychoanalysis was precisely what Jackson and Eckels needed to make their case.

Similarly, in her study of the relationship of African American women novelists to the ideological program espoused by Black Arts advocates during the 1970s, Madhu Dubey has discussed "three central oppositions—between individual and community, oppressive past and revolutionary future, and absent and present subjectivity—that structure black nationalist discourse" (21). In the process of demonstrating the numerous ways in which the Black Aesthetic paradoxically managed to adhere to the very bourgeois white value system that it was purported to critique, Dubey shows how black women were repeatedly construed in these discourses as a hindrance to the revolution. She points out, for example, that Larry Neal had "staunchly confirmed the oldest traditional opposition between the masculine and feminine principles: 'woman as primarily need / man as doer'" (20).[25] As Dubey succinctly explains, in Black Aesthetic ideology, black women are vilified as "the dead, static past, tainted with white values, which the militant black writer must destroy before he can articulate a new revolutionary black sensibility" (20).

Of course, it should come as no surprise that this fixation on the "revolutionary" future was most frequently expressed via the dispersal of pronatalist ideologies literally mandating black female—and therefore black male—reproductive sexuality. As Dubey has further pointed out, although many politically and artistically active African American men had attacked Daniel Patrick Moynihan for describing black families as a "Tangle of Pathology" (140) in his infamous study *The Negro Family*, "[t]he black nationalists' womb-centered definition of black women was, in a sense, their strongest tribute to the Moynihan Report, for Moynihan had been dismayed primarily by black women's insufficient inscription in the patriarchal reproductive system" (19). By celebrating black women as the breeders of revolutionary warriors, black nationalist discourses actually worked to mire "black women more firmly within white middle-class familial ideology" (Dubey 19). Expressing her frustration with this expectation in her 1976 novel *Meridian*, Alice Walker depicts black nationalist Truman Held commanding his ex-girlfriend Meridian Hill, "*Have* my beautiful black babies" (116). His command is futile, however, since by this point in the novel Meridian has not only aborted an embryo fathered by Held, but she has also undergone sterilization.

At the same time, we should not lose sight of the way that African American men's invocations of maternity frequently melded into an attack on white male authority. Here one thinks, for example, of the opening lines of H. Rap Brown's memoir *Die Nigger Die!* (1969): "My first contact with white america was marked by her violence, for when a white doctor pulled me from between my mother's legs and slapped my wet ass, I, as every other negro in america, reacted to this man-inflicted pain with a cry" (1). Like Jackson, Brown denies black mothers any instrumental role in the process of birth.[26] Rather than depicting himself as being *pushed from* the womb by a laboring black woman, Brown ascribes agency to a white male doctor. Although representations of female passivity were (and are) by no means uncommon under the prevailing medical model of childbirth, Brown's focus on the "white doctor" should serve as an important reminder that sociopolitical investments in the myth of black matriarchy ought to be understood in conjunction with fears about the future of white male dominance (and, indeed, white female reproductive practices) in the wake of the liberatory social movements of the late 1960s.[27]

The era was preoccupied, after all, with the reproductive rights and practices not just of African American women but of all U.S. women—most especially native-born white women of the middle class (Petchesky 101–38). This concern was animated by a variety of factors, including high-profile campaigns to legalize abortion and halt sterilization abuse, declining birth rates and increasing births outside of marriage, and the movement of (white) women into the (professional) workforce in the wake of Congressman Howard Smith's successful motion to include "sex" as a protected category under Title VII of the Civil Rights Act of 1964 (Graham 136–39). After acknowledging that "42 percent of white women" were employed in the public sphere, Moynihan himself fretted that if the then current reproductive "rate continues, in seven years 1 American in 8 will be nonwhite" (138), thus illuminating one important subtext for his overt obsession with black family structures. And though Puerto Ricans and Mexicans had been coming to the United States in fairly substantial numbers prior to 1965, when a less restrictive immigration act was passed, Moynihan was actually writing before the most sustained wave of eugenicist panic began to set in because of the failure of America's white population to keep reproductive pace with that of its increasingly multiethnic cohorts, including peoples of Asian as well as African and Latino/a descent (J. Patterson 326–27 and 577–79; Takaki 400–1).

Taking this historical context into account, it seems likely that the black male preoccupation with black maternity was (and continues to be) so widely resonant because it allowed the expression of anxieties about challenges to white as well as black racial identity, to white as well as black patriarchy. These challenges have emerged from diverse social groups, including feminists, lesbians and gays, Native

Americans, and immigrants whose racial identifications destabilize the conventional white/black analytic binary. By presenting the wombs of African American women as a battleground for phallus-driven interracial politics, men such as H. Rap Brown transformed long-standing investments in the myth of black female dominance into an opportunity for the public staging of fears about the future of whiteness, blackness, and the beleaguered manhood of both.

Working from this perspective, moreover, it becomes noteworthy that when Julian Mayfield proclaimed in 1971 that "I cannot—will not—define my Black Aesthetic, nor will I allow it to be defined for me," he was one of many who began refusing to define discursive practices stemming from the Black Arts movement precisely as black feminists launched their critiques of the era's masculinist posturing (27).[28] Given Mayfield's shift from "cannot" to "will not," such evasions could be construed as a pose of resistance to white appropriations of black culture. If, however, one takes into account the second half of his comment—"but I know that somehow it revolves around this new breed of man and woman who have leaped out of the loins of all those slaves and semi-slaves, who survived so that we might survive"(27)—it seems clear that this rhetoric of aesthetic indefinability was linked to Black Power's fixation on maternity. If one also notes that the slave mother is once again depicted as having no agency in her labor, then it seems likely that soul's articulation as a discourse of improvisational racial authenticity enabled black cultural nationalists to sidestep the ideological contradictions in their construction of black gender roles. The vilification of "slave" mothers by Black Arts and Black Power proponents was surely at odds with the era's valorization of soul.

"It's Everything That's Good"

> It's not soulful to try and spell out exactly what soul is . . .
>
> Jimmy Lee, *Soul Food Cookbook*, 1970

In their study of core belief systems in African American culture, Nicholas Cooper-Lewter and Henry Mitchell participate in this commonplace representation of soul as indefinable. "For many," they write,

> Soul has referred to . . . a style of cooking (Soul food), a complicated handshake, a widely popular genre of music, or an identity (Soul sister or brother). Some, if pressed, would define it more specifically as natural rhythm, emotive spontaneity, or a cultural compulsion to compassion. Still others would define Soul as the sum of all that is typically or uniquely Black. However, most would simply say that it really defies description, and that one who has to ask what it is can never know. Few terms in American English have assumed such a secure place in everyday language without being precisely defined. (ix)

By 1986, when Cooper-Lewter and Mitchell published this commentary, aphorisms that soul "defies description" and that "one who has to ask what it is can never know" were widely familiar. Holding fast to such precepts in the face of poststructuralist critiques of the humanist conception of authenticity, bell hooks claims in her essay "The Chitlin Circuit" (1990) that "[a] very distinctive black culture was created in the agrarian South" and that this culture offers lessons for survival for all African Americans (38). "Current trends in postmodernist cultural critiques devaluing the importance of this legacy by dismissing notions of authenticity or suggesting that the very concept of 'soul' is illusory and not experientially based are," she maintains, "disturbing" (38). Particularly given the rightward momentum of U.S. politics since the late 1960s, hooks's goal—to ensure that viable strategies of resistance to racism be passed on to younger generations—is clearly worth pursuing. Yet my presumption all along has been that precisely because of the potentially "disturbing" ramifications of such a critique, a central problematic of soul to be questioned is, nonetheless, the emergence of this consensus that it should not be questioned. Like black feminist criticism (as Hazel Carby has defined it), soul is not a site of closure but rather "a sign that should be interrogated, a locus of contradictions" (*Reconstructing* 15).

In this regard, it is important to bear in mind that when soul first began gaining wider circulation in the early 1960s, it was by no means defined as indefinable, nor, for that matter, was it associated with improvisation. Baraka, for example, had contended in *Blues People* that soul signifies not a "return" to but more precisely a "conscious re-evaluation" of black "roots" (218). Soul, he observes, "is as much of a 'move' within the black psyche as was the move north in the beginning of the century. The idea of the Negro's having 'roots' and that they are a valuable possession, rather than the source of ineradicable shame, is perhaps the profoundest change within the Negro consciousness since the early part of the century" (218). In Baraka's telling here, soul is not mysterious, not a "natural rhythm," not an essentialized identity. It is instead a "conscious" change in point of view, an intellectual exercise in reconceiving one's past. By noteworthy contrast, he defines "the very structure of jazz" as a "melodic statement with an arbitrary number of improvised answers or comments on the initial theme" (*Blues* 27). Not soul but jazz, in other words, was the black musical form which Baraka described using the language of improvisation and indeterminacy.

Once black nationalist fixation on racial separatism and masculinity became more pronounced during the late 1960s, however, soul emerged as a key site of contestation. Diverse voices—including those of numerous African American women—began to engage in a public debate over the proprietorship, origins, ingredients, and meanings of soul food; my argument has insinuated that this debate was in many ways also over the proprietorship, origins, ingredients, and meanings of blackness. Instead of confronting these challenges—as would Elijah Muhammad and Dick Gregory through their dietary prescriptions—many ideologues of soul food skirted the issue by constructing their cookbooks as a form of resistance to white appropriations of black culinary traditions.

Bob Jeffries claims in his *Soul Food Cookbook* (1969), for example: "Soul food, like jazz, was created in the South by American Negroes, and although it can safely be said that almost all typically southern food *is* soul (up until World War II nearly all the better cooks in the South *were* Negro), the word soul, when applied to food, means only those foods that Negroes grew up eating in their own homes" (ix). Like his contemporary Craig Claiborne, Jeffries too makes a distinction be-tween southern and soul food. But his distinction differs noticeably from that of the *New York Times* food critic. Soul, for Jeffries, is a quality that is more accurately said to inhere not in the food but instead in the cook and eater. By (this) defini-tion, then, racial outsiders such as Claiborne and his fellow displaced white south-erners can never be accurately said to eat soul food, since soul derives from the ex-perience of being black in white America. Whereas white people had traditionally biologized the cooking ability of African Americans in a dual gesture of racial envy and racist dismissal, many of the black cookbook writers appropriated the same strategy as a gesture of racial solidarity. They naturalized soul to construct a unified, albeit phantasmatic, racial whole. As Black Power historian William Van Deburg has put it: "Soul was sass—a type of primal spiritual energy and passion-ate joy available only to members of the exclusive racial confraternity" (195). Al-though Van Deburg seems at times unsure whether his goal is to perpetuate this doctrine or to analyze it, his ambivalence does suggest the extent to which the ide-ologues of soul were successful.

The difficulty of maintaining this fiction of the "exclusive racial confraternity" becomes apparent, however, whenever the writers broach the origin and meaning of the term "soul." "'Down South they used to say that rich folks ate food for the body while poor folks ate food for the soul,' reports a former resident of Louisiana" to *Soul Food Cookbook* author Jimmy Lee (8). In pointing toward class and region as much as toward race, the comment reveals some of the contradictions inherent in maintaining the fiction of soul as "a sum of all that is typically or uniquely Black" in the face of black geographic and economic diversity. Another person tells Lee that "'Soul comes from church.' . . . 'It's everything that's good—love, warmth, rhythm, happiness, feeling'" (8). This assertion helps explain why, in the context of a Civil Rights movement led in part by southern black Christian churches, soul food would come to be valorized in the South in a way which dif-fered from its emergence in the North and West. Yet Lee does not bother to note that it was primarily black Christian women, the "church sisters," who derived cul-tural authority and some financial autonomy from their knowledge of cooking. As Ruth Gaskins observes of her church's homecoming festivities in her 1968 cook-book *A Good Heart and a Light Hand*: "The men plan the events and the women do the cooking. . . . No woman ever enters the church empty-handed that Sunday of Homecoming" (x).[29]

My hypothesis is that it was in response to such fissures in the prevailing ideol-ogy of blackness that the champions of soul began to construe it as both indefin-able and improvisational. Pearl Bowser and Joan Eckstein write in *A Pinch of Soul* (1970), for instance, that "[s]oul food is a kind of music. . . . The tempo has been carried by the vitality of a people, migrating from the South to all points on the map, improvising, as in soul music, as they go along, creating, using what is at hand, all merging finally to produce a full concerto without really trying to" (11). The ironic aptness of their subsequent allusion to the stereotypically standardized white musical form of the "concerto" soon, however, becomes apparent: after read-ing this disclaimer, one encounters over 250 pages of very well-concerted recipes. "It took lots of experimenting," they acknowledge, "before we decided that 'a good palm pit full' is a tablespoon, or that the blade of a knife holds a fairly scant tea-spoonful, or that a bit of butter 'the size of your fist' is almost a pound" (14). In her introduction to Kathy Starr's *The Soul of Southern Cooking* (1989), Vertamae Grosvenor insists that her Aunt Zipporah "knew precisely how much was a pinch and how little was a dash" (xi). She might well have written the same assessment of Bowser and Eckstein.

This tension between assertions that soul food cooking is improvisational and the substantial evidence to the contrary points to the larger dilemma of what soul was understood to signify in the construction of African American identity. Even as soul was offered as paradigmatically inclusive within the undefined parameters of blackness ("it's everything"), it also entailed rendering judgment according to a Platonically elusive absolute ("it's everything that's good"). The contradiction be-tween the desires for indeterminacy and for the maintenance of a determinate schema of valuations (about morality, spirituality, taste, pinches and dashes, etc.) influenced the ways in which soul began to be defined in the late 1960s. The rep-resentation of soul as inscrutable functioned as more than a tactic of racial resis-tance to whites; it surely also masked a desire among African Americans (and oth-ers as well) for the containment of racial meanings. Assertions that "one who has to ask what [soul] is can never know" disguised a resistance to inquiries into the in-stabilities in all definitions of identity, including those of race.

What was most at stake in this resistance, I believe, is amply illustrated by a definition of soul that *was* offered in the preface to *Princess Pamela's Soul Food Cookbook* (1969):

> The aromas wafting from the grand plantation kitchen and the slave quarters could
> 'not help but comingle with the larger-than-life presence of the bandannaed mammy
> stirring the pots in both places. Pickaninny and white-linen plantation babe alike
> were nurtured from the milk and the spoon of The Black Mother. And that which,
> not by virtue of choice, remained unschooled and instinctive, found its greater en-
> couragement as a loving art rather than as a domestic science. . . . Call it Soul.
> (Princess Pamela 9–10)

Unlike Jimmy Lee, this anonymous (and quite possibly white) author does not hesitate to "spell out exactly" what soul food was widely thought to signify: the Black (Slave) Mother. At issue was not just that black women were perceived as the primary creators and preparers of soul food, though this clearly posed obstacles for many black male cookbook writers. Rather, because the "slave diet" helped call into question the boundaries and purity of the self, it also posed a more psychically threatening challenge to the ideal of black masculinity being propagated in the late 1960s. Hence soul's legacy as a constitutive rupture in the façade of U.S. black nationalist ideologies.

Had the contestation over the maternal inscriptions of soul simply faded away after the early 1970s, one might be tempted to downplay the issue as an historical aberration. It seems clear, though, that more recent discussions of soul have recu-perated some of the central assumptions underlying the earlier debate. In a 1991 study of African American women writers, for example, Houston Baker Jr. formu-lated a curious distinction between "soul" and "spirit":

A primary component of what might be termed "classical" Afro-American discourse is "soul." In more sacral dimensions, this component is labeled "spirit." Soul motivates; spirit moves. The generative source of style in Afro-America is soul; the impetus for salvation is spirit. *The spirit* is the origin of species, one might say, for countless black generations who did not choose material deprivation, but who were brutally denied, as I have suggested earlier, ownership or control of *material* means of production. If these generations had not possessed nonmaterial modes of production, there would have been no production at all. (*Workings* 75)

Inasmuch as Baker's book was offered as a contribution to African American feminist theory, I found it surprising that he would invoke a distinction between soul and spirit that replicates historically oppressive binaries, binaries which traditionally privilege masculine over feminine, white over black, intellect over body. Writing just before soul was appropriated by hypermasculinist Black Power discourses, Lerone Bennett Jr. had implicitly acknowledged precisely what Baker tries to deny. Soul has been understood to signify not just "the generative source of [black] style" but rather the perception that blackness itself is irrevocably inscribed, because generated, by women. At the time Baker published *Workings of the Spirit*, the resurgent 1990s' fixation on pure black manhood was already well under way. In retrospect, therefore, it seems only logical that soul had once again become a focal point of concern for observers of African American culture.

Just as Baker's distinction between soul and spirit is problematic from a feminist frame of reference, so also is the one often made between soul and jazz. Whereas Bob Jeffries had invoked the latter as his metaphor for culinary improvisation, Pearl Bowser and Joan Eckstein instead described their cooking technique via an allusion to the former. If one reads this discrepancy as reflecting a gendered binary—soul music being a more commercial and therefore "feminized" form than jazz[30]—Bob Young and Al Stankus's 1992 cookbook *Jazz Cooks* might, consequently, be construed as yet another early 1990s resurgence of Black Power's anxieties about the gender inscriptions of soul food. Except for the inclusion of a scattering of women and nonblacks, the book is devoted to representing the culinary forays of African American male "Greats" in the field of jazz. Stankus intones in the introduction to the book: "The artists have provided the inspiration, now it's your turn to improvise" (7). In this fashion, the book tries to reappropriate the language of culinary indeterminacy from an implicitly feminized soul in order to reinscribe it with masculine jazz potency. Yet the reader can only harbor suspicion toward Stankus's claim since his coauthor Bob Young had already acknowledged in passing that many of the musicians portrayed rarely find time to cook at all. Instead, they rely on "their wives, or grandfathers[!], or daughters [to] pinch hit" (6). Similarly, in his dedication to *The Black Gourmet* (1988 ed.), Joseph Stafford claims: "Just as the black musician injected his rhythm into traditional European music, the black gourmet injected new foods and a new flavor into traditional European cookery" (n. pag.). None of the African American women cookbook writers with whose work I am familiar use the obviously phallicized language of "injection" to describe their culinary endeavors.

In the face of such masculinist appropriations of black culinary history, many African American women have deployed discourses of (soul) food in ways that were and are sometimes politically reactionary but also potentially progressive. In fact, considering the extreme hostility of Black Power's social, cultural, and political climate toward black maternity, it is surely not insignificant that "authoritative" discourses of black culinary traditions were by 1970 not only emanating primarily from African American women, but often merging with or functioning as narratives of black grandmotherhood, motherhood, and daughterhood. The first chapter in Pearl Bailey's *Pearl's Kitchen*, to cite my favorite example, is called "Mama Looking over My Shoulder" (3), and the first sentence in her chapter "I Don't Iron Dust Rags" is "My Mama did" (74). Similarly, before relating one family anecdote in *A Good Heart and a Light Hand*, Ruth Gaskins acknowledges that "Mama is not going to like this" (xi).[31]

Viewed from this perspective, however, the details of the music metaphor that Bowser and Eckstein adopt become fascinating for another, more problematic, reason:

> The melody has been shaped by the land, mellowed by the many who have played its different tunes—from the chefs and cooks in the kitchens of the South, to the black cowboy cooks of the Old West, to the average momma keeping her own kitchen—and interwoven with the themes of many cultures. Blending into the medley are indigenous regional foods (fruits, grains, and nuts), with an occasional trill of French and English influence. The grace notes of Spanish food from Mexico and the Caribbean harmonize to produce richer flavors and tastes. And in the background the soft but persistent beat of Africa (with its peanuts, yams, okra, and pilli-pilli or hot pepper) and the American Indian (contributing herbs and corn) gives rhythm to the melody. (11)

This description is admirable to the extent that it seems intended to complicate the reader's understanding of not just soul food but also black racial identity. Yet Bowser and Eckstein's cheerful exposition of cross-cultural culinary hybridization tends to obscure the material practices of slavery, capitalism, and colonialism which have historically underwritten such dietary exchange. One cannot help but note, furthermore, that their musical metaphor manifests the everpresent problem of culinary sprawl: if soul food includes French and English and Spanish and Mexican and Caribbean and African and American Indian influences, what unifying conception could possibly hold it together? Though chitterlings did this work in many cultural contexts, the reductive fiction of "the average momma keeping her own kitchen" often sufficed just as well. Hence, Bowser and Eckstein end their introduction by invoking the iconic image "of learning at grandmother's elbow" so as to keep the centrifugal impulses in their culinary writing at bay (13). This is the sense in which black women's strategies of resistance to Black Power's misogyny sometimes furthered conservative cultural imperatives.

My hope, though, is that if we can unravel what Freud might have termed the convoluted "cloacal" connection between the era's fascination with chitterlings and black maternity, we will be better able to appreciate the ambivalence and ingenuity with which many African American women have participated in the debate over soul food.[32] When a 1982 *Essence* article announced, in simultaneously titillating and fretful language, that "[c]hitterlings are the 'gutsy' soul food!"

("Food" 94), the obviously class-inflected undertones were compounded by differences in how race and sexuality are mapped onto gendered bodies. Culinary "slumming" signifies very differently for black women than for black men. In this respect, the contestation surrounding soul food has much to teach us about both the emergence of "identity" politics and the ongoing struggle over the substance and boundaries of "American" identity. For this reason, too, it warrants our attention.

four

"Pork or Women"

Purity and Danger in the Nation of Islam

The cabbie was not a Muslim himself—he was unwilling to curb his
appetite for pork or women in accordance with Muslim doctrine.

Charles Silberman, *Crisis in Black and White*, 1964

I prefer my meats firm but tender
which goes for
chicken, pork chops, and men.

Princess Pamela, *Princess
Pamela's Soul Food Cookbook*,
1969

In fall of 1995, several of the most successful African American male rap stars—
Ice T, Ice Cube, Chuck D, 2Pac, Snoop Doggy Dogg, and others—joined forces
to release an album called *One Million Strong*. Intended as a show of support for the
October 1995 Million Man march in Washington, D.C., the album demonstrated
an important connection between Louis Farrakhan's Nation of Islam (NOI), spon-
sor of the march, and numerous black hip-hop artists. As Mattias Gardell has explained, although actual membership figures for the Nation remain small in
comparison to the total African American population, its black nationalist appropriation of Islamic doctrines has been dispersed throughout U.S. youth culture via
the pervasive influence of music: "What reggae was to the expansion of the Rasta-
farian movement in the 1970s, so hip-hop is to the spread of black Islam in the
1980s and 1990s" (295).

Though the liner notes for *One Million Strong* are at pains to point out that
"[s]ome of the lyrical content within this album does not reflect the views of the
Hon. Louis Farrakhan and/or the Nation of Islam," such an assertion of political
and creative independence is telling precisely by virtue of its necessity. In their
references to black men as the "original" men and their allegations that "dead"
(unconverted) black men are "deaf, dumb, and blind," several of the songs in-

cluded, such as X-Niggaz's "Wake Up," could have been transcribed directly from Farrakhan's speeches. Similarly, a substantial number of the rap albums released during the 1990s have been filled with allusions to the Nation and its teachings. The cover photo for Public Enemy's *Fear of a Black Planet* (1990), to cite one of the better known examples, includes several men dressed in the uniform of the Fruit of Islam (FOI), the Nation's aptly named (given the interplay between the homophobia of its teachings and the homoeroticism of its practice) paramilitary arm.

While the Million Man March may have resulted in the broadening of Farrakhan's base of support, renewed mass interest in the NOI itself actually began several years before the march, with the production and release of Spike Lee's 1992 film *Malcolm X*.[1] Much of the commentary about the film revolved around issues related to the appropriation of Malcolm X's legacy.[2] My own interest in both the film and the NOI, by contrast, has focused on the relationships among the dietary prescriptions, the conception of black selfhood, and the sociopolitical vision of longtime leader Elijah Muhammad. Especially given the most common critique of the Nation (one currently leveled with good reason at Farrakhan and his deputies), that it has been a primary proponent of anti-Jewish ideologies among African Americans, I have been intrigued by the way in which Muhammad's ban on pork is often jokingly construed, in general parlance, not in conjunction with Orthodox Jewish (or even Muslim) dietary practices, but instead in relation to his castigation of white female sexuality.

For instance, in the screenplay for *Malcolm X*, Lee has his character Shorty admit to Denzel Washington's Malcolm X: "My trouble is—I ain't had enough stuff yet, I ain't et all the ribs I want and I sure ain't had enough white tail yet" (Lee and Wiley 250). Earlier in the film, when Bembry had begun the process of converting his fellow inmate Malcolm Little into a follower of Muhammad, he had immediately conflated pork and women as equivalent "poisons":

BEMBRY   I read, study, because the first thing a black man must have is respect for himself. Respect his body and his mind. Quit taking the white man's poisons into his body—his cigarettes, his dope, his liquor, his white woman, his pork.

MALCOLM   Pork? Hm. Yeah, my mama used to say that. Don't eat no pork.

BEMBRY   Your mama was right. Cause that pig is a filthy beast: part rat, part cat, and the rest is dog.[3]

This particular scene is played, to an extent, for comic relief: Malcolm X's response to Bembry's information is to inquire whether by giving up pork he will "get sick" and "get a medical or something."[4] Such jocular treatment notwithstanding, it seems to me that the widely perceived connection between pork and white women needs to be understood as fundamental to—albeit also a fundamental misrepresentation of—the Nation's ideology of black manhood.

To explain why, this chapter will develop a detailed discussion of Elijah Muhammad's efforts to regulate the diets of his followers by banning not just pork but also other foods he associated with slavery. Anticipating many tenets of the liberatory social movements of the late 1960s and early 1970s, Muhammad was clearly insisting on the political nature of gastronomic desire, on the connection between so-called private practices of the body and social forces such as white supremacy. But having perhaps fallen through the gap that separates standard political scholarship about the civil rights era from post-1960s social histories, his dietary teachings have not been given serious scrutiny. My main line of argument will be that Muhammad used food as part of his effort to formulate a model of black male selfhood in which "filth" was displaced onto not white but black femininity and thus articulated within African American culture via discourses of gender and sexuality rather than class. He adopted the traditional Islamic ban on pork to pursue this rearticulation, while supplementing it with numerous other dietary recommendations which, through their stigmatization of the foods associated with "soul," seem to have been intended to purify the black male self of black female contamination.

Paradoxically, however, Muhammad himself was widely Orientalized, described in terms associated with femininity and homosexuality. The fascination with the Nation leader and his teachings thus perhaps stemmed, at least in part, from the fact that he was not simply addressing but also embodying the precarious status of black masculinity in U.S. culture. In this sense, a discussion of the NOI can provide further insights as to why black men are popularly associated with misogyny, homophobia, and anti-Judaism. They have historically functioned as a site of cultural anxiety in no small part because black masculinity has foregrounded the inevitable failures of the practices of othering through which hegemonic American identities have emerged.

"The Negro in the Mud"

Given the ongoing influence of Malcolm X (man, myth, and movie), as well as the more recent interest in Louis Farrakhan, it has seemed safe to assume thus far at least some cultural literacy with respect to the history and ideology of the NOI.[5] The movement was founded in Depression-era Detroit by Fard Muhammad, or the "mysterious" W. D. Fard, as C. Eric Lincoln tagged him (12). He is said to have disappeared, again "mysteriously," in 1934 (Lincoln 15).[6] The NOI was small and unknown during its early years when Fard's eventual successor, Elijah Poole, became one of his more devoted converts. Like most of these initial followers, Poole was a lower-class, poorly educated southern black man who had migrated to the urban North in search of employment. Renamed Elijah Muhammad, he gained legitimacy as a leader of the Nation after being imprisoned for draft resistance during World War II (Essien-Udom 80–81; Clegg 82–87). The movement grew slowly throughout the early years of the Cold War until 1959, when the documentary special *The Hate That Hate Produced* aired on national television. In conjunction with the emergence of Malcolm X as a leading spokesman for Muhammad, the publicity generated in the white press by journalist Mike Wallace's sensationalized portrayal of Muhammad's teachings brought the Nation to the forefront of attention during the 1960s.

By 1960 the Nation's membership probably hovered only between five thousand and fifteen thousand (Essien-Udom 84), as opposed to over nine million members of black Baptist and Methodist churches at this same time (Frazier, *Black* 88). By the end of the decade the number of Muhammad's followers had increased dramatically, but converts to the NOI were still only a tiny fraction of African Americans, the majority of whom remained loyal to Christianity.[7] Yet the Nation's ideology, which valorized black manhood, black nationalism, and black economic self-sufficiency, had (and, as we have seen, continues to have) an impact beyond its immediate membership. In addition to playing a key role in the rise of various strains of its secular counterpart, Black Power, the Nation's militarized practices have exerted an unusually strong appeal on the collective imagination of the American public—black as well as white.

To offer a sketchy overview of these features, besides advocating a rigidly controlled diet in which pork, alcohol, tobacco, and other drugs were most prominently forbidden, Muhammad also set forth a variety of other rules controlling almost all aspects of the lives of his followers: hygiene, dress, speech, worship, tithing, sexuality, marriage, children, education, and employment. Males and females were considered to be two ontologically different and hierarchically arranged, yet complementary, species. The male, one might easily infer from Muhammad's teachings, was intrinsically superior to the female; her weak, irrational, deceitful, insatiable nature required the controlling hand of the strong, wise, truthful, abstemious man. In accordance with the ideology of orthodox Islam, men were to be submissive to Allah and women were to be submissive to men (Sabbah 81). Men were to work outside the home, preferably in Muslim-owned enterprises to create more wealth for the Nation. In this fashion, Muhammad encouraged a form of modified capitalism aimed at redistributing the United States' wealth among his generally lower-class male followers. Private property was to be accumulated by Muslim men to bolster their authority in the family and community, as well as to enable them to tithe heavily to the Nation. In turn, the Nation was to use the money to purchase land, buildings, and supplies for communal purposes such as farms, schools, hospitals, and housing.[8]

Muslim women, by contrast, were encouraged to be economically dependent on men and responsible for domestic duties, including cooking, cleaning, and child-care. In practice, however, many worked outside their own homes, not infrequently as domestics for whites and also in subordinate positions in Muslim-owned businesses. Malcolm X even made a point of proselytizing on Thursdays, which were, he points out, "traditionally domestic servants' day off" (222). Whenever feasible, men were to dress in dignified suits and ties; women were always to dress "modestly" in clothing that covered their hair and limbs. All members, and especially new converts, were inspected for bodily cleanliness before entering a temple. Sexuality outside of marriage and interracial relationships were strictly forbidden, and heterosexuality was, needless to say, presumed. The Muslim woman's highest calling was to bear and raise children within the context of patriarchal marriage. These children were to be segregated by gender in Muslim-run schools, boys in the front of the room and girls in the back—or, if possible, taught in different classrooms entirely. This segregation was also observed in the worship services, the leadership of which was, again, solely male. Audience participation common to some black Christian denominations (e.g., call and response) was discouraged. Though clearly influenced by orthodox Islam, Muhammad also propagated many unorthodox ideas, including: the belief that W. D. Fard was "God in Person"; the deemphasis on the afterlife in favor of pursuing reparations and racial separatism on earth; and a theory of eugenics that construed black men as the "Original Man" and Caucasians as a "grafted" breed of "devils" (e.g., Muhammad, *Message* 31 and 118).

These last two teachings may have led to the initial white media fascination with the NOI, as did the practice of casting off the "slave" patronymic in favor of "X" until such time as Allah saw fit to reveal to Elijah Muhammad the convert's original name. But I would contend that whites have in fact been quite intrigued not just by the Nation's attitude toward Caucasians, but also by the extreme asceticism, self-discipline, and male dominance propagated by Elijah Muhammad as the ideal way to be black. To the extent that blackness has been situated in the U.S. imaginary as sensuous, promiscuous, rhythmic, impulsive, and improvisational—as, in short, soulful—the rigid demeanor and puritanical behavior of obedient converts presented a formidable challenge to the stereotype even while, paradoxically, helping to perpetuate it by default. To the extent, moreover, that blackness has also been situated in the U.S. imaginary as matriarchal, Elijah Muhammad's widely publicized efforts to institutionalize black patriarchy have likewise contributed to the myth that the Nation was engaged in what the movement's chronicler E. U. Essien-Udom called a "reversal of customary [African American gender] roles," rather than merely their perpetuation (102).[9]

To stress the hierarchical gender relations of African American culture is not to suggest that black men have, as a group, historically been either vested with or able to exercise the prerogatives of patriarchy in the same fashion as have white men (of property) in the United States. Black patriarchy is not the same as white patriarchy, and the African American men who joined the NOI were, by and large, among those least well situated to exercise many of its privileges. Nor is it to suggest that black women have, as a group, been party to the cult of true womanhood, an ideology long propagated as the essence of white middle-class femininity and to a great extent valorized by Muhammad as the model for black Muslim women as well.[10] It is, rather, to reiterate Spillers's contention that African American culture is not matriarchal "because 'motherhood' is not perceived in the prevailing social climate as a legitimate procedure of cultural inheritance" ("Mama's" 80). The institution of black matriarchy would entail, among other things, that black female access to power (wealth, education, institutional authority, etc.) be constitutive of the social structure, and in the United States this most certainly is not the case.

This approach to interpreting Muslim ideology regarding proper personal conduct and gender roles can also be applied to understanding the relationship between the dietary rules set forth by Elijah Muhammad and the emergence of soul food. Malcolm X's fond memory of the stir caused by his refusal to eat pork in prison is suggestive of how the two are linked: "One of the universal images of the Negro, in prison and out, was that he couldn't do without pork. It made me feel good to see that my not eating it had especially startled the white convicts" (156). Clearly he perceived Muhammad's dietary prescriptions to offer a cross-class strategy of resistance to white racist stereotypes about black people. Ironically, however, Baraka's inclusion of Muslim "bean pies" in his essay on "Soul Food" would suggest that as late as 1962 not only were the boundaries of soul still quite permeable, but that the Nation's efforts to proselytize about dietary practices had not been entirely successful. "The Muslim temple serves bean pies which are really separate," Baraka had advised the reader (103), thus obscuring the important distinction that for Muhammad the foods eaten by members of the NOI were "really separate" not just from white food, but from southern black food as well.

Viewed from this perspective, it seems significant that even though Muhammad never (to my knowledge) referred directly to "soul food" in his writings, he intensified his condemnation of traditional southern black dietary practices as the popularity of soul food began to peak. Most notably, in 1967 and 1972 Muhammad published two lengthy and repetitive dietary manuals called *How to Eat to Live* (132 pages) and *How to Eat to Live*, Book No. 2 (199 pages).[11] Muhammad's denunciation of what he called the "slave diet" for his followers thus appears to have operated (along with other factors such as the "gourmet plague" and the emergence of "natural" foods) in a dialectic with the black bourgeoisie's valorization of "soul" for itself.[12] Yet, whereas Baraka revealed a skewed awareness of the NOI's call for culinary separatism, when Muhammad opined on the topic of "Why They Urge You to Eat the Swine" (*How* 13), the "They" he had in mind were not the Radical Chic or Black Arts sets. "They" were African American "[p]reachers and priests" (*How* 13). It is important to recognize, therefore, that the foods associated with soul were stigmatized by Muhammad at least in part because they operated through, and perhaps even contributed to, the cultural dominance of his nemesis, black Christianity.

What this means is that to understand why food was central to the construction of Islamic selfhood, we need to focus less on Muhammad's inflammatory rhetoric about the "white devil" than on his positioning among underpublicized but equally charged intraracial fissures, particularly those of class, sexuality, gender, and religious affiliation. In *Black Nationalism*, Essien-Udom paraphrases Muhammad as having informed him: "The official policy of the Nation of Islam . . . is to recruit the 'Negro in the mud' into the movement and to 'alienate him from giving support to middle-class Negro leadership'" (201). "Negro in the mud" is Muhammad's phrase, a phrase also attributed to him by Malcolm X: "Always Mr. Muhammad instructed us, 'Go after the black man in the mud'" (262). In the context of my earlier discussion of the implications of black bourgeois *nostalgie de la boue*, it should not be difficult to understand the relevance of Muhammad's comment to the construction of lower-class African American selfhood.[13] In their public rhetoric, Muhammad and his ministers commonly targeted the white devil as the enemy of the black man. But as his remarks to Essien-Udom and Malcolm X reveal, Muhammad also viewed middle-class blacks—especially middle-class black Christians—with tremendous anger and distrust. Likewise, Malcolm X displayed a strong class-based resentment of the black bourgeoisie. For instance, in discussing his own efforts to recruit among black Christians, he recollects: "We by-

passed the larger churches with their higher ratio of so-called 'middle class' Negroes who were so full of pretense and 'status' that they wouldn't be caught in our
little storefront" (219).

The upwardly mobile Muhammad implied that members of the black bourgeoisie (and those working-class black "strivers" who identified up the class ladder)
were attempting to purify themselves by articulating filth via class rather than
race, thus displacing it on an intraracial plane from blackness onto poverty. It
would make sense, consequently, why many working-class black men might have
been drawn to Muhammad's teachings, because he was offering a model of selfhood that appealed to their feelings of disempowerment. But, of course, one important implication of the Nation's valorization of pure black manhood is that
black women—including, significantly, Muslim women within the NOI—functioned as a default site of sensuality, impulsiveness, and, as Baraka would have it,
Negro smell. Muhammad may have condemned Caucasians as grafted white devils
and derided the black bourgeoisie as their acolytes, but in the model of selfhood he
formulated it was black women who were, like Toni Morrison's Pecola Breedlove,
the black man's "*own plot of black dirt*" (*Bluest* 6). Or, to cite the now-notorious
phrase Muhammad himself used in his *Message to the Blackman in America* (1965):
"The woman is man's field to produce his nation" (58). By reducing all black
women to the status of womb-in-waiting and literalizing the equation of womb
and dirt, Muhammad's dictum stands as persuasive evidence for the validity of
Kristeva's argument that the maternal body provides the paradigm for that which
must be abjected because it threatens the boundaries of the self. African American
women were necessary to give birth to this social order of original black men, but
they were also the "filth" that had to be othered, lest the purity of that order be
undermined.[14]

"How to Eat to Live"

> Fast once a month for three days or four days—or for whatever length
> of time you are able to go without food without harming yourself—and
> you will feel good.
>
>   Elijah Muhammad, *How to Eat to Live*, Book No. 2, 1972

> Without calories, what have you got?
>   A glass of water, a barren plate, an empty pot.
> When I eat, I like to eat a lot.
>   Frankly, I think calories is the best thing
> that ever happened to any meal.
>   The more you consume, the better you feel.
>
>   Charleszetta Waddles,
>   *Mother Waddles Soulfood Cookbook*, c. 1976

Muhammad's equation of black women and filth through his dietary strictures is
obscured by the commonplace assumption that the second term in the "pork and

women" pairing refers to white rather than black female sexuality. It is also obscured by the fact that Muhammad's wide-ranging list of "Some of the Foods We Eat and Do Not Eat" was legitimated by discourses drawn from a variety of cultural locations, including sociology, religion, politics, and medicine.[15] To justify the ban on pork, he would typically refer to the Old Testament and Koran in one breath, trichinosis and high blood pressure in the next. Hence, in a 1961 article which appeared in the Nation's newspaper *Muhammad Speaks* on the topic of dietary practices, Muhammad informed readers:

> The Pig is the chief cause of many of the ills and mental deficiencies occuring [sic] among the so-called American Negroes and any other people who eat it.
> The pig is a mass of worms. Each mouthful you eat is not a nutritious food but a mass of small worms the naked eye cannot detect. . . .
> The scientific name for the ill-causing worm found in all pork is Trichinella spiralis which causes trichinosis. . . .
> In the Bible and the Holy Quran, it is the Divine will of God that the pig should not be eaten and God has never changed this instruction, despite the white man's setting up governmental bureaus to grade and approve the selling of pork. ("Truth" 5)

But though Muhammad had frequent recourse to both religion and science in explaining his dietary regulations, he repeatedly returned to the "filth" of the hog: "He is the foulest animal. He lives off nothing but filth. The only way you can get him to live and eat better food is to keep him from getting to filth. He is so poisonous (99.9 per cent) that you can hardly poison him with other poison" (*How* 14). Muhammad was obsessed not just with the filth of hog intestines but with the filth of what the hog itself ate and the filth of the environment the hog inhabited. In fact, for Muhammad, the whole hog in a sense was a chitterling: "He is so poisonous and filthy, that nature had to prepare him a sewer line and you may find the opening on his forelegs. It is a little hole out of which oozes pus. This is the filth of his body that cannot be passed fast enough" (*How* 14–15). Excrement was not just in the bowels but distributed throughout the body of the swine.

Only pork was banned in the Koran; consequently, Muhammad justified his aversion to or prohibition of other foods associated with the southern black diet by using a variety of nonscriptural tactics. When discussing animals, he often invoked analogies with the hog. Thus he insisted: "The catfish is a very filthy fish. He loves filth and is the pig of the water" (*How* 64). Similarly, chickens were "quite filthy (inasmuch as they do not eat the cleanest of food), but we eat them" (*How* 64). Nonanimal products such as bleached flour and canned goods were spurned because they had been deprived by the white-owned food industry of their original nutritional value, whereas cornmeal, by marked contrast, was "too rough" to be digested without physical risk: "It wears out the stomach like sand grinds away a delicate rug on your floor" (*How* II: 66). Other foods that Muhammad associated with the slave diet—including sweet potatoes, collard greens, and pinto beans—were, for similar reasons, also not fit for human consumption. Freshly baked bread was prohibited because "[i]t rises and buckles in the stomach" (*How* 67). One of the few foods Muhammad recommended was the small navy bean, which was used in making Baraka's "really separate" bean pies. Young squab that had not yet left the nest was also permitted (presumably because it would not have had an opportunity to eat filth), but ideally a Muslim should "not be a meat consumer. Be a vegetarian. This is the best menu for our health" (*How* II: 64). An optimal diet would consist of a single daily meal of thrice-baked bread and well-pasteurized milk, supplemented by cooked vegetables and those few raw fruits which were "good for our stomachs to digest" (*How* 43).

Because Muhammad's dietary teachings appear to have no logical development and little internal consistency, they initially frustrate efforts to comprehend his purpose. The comments on catfish quoted in the preceding paragraph, for example, are contained in a chapter from the first volume of *How to Eat to Live* titled "The Benefits of Eating Once a Day" (63). His frequent diatribes on "filth," particularly that of pork, are interwoven throughout his writings, often appearing abruptly as non sequiturs. Were Muhammad's motivations purely monetary, as Cleaver only half-jokingly suggested, why would he recommend both young squab, which was expensive, and fasting, which obviously was not? Yet, with the aid of Mary Douglas's analysis of pollution rituals, it is possible to formulate a plausible account not just of Muhammad's loathing for swine, but also of his other dietary strictures. Douglas, of course, famously argued in *Purity and Danger* that the seemingly arbitrary dietary laws set forth in the Old Testament book of Leviticus must be interpreted as a function of the rules governing emerging Israelite society as a whole. These rules derived from a division of practices into those which were "holy" and those which were "unholy" (51–54).[16] After analyzing the dietary rules in relation to this schema, Douglas deduces that "the underlying principle of cleanness in animals is that they shall conform fully to their class. Those species are unclean which are imperfect members of their class, or whose class itself confounds the general scheme of the world" (55).

This Yahwistic division of practices into the holy and the unholy finds an analogue in Muhammad's attempt to structure all of Muslim society according to the categories of "purity" and "filth." These categories encompass both ontology and actions: what one is, what one desires, what one eats, what one does. Thus we find that frequently Muhammad's discourse on diet melds into a discourse on morality. Fasting not only enables one to "feel good," as the epigraph from Muhammad claims; it also "takes away evil desires. Fasting takes from us filthy desires" (*How* II: 49). "Filthy" here clearly functions as a synonym for "evil," which makes sense only if we continue to conceive of filth as a relational designation rather than an ontologized substance. Muhammad's writings contain many extended examples of this tendency to conflate individual diet with social morality. For instance, in a chapter called "Do Not Eat Forbidden Food" (*How* II: 19), he offers the following series of commandments:

> VEGETABLES, MILK AND BUTTER are the right foods to eat, when they are *pure*. But my Dear Brothers, and Sisters do not think that you are getting *pure* products now from the dairy. Substitutions are added to butter, and much water is added to the milk.
>
> So, do not practice the *evil* things that the white race is doing, as you are following them now. If they pull off their clothes, you will pull off yours. . . . A doom is set

for the whole race of them and you will share their doom with them, if you follow eating and drinking intoxicating drinks just because you see them doing such things and going nude in public (women with dresses above their knees and men wearing just trunks in public).

YOU ARE FOLLOWING one of the *filthiest* things that even an animal wouldn't follow, by doing such things. (Muhammad's capitalization, my italics; How II: 20)

As this passage illustrates, the underlying message of Muhammad's teachings is to pursue purity and avoid filth in all their corporeal and spiritual manifestations. Following this model, it is possible to subsume Muhammad's concern for health under his even more encompassing obsession with purity. For Muhammad, a pure body was, prima facie, a healthy body, and vice versa. But having said this, we still need to ask what the relationship was between Muhammad's dietary prohibitions and his vision of social order and disorder. How, in other words, was filth articulated? Here is where the potential slippage of filth among discourses of race, ethnicity, sexuality, gender, class, and religion begins to operate.

Given the NOI's history of hostility toward Judaism, it is worth noting here that Muhammad actually praised Orthodox Jews for following the Old Testament ban on pork.[17] They are, he claimed, "excellent in protecting their health, even spiritually trying to do and eat like their prophet Mossa (Moses) taught them through the Divine teachings of Allah. If you respect yourselves as Muslims, the spiritual Orthodox Jew will respect you" (How 11). When Muslims were unable to purchase food from a Muslim-owned grocery or restaurant, Muhammad even advised them to patronize kosher Jewish-owned businesses instead (How 11). Such teachings might suggest that Muhammad's attitude toward Judaism was more complex than has been commonly recognized, that his attacks on Jews as prime exemplars of the "white devil" were underwritten by a vexed awareness of the contradictory positioning of Jewish people in relation to whiteness. Not surprisingly, his black nationalist politics led Muhammad to condemn the creation of Israel as a straightforward act of white imperialism committed against Palestinian peoples of color (Clegg 255).[18] Yet, in his perception, Orthodox Jews were still to be emulated because they had achieved the goals he was setting for his followers: bodily purity, religious piety, territorial nationalism, and patriarchy.

In keeping with this ambivalent fascination with Jewish practices of whiteness, the boundary that is generally understood to have most concerned Muhammad was one of race. As I have explained, he pursued racial separatism and taught that the white race was grafted and therefore impure. He likewise condemned the pig as a mixture of rat, cat, and dog (How 105). Created by the white man, the pig was also a hybrid, and thus both were filthy because they threatened Muhammad's boundaries of order and disorder. NOI scholar Martha Lee quotes him as insisting that "the hog has all the characteristics of a white man!" (30).[19] Muhammad's condemnation of other animals followed, as we have seen, a similar logic. It would be tempting to suggest that he was articulating the filth of selfhood via race rather than class, reversing the process of abjection by othering whites. As Muhammad taught his followers, "all of the diseases that trouble us today—from social diseases to cancer—came from the white race, one way or the other" (How 79). The problem with this reading, however, is that it does not take into account the prohibition of boundary violations within the NOI, boundaries which, I have made clear, were largely aimed at valorizing heterosexuality while maintaining a rigid, hierarchical division of the sexes.

Consider in this context how Malcolm X explained to potential converts the rationale for the rules of the NOI: "The white man *wants* black men to stay immoral, unclean and ignorant. As long as we stay in these conditions we will keep on begging him and he will control us" (221). Following Muhammad, Malcolm X viewed immorality, uncleanliness, and ignorance as part of a continuum, and the binary overtly informing his comment was one of race. But when he elaborated, his concerns were primarily oriented toward setting forth rules of behavior regulating internal gender relations and sexual practices rather than interaction with whites:

> Any fornication was absolutely forbidden in the Nation of Islam. Any eating of the filthy pork, or other injurious or unhealthful foods; any use of tobacco, alcohol, or narcotics. No Muslim who followed Elijah Muhammad could dance, gamble, date, attend movies, or sports, or take long vacations from work. Muslims slept no more than health required. Any domestic quarreling, any discourtesy, especially to women, was not allowed. (221)

Whereas the white devil represented a threat to the Nation's external boundaries of selfhood, black femininity represented a threat to the Nation's internal boundaries. Purity, simply put, was not just black; it was black and male. Impurity was not just white; it was also female. Certainly Malcolm X appears to have viewed women as detrimental to his mission: "I had always been very careful to stay completely clear of any personal closeness with any of the Muslim sisters. My total commitment to Islam demanded having no other interests, especially, I felt, no women" (225).

Malcolm X located black female sexuality and filthy pork on a continuum, but Muhammad was even more explicit in claiming that pork "takes away the shyness of those who eat this brazen flesh. Nature did not give the hog anything like shyness" (*How* 14). Muhammad expected "shyness" of his women followers, which is to say that by anthropomorphizing the hog, he was associating it with female, not male, sexuality. He was, moreover, constructing male desire and female desirability as complementary. Fatna Sabbah has pinpointed one way femininity is constructed as the object of male desire in orthodox Islam when she argues that the veil "represents the denial of the economic dimension of women, who, according to the tenets of Muslim orthodoxy, are exclusively sexual beings" (13). Such an analysis could easily be extended to the NOI, with its commitment to heterosexual patriarchy.[20]

Furthermore, by presenting his dietary dicta as being "From God in Person, Master Fard Muhammad," Muhammad attempted to subsume under sacred black patriarchal authority a domain that had long been the province of black women such as Princess Pamela, Mother Waddles, and the church sisters. This absolute male authority was central to Elijah Muhammad's sociopolitical agenda, an agenda which was anchored in his vision of black male selfhood, a selfhood which was in turn to be utterly independent of black female influence or control. When it came to diet, however, Muhammad knew that Allah was up against a formidable foe:

Allah (God) has pointed out to us in both the Bible and the Holy Qur-an the right foods for us to eat and He has pointed out the poisonous food and drinks. Follow His guidance or suffer the consequences.

Do not eat the swine—do not even touch it. Just stop eating the swine flesh and your life will be expanded. Stay off that grandmother's old fashioned corn bread and black-eyed peas, and those quick 15 minute biscuits made with baking powder. Put yeast in your bread and let it sour and rise and then bake it. **Eat and drink to live, not to die.** (*How* 116)

As this passage makes clear, all the foods that Muhammad associated with the slave diet had to be prohibited because they were associated not just with black women but with black women as mothers. Eating calls into question more than the boundaries of the self ("do not even touch it"). It calls into question the origins of self in the mother and grandmother, who are here rescripted by Muhammad as takers rather than givers of life. Muhammad was facing a problem common to all patriarchal religions: how to elide the role of women in procreation so as to locate the origins of life in a male god. Hence the significance of the rubric under which he usually situated his dietary teachings: Allah, not Mama, taught one "How to Eat to Live."[21]

Gestating Women

What would you think of Jesus if you saw him in his holy robes, over-weight, with a stomach that made him look eight months pregnant, fat jowls and a fat neck?

Louis Farrakhan, "Exercise to Stay Alive!" 1991

Even as he valorized a model of black manhood that was free of the taint of black female pollution, Muhammad acknowledged quite clearly his social and subjective need for control over African American women. In *Message to the Blackman in America*, he complained:

Our women are allowed to walk or ride the streets all night long, with any strange men they desire. They are allowed to frequent any tavern or dance hall that they like, whenever they like. They are allowed to fill *our* homes with children other than *our* own. Children that are often fathered by the very devil himself. . . .

We protect *our* farms by pulling up *our* weeds and grass by the roots, by killing animals and birds, and by poisoning the insects that destroy *our* crops in order that we may produce a good crop. How much more valuable are *our* women, who are *our* fields through whom we produce *our* nation. . . .

Have private pools for your women and guard them from all men. Stop them from going into bars and taverns and sitting and drinking with men and strangers. . . . Stop them from using unclean language in public (and at home), from smoking and drug addiction habits. (emphasis added; 59–61)

Writing in 1965, Muhammad was acknowledging the same black matriarchal anxieties to which Daniel Patrick Moynihan was simultaneously giving public policy legitimation. Hortense Spillers's careful dissection of the myth of what E. Franklin

Frazier had dubbed "The Matriarchate" (*Negro* 125–45) once again has relevance for understanding the appeal of the NOI for black men who wish to affirm what we might term the Law of the Black Father.[22]

Following Spillers, I would argue that the Nation represents a community of African American males who made (and are continuing to make) a systematic, organized effort to insert themselves into public consciousness as legitimate partners with white men in the imposition of Phallic Law. In this context, we can perhaps understand the significance of Essien-Udom's observation that "[o]ne minister has even referred to [Elijah Muhammad] as 'father and mother'" (92). Muhammad's goal seems to have been not just to insert the black father into view but to render invisible the legacy of black women in generational continuity. According to the historiography of the NOI, Fard had initially mentored Muhammad by visiting him daily "for a period of nine months, corresponding to the length of pregnancy" (Gardell 50). The motivation behind this desire to displace black women from the scene of maternity was perhaps best summed up by Ossie Davis in explaining why he offered a eulogy at the funeral of Malcolm X. Regardless of "whatever else he was or was not," Davis famously observed, "*Malcolm was a man!*" (457). In this reading, the claim to sociopolitical equality becomes a function of unambiguously gendered identity (Wiegman 75–76; Harper 68–69).

At the same time, Sabbah has also argued that in orthodox Muslim discourse "the possession of the female body [is] the model for all forms of possession" (42). Muhammad's repetition of "our" in the passage quoted earlier would suggest that this assumption was operative in his mind as well. He even claimed that control over black women provided the paradigmatic model of black male self-knowledge: "Allah, Himself, has said that we cannot return to our land until we have a thorough knowledge of our own selves. This first step is the control and the protection of our own women" (*Message* 59). Muhammad's admission that black men can know themselves only via black women surely foregrounds the contradictory underpinnings of his more widely acknowledged contempt for racial hybridity. One could easily infer from Muhammad's own dictates that the male, having emerged from a female body, would be the grafted species, and the female would be the "original."

His anxiety about female contamination of black manhood might explain why Muhammad expressed a desire not just to control the reproductive practices of African American women (and hence to guarantee paternity), but also to dictate what black women put into their own bodies. Like many African American men of the era, Muhammad attacked the birth control pill as a form of racial genocide. In "Birth Control Death Plan!" for example, he emphatically warns that "STERILIZATION IS NOT BIRTH CONTROL BUT THE END OF ALL POSSIBILITY TO BEAR CHILDREN" and refers his readers to a notorious example of involuntary sterilization that occurred in Fauquier County, Virginia (*Message* 64). Muhammad is surely quite justified in indicting not just the forced sterilizations but also the racist underpinnings of much population-control ideology. But though his rhetoric might seem to have much in common with that of women who were (and still are) fighting sterilization abuse, Muhammad's motivations were not to secure reproductive autonomy for African American women. "No man wants a non-productive woman," he writes (*Message* 64). "Though he may not want children for a time, he does want a woman who can produce a child if he changes his mind. Using birth control for a social purpose is a sin" (*Message* 64). Sterilization abuse of African American women and the availability of the birth control pill were a problem in Muhammad's eyes because they interfered with the reproductive autonomy of black men.[23]

Despite his rhetoric charging the white devil with attempting to destroy the black race, Muhammad also expressed anger at black women for their efforts to control their own reproductive destinies. "It is," he claimed, "a disgrace upon us black people of America to permit ourselves and our future generations to be cut off and destroyed by ignorant, foolish, pleasure-seeking girls and women of our own, who do not know what they are doing when they swallow the birth control pill" (*How* 93). This diatribe makes clear that his attacks on the white devil were underwritten by the assumption that African American women were acting in complicity with white men and women—and particularly with white feminists— to destroy black men. Just as his attack on pork foregrounds white devils and white female sexuality while assuming black female filth, so his attack on the pill foregrounds a white-sponsored "death plan" while assuming black female selfishness and promiscuity.

These two obsessions converge in Muhammad's concern for the dietary practices of pregnant and nursing women. Muhammad was worried not just about controlling the number, timing, and paternity of children born to each African American woman; he also strove to achieve black fetal quality control. In the passage quoted earlier, we saw that he told his male followers to "[s]top [black women] from . . . smoking and drug addiction habits." His concern, however, was not for the health of black women. It was for the effect of their purported impurity on black men. Thus, in the second volume of *How to Eat to Live*, Muhammad advised pregnant women:

> EAT GOOD FOOD so that you will be able to give your baby good, pure milk.
> You can drink cows' milk; your own milk glands will put it into the right stage for your child. Be careful as to what kind of drugs you take while nursing your baby. And do not take fasts while you are breast-feeding an infant or even while you are pregnant. If you like, you may eat once a day while pregnant or breast-feeding your baby, but you are not forced to do so. You should not go for two or three days without eating. (90)

The fact that from a contemporary vantage point these strictures seem quite mild surely suggests the extent to which we have increasingly become accustomed to treating the bodies of pregnant women as having value only in subordination (as a "maternal environment") to the zygote, embryo, or fetus they carry. Though this womb-centered perspective is by no means of recent vintage, new technologies enabling us to visualize the fetus in utero have made it more difficult to combat the trend toward viewing the pregnant body as two separate human beings, with the fetus being by far the more interesting of the two. Muhammad's directive to "EAT GOOD FOOD so that you will be able to give your baby good, pure milk" calls to mind a telling question posed by legal theorist Patricia Williams. In the context of discussing a Washington, D.C., case in which a judge imprisoned a pregnant woman, "ostensibly in order to *protect* her fetus," Williams muses: "Why is there no state interest in not simply providing for but improving the circumstances of the woman, whether pregnant or not?" (*Alchemy* 184).

Indeed, Muhammad's strictures presage the contemporary resurgence of efforts to place the blame for so-called social pathology on the behavior of pregnant women—particularly impoverished, unmarried women of color—rather than on structural forces of discrimination such as regressive tax policies, declining wages and benefits, cuts in social spending, and concentration of toxic wastes in areas with large minority and poor populations. In the first volume of *How to Eat to Live*, Muhammad begins by chastising black women for their failure to breast-feed but rapidly escalates his rhetoric:

> The baby eats poisonous animals, fowls and vegetables and drinks milk that is not his milk—it belongs to the cow's baby, goat's baby and horse's baby. Here the child is reared on animals' and cattle's food.
> This is why we have such a great percentage of delinquency among minors. The child is not fed from his mother's breast—she is too proud of her form. . . .
> When the baby reaches the age of 10, and if it is a male, most of them begin to indulge in drinking alcoholic beverages and using tobacco in one form or another.
> Alcohol and tobacco, with their poisonous effect upon the male, cut his life down, as far as his reproductive organs are concerned. He is unable to produce his own kind. (88–89)

The vanity of the black woman in refusing to breast-feed her son leads inexorably to his "delinquency," his alcohol and drug addiction, and then to his impotence or sterility. Mirroring central aspects of contemporaneous discourses of white racism, this polemic implies that the responsibility for black social problems rests with the failures of African American mothers.

Muhammad's conflicted effort to formulate a model of pure black manhood through the twinned valorization and pathologization of black maternity was, as we have seen, recuperated in the secular realm via the Black Arts and Black Power movements. It has also been perpetuated within the NOI by Louis Farrakhan in the years since Muhammad's death. The current Nation leader celebrates maternity while insisting that pregnant women must be held under male authority and denied access to public places of "vice" such as bars and dance halls; he does not think they should be allowed to consume tobacco, alcohol, drugs, or "junk" food either (Gardell 335). According to Mattias Gardell, black male control over gestation is very important for Farrakhan since he believes that women have "the ability to write on the brain of the fetus, as if it were a blank piece of paper. The prenatal engraving can determine whether the offspring is born god or beast" (334). Farrakhan not only condemns abortion as a practice of racial genocide, but he actually contends that even the (thwarted) desire to have an abortion will harm the mind-set of the fetus.[24] His own mother had wanted to terminate her pregnancy, Farrakhan claims. As a result, "she marked me with her own thinking. And this is what led to my fall from the Honorable Elijah Muhammad" ("How" 102). In this scenario, even the merely fantasized "sins" of black mothers are visited upon the sons.

Bussing Men

> And there is something in the man, the real man, that God put in that
> no woman can give you—ain't it sweet?
>
> Louis Farrakhan, "The Re-Unification of the Black Family," 1990

The seeming paradox in all this is that the Nation's hyperbolized fixation on black manhood and abjection of black maternity have been underwritten by a widespread preoccupation with what was perceived as Muhammad's own racial and sexual ambiguity, and indeed that of his predecessor, W. D. Fard, as well. Earlier we saw that C. Eric Lincoln (writing in 1961) repeatedly described the latter as "mysterious." Malcolm X echoed the Orientalizing aspects of Lincoln's discourse about Fard when he recollected that while he was in prison, a man with "an Asiatic cast of countenance" appeared to him in a vision (186). Subsequently, Malcolm X identified the man as Fard (189).

Descriptions of Elijah Muhammad present him as no less exoticized than his teacher. For instance, Essien-Udom records the response of a young black woman to her first sighting of the famed Nation leader: "I could not believe my eyes. . . . I was waiting to see a really black man. But who came in? A Chinese. He looks very much like an Oriental" (393, n. 32). In his biography of Muhammad, Claude Clegg III both summarizes and participates in such characterizations when he writes that Fard's successor

> was an unimposing man, standing five and a half feet tall and weighing less than 150 pounds. Balding, the leader was a fair-skinned man with a disarming gentleness. His slender body was almost delicate in form and, according to a contemporary, appeared "tiny and transparent and breakable as a china doll." . . . To some, Muhammad's thin lips, pronounced cheekbones, and deep-set brown eyes were reminiscent of Oriental features. His appearances in fezzes, indeed, gave him a decidedly Eastern look. (117)

Providing further evidence for Edward Said's understanding of Orientalism as a discursive formation through which the white West's racial Others are rendered not just "mysterious" but also "feminine," much of the commentary about Muhammad registers anxiety about the status of his masculinity.[25] Even Malcolm X allows that Muhammad "seemed fragile, almost tiny" by comparison to his bodyguards in the FOI (196). Leaving little question about what was at stake in at least some of these descriptions, journalist Louis Lomax observed in 1962 that Muhammad spoke "with a disturbing lisp" (*Negro* 168). Since extant recordings of Muhammad's speeches do not confirm Lomax's diagnosis (Clegg 313, n. 19)—and here I am admittedly begging several questions regarding the social construction of lisping—he perhaps described Muhammad's unusual speaking style using this stereotypical signifier of homosexuality precisely because to do so was also to convey his unease with Muhammad's apparent effeminacy.

If Lomax's comment can be construed as an expression of homosexual panic, James Baldwin's contemporaneous recollection of his dinner at Muhammad's Chicago home communicates instead the homoerotic possibilities that were evoked for him by the Nation leader's presence:

I had read some of his speeches, and had heard fragments of others on the radio and on television, so I associated him with ferocity. But, no—the man who came into the room was small and slender, really very delicately put together, with a thin face, large, warm eyes, and a most winning smile. . . . He teased the women, like a father, with no hint of that ugly and unctuous flirtatiousness I knew so well from other churches, and they responded like that, with great freedom and yet from a great and loving distance. . . . I had the feeling, as he talked and laughed with the others, whom I could only think of as his children, that he was sizing me up, deciding something. Now he turned toward me, to welcome me, with that marvellous smile, and carried me back nearly twenty-four years, to that moment when the pastor had smiled at me and said, "Whose little boy are you?" (Fire 63)

Earlier in The Fire Next Time, Baldwin had informed the reader that "Whose little boy are you?" was "precisely the phrase used by pimps and racketeers on the Avenue when they suggested, both humorously and intensely, that I 'hang out' with them" (28). Given his portrayal of Muhammad's relationship to the Muslim women as asexual and his elliptical reference to being "sized up," Baldwin surely intends to queer, as it were, the reader's impression of Elijah Muhammad's personal appeal. The open secret of Muhammad's sexual relationships with a series of Muslim women, relationships which resulted in the birth of numerous children (Clegg 184–89), could even be understood to have functioned as a "beard" which obscured widespread discomfort over Muhammad's perceived lack of masculine virility. At issue here, let me stress, are not Muhammad's actual sexual practices but rather the social, cultural, and political ramifications of how his sexuality was represented and understood.

Certainly it seems likely that the rapidity with which Malcolm X gained a following was not unrelated to his ability more straightforwardly to embody black manhood than did Muhammad. The controversy over Bruce Perry's claim that the young Malcolm Little slept with men for money is indicative of the ongoing investment in his heterosexuality (77–78).[26] At the same time, the perceived ambiguity in Muhammad's appearance and mannerisms was obviously quite central to his own particular appeal. If Malcolm X was held up by Ossie Davis as an unquestioned example of "a true man" (459), then Muhammad, by contrast, more nearly manifested what Judith Butler has referred to as the "impossible impermeability" of the self (Gender 134), the inability of binaries such as black/white, homosexual/heterosexual, and female/male adequately to account for the intricate processes through which American identities are created and sustained. In this context, we can see that Essien-Udom's anecdote about the minister who labeled Muhammad "father and mother" warrants a different interpretation than I gave it earlier. In keeping with Kristeva's understanding of the abject as that which threatens one from within, Muhammad might be said to have bolstered the Law of the Black Father not so much by rendering invisible the symbolic function of black mothers as by seeming to have internalized black maternity.

Released just over two decades after Elijah Muhammad's death, Spike Lee's tribute to the Million Man March, Get on the Bus (1996), participates in this construction of the NOI as less an answer to than a privileged site of ongoing trepidation about the status of African American masculinity. As such, the film provides a perfect opportunity to conclude this chapter by returning to the mid-1990s cultural moment with which we began. *Get on the Bus* allows us to speculate that even the most blatantly reactionary of black nationalist discourse, such as that represented by the NOI, speaks not just to the investments of many African American men in bourgeois patriarchy but also to their desire to be freed from the overwhelming psychic burden of having constantly to assert their masculine authenticity. If in many respects black manhood has been constructed as a condition of continual homosexual panic, *Get on the Bus* suggests that African American men who assume the role of financial provider in patriarchally constituted families will be able to relax, at last, in their sexual and gender identities.

Independently funded, to great fanfare, by numerous prominent African American investors, such as Danny Glover, Wesley Snipes, and Johnnie Cochran (Maslin), the film begins in South Central Los Angeles with a group of African American men boarding a bus headed for the march. Lee has intentionally assembled an incompatible group of passengers including: an elderly Christian ex-businessman, Jeremiah (Ossie Davis), who has been downsized out of his job and has lost his family; a biracial policeman, Gary (Roger Guenveur Smith), whose own black policeman father was killed by a gang member; an ex-gang member, Jamal (Gabriel Casseus), whose conversion to Islam enabled him to repudiate his "outlaw" past; a gay couple, Randall and Kyle (Harry Lennix and Isaiah Washington), who are in the process of ending their relationship; an egotistical actor, Flip (Andre Braugher), who questions the racial authenticity of the light-skinned policeman and the manhood of the "faggots"; an absentee father, Evan Sr. (Thomas Jefferson Byrd), who has chained himself to his (newly reclaimed) son, Evan Jr. (DeAundre Bonds), in accordance with the youth's probation order; a film-school student, Xavier (Hill Harper), who seems to be intended as a stand-in for the young Spike Lee; a Republican automobile dealer, Wendell (Wendell Pierce), who joins the group in Tennessee only because he views the march as a business opportunity; the head bus driver, George (Charles Dutton), who says that the women in his house would have forced him to attend the march even had he preferred not to; and his substitute Jewish codriver, Rick (Richard Belzer), who, after asserting his liberal credentials to the passengers and condemning Farrakhan's anti-Jewish statements privately to George, reaches the conclusion that his helping transport these men to the march is analogous to asking a black man to drive him to a KKK rally.

This cast of characters allows Lee to offer a cursory treatment of the controversy surrounding the march, as well as of the barriers to African American male affective and political unity.[27] Over the course of the cross-country trip, the men are shown debating, and at one point fighting over, issues such as whether gay and biracial men should be accepted as legitimate participants in black communities, whether welfare and affirmative action are strategies for perpetuating white dominance, and whether attending the march signifies support for Farrakhan's politics. (The Nation's ban against pork warrants only one brief, and comic, mention.) As are Farrakhan's anti-Jewish statements, the exclusion of black women from the march and the Nation's advocacy of patriarchy are addressed only in passing. Terry's light-skinned, convertible-driving "girl" Shelley is shown condemning the march as "sexist" near the start of the film. Later, when the bus pulls into a rest stop in Arkansas, two young black women whom Gary and Flip pursue seem to disagree with one another over the implications of Farrakhan's males-only decree. Both women, perhaps not insignificantly, are darker skinned and less bourgeois in appearance than Shelley. One offers lukewarm criticism of the march while the other expresses her wholehearted approval; by the end of the conversation, the former's resistance appears to have been overcome. The film allows the viewer to infer that Shelley's lack of support for Terry's pilgrimage has left him no choice but to seek solace elsewhere, among the real "sisters" who understand that sometimes the "brothers" simply need to be (with) men.

This particular assemblage of men is fated by Lee and screenwriter Reggie Rock Bythewood, however, never to reach its destination. As the bus nears Washington, Jeremiah (portrayed, one should note, by Malcolm X's eulogizer) is found unconscious and taken to a hospital. In a show of solidarity that is said to demonstrate the true principles of the march, several of his fellow passengers choose to stay with him. They end up watching actual footage of the march on television as the "great woman" Maya Angelou addresses the multitudes.[28] Lee's decision to excerpt the speech of Angelou, one of several African American women asked to participate in the public spectacle of the march in order to defuse black feminist criticism of women's exclusion (Boyd, "Million" 877), allows him to further disavow Farrakhan's conservative agenda. A more comprehensive representation, after all, would have revealed that the majority of black women were urged to support the march by undertaking the "invisible" work of raising money to finance a get-together to which they were not invited. Jeremiah dies anyway, having literally given his life in a failed attempt to march, finally, on Washington—for, as it turns out, he was too busy pursuing the American bourgeois dream to have attended the earlier one in 1963.[29]

Conjuring in many ways the impulse Ishmael Reed had encoded in *Mumbo Jumbo*'s "jes' grew," the men on the bus are presented as seeking their text in D.C.—and displacing Louis Farrakhan's leadership in the process. The fact that they end up not marching on the Mall but rather reciting Jeremiah's prayer in the Lincoln Memorial perhaps reflects Lee's personal ambivalence about his subject matter, if not the ambivalence of African Americans in general. Whatever the explanation for such a narrative decision, the desire of many of the march's real-life supporters, like Cornel West, to distance themselves from its sponsorship by the Nation is surely reflected in the liminal status of the one man on the bus who is clearly coded as a follower of Farrakhan.[30] Clean-shaven and attired in a black suit, white shirt, and bow tie, the man—whose appearance distantly and perhaps not coincidentally evokes that of Elijah Muhammad—is neither named nor allowed to speak. He is presented only as the "mysterious," fleeting object of the viewer's gaze: unknown and (at least in this film) quite unknowable.[31]

Yet Lee defuses any potential threat the man might pose by using his presence to elicit laughter, almost as though he and not the Jewish driver Rick were functioning as the out-of-place "white" man on the bus. The camera lingers on the Nation member at key moments when the "named" characters are interacting (most notably during a sing-along to a James Brown recording), leading the viewer to perceive him as Other to Lee's true subjects—the men who manage to transcend their differences of color, generation, sexuality, and (for the most part) class as they pray, rap, fight, weep, and embrace. Of the named characters, only the boastfully bourgeois Republican Wendell is emphatically exiled from the predominantly working-class bus community, while the more discretely middle-class Xavier, who as a surrogate for Spike Lee would be destined to achieve wealth far greater than Wendell could ever derive from his automobile dealership, is accepted into the fold. Though the Nation member is present during the brief closing segment at the Lincoln Memorial, and thus briefly included in the film's final vision of (as it were) black brotherly bussing, Lee's representation of a disjunction between the man's restrained demeanor and the sorts of cultural practices which he typically valorizes in his films means that the Nation itself ends up being scripted as inauthentically black. Intriguingly, moreover, since Randall also shares Elijah Muhammad's light-skinned appearance and "gentle" mannerisms, Get on the Bus creates a potential semiotic slippage between the mysterious Nation member and one of the two gay men on the bus. This similarity is underscored during the final Lincoln Memorial scene, when the two men are positioned side by side.

It comes as no surprise, accordingly, that the film's contradictory investment in homosocial bonding (which I am signifying here by my pun on "buss") ends up more nearly reinforcing than questioning the antigay bias inherent in the Nation's politics of black "realness." Lee's opening credit sequence can be seen to offer a paradigm for how the homoerotic possibilities of the film (and, by extension, of the march itself) are invoked only to be foreclosed. The sequence features a youthful, dark-skinned, muscular man, his nude body encased in chains. In what might be construed as an allusion to Robert Mapplethorpe's controversial photographs of African American men, the camera offers up this man's body, part by fetishized part, as the object of the viewer's gaze.[32] But because this is a dark-skinned body encased in chains, the sequence is obviously also intended to conjure for the viewer the iconography of the auction block. By subordinating the (sadomasochistically) erotic underpinnings of the opening shots to the historical narrative of chattel slavery, the film does more than force us to recognize that the sexuality of black men, like that of black women, was expropriated and exploited under slavery. It also effectively stigmatizes any homoerotic pleasure the male viewer might derive from taking this nude black male body as the object of his gaze. To participate in the sexual objectification of black men, the opening sequence suggests, is to perpetuate white domination.

Once the film is under way, moreover, the erotically charged shackles of the opening sequence are transmuted into the chain linking Evan Sr. to Evan Jr., who prefers to be addressed as "Smooth." The former is soon criticized by his fellow passengers for carrying out what they view as a blatantly racist court order, but he insists upon his right, as a father, to discipline his namesake as he chooses. In this fashion, Get on the Bus uses the visual iconography of the chain to associate the opening credit sequence with its narrative quest to affirm both black patriarchy and the black patronymic. Smooth's refusal to be called "Junior" operates as a critique not of the social system of patriarchy (and its attendant naming practices, which elide women's roles in reproduction) but rather of the senior Evan's failure to have assumed his proper role as patriarch when his son was born. The film implies that the inappropriate positioning of black men as sexualized objects of the gaze has somehow resulted in this putative crisis of fatherhood in contemporary black communities.[33] As a result, the viewer is allowed to acknowledge the homosocial impulses that structure *Get on the Bus* as a narrative of black male bonding, while also being asked to disavow that bonding ritual's homoeroticism. The film affirms instead the institution of black patriarchy under the Law of the Black (Wage-Earning) Father.

Without discounting in toto the progressive possibilities of Lee's treatment of black male same-sex desire, one might consequently be inclined to hypothesize that the subplot about Randall and Kyle (who, curiously, are never located by the film in terms of their employment status in the way that most of the straight men are) serves primarily to avert the greater anxiety raised by the homoerotically charged setting of the bus. Marking two of the men as gay, in other words, helps foreclose speculation about the sexuality of their seatmates. Working from this perspective, we can also see that Shelley functions in the film not simply to offer a feminist critique of the march, but also to exclude one possible explanation for Gary's determination to spend six days in the company of other men. His fellow passengers' propensity to make their wives and girlfriends a frequent topic of conversation could be interpreted in an analogous fashion.[34]

By using Kyle and Randall as an occasional target of laughter, moreover, Lee provides a moment of release from any rising homosexual panic among his viewers. During the screening I attended, when Flip announces that the two should be ejected from the bus and another passenger suggests that they can "skip" cross-country to the march, the racially/ethnically mixed audience surrounding me responded with loud and appreciative laughter. A fundamental contradiction of the film, needless to say, is that the exclusion of black women operates simultaneously to confirm the manhood of the bus passengers and to destabilize the status of their sexual desire. In this, it reflects a fundamental contradiction of the homosocial practices promoted by the NOI as a strategy for asserting black masculinity, including the Million Man March. If, however, the two gay men provide a resolution of this contradiction by enabling the viewer to perceive a clear disjunction between hetero- and homosexuality, it is important to recognize that the film also works to recuperate maternal power for an "unpanicked" black manhood.

This recuperation operates most clearly in the character of the head driver, George, the primary figure of authority in the film. George's integrity, values, and physical appearance are never called into question: he is a reliable, working-class family man who does not aspire to bourgeois (read: assimilationist) success; he is sufficiently dark-skinned so that his racial identity is taken for granted in a way that Gary's is not; he supports Farrakhan's leadership without himself espousing overtly sexist, homophobic, or anti-Jewish sentiments; he maintains solidarity with his coworker Rick even when the latter bails out. At home in his racial, sexual, gender, and class identities, George is surely intended to provide a moral compass for the film's viewer. For this reason, I am particularly intrigued by an exchange between him and the passengers which takes place near the outset of *Get on the Bus*. Just prior to departure, George announces a series of behavioral rules, only to be (good-naturedly) heckled by Gary with the accusation: "This guy sounds like my mother." Unfazed, George responds, or perhaps more accurately threatens them, with the decree: "Well, good, because for the next six days I am your mother. Don't make me use my belt."

Given my earlier discussion of Elijah Muhammad's ambiguous gender identity and perceived maternal qualities, my interest in this assertion should not be hard to understand. On one level, the exchange reminds us of the strategies of disavowal through which "authority" in African American culture is repeatedly constituted as the domain of black women, as (belt-wearing) maternal rather than paternal power. To cite the most apt of recent examples, in a 1997 memoir, Sonsyrea Tate writes of her childhood experiences as the daughter of NOI members: "I never really understood who wore the pants, so to speak, between Ma and Dad. As far as I could tell, Ma put Dad in control, like she was saying, 'Okay, you be the man, and this is what the man's supposed to do, okay, honey? Kiss, kiss'" (68). In a 1996 essay written to defend the Million Man March from its detractors, Clyde Taylor deploys a somewhat analogous narrative to describe the African American women who supported the Million Man March. "Doubtless," he writes, "many of these women shared the view of one Sister I heard about who told her mate: 'You've got so much to atone for, I'll pay for your fare to D.C. myself!'" (91). George's joke that his wife and daughters "insisted" he attend the march similarly implies that black patriarchy is not just desired by but also actually implemented by black women.

At the same time, George is also presented as an African American man who is so confident of his identity and authority that he need not be threatened by the prospect of being interpellated—literally "hailed," in Althusserian terms (162)— as a black mother. Whereas Flip seems almost an exemplary model of black homosexual panic, George opens up the possibility of a black manhood whose boundaries are so secure as to allow for incursions of femininity. If anything, his willingness to assimilate maternity renders him more masculine. The allure of George's character is perhaps intimated by Malcolm X's fond recollection of the "feminine" aspect of domestic life in patriarchal Muslim households. After being released from prison, he marveled at how "softly and pleasantly" his brother's family interacted (193). Empowered in both the public and private spheres by their status as financial providers and recognized heads-of-households, black men would, in this fantasized scenario, be enabled to serve as models of patriarchal restraint, "genteel" in their uncontested dominance.[35]

Taylor suggests that the dynamics I have outlined in the film were, for him at least, operative in the actual march as well. Claiming that black feminists in particular were angry because they "have a history of controlling the agendas they get involved with" (92), he insists that the real "Sisters" (a category that is deployed in the essay so as to exclude black feminists) were happy to show their support. They "did not build their reality around a commitment to seeing Black men as the competitive other," he opines (91). While disavowing a patriarchal agenda, Taylor further claims that he "recognized in D.C. that autumn day a hunger for leadership from Black men in Black women" (91), a hunger which he presumably now feels compelled to satisfy.

Having thus legitimated his participation in the march by excluding black feminists from the family grouping of Brothers and Sisters, Taylor describes how his experience in Washington altered his thinking about the relationship of femininity to black masculinity:

> What also came unhinged for me was a certain formalist symmetry in what has been called the politics of difference. Through the existentialist psychology of Jean-Paul Sartre and the dialectical reasoning of Marx, there has arisen the concept of co-defining identities: Whites get their identity as being Other than Black, and men see themselves as manly only as opposed to women or gays. So, the narrative goes, one could only get rid of one's homophobia by accepting the homophile or woman within one's masculine self.
>
> But after the Mall, I began to see how this kind of equation, though basically persuasive, could easily be overworked. It suffers by making someone else [in Taylor's case, women and gay men] the guardian of one's conscience. It discounts the capacity to respect another's difference simply because that's the decent thing to do. . . . After the Mall, I came to believe that Black men, after the sometimes sharp-edged prompting and protests of women and gays, could widen their moral vision without submitting to the predesigned psychological make-over that some would impose on them as if from some higher external authority. (94–95)

Although he insists that the march "embraced straights and gays" (94), this passage makes it clear that, for Taylor, the category of "Black men" as a "core identity" (100) relegates homosexual men to the implicitly feminized Other grouping of "women and gays." And just in case the reader has any doubts about the sexuality of the participants, Taylor sprinkles his essay with numerous references to the girlfriends, wives, and daughters who were on hand to offer support. Having symbolically configured the scene on the Mall as one of nonhomoerotic homosocial bonding, Taylor can thus make his admission: "All right, I confess. We liked each other" (93). Whereas Spike Lee at least attempted to articulate a space for black gay men on the bus, Taylor maintains that the march's "single most striking achievement . . . was the instant reconstruction of the identity of the moral and serious heterosexual Black male" (101).

One can only hope that Taylor is indeed "serious" in his commitment to ensuring that the widespread fixation on hyperbolically heterosexual black manhood during the 1990s does not simply rehabilitate what Angela Davis has referred to as "some of the more unfortunate ideological convergences of" the 1960s ("Black" 317). Since the sexist biases of earlier eras in African American history have been repeatedly justified by a version of the claim that black women desire and deserve but have been denied the luxury of patriarchy—as though black male dominance were an obviously just reward for centuries of struggle against white racism—it is frankly hard for me to see how this new wave of masculinist posturing signifies anything different from what it did the last time around.

Let me conclude, though, by pointing out that in his book of interviews with young African American men, *Living to Tell about It* (1996), journalist Darrell Dawsey goes out of his way to contest the common representation of young black men as sexist. One of the interviews he includes is with Bilal Allah, a member of the Five Percent Nation of Islam. When discussing his feelings about women and gender roles, Allah affirms his commitment to ending sexism. Speaking of a hypothetical girlfriend, he acknowledges his desire that she know how to manage a house. "However," he continues, "I got to be up on it as well, I got to be able to equate that on the same level. I have to be able to clean, clean the food, whatever, so we can build together" (176). Though his investments in "cleaning" warrant attention for all the reasons I have explained and his reference to male/female "duality" (177) inscribes a presumption of heterosexuality that needs to be critiqued, I do not want to discount the potentially progressive impulses that also underwrite his commentary. White men clearly benefit from the prevailing representation of black men as sexist (and homophobic and anti-Jewish) since it serves to deflect attention from their own more secure position of domination over disempowered groups.

At the same time, in keeping with the overall premise of this book, I also wanted to end this chapter with Bilal Allah because his commentary reflects the resilient perception that black women embody and enact a "special" relationship to food:

> I feel what happens is that, as the mother, she's going to be able to bring a special vibe when she cooks dinner that night. She's a woman; she got that special spiritual connection and she got that mental vibe where she knows how the family wants it, more so than I'm going to bring to it. She's more in tune with her thing inside than I am. Then that's what I have to learn about myself; then we can learn from each other.
> I think the roles should definitely be shared. (176–77)

It admittedly strikes me as unlikely that egalitarian gender relations are presaged by a comment such as this, which in naturalizing black women's labor in the kitchen could easily provide Allah with a justification for evading his responsibility for domestic labor. Nonetheless, I happily affirm his stated commitment to mutual teaching and to the necessity of creating "shared" roles.

five

Of Watermelon and Men

Dick Gregory's Cloacal Continuum

> She dreams the baby's so small she keeps
> misplacing it—it rolls from the hutch
> and the mouse carries it home, it disappears
> with his shirt in the wash.
> Then she drops it and it explodes
> like a watermelon, eyes spitting.
>
> Rita Dove, "Motherhood," 1986

In 1988 an employee of the Texaco corporation, Sheryl Joseph, informed her colleagues that she was expecting her second child. At an office party the following day to celebrate her birthday, Joseph was presented by her boss with a cake decorated with an image of a dark-skinned, Afro-wearing woman far advanced in pregnancy (figure 5-1). (Joseph, a light-skinned African American woman, had never worn an Afro and was still in her first trimester.) Inscribed on the cake were the innocuous words "Happy Birthday, Sheryl," followed by the ideologically loaded speculation: "It must have been those watermelon seeds." According to a 1996 *New York Times* account of a subsequent employment discrimination lawsuit brought against Texaco by minority workers, the stunned Joseph "did her best not to react" at the time since she feared a response would cause her to lose her job (Eichenwald 11).

Joseph's story serves as a particularly vivid manifestation of the pattern that we have been tracing, through which cultural stereotypes regarding dietary habits become imbricated in broader social ideologies of sexuality, gender, race, and class. The cake's inscription not only invokes the long-standing association of watermelon with African Americans (and particularly with African American children), but it also hypothesizes that Joseph's pregnancy was itself caused by "those watermelon seeds."[1] Recuperating a central assumption underlying the myth of black matriarchy, that black women have rendered black men superfluous, the message implies that the fetus she was carrying had no father; presumably it "jes'

FIGURE 5.1 Birthday cake for Sheryl Joseph. 1996 *The New York Times*. Photograph of newspaper visual by the University of Iowa Audiovisual Center Photo Service.

grew" of its own accord. In this respect, the birthday cake surely participates in the widespread erasure of African American men from the scene of reproduction, which Elijah Muhammad, among others, attempted to remedy.

Curiously, despite his unrelenting attacks on what he called the slave diet during the 1960s and early 1970s, Muhammad had little to say about watermelon. Many of his contemporaries, however, readily adopted it as a trenchant symbol of the oft-precarious status of U.S. racial and gender identities. Perhaps most memorably, Melvin Van Peebles's 1970 film *Watermelon Man* follows the fortunes of its protagonist, Caucasian insurance agent Jeff Gerber, played in whiteface by African American comedian Godfrey Cambridge, after he awakens in the middle of the night to find himself transformed into a black man. At the start of the film Gerber is, as Eric Lott claims, a "devoted racist whose compulsive engagement with 'blackness' undergirds or buttresses his whiteness" ("White" 488). He mimics black vernacular while exercising, for example. Over the course of *Watermelon Man*, Gerber slowly comes to identify himself with his unwonted black subject position, and he grows increasingly angry at the discrimination faced by African Americans in U.S. society. Lott thus claims that the film operates as an allegory about Black Power, as a conversion fantasy in which the newly black protagonist moves from a position of racial self-hatred into a black nationalist assertion of racial pride.

But though *Watermelon Man*'s initial portrayal of Gerber might indeed be said to demonstrate "that white supremacy has as one of its constituent (if unconscious) elements an imaginary closeness to black culture" (Lott, "White" 488), it is also worth noting that Gerber's experience of black masculinity is further mediated in the film by an imaginary closeness to (black) femininity. Upon waking to find himself black, he quickly undertakes a series of "beauty" rituals designed to erase or disguise the unwelcome pigmentation: he bathes in milk and raids the local drugstore for skin-bleaching creams. His morning calisthenics ritual fallen by the wayside, this new Gerber is in fact feminized by his racial alteration, far more concerned with his skin tone than his muscle tone. Nor does his altered racial identity bring with it a compensatory enhancement of penis size. "That's an old wives' tale," he admits, after peering down his pants. Watermelon itself functions in the film mainly as a trope for a simultaneously desired and disavowed blackness: self-conscious about the fruit's racial associations, Gerber is unwilling to eat it after his reincarnation as an African American man. "What? Are you crazy? Is that supposed to be funny?" he demands of his wife, Jeannie, after she offers him a wedge of watermelon. When she protests her innocence, Gerber invokes the Quaker Oats trademark to insinuate that Jeannie's white racial credentials will now also be considered suspect: "Well, listen, Jemima, you're in this too."

But meanwhile, in real life, Godfrey Cambridge was claiming comedian-turned-diet guru Dick Gregory as his professional mentor and "spiritual leader" (quoted in Jarrett, "One"). The connection between these two African American men is significant for my study because by the early 1970s Gregory was anointing himself "watermelon man" in a quite literal fashion. In articles, interviews, and a 1973 cookbook, Gregory proselytized for watermelon as a mainstay of the fruitarian regimen which he believed African Americans (and everyone else, for that matter) should embrace. Whereas Elijah Muhammad had condemned pork and other soul foods as part of an effort to propagate a vision of black masculinity untainted by black femininity, Gregory actually used watermelon in a symbolic appropriation of pregnancy for himself. This strategy allowed him to parody white America's fearful attribution to black America of an out-of-control birthrate, while ignoring black feminist challenges to the black nationalist dismissal of birth control and abortion as practices of racial genocide. Despite what I will delineate as the thoroughly problematic aspects of such an undertaking, Gregory's gender-bending teachings and practices provide a potentially progressive alternative to the historical tendency of African American liberation struggles to be framed in terms of the pursuit of nonhybrid gender identities.

Nigger

> That family has one foot in the ghetto and the other on a watermelon rind.
>
> Gloria Naylor, Linden Hills, 1985

In a December 1992 letter to the editor of the Nation, Grover Sales recounts a night in 1962 when he and fellow comedian Gregory "walked in on Lenny Bruce in mid-performance in a San Francisco nightclub" (686). After spotting the pair, the embattled counterculture icon proffered the following now-famous query: "Are there any *niggers* here tonight?" (quoted in Sales 686). Stunned silence ensued. Bruce then proceeded to explain his rationale in repeating the racist epithet, initially by mocking his audience:

"Omygod! Did you hear what he *said!* 'Are there any *niggers* here tonight?' Is that rank! Is that cruel! Is that a cheap way to get laughs? Well, I see a couple of niggers at the bar talking to the guinea owner, and next to them are a couple of lace-curtain micks, two wops, one square-head, three greaseballs, two kikes, one hunky-funky boogie, a couple of gooks, one sheeny, one dago—Bid 'em up! Bid 'em up! I pass with three dykes, four kikes, and eight niggers!"

The frozen audience gave way to hysteria, the sweet laughter of liberation only Lenny Bruce could unloose. "Now why have I done this? Was this only for shock value? Well, if all the niggers started calling each other 'nigger'—not only among themselves, which they do anyway, but among the ofays, the whites—and if President Kennedy got on television and said: 'I'm considering appointing two or three of the top niggers in the country to my Cabinet,' in six months 'nigger' wouldn't mean any more than 'goodnight,' 'God bless you' or 'I promise to tell the truth, the whole truth and nothing but the truth so help me God'—and when that beautiful day comes, you'll never have another 6-year-old nigger kid come home from school crying because somebody called him a nigger." (686)[2]

Gregory, according to Sales, responded by calling Bruce "the eighth wonder of the world" and predicting that "if they don't kill him or throw him in jail, he's liable to shake up this whole fuckin' country" (quoted in Sales 686). His prediction came at least partly true: Bruce ended up in court on obscenity charges and died of an apparent drug overdose in 1966. The country was also in for some shaking up, though the 1960s can hardly be laid solely at the feet of Lenny Bruce. Two years after this encounter, Gregory published his autobiography. Sales speculates that its title, *Nigger*, was inspired by Bruce's polemic. The memoir is dedicated as follows: "Dear Momma—Wherever you are, if you ever hear the word 'nigger' again, remember they are advertising my book" (n. pag.).

As the dedication's reference to a single parent indicates, *Nigger* chronicles Gregory's rise from "fatherless" poverty in St. Louis, Missouri, to fame and fortune as a comedian, social activist, and natural foods advocate. Born in 1932, the second of Lucille and Presley ("Big Pres") Gregory's six children, he spent his early years scavenging for food, working for small change, trying to keep warm through the winter, and waiting for his peripatetically inclined father to come home. Big Pres rarely obliged. Despite health problems exacerbated by an often meager, sugar-laden diet, Gregory was a gifted sprinter and received an athletic scholarship to attend Southern Illinois University. Successful at S.I.U.—he was named "Outstanding Athlete of the Year" there in 1953—Gregory nonetheless left school midway through his senior year, distraught over the death of his mother and angered by the racial segregation he experienced in the predominantly white environs of Carbondale, Illinois. "That piece of white paper isn't enough unless they graduate you with a white face, too," he observes of his decision to forgo receiving a diploma (*Nigger* 92). For the next few years Gregory struggled to make ends meet while working sporadically in black Chicago nightclubs as a stand-up comic. In the late 1950s he began borrowing money from and dating a secretary at the University of Chicago, Lillian Smith. They married after Smith informed him that she was four months pregnant with the first of what would eventually be their eleven children (*Nigger* 115–16).

By the time he encountered Lenny Bruce, Gregory had received national recognition for his appearances in front of well-heeled white audiences at Hugh Hefner's Playboy Club, recorded a best-selling album, *Dick Gregory in Living Black and White* (c. 1961), and published a book of caustic humor about segregation, *From the Back of the Bus* (1962). The latter contained an introduction written by Hefner. Ironically, in retrospect, Gregory's first performance at Hefner's Playboy Club in January 1961 had been for "a convention of frozen food executives from the South," and he was almost denied the job because of his race (*Nigger* 142). Far from wanting to boycott establishments that banned nonwhites, Gregory's early goal was to perform in them, mainly because of their lucrative salaries. Though politicized, his brand of humor tended to be less confrontational than was that of Bruce, and it often relied on self-deprecation: "Just my luck, bought a suit with two pair of pants today . . . burnt a hole in the jacket" (*Nigger* 132). Here he thwarted potential hecklers by, in effect, heckling himself.

Having thus lured potentially hostile white audiences into complacency, Gregory might turn the tables by satirizing the cultural institution that has traditionally mediated white access to African American humor: "Wouldn't it be a hell of a thing if all this was burnt cork and you people were being tolerant for nothing?" (*Nigger* 132). To the extent that minstrelsy had been a principal form through which white envy of, as well as contempt for, blackness was expressed, such an aside exposes the precarious psychic underpinnings of "whiteness" itself.[3] Mel Watkins argues that Gregory actually succeeded with white audiences not because his humor was particularly innovative—indeed other black "funnymen" viewed him as having "pirated some of their best lines" (*On* 498)—but rather because his lack of experience performing in black clubs had allowed him to develop a style more similar to that of the "cerebral" Mort Sahl than the "bawdy" Redd Foxx.[4] In the context of the social upheavals of the 1960s, Watkins further claims, many whites would have been made uncomfortable by the minstrel-influenced mannerisms and sexually explicit humor that still tended to predominate on the black "chitlin circuit" stage (*On* 499). In fact, as his act progressed, Gregory would satirize almost every controversial social and political topic but sex. "If you mix blue and topical satire that white customer, all hung up with the Negro sex mystique, is going to get uncomfortable," he concluded (*Nigger* 132–33).[5]

Even as his career flourished in segregated clubs, Gregory became increasingly active in the Civil Rights movement. In the process, he says, his humor became "more topical, more racial, more digging into a system I was beginning to understand better and attack more intelligently" (*Nigger* 155). The growth of his political sophistication is evidenced by his writings from this period. *What's Happening?* from 1965, offered humor similar to that in *From the Back of the Bus*. But in his next series of books—*The Shadow That Scares Me* (1968), *Write Me In!* (1968), *No More Lies* (1971), *Dick Gregory's Political Primer* (1972), and *Up from Nigger* (1976)—Gregory began to develop a more consistent and comprehensive critique of the racialized ideology of "America" and of the U.S. sociopolitical system, including the intertwined forces of capitalism, colonialism, and patriarchy. He was attuned, for example, to the originary violence through which Native Americans were displaced from their land (e.g., No 50–87). Of course, the substantial income Gregory was earning from this same system enabled him to attend sit-ins, marches, and demonstrations all over the country. The irony of this situation was not lost on Gregory. "Isn't this the most fascinating country in the world?" he would inquire. "Where else would I have to ride on the back of the bus, have a choice of going to the worst schools, eating in the worst restaurants, living in the worst neighborhoods—and average $5,000 a week just talking about it?" (From 21).[6]

Jailed frequently for civil disobedience between engagements, the former track star was also eating heartily for the first time in his life and losing his trim, athletic physique in the process.[7] By 1965, though, Gregory had decided to modify his meat-eating, chain-smoking, heavy-drinking habits. Motivated initially by a commitment to nonviolence stemming from his civil rights activism, he became a vegetarian after deciding "that the killing of animals for food was both immoral and unnatural" (Dick Gregory's Natural 16). Somehow, Gregory claims, he managed to gain over one hundred pounds after ceasing to eat meat. "If it is possible to be an omnivorous vegetarian," he muses wryly when reflecting on his insatiable appetite, "I was it!" (Dick Gregory's Natural 16). Two years later, while waging independent write-in campaigns for the 1967 Chicago mayoral race and, subsequently, the 1968 presidential election, Gregory decided to embark on a fast to protest the Vietnam War. The catalyst for his resolution was a visit he paid to Dr. Alvenia Fulton, a Chicago nutritionist and health food restaurant owner who had "dropped off" a gift of salads for Gregory and his staff at his campaign headquarters several weeks earlier (Dick Gregory's Natural 17–18).

Fulton became Gregory's nutritional advisor, and thereafter the morality and the healthfulness of the American diet (or, more precisely, what he perceived as the lack both thereof) remained a focal point of his sociopolitical agenda. He narrates this gastronomic conversion in his 1973 dietary manual, Dick Gregory's Natural Diet for Folks Who Eat (hereafter Natural Diet). Gregory evolved, as he puts it, "From Omnivore to Fruitarian in Seven Short Years" (Natural 7). Eventually shunning not just meat and alcohol but also cooked foods and dairy products, Gregory became an ardent proponent of raw fruits, vegetables, and nuts. As Natural Diet went to press, he was engaged in yet another fast to protest the Vietnam War, his weight having dropped to around 90 pounds from a high of 288 ("Gregory"; Petersen; Natural 25–26). Gregory also abandoned stand-up comedy in 1973 because he felt that he could no longer associate himself with a nightclub scene that encouraged patrons to "consume alcohol" and otherwise engage in practices "that might be damaging to one's personal health" (Jarrett, "Dick"). As Chicago Tribune columnist Vernon Jarrett observed at the time of Gregory's decision to curtail his career as a comedian, "Dick's near full-time commitment today is to the human body and what is done to it and with it. And there is nothing funny about this commitment" ("Dick").

Since turning his attention to the "human body," Gregory has worked as a progressive community activist, purveyor of natural foods, and capitalist entrepreneur. During the early 1990s, he received media attention for, among other things, protesting the Persian Gulf War (Levinson), overseeing Riddick Bowe's diet prior to the boxer's world heavyweight championship fight with Evander Holyfield (D. Anderson), and performing "his first stand-up routine in 20 years" at a comedy festival in Manhattan (Pener). Unlike Bruce, then, Gregory has lived to see the aftermath of the cultural and political insurrection they both helped to instigate. Still in awe of the "eighth wonder," he remarked to a New York Times reporter in 1993 that Bruce "said things that no one would dare say and many were scared to even listen to" (Pener). Gregory, too, challenged his listeners by dwelling on the contradictions and hypocrisies of U.S. society. But whereas Bruce became obsessed with obscenity statutes and his First Amendment right to free speech, Gregory's determination to "corporealize" his sociopolitical beliefs through his dietary practices uniquely positioned him at the nexus of counterculture, black nationalist, second-wave feminist, and gay liberation politics.

"The Raw and the Cooked"

As is suggested by the subtitle of his dietary manual—Cookin' with Mother Nature—Gregory eventually associated himself with the "natural" foods movement which had its base in California. This counterculture cuisine had gained some public notice in October 1966, when the Diggers began yelling "Food Is Medium" in Haight-Ashbury, and developed a larger following after the taking of People's Park on 20 April 1969.[8] Warren Belasco writes in Appetite for Change that members of the counterculture invoked the term "natural" to expose what they saw as the fakeness—or plasticity—of modern culture: "Beyond defining the content of food, natural was a liberated state of mind, a symbol of opposition to mass production, efficiency, rationalization, limits" (40). It signified a revolt against "preservatives, pesticides, chemicals, packaging" (41). Foods such as yogurt, brewer's yeast, miso, and tempeh were valorized because they contained microbes, not artificial additives. While some used the term "natural" to denigrate the homogeneity of middle-class white suburbia, others used it to praise lifestyles marked by simplicity and lack of sophistication.

Because of such seeming discrepancies, "defenders of mainstream cuisine liked to point out how ill-defined, indeed contradictory, the concept of natural could be," but Belasco maintains that "within the countercuisine the adjective was attractive precisely because it was so expandable" (41). On the whole, he concludes, "natural seemed a useful oppositional category because it was defined by what it was not" (41). One should note, though, that if by the late 1960s "natural" had become synonymous with "soul" in some discursive contexts, the natural foods movement was not one of them. Belasco points out that "despite the obvious propinquity and political romance, black American cooks were not often discussed or recommended in white underground columns and books" on counterculture cuisine (63). He speculates: "While soul food was oppositional for blacks, at a time of rising tensions between black and white radicals, it may have been off limits for whites" (63). Hence one of the differences in how whites responded to soul food on the east versus the west coast.

Obviously opposition was no less fundamental to counterculture than to Black Power ideology, but the former movement did affirm some beliefs, the most pivotal of which was summed up by the equally ambiguous slogan "the personal is political." Purveyors of natural foods espoused this dictum along with feminists, lesbians, and gays because they understood private dietary practices to be "a medium for broader change" (Belasco 28). Unlike attending, for example, a protest rally, altering one's diet was an ongoing endeavor, requiring a thrice-daily renewal of resolution. Each meal became, moreover, a consciousness-raising session: "Compared to other cultural adaptations, the emerging countercuisine seemed less co-optable because it demanded greater personal commitment. . . . Examining and altering one's tastes was somewhat akin to psychoanalysis: a confrontation with subconsciously ingrained values, tastes, and behaviors" (Belasco 28). To alter one's patterns of eating was, in a sense, to alter one's state of being.

Gregory sounds similar themes. For instance, in Lesson Fourteen, "A Turnip in Every Pot," from *Dick Gregory's Political Primer*, he writes:

> I have experienced personally over the past few years how a purity of diet and thought are interrelated. And when Americans become truly concerned with the purity of the food that enters their own personal systems, when they learn to eat properly, we can expect to see profound changes effected in the social and political system of this nation. The two systems are inseparable. (262)

Like his California-based counterparts, Gregory believed that local actions would lead to global changes. In the process of purifying their bodies, Gregory's readers would become concerned with purifying society as a whole—purging corruption from the body politic. Of course, as Mary Douglas would doubtless point out, the meaning of "purity" is just as contingent as are the meanings of "natural" and "filth." Gregory's understanding of what constitutes a "pure" society would by no means be universally shared. But it is certainly worth noting that his perception of the body as a symbol for the social order—this being an argument to which Douglas had given scholarly legitimation in her contemporaneous book *Natural Symbols* (1973)—is highly reminiscent of the teachings of his fellow Chicagoan, Allah's temporal guide to godly gastronomy, Elijah Muhammad.[9]

Working in Chicago from the late 1950s through the 1970s, Gregory could hardly have avoided familiarity with the Nation of Islam. Malcolm X recalls that it was Gregory who first forced him to acknowledge Muhammad's sexual relationships with several of the young women who had become pregnant while employed as his secretaries: "Backstage at the Apollo Theater in Harlem one day, the comedian Dick Gregory looked at me. 'Man,' he said, 'Muhammad's nothing but a . . .'—I can't say the word he used. *Bam!* Just like that" (296).[10] Malcolm X's recollection is intriguing because Gregory himself has little to say in his writings from this period about either the Nation of Islam or its controversial leader.[11] Yet, given that Alvenia Fulton—listed as a contributor to *Dick Gregory's Natural Diet for Folks Who Eat*—also advertised regularly in the Nation's newspaper, *Muhammad Speaks*, it seems possible that Gregory's indebtedness to Muhammad's dietary fixations is greater than he has been willing to admit.[12] If his secular, integrationist politics are incompatible with Elijah Muhammad's advocacy of theistic black nationalism, their dietary concerns share a number of striking similarities.

Like (and perhaps following) Muhammad, and unlike the west-coast proponents of natural foods, Gregory became a harsh critic of soul food, "the diet of Blacks during the period of slavery" (*Natural* 78). "Nothing but garbage," was the phrase he used to describe it when questioned by Vernon Jarrett, himself one of soul's unrepentant devotees (quoted in Jarrett, "Dick"). Whereas the white counterculture had largely refrained from discussing soul food, Gregory echoed the Nation of Islam leader in labeling it a form of racial "genocide":

> I personally would say that the quickest way to wipe out a group of people is to put them on a soul food diet. One of the tragedies is that the very folks in the black community who are most sophisticated in terms of the political realities in this country are nonetheless advocates of "soul food." They will lay down a heavy rap on genocide in America with regard to black folks, then walk into a soul food restaurant and help the genocide along. (*Natural* 81)

Gregory claims that soul food in its original form—which he terms "soil food" (*Natural* 78)—was far more healthful than the version popularized starting in the 1960s. Slaves, he contends, ate primarily a diet of pesticide-free vegetables seasoned with pork fat, cornmeal breads unenriched by eggs or dairy products, wild fruit, and unrefined sugar in the form of molasses. Most slaves, moreover, led far from sedentary lives. Gregory says that his largely inactive contemporaries consumed, by contrast, far too much meat, lard, starch, sugar, salt, alcohol, and tobacco. As a result, they were suffering from a variety of illnesses, including high blood pressure, diabetes, and heart trouble (*Natural* 79–80). These claims parallel many of Muhammad's pronouncements in *How to Eat to Live*.

But whereas Muhammad tended to focus on the filthiness of the hog and the "sewer lines" in its forelegs, Gregory was quite explicit in his obsession with human bowels and human excrement, particularly his own. This fixation culminates in a section from his dietary manual titled "The Sewage System":

> It has been claimed that nine-tenths of the physical disorders and diseases of body owners have their origins in the STOMACH and INTESTINES. The two great abuses body owners inflict upon the machine Mother Nature has given them are the failure to *nourish* the organs in the body responsible for the proper elimination of waste matter and the failure to give *careful* and *immediate* attention to Mother Nature's call that waste matter must be eliminated. (44–45)

Gregory continues by delineating in great detail the dangers of allowing fecal matter to remain in the colon. The bacteria in the intestinal tract produce, he says, "some very toxic by-products" that tend to be reabsorbed into the body "if proper elimination does not take place" (47). As a result, "the whole body is poisoned" (47). Gregory recommends that, as a first step in altering their dietary practices, his readers flush waste matter from their bowels via several colonic irrigations or enemas; then they should establish a regimen of "internal baths" to maintain the purity of their intestinal tracts (49).[13] "When the outside of your body machine gets dirty, you give it a bath," he points out. "So if the *inside* of your body is 'dirty,'

why not give *it* a bath?" (49). Gregory's obsession might well be construed as a displacement of the Black Power chitterling fetish: he internalizes the debate over
soul food, in a sense, by "relishing" human rather than hog bowels.

Both Muhammad and Gregory advocated "purifying the system" of such dietary
dangers via fasting; unlike Mother Waddles, they believed that the less one ate,
the better one would feel.[14] But each also recognized that his readers were likely to
wish to partake, at least periodically, of food. Where they disagreed was over what
sort of diet was least likely to pollute the body. Though in his *Political Primer* Gregory does follow Muhammad by advocating the navy bean (273), he claims that
raw foods such as fruits and nuts provide all the nutrients the body needs naturally
and that they are, furthermore, preferable to cooked foods because they leave little
residue in the intestinal tract. He inveighs in particular against dairy products because they result in a buildup of "mucus" in the body (*Natural* 62). The sole exception to his ban on animal products is plain yogurt: "It establishes an acid medium
in the intestinal tract which inhibits the growth of harmful and putrefaction-
causing bacteria" (*Natural* 62).

Muhammad, by contrast, thought that cooked foods were least harsh on the digestive system and that their nutrients were more readily absorbed. As we saw in
the last chapter, he believed that an optimal diet would consist of thrice-cooked or
stale bread, pasteurized milk, and a few well-cooked vegetables. Perhaps referring
obliquely to Alvenia Fulton (or possibly Gregory), Muhammad dismisses the
fruitarian diet in the second volume of *How to Eat to Live*: "This civilization is
rapidly turning back to raw food and raw juices, but our God and Saviour Allah
(God), in the Person of Master Fard Muhammad, taught me to cook our food and
most of the doctors agree that cooked food is better" (85). Whereas Gregory
claims the counterculture patron "Mother Nature" as his authority for advocating
raw food, Muhammad justifies his antithetical dietary prescriptions by citing patriarchal Islamic divinity.[15]

It would perhaps seem logical to invoke a gendered binarism here to conclude
that Muhammad was a proponent of male "culture," and Gregory, of female "nature." Muhammad's disdain for manifestations of black primitivism and fear of
black female pollution underwrote his desire that African Americans be perceived
as the possessors of a refined patriarchal culture. Gregory, by contrast, presented
himself as a critic of anything "man-made" and repeatedly deployed the metaphorical language of motherhood as a term of approbation. Many of the political positions Gregory espoused would appear to follow from this conviction. For example,
he dedicated his 1972 book *No More Lies* "to Women's Liberation" (v)—a movement that was, of course, at the time anathema not just to Elijah Muhammad but
also to a majority of all U.S. men. In her study *The Sexual Politics of Meat*, Carol
Adams even invokes Gregory to support her linkage of vegetarianism and feminism. In particular, she quotes a comparison Gregory had drawn between the
ghetto and the slaughterhouse.[16] Though Adams acknowledges that there are some
vegetarian exceptions to the feminist rule (Hitler, most notably), she suggests that
an ethical, rather than health-related, commitment to vegetarianism should be in
keeping with a feminist ideological perspective (152).

The remainder of this chapter addresses in greater detail the political ramifications of the fact that Gregory's interest in vegetarianism was indeed motivated by a desire for bodily "purification" rather than only a concern with the ethics of eating meat. Here, though, we need to pause to consider how this nature/culture binary was being reconfigured in contemporaneous discourses emanating from the academy. As it turns out, Gregory's culinary ideology actually replicates in some intriguing ways the structural logic of "tangible qualities" which Claude Lévi-Strauss famously, but misleadingly, referred to as "the raw and the cooked" (*Raw* 1). In his essay "The Culinary Triangle," published in the United States in 1966, Lévi-Strauss claims that cooking operates

> within a triangular semantic field whose three points correspond respectively to the categories of the raw, the cooked and the rotted. It is clear that in respect to cooking the raw constitutes the unmarked pole, while the other two poles are strongly marked, but in different directions: indeed, the cooked is a cultural transformation of the raw, whereas the rotted is a natural transformation. (587)

Working in the early 1970s, feminist anthropologist Sherry Ortner elaborated on this work in structural anthropology in her own germinal article "Is Female to Male as Nature Is to Culture?" (1974). Ortner's conclusion—that woman is "seen as intermediate between nature and culture" (87)—leads me to believe that we should be hesitant to adopt a binaristic model for understanding the gendered underpinnings of the dietary dictates of Muhammad and Gregory. Lévi-Strauss's and Ortner's triangulated schemata allow us to formulate a more complicated interpretation of Gregory's belief system than that which he himself advocated. Rather than associating raw/nature/feminine and cooked/culture/masculine in a simplistic series of binary substitutions, we can follow Lévi-Strauss by positing a third poll, the "rotted." In this model, the "rotted" is associated with nature and, I think, femininity. The "raw" is an "unmarked pole."

Tellingly, Lévi-Strauss concludes "The Culinary Triangle" by observing that "the cooking of a society is a language in which it unconsciously translates its structure—or else resigns itself, still unconsciously, to revealing its contradictions" (595). In the next section, I will extrapolate from Lévi-Strauss's claims to suggest that though Gregory consciously understood himself to be celebrating femininity via his valorization of rawness and nature, femininity nonetheless threatened the boundaries of the self as the maternal and so had to be abjected as the "rotted." Gregory tried to resolve the contradiction between his psychic fears and his avowedly profeminist sociopolitical positions by appropriating the Law of the Mother for black masculinity. He posited a hybrid entity—his own purified, fecund body—to occupy the "unmarked pole" of the raw.

"Fruit-full and Multiplying"

> Be a watermelon up under that one's dress by summer.
>
> John Edgar Wideman, *Sent for You Yesterday*, 1983

If Gregory made manifest the psychic underpinnings of the Black Power fixation on chitterlings by fetishizing his own bowels, as a fruitarian he was, as we have seen, far more willing to embrace and redefine another food stereotypically used to denigrate African Americans: watermelon. In his second autobiography, *Up from Nigger*, Gregory writes that he "often used a watermelon as a sort of personal symbol and a private joke. For years, white folks have enjoyed poking fun at Black folks' fondness for watermelon. I reversed the process and made the watermelon a symbol of pride in Blackness" (47). By way of illustrating his tactics, Gregory recounts one occasion when he

> booked two first-class seats on a plane back home to Chicago. The tickets were in the names of D. Gregory and W. Melon. No doubt the ticket agent thought I was traveling with a wealthy friend from Pittsburgh. I boarded the plane with my watermelon under my arm. I carefully fastened the seat belt around the melon in the seat next to me and acted like there was nothing unusual. Every time someone would look as though he were getting up the nerve to ask about it, my expression discouraged the question. I guess folks were thinking, "We knew Dick Gregory had a lot of kids, but this is ridiculous!" (48)

While Gregory—with surrogate offspring in tow—was flying all over the country performing stand-up comedy and protesting segregation, his wife Lillian was in Chicago bearing and rearing the "kids" to which he refers: Michelle, Lynne, Richard Claxton Jr. (who died at age two and one-half months), twins Pamela and Paula, Stephanie, Gregory (the child's sole name), Miss, Christian, Ayanna, and Yohance. While Gregory was becoming increasingly preoccupied with food, gaining and losing several hundred pounds on his early feasts and subsequent fasts and in the process developing what might be construed as an "anorectic" relationship to his body, Lillian Gregory's body was regularly expanding and contracting as well. In the colloquial usage of John Edgar Wideman, she spent the interval from 1959 through 1973 growing "a lot of" watermelons up under her dress.

The size of their family was no accident—at least not in Gregory's opinion. Like many of his contemporaries, including Elijah Muhammad, Gregory viewed the birth control pill as a white-sponsored method of black racial genocide. He expressed these views most directly in a controversial 1971 *Ebony* article, "My Answer to Genocide," the opening comment of which summarizes his advice: "My answer to genocide, quite simply, is eight black kids—and another baby [Ayanna] on the way" (66). To justify his pronatalist stand, Gregory not only condemns the long history of white efforts to "control" African Americans via slavery and segregation, but he also invokes his devotion to "Mother Nature": "Of course, I could never participate in birth control, because I'm against doing anything that goes against Nature. That's why I've changed my eating habits so drastically over the years and have become a vegetarian. And birth control is definitely against Nature" (66). Only in passing does Gregory acknowledge that his answer to genocide requires a pregnable black woman: "In fact, my wife had so many babies at the same hospital in Chicago that they put a revolving door on her room in the maternity ward" (66). More often his usage would lead one to infer that he created the children unassisted. Thus, at the outset of the article Gregory refers to himself as "one black cat who's going to have all the kids he wants" (66).

This elision of female agency in reproduction returns in the watermelon anecdote as an overt appropriation of childbearing for masculinity. Gregory carries his watermelon "under his arm" rather than under a dress. Certainly the analogy is not lost on the comic-activist, who observes in a chapter from *Natural Diet* (called "On Being Fruit-Full and Multiplying") that he and Lillian "chalked up quite a record of fruitfulness before we became full of fruit" (24). Chitterlings and watermelon might thus be said to define the parameters of Black Power's cloacal continuum. Whereas Freud had described the cloacal theory as the childhood belief that "babies are born through the bowel like a discharge of faeces" (*Three* 62), Gregory implies that watermelon are born through his bowel like a discharge of babies. In an era during which most of the African American men featured in the mainstream press were valorizing black male autonomy when not condemning black women for attempting to "emasculate" them, Gregory stands out in his embrace of maternity as a paradigm for black masculinity.

Opposition to birth control and abortion were, of course, by no means universal among African Americans—and particularly not among African American women. Indeed, as Robert Weisbord points out, "*Ebony*'s offices were deluged with correspondence in response to Gregory's article," much of it critical of his position (92). Gregory's fixation on pregnancy thus needs to be understood, at least in considerable part, as a politically conservative reaction to cross-racial women's demands during the 1960s and early 1970s for greater reproductive autonomy.[17] While acknowledging the eugenicist underpinnings of much population-control ideology, many black feminists insisted on their need and right to decide whether to bear children. Thus, in their "Statement on Birth Control" (1970), the Black Women's Liberation Group takes issue with claims of "militant black brothers" that birth control is "a form of Whitey's committing genocide on black people" (405). They agree that "Whitey's" motives are suspect but point out that "it takes two to practice genocide and black women are able to decide for themselves, like poor people all over the world, whether they will submit to genocide" (405). The group concludes that "birth control is the freedom to *fight* genocide of black women and children" (405). Writing in the same year, then–U.S. Representative Shirley Chisholm insists: "To label family planning and legal abortion programs 'genocide' is male rhetoric, for male ears. It falls flat to female listeners, and to thoughtful male ones" (604). Echoing the sentiments of members of the Black Women's Liberation Group, Chisholm maintains "that two or three children who are wanted, prepared for, reared amid love and stability, and educated to the limit of their ability will mean more for the future of the black and brown races from which they come than any number of neglected, hungry, ill-housed and ill-clothed youngsters" (604).[18]

In condemning birth control and abortion, Gregory was clearly at odds with many leading black as well as white feminists.[19] This did not prevent him from professing support for women's rights, however. *No More Lies* contains a sympathetic discussion of issues pushed by feminists, such as sexual objectification and wage discrimination (236–41); as we saw in the preceding section, moreover, he dedicated the book as a whole to women's liberation. But it is instructive to look at the full text of the inscription: "This book is dedicated to Women's Liberation, the movement of the 1970's which will make all Americans proud to call the Statue of Liberty their momma. The book is further dedicated to the Indian Americans who once owned the harbor in which Miss Liberty stands and all of the

land her children now occupy." Just as second-wave feminists were most strin-
gently criticizing the primacy accorded childbearing and childrearing in women's
lives—indeed, only two years before they helped push the Supreme Court to recognize a constitutional right to abortion—Gregory conflated feminism with
motherhood.

Gregory tried to resolve the contradictions in his stance by elevating motherhood—reversing Western hierarchical gender relations and claiming sexual difference as a sign of female superiority. Flying in the face of contemporaneous feminist
politics, he devoted an entire chapter of *Natural Diet* to the dietary practices of the
conflated entity "Women and Mothers":

> In his marvelous little booklet, *Your Vegetarian Baby*, Dr. Pietro Rotondi reminds:
> "Women and Mothers of today have the power to save mankind from further trou-
> ble, future wars, pestilence and disease, and to redeem man to his rightful place on
> earth, especially in relation to his Maker. The Mother-to-be should at all times re-
> member her high calling fearlessly, and with great joy await her time of fulfillment."
> (127)

Rotondi's (and Gregory's) advice could easily be attributed to nineteenth-century
"separate sphere" advocates such as Catharine Beecher. Women, according to
Beecher and her cohorts, did not need political rights such as suffrage because they
were better suited to exercise moral suasion over men via their maternal instincts.[20] His tribute to the Women's Liberation movement notwithstanding, Gregory propagates many aspects of this ideology. Yet, throughout his writings, it is also
clear that the maternal body poses a threat for him: it undermines his efforts to purify his own body of filth.

Like Elijah Muhammad, Gregory literalizes the equation of African American
women with dirt. He jokes in "My Answer to Genocide," for example: "Some of
the Southern white folks used to bad-mouth me for having so many kids. Governor Wallace even accused me of trying to grow my own race" (66–67). In *Natural
Diet* the comedian-activist is even more explicit in drawing the analogy between
woman and "soil." After advising his female readers to "vow to try to be a reflection of the Supreme Mother of all—Mother Nature," Gregory continues: "In the
order of nature, it is extremely important to plant seeds in the proper season.
The conditions of the soil and the climate for growth will determine the quality
of the crop. Seeds planted 'out of time' yield an undesirable harvest" (128). Unlike
Elijah Muhammad, Gregory is at least addressing women directly, but his pronouncements are still reminiscent of *Message to the Blackman in America*: "We love
a crop that we can produce every year, every season, so well that we will kill every
enemy that we find seeking to destroy it. . . . Is not your woman more valuable
than that crop of corn, that crop of cotton, that crop of cabbage, potatoes, beans,
tomatoes?" (58).

Then again, in Gregory's schema, "soil"—if pure and natural—is a privileged
term and would not necessarily pose a threat of bodily pollution. His anxiety
about the maternal body is thus perhaps more readily apparent in his comments
about nursing mothers and milk. Gregory shares Muhammad's disapprobation for
women who do not breast-feed their infants. "Few human mothers," he says,

"would consent to nurse a calf, but they let the cow nurse their own babies" (*Natural* 61–62). To explain his disdain for bottle-feeding, he further claims that cow's milk contains too much casein for human infants and is therefore harmful: "Cow's milk is designed to double the weight of the calf in a period of six to eight weeks. A human baby requires six to seven *months* to double its weight. It is little wonder that so many babies fed on cow's milk have an excess of mucus, as in running noses, congested chests, etc." (*Natural* 62). But what is intriguing is that mucus—including, significantly, that generated by human milk—turns out to be a form not simply of fetal endangerment, but more specifically of *male* fetal endangerment:

> For some strange reason, girl babies are better able to survive the abundance of mucus in the mother's system than boy babies. But Nature's way seems to be that more boy babies are born than girl babies. It has been said that Nature's ratio is three to one. Yet the female population of the United States is larger than the male population. The reason is that more boy babies die at birth or shortly thereafter than girl babies, because they are unable to survive the mucus in the mother's system. (*Political* 260)

Gregory is not concerned simply that milk-fed infants develop too much mucus in their systems. Rather, the maternal body—and, by extension for him, the female body—is itself defined by its ability to generate and "survive the mucus." This body becomes in Gregory's mind an a priori threat to the survival of any male fetus that it carries.

One way Gregory responded to this threat was by a renewed emphasis on the male role in reproduction. Rather than insisting only that his wife Lillian change her eating habits, he also claimed that paternal dietary practices could have an impact on the health of the offspring. "The child should first be conceived in the minds of the mother and father and the proper climate should be established in the home," Gregory opined (*Natural* 128). "The condition of the bodies of the parents is very important to the growth and development of the new life they are planning to bring into the world, just as the condition of the soil determines the growth of the seedling" (*Natural* 128). Following this logic, Ayanna, whose name means "beautiful flower," is "the child closest to Mother Nature from birth, having been conceived and born during the most advanced period of her parents' nutritional awareness and appreciation of the natural way of life. As a true child of Mother Nature, she shares kinship with a beautiful flower" (*Natural* 25).

In keeping with his determination to create children whose bodies were uncontaminated by parental dietary impurities, Gregory appropriated for himself the authority to regulate not just the bodily functions of himself and Lillian, but also of his offspring, this being a typically devalued responsibility traditionally delegated to mothers and servants. "I am often asked if I get a lot of family resistance when I make a dietary change in the household," he muses in *Natural Diet* (26), thus extending the domain of black patriarchy into the kitchen. "Over the years," he continues, "I have developed a system for making those changes which seems to work very well" (26). Control over his family's gastronomic practices seems to have functioned as a way for Gregory to purge himself, psychically, of the impurities of his own childhood diet. After all, he could not *not* have eaten what he grew up eating; he could not control what his mother ate before and during her pregnancy with him. What he could control—in theory if not in practice—was the food intake of his own family.

"Pregnant with Hunger"

That the adult Gregory's dietary and reproductive fixations were related to his memories of childhood hunger is amply illustrated in his first autobiography. Many of the events he records therein are associated with food. When describing a particularly happy Christmas from his youth, for example, Gregory recollects: "Did we eat that night! It seemed like all the days we went without food, no bread for the baloney and no baloney for the bread, all the times in the summer when there was no sugar for the Kool-Aid and no lemon for the lemonade and no ice at all were wiped away" (*Nigger* 5). Yet, for the most part, Gregory also perceives his early diet as unhealthful. In a brief introductory epigraph to *Nigger*, he describes himself as a "welfare case":

> You've seen him on every street corner in America. You knew he had rhythm by the way he snapped his cloth while he shined your shoes. Happy little black boy, the way he grinned and picked your quarter out of the air. Then he ran off and bought himself a Twinkie Cupcake, a bottle of Pepsi-Cola, and a pocketful of caramels.
> You didn't know that was his dinner. And you never followed him home. (n. pag.)

In this anecdote, Gregory associates the poverty of his childhood with what he would later view as an impure, pollution-laden diet. And no matter how much the adult Gregory fasted, no matter how many colonic irrigations he underwent, he seems unable to satisfy himself that he has cleansed his body of the foods he ate as a child.

What most intrigues and concerns me here is that while Gregory is clearly aware of the overdetermined relationship between his race and his childhood poverty, he attributes responsibility for his malnourishment not to white racism but instead to his own mother. In the course of discussing his early resistance to the teachings of Alvenia Fulton, for instance, he writes: "Out of ignorance, I argued, rationalized and repeated all the wrong notions about food I had been taught" (*Natural* 4). His reason is that he "just couldn't believe my momma would have fed me meat if it was wrong, or given me cow's milk if it was wrong. And here was a stranger, a woman I had just met, telling me that my own momma had fed me wrong!" (*Natural* 4–5). Subsequently, Gregory allows that his "momma never had the benefit of learning the Truth about proper diet, and as a result she suffered many of the physical results of improper eating habits" (*Natural* 5). But the insinuation that she is somehow to blame still lingers in the reader's mind.

More tellingly, even as Gregory implies that his early health problems stemmed from his mother's lack of familiarity with proper "eating habits," he also interprets his own childhood cravings using the metaphor of pregnancy. Teachers, he says, thought he was "stupid":

Couldn't spell, couldn't read, couldn't do arithmetic. Just stupid. Teachers were never interested in finding out that you couldn't concentrate because you were so hungry, because you hadn't had any breakfast. All you could think about was noontime, would it ever come? Maybe you could sneak into the cloakroom and steal a bite of some kid's lunch out of a coat pocket. A bite of something. Paste. You can't really make a meal of paste, or put it on bread for a sandwich, but sometimes I'd scoop a few spoonfuls out of the paste jar in the back of the room. Pregnant people get strange tastes. I was pregnant with poverty. Pregnant with dirt and pregnant with smells that made people turn away, pregnant with cold and pregnant with shoes that were never bought for me, pregnant with five other people in my bed and no Daddy in the next room, and pregnant with hunger. Paste doesn't taste too bad when you're hungry. (*Nigger* 30)

Gregory represents himself as "pregnant" (using the gender-obscuring misnomer "pregnant people") precisely to demonstrate that he was incapable of exercising control over his cravings. The gravid body in this scenario is both needy and demanding. Its desires are not to be trusted. For all of Gregory's subsequent valorization of "motherhood," pregnancy seems clearly to function in his subconscious as a metaphor linking black female "dominance" in the home with poverty and, therefore, with bodily pollution as well.

In fact, Gregory quite explicitly associates his "pregnant" desires with fatherlessness. He was pregnant with "no Daddy in the next room." His recollections of hunger are, however, not just about his desire for a father but rather for the Law of the Black Father, for patriarchy and (what he perceives as) patriarchal order. In his putatively matriarchal household, Gregory recollects, "There never was any mealtime. . . . If you were there, you ate. Grab a hot dog, a piece of baloney, bread, and run out again" (*Nigger* 42). To explain what he was missing, he then recounts one brief period when he took part in a traditional patriarchal family. Gregory had been wont to wait outside when his friend Robert was called in from their play to dinner. "It's a funny feeling to be by yourself on a back porch and hear people eating, people talking," he observes (*Nigger* 42). "There's no talk in the world like the warm, happy talk of a family at the dinner table. I'd peep through the window and see my friend Robert in there, close by his Daddy. Then his Daddy'd get up and stick a toothpick in his mouth, pick up the paper, light a cigar, and walk around like he owned the world" (*Nigger* 42). One night Robert's father invites Gregory in for dinner, an offer he repeats several nights in a row. On these nights "Robert's little sister jumped up so quick to wash the dishes and bring me water that everybody teased her" (43). Gregory was pleased to feel part of the family and to have found, moreover, a potential surrogate father. "Bet he wouldn't have minded it too much if I was his son, too" (43), he recollects thinking at the time.

But Gregory acknowledges that he soon became "ashamed of how dirty I was, dirty from the top of my head to the bottom of my feet" (43). After encountering Robert's father on the streetcar one day, he decides he wants to impress his new family and "go clean" to dinner at Robert's house: "Then I ran home and took a bath. I had polished my tennis sneakers and put them up on the roof so they wouldn't stink so bad. . . . I wanted to sit at that table as clean as they were" (43). Yet, despite his best efforts, the evening goes poorly. Robert's mother invites Gregory in that night only after being instructed to do so by Robert's father, and his friend's parents quarrel during dinner. Later, while helping to clean up, Gregory accidently drops and breaks a dish. Trying to redeem himself, he goes outside to help Robert's father sharpen a lawn-mower blade. Then, he recalls, "I heard it"— "it" being a conversation between Robert and his mother: "Robert, I'm sick of that Gregory boy in here eating every night. Doesn't even say thanks any more. Ain't he got no mother and father?" (44). Gregory starts to cry before fleeing: "And I run and I run and I run. . . . Why'd she have to go say that? Ain't he got no mother and father?" (44). As if to be certain that the reader not misconstrue the meaning of his loss, he opens the next chapter with the comment: "There were other fathers along the way, men who reached out and gave me their hands" (45).

Just as his own mother was unable to provide him with a biological father, Gregory implies that Robert's mother is responsible for his loss of a surrogate. But for all this emphasis on his desire for a father figure, Gregory himself was largely absent from his own family. His social activism almost always took precedence. When he learned that Lillian was pregnant with their first child, he thought to himself "that as poor as the Gregory kids were, and as ornery and as rotten and as no-good as Big Pres was, at least we all had a name. Big Pres had given us that" (*Nigger* 116). Significantly, the "rotten" is associated in this memory not with maternity but rather with the ersatz patriarch, Big Pres, who by failing to uphold the Law of the Father clearly lost his right, in Gregory's mind, to feign possession of the phallus. (Robert's father, by contrast, had "walk[ed] around like he owned the world.") When Lillian had the temerity to refuse Gregory's offer of marriage, saying "she didn't want to do anything to stand in [his] way," the comic responded by invoking male authority: "This time I didn't ask her, I told her" (*Nigger* 116). Four days later, on 2 February 1959, they were married, and Gregory immediately sent his new wife to St. Louis to carry the pregnancy to term while he stayed in Chicago to work. Like her mother-in-law, Lucille, Lillian raised the Gregory children almost single-handedly. By his own account, Gregory's contribution to their upbringing consisted primarily of financial support and, in honor of his "rotten" father, "a name."

The story of childhood poverty that Gregory recounts in *Nigger* is not unfamiliar to readers of African American literature. Perhaps most noteworthy is the similarity it bears to Richard Wright's recollections of his upbringing in *Black Boy* (1945)—originally and more aptly titled *American Hunger*. To explain what it meant for him to grow up without a father, Wright recounts a conversation which ensued after he, then a young child, began badgering his mother for something to eat:

> "Who brings food into the house?" my mother asked me.
> "Papa," I said. "He always brought food."
> "Well, your father isn't here now," she said.
> "Where is he?"
> "I don't know," she said.
> "But I'm hungry," I whimpered, stomping my feet.
> "You'll have to wait until I get a job and buy food," she said.
> As the days slid past the image of my father became associated with my pangs of

hunger, and whenever I felt hunger I thought of him with a deep biological bitterness. (17)

In these early writings, both Wright and Gregory associate their childhood deprivations with the failure of their fathers to fulfill the role of financial provider. As it had for Gregory, "hunger" encodes for Wright both literal starvation and a desire for black patriarchal presence in the home. Their autobiographies could, as a result, easily be understood to lend credence to antifeminist propositions that the solution to poverty in black America is the bolstering of black male authority in the family, primarily by giving black men (rather than black women) access to better paying jobs.[21]

Yet Gregory, at least, was not utterly oblivious to the ramifications of this tendency to attribute black indigence to the supposed matriarchal structure of black families.[22] In *The Shadow That Scares Me*, for example, he offered an elaborate rebuttal to the Johnson Administration's willingness to blame black women rather than white racism for African American inequality:

> President Johnson, backed by the statistics and findings of the Moynihan Report, has said that a breakdown of the family is responsible for the plight of the Negro in America. He is absolutely correct. America is my momma. And my momma was America to me. Since the United States Constitution is the farthest thing from the Negro in America, it is the last thing to be blamed for his plight. State, city, and county governments are closer, but they are still distant. My momma, as head of the family, was the only authority my America allowed me to touch. When my momma stole food from white folks, and justified it as necessary for survival, I did not blame the system. . . . I blamed Momma. (77)

In this passage, Gregory critiques the combination of social and psychic forces through which the most disempowered of black women, including his own mother, come to bear the burden of blame not just for their own oppression, but for the oppression of all lower-class African Americans. These ruminations lead him to announce that he is "going to place the blame for injustice and wrong on the right momma" (*Shadow* 77). Rather than relinquishing the "mother" metaphor entirely, in other words, Gregory wants to alter its referent: to the state, as epitomized by "the Statue of Liberty" (*Shadow* 78). He spins out a fantasy scenario according to which he would "show her the 'tired, the poor, the huddled masses yearning to breathe free.' I want to show Momma what she has been doing to her children. And Momma should weep. For the grief of the ghetto is the grief of the entire American family" (*Shadow* 78).

Gregory's expressed goal here, to find ways of demanding more positive government responsibility for the lives of all Americans, is no less laudable today than it was in 1968. Unfortunately, however, the contempt shown recipients of public assistance since the 1960s—inaccurately exemplified by African American women —would indicate the formidable difficulties involved in mobilizing the traditionally right-wing discourse of the "family" in service of leftist political aims (Abramovitz 349–88).[23] Indeed, the practice of rescripting the state as a macrocosm of the family has historically been far more amenable to conservative than to progressive political priorities. Witness the fact that Gregory's deployment of the

"America is my momma" rhetoric not only perpetuates the assumption that care-giving is properly the responsibility of women rather than men, but it renders normative the heterosexual reproductive matrix.[24]

The Nutty Fruitarian

> But more important, I'm just gonna have to accept myself for who I am.
>
> Eddie Murphy, *The Nutty Professor*, 1996

Gregory's refusal to acknowledge the profoundly antifeminist and antihomosexual underpinnings of his obsession with mothering clearly warrants a strenuous critique. By taking up a stance which denied African American women the right to determine their own reproductive futures, by taking up a stance which literally conflated womanhood with motherhood, he was supporting African American women's continued social and economic subordination to African American men. Yet, given his expressed commitment to progressive political change, Gregory does at the very least provide a useful counterpoint to the men who are typically understood to comprise Black Power's nationalist cultural and political scene. Not surprisingly, as a result, contemporaneous commentators often betrayed ambivalence when discussing Gregory and his writings, and they frequently couched their articles in a slightly satirical tone, almost as though they feared that his dietary practices were a joke concocted at their expense. For instance, a brief, unsigned *New York Times* review of *Natural Diet* presented the book primarily as a source of humor, noting that "Gregory's discourse on the typical mistreatment of the digestive tract should be informative—it certainly is amusing" (*Dick*).[25]

As this clumsy assessment suggests, social observers were largely unsure how to interpret Gregory's progression from thriving stand-up comic to fasting political activist. One source of their agitation, though, is readily apparent: he was wreaking havoc on the era's fascination with a hyperbolically phallicized black masculinity. A 1972 *Chicago Tribune* interview with Gregory illustrates why. Author Clarence Petersen recounts in an only half-jesting tone his efforts to discern the effects of fasting on Gregory's physical stamina:

> "But without any nourishment," I said, "you must be losing something. There has to be some toll." I was groping, frantically. "Um, uh, what has it done to your . . . uh . . . your sex life?"
>
> "It increases it!" said Gregory. "That's very interesting. If men knew what fasting does for sex, they would sell more water in this country than whisky. If most people knew how it rejuvenates the glands and increases sex potency, we would have water *bars*, man, with cats sitting around drinking water by the gallon!" (Petersen's ellipses and emphasis)

In appropriating for his ninety-eight-pound self the valorized image of the virile black stud, Gregory warded off anxieties that his dietary regimen reflected his sexual orientation—i.e., that a man who *eats* fruit must himself *be* one. But in the process, he still managed to carnivalize America's foundational obsession with black male phallic potency. As Petersen subsequently observed, at the time he made this comment, the self-professed sex machine "looked like Sammy Davis Jr. doing an impression of the Shadow."

If comedian Eddie Murphy's highly successful 1996 remake of *The Nutty Professor* is any indication, Gregory's ability to caricature prevailing stereotypes of black masculinity is as relevant to the black cultural politics of the 1990s as it was to those of the early 1970s. In keeping with my efforts in the preceding chapter to draw some parallels between the two eras, I want to conclude, then, with a brief discussion of how both this film and the recent resurgence of interest in vegetarian soul food might be construed as recastings of black nationalism that perpetuate Gregory's legacy. The original 1963 version of the film starred Jerry Lewis as a socially inept chemistry professor who, obsessed with a woman student, concocts a potion that transforms him into the arrogant and suave Buddy Love. The 1996 version makes a significant alteration, casting Murphy as obese chemistry professor Sherman Klump; he pines for the petite Carla Purty (Jada Pinkett). Throughout the film, Murphy oscillates between the Klump and Love personas, gaining and losing several hundred pounds in a feat of high-tech wizardry which might be construed as a fast-forward retrospective of Dick Gregory's life.

At the time *The Nutty Professor* was released, it was widely noted that Murphy himself was responsible for the new story line, that he had agreed to star in the film "only if it took on society's unfairness toward fat people" (Friday). Yet, inasmuch as he had achieved celebrity status during the 1980s as a performer of notoriously misogynistic and homophobic comedy routines, the motivation behind his desire to take a stand on this issue left many people more than a little mystified.[26] Certainly the National Association to Advance Fat Acceptance (NAAFA) was by no means willing to take Murphy's intentions at face value: among other criticisms, the group claimed that the film perpetuated the stereotype that fat people are fat because they eat too much, rather than because of a biological predisposition (Verzemnieks). In the film, Klump is frequently shown bingeing on food in a fashion which does imply that if fat people were sufficiently motivated, they could indeed achieve "normal" size. At the same time, it is worth noting that the film ends with Klump choosing his kindly fat incarnation over that of the egotistical Love by announcing, "I'm just gonna have to accept myself for who I am."

Given my discussion in chapter 3 of the slippage between ontologizing discourses of gastronomic and libidinal desire, my interest in NAAFA's critique of *The Nutty Professor* should be readily apparent. At stake for its members is the social construction of obesity, whether fatness will be understood as a failure to exercise proper control over one's appetite or as a manifestation of who one immutably is. What I want to suggest, though, is that the film needed to keep this ambiguity operative because the transcoding between the epistemological domains of hunger and sexuality is fundamental to its narrative trajectory. Murphy portrays the updated "nutty professor" as a man caught between competing desires: for normative, public black heterosexuality, on the one hand, and for non-normative, closeted white orality, on the other. Since the prerequisite for the former is a muscular, hyperphallic body, the punishment for indulging in the latter is life as, in effect, a fat black fag.

Starting with the opening scene, in which Richard Simmons is shown on Klump's television screen encouraging his audience to "vogue" to the tune of the Village People's "Macho Man," *The Nutty Professor* invites us to draw on the metaphorics of homosexuality and the closet to interpret Klump's passion for food. Throughout the scene, the camera pans back and forth between the flaming white exercise queen and the obviously feminized body of the obese black man. Lest the viewer somehow miss the point, as the opening winds to a conclusion we are offered a close-up of the buttocks of each man. This scene is followed by a sequence in which Klump's lab hamsters, having escaped from their cages, are shown terrorizing the college campus. At one point the camera lingers on a billboard as one of the hamsters burrows through the buttocks of a white male BVD underwear model, thus reinforcing the association already made between whiteness and homosexuality. Upon arriving at his lab, Klump is informed by his nerdy white assistant Jason (John Ales) of what has transpired: the professor had inadvertently unlatched the hamster cages with his buttocks prior to leaving the preceding day. The film uses the obvious physical resemblance between Jason and Richard Simmons to code the former as a potential love interest for Klump.

This construction of the "nutty professor" as a closeted gay man is continued when, after dismissing a class of his students, he is shown stealthily retrieving a chocolate bar from a private stash in a hidden desk drawer. As the soundtrack swells with romantic music, Klump opens his mouth wide to eat (or fellate) the (simultaneously excrementalized and phallicized) bar just as Purty enters the room, disrupting his oral indiscretion. Caught in the homosexual act, as it were, Klump has little choice but to take up the normative male role in a standard heterosexual script: the scene finishes with Purty as the object of his desiring gaze. The film subsequently portrays Klump as vacillating between private homosexual longings and public heterosexual imperatives, with Jason being positioned as Purty's main rival for Klump's affections. Indeed, after learning that the heterosexually voracious Buddy Love is actually Klump's alter ego, Jason discourages the professor from drinking his own potion, fretting that Love's "testosterone levels are way too high."

The film's linkage of homosexuality with whiteness and of heterosexuality with blackness is complicated, however, by the scenes in which Klump shares dinner with his family. When alone and in the throes of same-sex desire, Klump binges in shame on commodified (and therefore, I would argue, presumptively "white") foods such as ice cream and M&Ms. His family, by contrast, savors heterosexualized cross-generational relationships along with collard greens, fried chicken, and other soul foods. This distinction between the two modes of oral gratification is significant because it helps to foreground an important subtext in *The Nutty Professor*'s portrayal of the source of Klump's homosexuality. Prodded by his family to eat, he loses his appetite and grows dejected. The viewer is invited to infer that Klump perceives the consumption of soul food to be incompatible with his pursuit of a relationship with Carla Purty. This interpretation is supported by a subsequent dream sequence in which Klump fantasizes himself as a marauding King Kong. Although the sexually available Purty is arrayed on a bed in a futile imitation of Fay Wray, the monstrous Klump chooses a leg of fried chicken instead, revealing a no-

ticeably delicate touch in the process. What this scene suggests is that, notwithstanding Klump's inability to come out of the closet with his family, his latent homosexuality is actually equated with a desire for soul food. If we bear in mind the
connections I have already established between soul food and "slave" maternity, it
seems clear that the film wants to insinuate that the source of Klump's attraction
to (white) men is the castrating love of his black mother.[27] Sherman, after all, is in
Carla's accounting "sweet," which is to say that she recognizes him first and foremost to be a black Mama's boy.

The roles of the obese Mama, Papa, Grandma, and Ernie Klump are played, of
course, by Eddie Murphy. This casting tactic gives him an excuse to don drag and
thus literalize the equation between black male homosexuality and black maternity.
Lest the viewer harbor any doubts as to the intended signification of Klump's fat,
after transforming himself into Buddy Love, the professor gloats that he no longer
needs to wear a brassiere: "No titties! No titties! No titties!" In this fashion, current
film technologies have enabled *The Nutty Professor* to create a visual analogue for
the long-standing cultural narrative according to which black men have been
emasculated by black mothers. When Klump's decision to kill off the uncoopera-
tive Love results in a literal battle of bulges—a battle which, of course, Love eventually loses—the film's investment in this narrative is hard to miss. The victory of
Klump's breasts, ass, and belly over Love's crotch implies that sooner or later the
truth of the maternal black male body will out, at the expense of virile black masculinity. In this respect, *The Nutty Professor*'s portrayal of Sherman Klump recuper-
ates the central feature of Eldridge Cleaver's homophobic attack on James Baldwin.
All Klump really wants, the film implies, is to have a baby by a white man.

This narrative line is developed primarily through the subplot requiring
Klump to court Harlan Hartley (James Coburn), the rich white man who is a potential "donor" to the school's science program, thus lending credence to Freud's
argument for the connection between anal-eroticism and money.[28] Their relationship is woven into the film's climactic ending, when Buddy Love plans to secure Hartley's money by staging an elaborate "murder" of Klump at the college
banquet. Just in time, however, the ever-faithful Jason escapes from the laboratory closet in which Love has, aptly enough, locked him. Rushing up the aisle to
the stage where Love is preparing to drink the fatal dose of potion, Jason yells, "I
cannot let you do this anymore. This has got to stop." The question of just whom
Jason is "outing" turns out to be vexed, though, for during the subsequent struggle
between Klump and Love for control over Klump's body, Klump refers derisively
to Love as "Tinkerbell."

The implication that Buddy Love rather than Sherman Klump is actually the
closeted homosexual is, of course, anticipated by the film in numerous ways—the
former's name being only the most obvious. One thinks, in addition, of the scenes
when Love dons "spandex" in order to indulge in narcissistic spectatorial pleasure.
In other words, he ogles himself in the mirror. Though Love is finally allowed to
reappropriate aerobics for heterosexual black masculinity, the status of his sexuality is still destabilized because of the film's earlier treatment of Richard Simmons
and the homoerotic iconography of the muscular BVD model. It comes as no surprise, then, when the gay subplot pairing Klump with Jason is thwarted in the end

by Purty, who informs the professor that she lacks a date and invites him to dance. Despite having conveniently come to the banquet equipped with a large-size tuxedo for Klump, Jason is exiled from the dance floor so that *The Nutty Professor* can end, unconvincingly, with intraracial heterosexual closure. The film's "real" fag, we are asked to believe, has been banished after all, in the body of the testosterone-driven Buddy Love. Nonetheless, Klump's vow to accept himself for who he is still leaves open the possibility that he and Jason might eventually get together after all—if only they can escape the heterosexualizing pressures of black women such as Carla Purty. In this fashion, African American women are doubly scapegoated for Sherman's predicament. Emasculated by one, he is denied the opportunity to act on his homosexuality by another.

This reading of *The Nutty Professor* as a contradictory parable about black gay male self-acceptance will take on added meaning for readers familiar with events that transpired in May 1997, almost a year after the film was released. Eddie Murphy was himself caught with a transvestite whom he had picked up in an area of Santa Monica "known for its homosexual prostitute trade" (police sargeant Robert Harms, quoted in K. Smith 94).[29] Not surprisingly, his attempts at damage control centered around an affirmation of his heterosexuality. Murphy insisted in an interview with *People* reporter Kyle Smith that he had perceived Atisone Seiuli to be a woman, and he asserted in typically homophobic language: "I know I'm a man. I'm a man. . . . I'm not a degenerate either" (quoted in K. Smith 96). Curiously, though, Murphy also admitted during this same interview that subsequent to the encounter with Seiuli, he had indulged in a ritual act of purification: "I'm obsessive-compulsive with cleanliness. . . . After I got home, I wiped off the door handle and the stuff that person had touched" (quoted in K. Smith 94). In his final speech Sherman had allowed that "Buddy's who I thought the whole world wanted me to be. He's who I thought I wanted to be." Notwithstanding Murphy's later disavowal of homosexuality, one is tempted to interpret this speech autobiographically as an implicit admission of Murphy's desire to confront the sources of his own obsessive hostility toward gay men.

Even though Murphy has thus far refused to follow through on the queer-friendly possibilities he himself was opening up, one might still explain the success of *The Nutty Professor* by speculating that the 1990s' fixation on militant black masculinity generated a psychic need for precisely such parodic recastings of black male bodies and black male sexuality. The grotesque trope of the expanding and contracting black man—incarnated literally by Gregory and cinematically by Murphy—should perhaps be construed as a function of the prevalence of black nationalist discourses during a given historical era. From this perspective, we can also understand the logic of basketball star Dennis Rodman's rise to fame during the mid-1990s as well. He both inhabited and strategically exploited a cultural moment in which black masculinist posturing had itself become a kind of camp. Rodman's dyed hair, makeup, and frequent public appearances in drag surely mocked, moreover, the homoerotic longings that have historically underwritten (white) male spectatorial investments in the bodies of black male athletes.

Not surprisingly, the 1990s have witnessed a concomitant renewal of interest in vegetarianism and/or fruitarianism as an always potentially carnivalesque discourse

FIGURE 5.2 Keith Jenkins, Vegetarian Chefs and Restaurant Owners. © 1994 *The Washington Post*. Photograph of newspaper visual by
the University of Iowa Audiovisual Center Photo Service.

of black sexuality. Most memorably, in 1994 the *Washington Post* published an article by Carole Sugarman on African American vegetarian restaurants and health
food stores in the Washington, D.C., area. In a photograph accompanying the article, restaurant owner Yokemi Ali is shown in (what might be construed as) a
pregnant crouch, balancing a watermelon carefully on his thigh (figure 5–2).
Kneeling beside and slightly above him, cafe manager El Rahm Ben Israel cradles
an armful of sugarcane stalks, which appear to protrude from between his legs as a
gigantic phallus; their tips point vertically in the air, well above the heads of Ben
Israel and Ali. Given the apparent implications of such culinary iconography, the
article's title, "Fruitful and Multiplying," is quite apt. Further ironizing the deployment of this procreative metaphor, all of the restaurant or store owners pictured
and profiled are men. The article enacts a fantasy of erasing African American
women from their putatively solitary positioning in the scene of black reproduction. In their stead, African American men are inscribed as both father and
mother, phallus and womb.

   Though Sugarman herself never refers to Gregory as a catalyst for the revival
of African American interest in natural foods, she notes that one of the article's
subjects, market and cafe owner Aris La Tham, was "influenced by the teachings
of Dick Gregory" in deciding to embrace a largely fruitarian diet (E11).[30] Yet, as
Sugarman also mentions, when La Tham was growing up in Panama, "it was his

grandmother who supervised all the cooking, who molded his culinary curiosity and affinity for fresh fruits and vegetables" (E11).[31] Once again, the fantasy of a world in which black masculinity can be rid of black female influence and control is haunted by the specter of the ever-present black (grand)mother in the kitchen. Necessary to affirm black male heterosexual potency, but consequently an obstacle to the fulfillment of black male homosocial desire, this black woman can be neither embraced nor entirely disavowed.

Let me conclude, though, by stressing that my critique of Gregory's participation in the abjection of black femininity has not been intended as a dismissal of his entire sociopolitical agenda. The psychoanalytic reading I have developed aims primarily to further my overarching claims about the centrality of the connection between African American women and food for U.S. culture. It has not by any means been intended as a comprehensive assessment of Gregory's contributions to twentieth-century U.S. social and political history. Such an assessment would need to understand Gregory as a person of great complexity, someone whose political passions have been enabled but also dramatically circumscribed by his private obsessions, someone whose often admirable stances against the hypocrisies of the U.S. government have been compromised by heterosexism and other lapses. To insist that Gregory be held responsible for his personal and political limitations does not, however, render meaningless his efforts to foster social change, nor does it justify the relative inattention to his legacy. Though the "shadow" Gregory casts over late twentieth-century U.S. history may indeed be parodically thin, it emanates from a man who has carried not-insubstantial social, cultural, and political weight.

PART III

BLACK
FEMALE
HUNGER

six

"My Kitchen Was the World"

Vertamae Smart Grosvenor's Geechee Diaspora

The question I was most often asked was why didn't I consider myself a "soul food" writer. Over and over I would try to explain my philosophy on the nonracial aspects of blackeyed peas, watermelon, and other so-called soul foods on TV, radio, and in lectures. It seemed to me while certain foods have been labeled "soul food" and associated with Afro-Americans, Afro-Americans could be associated with all foods.

I would explain that my kitchen was the world.

> Vertamae Smart-Grosvenor, introduction to
> the second edition of *Vibration Cooking*, 1986

In her critically acclaimed 1991 film *Daughters of the Dust*, Julie Dash explores the lives of Gullah peoples on the Sea Islands off the coast of South Carolina and Georgia. Brought from Africa to the United States as slaves, they cultivated indigo and later cotton while creating "a distinct, original African-American cultural form" because of their relative isolation from outside influences (Creel 69). Dash's film focuses on a single day in 1902, when members of the Peazant family are planning to leave their home on Ibo Landing to begin a new life on the mainland. Family "matriarch" Nana Peazant cannot understand why her relations would want to abandon the land and the cultural traditions which, in her opinion, constitute their rightful heritage. Throughout the day, many of the Peazant women are shown engaging in one of those traditions, the preparation of food for a feast the family will share before taking leave. Images of fresh okra, shrimp, rice, and other island delicacies contribute to the film's somewhat nostalgic portrayal of Ibo Landing as a site of authentic pleasure outside the realm of commodity capitalism. The women's labor is presented not as alienating or oppressive but rather as a natural accompaniment to their socializing.[1]

At the center of these culinary rituals is the "hair braider," a character portrayed, fittingly, by South Carolina native and "Geechee" popularizer Vertamae Smart Grosvenor. A longtime commentator on National Public Radio (NPR) and host in the mid-1990s of the Public Broadcasting Service (PBS) series *The Ameri-*

cas' Family Kitchen, Grosvenor was one among at least two dozen African Americans who published nationally distributed cookbooks during soul food's peak years from 1968 to 1971.[2] But in her underground classic *Vibration Cooking, or the Travel Notes of a Geechee Girl* (1970), Grosvenor distanced herself from the term "soul" while proselytizing for many of the foods associated with it. The dishes she included in her cookbook ranged from the standard chitterlings, watermelon rind preserves, and hoppin' john to by no means typically soul fare such as feijodas, Irish potato soup, salade niçoise, and stewed Jerusalem artichokes. On a generic level, moreover, *Vibration Cooking* is memorable as a hybrid of cookbook, autobiography, and travelogue similar to *The Alice B. Toklas Cook Book* (1954)—which, Grosvenor acknowledged in a 1971 *Ebony* interview, she used as a model for her own writing (Garland 90). Recipe gives rise to anecdote, and anecdote to recipe. Both are integral to the text. *Vibration Cooking* thus stands out from many contemporaneous African American cookbooks in its attempt to disrupt normative categories of racial identity and textual genre alike. Indeed, the book's generic plasticity might be viewed as an analogue to Grosvenor's formulation of what I will call a protodiasporic model of black American culture.[3]

Since the publication of Paul Gilroy's *The Black Atlantic* in 1993, scholars of race have been giving renewed attention to the ramifications of black migration for our understanding of how the nation-state has developed in tandem with ideologies of racial difference. Working to critique the exclusionary logic that renders whiteness the normative condition of Western citizenship, Gilroy formulates an alternative theorization of black modernity as a phenomenon of transatlantic, cross-cultural exchange. Movement and music operate as privileged terms in *The Black Atlantic*, the latter providing for Gilroy perhaps the exemplary manifestation of the former. Whereas traditional conceptions of the black diaspora are preoccupied with movement from east to west, primarily from Africa to Europe and the Americas, Gilroy's understanding of the term offers up a more complicated dynamic in which black Americans and Europeans talk back, as it were, to Africa. He explores, for instance, the influence of black American musical styles on black British and African cultures.

This chapter will work from Gilroy's model in order to reframe my exploration of African American culinary debates during the post–World War II era. Taking Vertamae Grosvenor as my focal point, this time I want to interrogate more carefully the often vexed relationship between black women and soul food. Having presented her first cookbook as a "travel" narrative and having hosted a television series devoted to "Afro-Atlantic" cookery, Grosvenor provides an especially apt opportunity to consider the ramifications for feminist work on racial identities of a critical theory that celebrates motion over stasis and syncretism over cultural isolation. At issue will be the interplay between Grosvenor's attempt to lay the groundwork for a nonessentializing study of African American culinary history and her personal mutability—her somewhat ambiguous positioning between poverty and affluence, between black nationalism and white feminism, even between the historically isolated Sea Islands and the small town of Fairfax, South Carolina, located at least forty-five miles inland, where she was born.

Grosvenor might be understood to have embraced a diasporic aesthetic not only to subvert the equation of African American culinary traditions with southern black poverty, but also to undermine stereotypical representations of African American women as domineering mammies and emasculating matriarchs. Yet the seeming paradox is that in the process of critiquing soul's positioning of black women as paradigmatic threats to the boundaries of the self, Grosvenor represents herself as the abject. What I will speculate is that this paradox is actually foundational to the discourses of diasporic black identity. And to the extent that the cultural logic of (maternal) abjection does continue to underwrite even progressive conceptualizations of the diaspora, African American women such as Grosvenor will indeed find it necessary to engage in a series of complex negotiations of position to find a psychically and politically liberatory "home" in a theory of black homelessness.

"The Truth Will Out"

> White folks be talkin' about classic and they mean Beethoven (he was supposed to be a brother, anyhow) and French cooking. Classic to me is James Brown and soul food.
>
> Verta Mae, *Vibration Cooking*, 1970

Born Verta Mae Smart in 1939, Grosvenor actually grew up not in South Carolina but rather in North Philadelphia, where her paternal grandmother Estella Smart had migrated after being widowed (*Vibration* 11). Though by no means as poor as the young Dick Gregory, she claims that her working-class parents were "behind in the rent (most of the time)" (*Vibration* 30). Referring to herself as "one of those 'key' children" (31), Grosvenor says that she would often amuse herself while alone after school by putting on plays: "I was actor, director and audience all in one" (*Vibration* 30). As she matured from a frail, prematurely born infant into a robust and precocious adolescent, Grosvenor feared that she would never be able to fulfill the first and foremost expectation of her gender: "I knew that I was destined never to marry. What man would want a six-foot-tall woman?" (*Vibration* 54). Accordingly, after finishing high school she decided to travel to Paris to become a "bohemian" and pursue her love of the theatre. While there she became acquainted with Robert Strawbridge Grosvenor, a white sculptor-to-be from a prominent and wealthy U.S. family. They were married and eventually settled in New York City. By the time the marriage ended around 1964, Grosvenor had given birth to two daughters, Kali and Chandra.[4] Shortly after *Vibration Cooking* was published, she was married again, this time to African American artist Ellsworth Ausby (Garland 94).

During the late 1960s, Grosvenor—who has published works as "Verta Mae," "Verta Grosvenor," "Vertamae Grosvenor," "Vertamae Smart Grosvenor," and "Vertamae Smart-Grosvenor"—worked at a variety of jobs while trying to succeed as an actress.[5] She was a cook known as "Obedella" at Pee Wee's Slave Trade Kitchen (*Vibration* 89); she was "a clothing designer and seamstress, creating bizarre six-legged and four-armed outfits for advertising photographers" (Garland

88); and she was a "'space chantress' and 'cosmic force'" with the musician Sun Ra and his Intergalactic Solar Myth Science Arkestra (Garland 88). The only occupation she always avoided was domestic labor, which not coincidentally was also the occupation of her mother. After having worked briefly in that capacity for one of her high school teachers, a job that ended when her "father found out" (Grosvenor, *Thursdays* 9), Grosvenor was determined to steer clear of the main employment opportunity traditionally open to African American women. Though her largely unfulfilled theatrical aspirations had already made her known among many avant-garde musicians, artists, actors, and writers in New York and abroad, she did not achieve wider notice until after *Vibration Cooking* appeared.

The catalyst for its publication was her elder daughter, Kali, herself a precocious writer. After seeing Kali's poetry displayed in their apartment, one of Grosvenor's friends asked to show it to his agent at Doubleday. The result, *Poems by Kali* (1970), was published when its author was only eight years old.[6] Meanwhile, Grosvenor had been doing some writing of her own:

> While reading the Alice B. Toklas Cookbook, I'd been impressed with the way she had captured the feeling of her times in Paris during the 20s and people she had known, of Gertrude Stein, the salon and Picasso. So I thought I'd do a little cookbook for the people *I* knew in Paris, New York, and even back home in South Carolina and Philadelphia. Maybe I'd have a couple hundred copies printed up myself and give them to my friends so we could remember the experiences we'd shared. I'd tell them about the food, but I'd also tell them about what went down. But the people who were doing Kali's book seemed to think it could sell and that's the way it all happened. (quoted in Garland 90)

Part autobiography, part travelogue, part culinary anthropology, part social history, part political commentary, *Vibration Cooking* undertook the paradoxical task of attempting to carnivalize the generic conventions of the standard cookbook even as it emulated Toklas's famous text. Whereas Fanny Farmer's *Boston Cooking-School Cook Book* had been organized under rubrics such as "Cereals," "Eggs," "Soups," "Soups with Meat Stock," "Soups with Fish Stock," and "Soups without Stock," Toklas offered up "Murder in the Kitchen," "Food to Which Aunt Pauline and Lady Godiva Led Us," and "Food in the Bugey during the Occupation." The stakes were thus high for Grosvenor, but she clearly held her own: *Vibration Cooking* is comprised of a memorable series of set pieces, including "The Demystification of Food," "Birth, Hunting and Gator Tails," "The Smarts, the Ritters and Chief Kuku Koukoui," "First Cousins and the Numbers," "Forty Acres and a Jeep," "Taxis and Poor Man's Mace," "White Folks and Fried Chicken," and so on.

Albeit somewhat derivative of Toklas's, Grosvenor's approach to writing a cookbook was, in other words, still idiosyncratic. As a result, *Vibration Cooking* developed a strong word-of-mouth following, and its author's career quickly began to flourish. Her brief essay "The Kitchen Crisis" was included in *Amistad 1* (1970), a collection of "Writings on Black History and Culture" by a group of prominent (and otherwise all-male) black intellectuals and artists; a lengthy article about her was featured in *Ebony* magazine (Garland); she appeared on television with, among others, the Galloping Gourmet, Barbara Walters, and Dick Cavett (*Vibra-*

tion 1992 ed., xv); and she published a second book, this one a stinging indictment of the exploitation of African American women as domestic servants, called *Thursdays and Every Other Sunday Off* (1972). By the mid-1970s, however, when "blackness" had become a somewhat less valuable commodity in the late-capitalist marketplace, *Vibration Cooking* had gone out of print. The late 1970s and early 1980s witnessed an explosion of attention to African American women writers such as Toni Morrison, Ntozake Shange, and Alice Walker. Perhaps not coincidentally, Ballantine issued a revised and expanded edition of *Vibration Cooking* in 1986, and Marian Burros profiled Grosvenor in the *New York Times* in 1988. By then she had established a career as a commentator with NPR and was involved in the filming of *Daughters of the Dust*. The year after Dash's film was released, Ballantine brought out the third edition of the now-legendary cookbook, this time under its "Many Cultures, One World" imprint. "There is," as Grosvenor acknowledged in the introductions to both the 1986 and the 1992 editions, "nothing like having a book published to change your life" (xiii; xiv). In her case, at least, she was right.

Of course, there is also nothing like having a book republished to tempt one to change the story of one's life. In the 1986 edition, for instance, Grosvenor disavowed the influence of Toklas on her initial conceptualization of *Vibration Cooking*, asserting in the new introduction: "The only thing I have in common with Alice B. Toklas is that we lived on the same street in Paris" (xv). She repeated this disclaimer in the 1992 edition as well (xvi).[7] As the epigraph to the opening of this chapter illustrates, moreover, by 1986 Grosvenor was also maintaining that at the time she first published *Vibration Cooking* she did not "consider" herself to have been "a 'soul food' writer." Although her attitude toward soul food was clearly far more complicated than was that of many of her peers, Grosvenor's writings from the early 1970s reveal her to have been rather less equivocal in her estimation of the term than she has later wanted to allow. Indeed, the last sentence of "The Kitchen Crisis" was the thoroughly unambiguous pronouncement "Long live Soul Food" (300).

One important motivation underwriting her embrace of soul food is not hard to understand. As Rafia Zafar has concisely argued, "people may proclaim a love for a particular kind of food *because* a preference for such marks one as a member of a particular group" ("Proof" 144). To celebrate soul food in 1970 was to proclaim oneself black, proud, and opposed to a white-dominated social order. *Vibration Cooking* included, accordingly, a copy of a letter Grosvenor wrote to the editor of *Time* magazine in response to "Eating Like Soul Brothers," the 1969 article in which chitterlings were labeled the "stone soul" food. Angry that the unnamed author had labeled soul food "tasteless" (*Vibration* 175), she informs the editors of *Time* that their "taste buds are so racist that they can't even deal with black food" (175). After indicting white culture as nothing more than an amalgam of "short-lived fads" (175), Grosvenor then proceeds to mount a defense of soul food, announcing that she will remain loyal to the cuisine that nourished her "ancestors through four hundred years of oppression" (175):

> Collard greens are thousands of years old and in the days of the Roman Empire were considered an epicurean delight. French restaurants too widely renowned even to de-

pend on stars given by Guide Michelin serve chitlins sausages, only they call it *andouillette*. Soul food is more than chitlins and collard greens, ham hocks and black-eyed peas. Soul food is about a people who have a lot of heart and soul. (175)

Grosvenor's desire to defend soul food clearly stemmed, at least in part, from her disdain for the same white radical chic set that Tom Wolfe was simultaneously skewering.

Like many of her peers, Grosvenor understood white patronage of soul food to be part of an ongoing set of practices whereby a sterile, artificial white culture renewed itself through parasitic dependance on black cultural innovation: "White folks always discovering something . . . after we give it up. By the time they got to the bugaloo, we were doing the 'tighten up.' By the time they got to pigs' feet, black people were giving up swine" (Grosvenor's ellipsis; *Vibration* 41). Yet her letter is geared less toward critiquing radical chic's reductive equation of soul food with "chitlins and collard greens, ham hocks and black-eyed peas" than toward exposing the racist disparities in how identical foods are treated cross-culturally. By reminding the editors that *andouillette* is considered a delicacy in France, she demonstrates how our valuations of food are a function of our cultural preconceptions. Grosvenor's treatment of the late 1960s' popularity of soul food needs to be understood, then, in conjunction with her more encompassing critique of how racial boundaries are used by members of the dominant classes to consolidate and perpetuate their power. She foregrounds the hypocrisy of a system which constructs racial boundaries so as to ensure that the dominant group will have power to determine the circumstances under which those boundaries will be crossed, as inevitably they are. Hence her closing directive to the editors of *Time*: "Ask Doctor Christiaan Barnard about them black hearts" (175).[8]

Grosvenor also demonstrated a conflicted willingness to capitalize on white fascination with black dietary practices, even while censuring its racist underpinnings, in a September 1970 article titled "Soul Food." Published in *McCalls* magazine and clearly intended for a white female audience, the article manifests a didactic tone similar to that of her letter to *Time*. She begins by observing that "[e]verybody talking about what soul food is; fore we even get into that lets talk about what it aint" (72):

> Soul food aint frozen collard greens.
> Soul food aint fresh turnip greens and smoked pigs tails cooked together for three hours. Thats tasteless.
> Soul food aint when you are white and you invite the token negro from your job to guest for dinner on thursday (black maid's night out) and when he arrives you serve portuguese sardines on crackers, south african rock lobster tails, greek wine, and california grapes. Thats bad taste. (72)

Having not only dismissed most of what constituted the radical chic perception of soul food but having also ridiculed the discrepancy between the public posturing and the private lives of many white liberals, Grosvenor proceeds to enumerate example after example of what, in her view, soul food is: "Soul food is onions chopped up on collard greens" (72); "Soul food is plantain served with bacalao and ackee" (72); "Soul food is vanilla wafers" (72); "Soul food is farina de manioc"

(73). This expansive listing of foods to be associated with soul clearly operates as a strategy for disrupting racist stereotypes about black culture. Carefully distancing her understanding of soul food from popular interest in the "slave" diet, she relocates African American dietary practices in the context of the culinary history of peoples of color around the world.

At the same time, Grosvenor offers a series of (presumably) autobiographical accounts of food-related experiences that she claims are constitutive of soul food, for example, "Soul food is when you go hunting with your daddy and cousin haygood and you walking alongside your daddy, your nine years old to his thirty one, your four foot eight to his six foot three, and he tells you he dont care if you are a girl you got to learn how to hunt because the smarts are the best hunters in hampton county" (73). Grosvenor's discussion evolves from clear assertions as to which foods do and do not constitute soul, to seemingly personal reminiscences, to a final suggestion that anyone who is reading her article to find out what soul is obviously will never have it: "Soul food is an attitude and if your attitude is natural and imaginative and creative, soul food will be served at your table, whatever you cook. Soul food are found where the soul peoples is" (75). The grammatical reversal of "are" and "is" in the last sentence mirrors the polemical reversal of cause and effect. People do not become "soulful" by eating soul food; food becomes "soulful" when it is eaten by "soul peoples." As one of the article's pull-quotes reads, soul food "is a natural feeling—either you got it or you dont" (72).

What this means, obviously, is that while criticizing reductive portrayals of soul food and offering a protodiasporic model for how it should be understood, Grosvenor also propagates a good many of soul's stereotypical precepts. Even her definition of "vibration" is evocative of the way many of her contemporaries were defining soul. Thus, for example, in an introductory chapter to *Vibration Cooking* called "The Demystification of Food," she insists that when cooking she does not "measure or weigh anything. I cook by vibration. I can tell by the look and smell of it. Most of the ingredients in this book are approximate. Some of the recipes that people gave me list the amounts, but for my part, I just do it by vibration. Different strokes for different folks. Do your thing your way" (xiii). Notwithstanding her later disavowals, Grosvenor did participate in the soul food "fad," and notwithstanding her disdain for white people who are "always discovering something" after black people "give it up," she too was a latecomer to the commodified celebration of black dietary practices. Her cookbook appeared, after all, eight years after Baraka had first penned his own germinal essay on "Soul Food."

It should therefore come as no surprise that in the process of continuously embracing and distancing herself from the rubric of "soul" during the early 1970s, Grosvenor also tendered a variety of contradictory assertions about the relationship of black and white American culinary traditions to modern consumer capitalism. In *Thursdays and Every Other Sunday Off* she condemns in no uncertain terms the racist stereotype of Aunt Jemima (63–70). Yet, two years earlier in *Vibration Cooking* she had advised readers who want to make pancakes to "go and use Aunt Jemima and they always come out right" (17).[9] Similarly, in her letter to *Time* magazine, Grosvenor castigates Caucasians for using "Minute Rice and instant potatoes, instant cereals and drinking instant milk" and admonishes them to "stick to your instant culture" (*Vibration* 175). This indictment of white standardization is preceded, however, by an acknowledgment that she herself is a consumer of cake mixes: "You won't find any heavy baking recipes in this book cause I'm not a good baker. I have never lived in a place that had a decent oven" (*Vibration* 18). Consequently, Grosvenor continues, "I use cake mixes and doctor them up. That way if they don't work out I don't feel as bad as when I start from scratch" (*Vibration* 18).

Shortly thereafter she records a recipe for "Spongecake" from Mrs. Greenstein, "of late my mother's former employer" and one of the few white people listed as a source of recipes in *Vibration Cooking* (34). The recipe includes, among other ingredients, "1 box Duncan Hines Yellow Cake Mix" and "1 3-ounce box lemon-flavor Jell-O" (34). Since Grosvenor was a harsh critic of women such as Mrs. Greenstein—the "Miss Anns" who employ black women domestics—perhaps she presumes that the quality of this "instant" recipe speaks for itself. Such an interpretation is supported by the fact that Grosvenor also includes in *Vibration Cooking* a recipe for "Cracker Stew," which reads as follows: "Take a can of any kind of soup and add 1 box of any kind of frozen vegetables and then add 1 cup of Minute Rice. Heat and serve with toasted crackers on top" (77). "Cracker," as Grosvenor was well aware, is a common African American appellation for (poor southern) whites. One might thus surmise that her goal is not only to associate mass-produced, instant, and "unnatural" food with the dominant white culture but also to insinuate that whiteness itself is artificial, insipid, and bland. One can of soup is the same as the next; one "cracker" is indistinguishable from another.

If, as I argued in chapter 3, key ontologies of blackness have been thought to reside not in black bodies but rather in foods said to nourish those bodies, namely hog entrails and extremities, then it makes sense that Grosvenor would be locating key ontologies of whiteness in food as well, namely in the standardized culinary commodities of crackers and canned soup. Such an interpretation should remind us, however, also to be skeptical of her claim in the 1986 edition of *Vibration Cooking* that she devoted much time to explaining her "philosophy on the nonracial aspects" of soul food when the book first appeared.[10] In the 1970 essay "The Kitchen Crisis," Grosvenor had, in fact, offered precisely the opposite culinary philosophy, proclaiming with characteristic dramatic flair that "the truth will out. Yes! Food is colored. Peaches are Chinese. Watermelons are African. Mangos is Indian. Avocado is Mexican. Carrots are Arab. If you check it out, ain't too many things, food or people, REAL WHITE-AMERICANS" (299). She invokes "natural" foods (or, rather, foods less immediately associated with modern technologies than crackers and canned soup) to signify the "unreality" of whiteness as a racial designation which is equated with a lack of color. By "outing" peaches, watermelons, mangos, avocados, and carrots, Grosvenor foregrounds the quixotic impossibility of white America's pursuit of racial purity via the consumption of chemically "processed" foods.[11]

Outing, of course, is structurally connected to the practice of "passing" in that both rely on the ontologization of (what I take to be) socially constructed identities. As Amy Robinson has explained, passing generally operates in a triangulated social field: "Three participants—the passer, the dupe, and a representative of the in-group—enact a complex narrative scenario in which a successful pass is per-formed in the presence of a literate member of the in-group" (723). Alternatively, outing becomes meaningful when the member of the in-group successfully enlight-ens the dupe. In the Invisible Man's dream vision of outing Bledsoe, for example, it is significant that the setting is the "crowded lobby of Men's House." Not unlike the joke, as Freud has defined it, both passing and outing require the presence of a third party to reach completion (*Jokes* 171–93). In thinking about Grosvenor's motivations in claiming to tell the "truth" about culinary history even while re-peatedly contradicting herself, it seems worth paying attention not only to the question of whom she conceives of as members of the in-group and whom as dupes, but also to the possibility that she herself is the one engaged in a complex performance of passing.

The (Dis)Guises of a Geechee Girl

> I was sitting there minding my own business when I hear this cracker voice say, "Do you speak English?" and I said, "I sho do honey." "Well, why are you wearing those African clothes, you are a Negro." I said, "I am who I think I am." "I am free and free to define myself." "No you are not. You are a Negro. You are of American descent. I'm from Georgia and have spent all my life with Negroes and had a black mammy when I was a child." So I got mad and said, "So did I."
>
> Verta Mae, *Vibration Cooking*, 1970

Grosvenor's early references in *Vibration Cooking* to her desire to become an actress set the stage, as it were, for one of the book's recurrent themes: her penchant for the-atricality and self-dramatization. As Quandra Prettyman has succinctly put it: "One doesn't know whether to speak of Grosvenor or Verta Mae, the writer or the crafted persona. Sometimes she poses, sometimes she poses at posing" (132). Grosvenor's recollection of being "actor, director and audience all in one" in her childhood play productions presents this aspect of her personality as an individual idiosyncrasy. However, many of the stories Grosvenor recounts instead seem intended to situ-ate her performances in the context of a broader historical narrative of African American investments in Africa as a source of an authentic black identity.

Early in *Vibration Cooking*, for example, Grosvenor describes how during her first stay in Europe she "posed" as "Princess Verta":

> A lot of people like to say they are the descendants of African chiefs. I have been through that stage. Did I tell you all about that? We put out a magazine and it was cheaper to do it in England—so we went to Dover. While we were there, it was so dull that we wanted to do something to liven the place up so we said that I was Princess Verta from Tabanguila, an island near Madagascar. (22)

This ruse was so successful, she maintains, that a story titled "Princess Verta Stud-ies Our Way of Life" was published in the 30 January 1958 issue of the *Kent Ex-press* of Dover, England. Presumably to impress upon the reader the veracity of her account, she "reprints" the entire article in *Vibration Cooking* (23).[12] In relating this anecdote, Grosvenor invites the reader to share in the joke she and her friends have concocted at the Doverites' expense, a joke that entailed a fair degree of condescension toward her fictive subjects: "She said that her own tiny community lived a simple life and that she would not try to impose any modern ideas upon her return," the news article reports (quoted in *Vibration* 23). Having passed successfully as an African princess, now she seems to be sharing with the reader the "truth" of her identity as an American fraud.

Curiously, though, the narrative of her encounter with the "cracker" who contested her right to wear African clothing operates to undermine this assumption. Recorded later in *Vibration Cooking*, the second exchange took place in 1968, when Grosvenor was once again in Europe, this time selling *pouvoir noir* materials at the Sorbonne (117). Whereas the first anecdote had appeared to mock the Dover residents' inability to distinguish a real African princess from an aspiring black American actress, the second expresses irritation at the white man's refusal to go along with her efforts to pass—visually if not aurally—as an African. At issue, she implies, is not so much the man's recognition that Grosvenor was stylizing a self, but rather his refusal to accept her right to perform her identity as she chose. Again to have recourse to Amy Robinson, the encounter situates passing as a collision between "two competing discourses of recognition" or "between two epistemological paradigms" (724). The cracker was insisting on the primacy of his paradigm and thus denying Grosvenor the option of defining her own sense of self. In comparison to his adherence to rigid stereotypes of black American identity, the Doverites' unquestioning acceptance of Princess Verta's disguise might be retrospectively construed as an admirable exercise in epistemological flexibility.

In addition to foregrounding further inconsistencies in how Grosvenor conceptualizes her identity, the "cracker" story is telling in the way that it connects Grosvenor's pleasure in the performance of African-derived selfhood to the typecasting of African American women as mammies. In her writings, she repeatedly expresses intense irritation at being mistaken for a servant. The most common target of her wrath, however, is not white men but rather economically privileged white women. For instance, in *Thursdays and Every Other Sunday Off*, she describes an occasion in 1965 when she had gone to a "citadel of white supremacy" to pick up Kali, "who was visiting a little girl in her class" (12). Despite being dressed in the "first Vogue Couturier pattern" that she had ever sewn, Grosvenor was directed toward the servants' entrance and subjected by a "middle-aged white woman" to the inevitable question: "Going in late today, aren't you?" (12). Taken aback by her realization that bourgeois clothing was insufficient to counter the woman's ingrained prejudices, Grosvenor offered the following response: "I am not a maid. . . . All of us aren't maids, you know" (12).

Through anecdotes such as this, Grosvenor mobilizes her fascination with clothing and performance as a strategy for critiquing the demeaning stereotypes imposed on African Americans by racist whites. She insinuates that, regardless of their class status, all black women are subject to being perceived as servants. Yet, as her complaint never to have "lived in a place that had a decent oven" might suggest, at other times she also goes further by explicitly representing herself as a lower-class African American woman. The next-to-last section of *Vibration Cooking* consists, for example, primarily of an exchange of letters between her and a friend (or alter ego?) named Stella, the latter of whom at the time was traveling around the world. At one point Stella writes to Grosvenor of her difficulties locating an apartment in Paris because of the racist discrimination she has encountered. Stella admits to having had "a white girl . . . front for" her in order to find a "decent" place to live (163). She is distressed, however, that some of her friends are giving her "static. They say that I have gone middle class" (163).

Grosvenor uses this "private" dialogue between her and Stella as an opportunity to record the following philippic as her response:

> Don't worry about being called middle class. Child, just go on and do what you got to do. What's so middle class about wanting enough to eat and a decent place to live? I am sick of the roaches and mice. I'm tired of cleaning the dirt off the floors so that when the children walk barefoot and get into bed the sheets won't get dirty cause when you go to the laundry and have dingy sheets white folks look at you like you was born nasty. . . .
>
> I'm tired of being poor. . . .
>
> If decent living is middle class, then they can sock me some from the middle. (163)

Despite this assumption of a working-class black female identity, it seems important to recognize that Grosvenor had intentionally sought out a "bohemian" way of living, even acknowledging at one point: "To tell the truth I ain't never really had no serious job working from nine to five" (*Vibration* 89). Her justification is that "[i]t's just not my rhythm . . . not my style" (*Vibration* 89). Perhaps as a legacy of her marriage to Robert Grosvenor, though, her "style" was by no means typically "poor." Only after mother and daughter became known as authors did Kali begin attending a "predominantly black and Puerto Rican public school" near their apartment in the East Village (Garland 92). Prior to the publication of *Poems by Kali* and *Vibration Cooking*, Kali had been "enrolled in an exclusive private school in midtown Manhattan" (Garland 92). Yet, although at one point in *Vibration Cooking* Grosvenor includes her ex-husband in a list of fourteen people she met in Paris, her sole observation pertaining to him is: "One of them I married" (55).[13]

Grosvenor's celebration of her personal mutability functions to distract the reader from paying too much attention to the relationship between her intentional choice of an "avant garde" lifestyle and traditional understandings of what it means to be working class or poor. Clearly, though, she felt a cultural imperative to identify "down" with less privileged African American women, perhaps because of the antibourgeois ethos of the era. In fact, all three editions of *Vibration Cooking* are "dedicated to my mama and my grandmothers and my sisters in appreciation of the years that they worked in miss ann's kitchen and then came home to TCB [take care of business] in spite of slavery and oppression and the moynihan report." As her reference to being thought "born nasty" would suggest, Grosvenor explicitly understands "dirt" to be the cultural justification of her forebears' oppression. In her view, dirt might be defined as a nonontological function of (lower-)class status that is mistakenly attributed to and ontologized as (black) racial identity. And in keeping with the differential positioning of black women and black men in relation to the ontologization of race, most of her discussion of cleanliness and dirt revolves around African American women.

Most notably, she foregrounds the importance of sanitation to her grandmother and her mother. In a passage that anticipates *Pearl's Kitchen*, Grosvenor reminisces about how her grandmother would not attend a movie without taking her own "water and pillows" (*Vibration* 12). She "didn't think it was healthy to drink behind other people. . . . She didn't believe in sitting directly behind somebody else, either. When we visited people she would turn the sofa seats over or spread a piece of cloth to sit on. Sometimes now I find myself doing that" (*Vibration* 12). Similarly, her "mother would be so tired when she came home from cleaning up Mrs. Krader's house all day that she didn't feel like scrubbing pots and she didn't trust me to clean them well enough. If she found a speck of grease on a glass or a dish she scalded it three more times" (*Vibration* 32). Her mother was "so tired" from cleaning the house of her white employer that she "didn't feel like" cleaning her own, but—vividly illustrating what Grosvenor means by the phrase "TCB" in the dedications—she did it anyway.[14]

In a sense, dirt is for Grosvenor that which structures the relationship between white and black women. The former generate it; the latter clean it up. At one point in *Thursdays and Every Other Sunday Off*, she fantasizes about inverting this scenario, announcing to the reader that "when I move in my new apartment, I'm gonna get me a white cleaning lady. That may seem strange to some of yall, but after all the years my mama spent on her knees, it would make me sick to have anyone in her image cleaning my house" (11). But even as she envisions employing a white woman who would bear the cultural burden of being perceived as "nasty," Grosvenor also suggests that overly clean women are not to be trusted. In *Vibration Cooking*, for example, she recalls being invited for dinner by a white actress, "now a leading young ingénue in the theater" (99). Immediately upon arriving, Grosvenor realized that "something was wrong. No smells of food cooking or having been cooked. The kitchen was spotless. My daddy always told me that you had to watch those people who never dirtied the kitchen. He said if they don't make a mess in the kitchen they ain't cooking nothing fit to eat" (*Vibration* 100). The un-"dirtied" kitchen clearly signifies the white woman's artificiality, her lack of soul. But, of course, having a dirtied kitchen puts black women at risk of being labeled "nasty."

Men, however, turn out to be central to this catch-22 ideology of dirt. Though Frank Smart had warned Grosvenor as a child to be wary of overcleanliness in the kitchen, her own scrupulous adult sanitation practices resulted in an offer of marriage. The prospective mate "said that he had a thing for girls who get on their hands and knees to scrub floors (I never use a mop) and who can cook. The dude asked me to marry him but I didn't" (*Vibration* 19). To be her father's honorary son—"a Smart" whom he will teach to hunt—she must embrace the filth of soul. To be her suitor's wife, she must bear the ongoing burden of keeping the race clean. Rather than face this contradiction, Grosvenor indicts the more immediate symbol of oppression, the person who most obviously benefits from the oppression of women of color. "Is there enough money to send for a girl from the South or the Islands, or, as of late, South America, to keep house for you, mind your overindulged brat, while you go to Women's Lib meetings?" she asks rhetorically of white women in *Thursdays and Every Other Sunday Off* (9).

In keeping with her hostility toward second-wave white feminism, Grosvenor's attacks on technology and standardized food products were often aimed directly at white women. Her contempt is perhaps nowhere more vividly expressed than in "The Kitchen Crisis." Reiterating the claim that she made in the letter to *Time* magazine, Grosvenor critiques the widespread use of "instant" foods, but this time she uses more precisely gendered language. "Everything is prepared for the unprepared woman in the kitchen," Grosvenor opines (295). "The chicken is precut. The flour is premeasured, the rice is minute. The salt is preseasoned, and the peas are prebuttered" (295).

> Just goes to show you white folks will do anything for their women. They had to invent instant food because the servant problem got so bad that their woman had to get in the kitchen herself with her own two little lilly-white hands. It is no accident that in the old old south where they had slaves they was eating fried chicken coated with batter, and biscuits so light they could have flown across the Mason-Dixon line if they had wanted to. There was pound cake that had to be beat eight hundred strokes. Who do YOU think was doing this beating? It sure wasn't Missy. Missy was beating the upstairs house nigger for not bringing her mint julep quick enough. Massa was out beating the field niggers for not hoeing the cotton fast enough. (295–96)

Grosvenor not only anticipates and rescripts the flagellatory resonances contained in Craig Claiborne's memories of the "whack after whack after whack," but she also makes clear some of the connections between the development of a cuisine and the socioeconomic structure of a society. Antebellum cooking was slave-labor intensive, and the fame of southern white "hospitality" is inarguably contingent on a social system in which southern blacks were forced to do that which technology had yet to render less back-breaking. Thus the entire polemic concludes, fittingly, with one of Grosvenor's most memorable punch lines: "Meanwhile up in the north country, where they didn't have no slaves to speak of, they was eating baked beans and so-called New England boiled dinner. It ain't no big thing to put everything in one pot and let it cook" (296).

Her reinterpretation of southern culinary history as a function of black women's availability for domestic labor is worth noting in and of itself, but what also interests me here are some implicit assumptions that Grosvenor seems to be making about her audience. As I have already mentioned, "The Kitchen Crisis" was published in *Amistad 1*, a volume of essays whose generally well-known contributors included Charles Harris, John Williams, Addison Gayle Jr., George Davis, C. L. R. James, Ishmael Reed, Calvin Hernton, Oliver Jackman, and Vincent Harding. Not surprisingly, given the masculinist biases of the Black Power and Black Aesthetic movements, Grosvenor's essay occupies the next-to-last spot in the volume, just before Langston Hughes's "The Negro Artist and the Racial Mountain." (The volume was dedicated to the late Hughes.) In keeping with a common political gesture of the era, the implied reader of "The Kitchen Crisis" was black.

But the query "Who do YOU think was doing this beating?" conveys some suspicion as to whether her audience can be trusted to recognize the "truth" of U.S.
culinary history even as she is spelling it out. Grosvenor insinuates that she is by
no means sure her readers understand the extent of black women's oppression at
the hands of white women, by no means sure that her readers share her contempt
for the latter. In the next section, I will speculate that her repeated critiques of
second-wave feminism might be construed as a performance put on primarily for
the edification of African American men, including the purveyors of the Black
Aesthetic. It turned out to be a performance, though, that would challenge to the
core many of their most fundamental tenets about the role of black women in the
Black Power revolution.

Verta

> Because each had discovered years before that they were neither white
> nor male, and that all freedom and triumph was forbidden to them,
> they had set about creating something else to be.
>
> Toni Morrison, *Sula*, 1973

Grosvenor was only one among many African American women who were critical
of second-wave feminism as it emerged during the Black Power era. Toni Morrison had perhaps most famously articulated this position in a 1971 *New York Times
Magazine* essay called "What the Black Woman Thinks about Women's Lib." After
pointing out black women's skepticism about the class biases of the early movement, she condemns white feminists for talking about liberation while abdicating
"the management of the house and the rearing of children to others. . . . The one
great disservice black women are guilty of (albeit not by choice) is that they are
the means by which white women can escape the responsibilities of womanhood
and remain children all the way to the grave" (64). At least in this early essay,
Morrison fails to question her presuppositions about why the "responsibilities" of
housework and childrearing should fall on the shoulders of women and not men.
When she refers to how black women servants have moved white women's "dirt
from one place to another" (64), it seems clear that she, like Grosvenor, is holding white women responsible for the "dirt" generated by white men and white
children as well.[15]

Morrison also states quite clearly that black women's dislike of "women's liberation" was due not only to their pre-existing "feeling of superiority" to white women,
but also to "the very important fact that black men are formidably opposed to their
involvement in" feminist politics (64). Without fully allying herself with the positions she is attributing to other African Americans, she claims: "The consensus
among blacks is that their first liberation has not been realized; unspoken is the
conviction of black men that any more aggressiveness and 'freedom' for black
women would be intolerable, not to say counterrevolutionary" (64). By the end of
the essay, Morrison affirms the value of "women talking about human rights rather
than sexual rights" and allows that "the air is shivery with possibilities" because of

the way that black women activists such as Shirley Chisholm and Fannie Lou Hamer were reconfiguring the public face of the women's movement (66). Still, the essay's complicated rhetorical gesture of attempting to describe "what the black woman thinks," while also insisting on how "consistently" black women "have (deliberately, I suspect) defied classification" (15), finally allows her to avoid staking out a clear position with respect to black feminist politics.

If Morrison did equate "housework" with "drudgery," even when done in one's own home (63), Grosvenor, by contrast, initially seems much less ambivalent in her adherence to traditional gender role ideologies within African American communities. Cooking and cleaning were only problematic for her if done for a white family. Like fellow cookbook writer Princess Pamela, moreover, Grosvenor locates food preparation within a heterosexual matrix of desire. Whereas the former had insisted that "[e]very woman should learn / to cook for her man / 'cuz love and indigestion / don't mix" (190), the latter observes that "[c]ooking for a man is a very feminine thing, and I can't understand how a woman can feed her man TV dinners" (*Vibration* xiv–xv). Similarly, in the *McCalls* article, Grosvenor idealizes women's labor in the kitchen as a tactic for creating male sexual as well as gastronomic desire:

> Soul food is when a fine brother hurts his back playing basketball and a fly sister comes to bring him a jar of homemade oxtail soup and another brother is there and he eats two bowls and the next day he calls the first brother asking for the sisters phone number and the first brother is mad cause he only offered the brother to be polite and give the illusion of solidarity anyhow. He say "hell no" cause he impressed that she cooked the oxtails for two hours, let them cool, stripped the meat off the bones, took off the excess grease, added barley, noodles, potatoes, whole tomatoes and frozen mixed vegetables and he decide to hit on her himself. (75)

In this scenario, women who rely on modern food technologies are seen as failing to fulfill their normative role in establishing heterosexuality. Male desire is stimulated by labor-intensive soul food cooking, not by opening a can.

It is worth pausing here to note that Grosvenor's efforts to foreground the heterosexual inscriptions of soul food received a fictional reworking four years later in Ann Allen Shockley's novel *Loving Her* (1974), which Madhu Dubey has described as "the only novel published by a black woman in the 1970s that follows its critique of heterosexuality [with] an unapologetic affirmation of lesbianism" (152). Shockley's protagonist, Renay, treats interracial lesbian relationships and soul food as though they are mutually exclusive propositions. As Dubey explains, "All traces of Renay's black past, including . . . her love of soul food, . . . have to be expelled from her life before her lesbian relationship with a white woman can be established and affirmed" (152). Thus, when in the company of her lover at a restaurant, Renay ends up seconding Terry's order of "[v]enison, baked potato and tossed salad. And a big mug of that delicious draft ale!" (Shockley 70). Shockley goes out of her way to contrast this "Sherwood Forest special" (70) to the chitterlings, pig's feet, and "rotgut whiskey" served at the "wild parties" to which Renay has been accustomed (68). Shortly thereafter, when Renay cooks a soul food dinner for Terry, the latter takes a whiff of a pot of chitterlings and pronounces, "Whew! They *do* have a distinctive odor, don't they?" (86). Renay jokingly adopts black southern vernacular in affirming, "They sho' do!" (86), but it soon becomes clear that Terry is not likely to consume them again. "Maybe it's the thought of what they are," the white woman acknowledges (87).[16] In this fashion, Shockley developed the implications of Grosvenor's presumption that soul food was inextricable from black nationalist valorization of intraracial reproductive heterosexuality—particularly for black women. Readers of the 1992 edition of *Vibration Cooking* will not, however, be privy to Grosvenor's most explicit alliance with the heterosexism of early 1970s black nationalism—a homophobic deployment of the term "faggot"—since this was another aspect of the text which was subsequently altered.[17]

Grosvenor's embrace of her African heritage, her hostility to second-wave white feminism, her refusal to question assumptions about women's responsibility for domestic labor, and her homophobia all clearly mark her affiliation with the prevailing black nationalist ideology of the early 1970s. *Vibration Cooking* is, in fact, riddled with allusions to her close ties with prominent proponents of the Black Aesthetic. The book's epigraph is a poem by Amiri Baraka, whom Grosvenor would eventually count among her good friends. Subsequently, she refers fondly to her encounters with William Melvin Kelley and Carlene Polite in Paris (61). The latter, whose 1966 novel *The Flagellants* has been characterized as "obsessively re-cycl[ing] the stereotypes of the matriarch and the emasculated black man" (Dubey 151), fixes Grosvenor a meal that is memorialized in *Vibration Cooking* as "Chicken Carlene Polite" (155).[18] Grosvenor also announces that Larry Neal "is one of the oldest friends I got" (148). At the same time, notwithstanding her intimacy with the Black Arts scene in New York and abroad, if we read *Vibration Cooking* as a precursor not just to Shockley's *Loving Her* but also to other fiction published by black women during the 1970s—namely Toni Morrison's novel *Sula*—Grosvenor's position with respect to the prevailing black nationalist aesthetic emerges as more complicated than is otherwise readily apparent.

In her work on black women novelists and the Black Aesthetic, Dubey explores different strategies through which novelists such as Morrison, Gayl Jones, and Alice Walker resisted the compulsion to present a unified vision of blackness that elided differences of sexuality, gender, and class. She suggests that "black feminist theorizations of identity" need to combine "a continuing appreciation of the cultural history that has produced the black writer's strong investment in the model of a whole, cohesive self " with "a vigilant attention to the differences within the black experience that confound any totalized, unitary definition of black identity" (4). As Dubey acknowledges, Deborah McDowell had already pursued this line of thought in an influential analysis of Morrison's *Sula*. McDowell focuses on Sula's indeterminate selfhood to argue that the novel as a whole can be read as Morrison's response to black nationalist literary critics who were demanding that black writers offer only "positive" representations of African American characters. Insisting that in the Black Aesthetic vocabulary "positive" was largely synonymous with black female submission to patriarchy, she shows how "*Sula* complicates the process of identification in the reading process, denying the conventional Afro-American critic a reflection of his or her ego ideal" ("Boundaries" 104).[19]

Morrison's *New York Times Magazine* essay certainly lends credence to both critics' claims. Using language which she would recycle in *Sula* two years later, she contends that "out of the profound desolation of her reality," the black woman "may very well have invented herself" (63). Yet what intrigues me are the numer-ous ways in which the self-inventing Verta Mae Smart seems to have provided a template for the famously mutable Sula Mae Peace. When Morrison had written that Sula's "was an experimental life" (*Sula* 118), she could easily have been de-scribing the author of *Vibration Cooking*. We even learn in *Vibration Cooking* that Grosvenor's maternal grandmother was named Sula (15).[20] Because Morrison has responded to my private inquiries by indicating that she was in fact not aware of Grosvenor as a possible prototype for Sula, I would admittedly be hard-pressed to try to argue that she was.[21] Nonetheless, it does still strike me as worthwhile to in-terpret Grosvenor's contradictory self-representation in her cookbook in a fashion analogous to the way that McDowell, Dubey, and others have interpreted *Sula*. Grosvenor's penchant for inconsistency and disguise might be read, in other words, as part of a strategy she deployed with considerable skill to negotiate a place for herself, for *Vibration Cooking*, and even for her female forebears within the black-male-dominated terrain of the Black Arts movement.

Sometimes her critique of Black Aesthetic ideology is easy to discern. For ex-ample, though black nationalists generally viewed black mothers as mired in the past and therefore a barrier to black men's revolutionary pursuits, Grosvenor an-nounces early in *Vibration Cooking* that her paternal grandmother Estella Smart "is avant-garde. . . . Last year she was engaged and I had already bought the fabric to make her wedding dress to this dude but she broke it off. I don't think she is ready to give up her freedom" (11). Even more tellingly, Grosvenor begins *Vibration Cooking* with a section called "Birth, Hunting and Gator Tails," which describes the scene of her birth. Weighing in at three pounds, she was half the size of her twin brother, and she was not expected to live. Her parents deposited the tiny newborn in a makeshift incubator, a shoe box, on the wood-stove oven door. Ac-cording to Grosvenor's mother, "it was a case of touch and go for a while, cause she got the childbirth fever" and nearly threw her daughter into the fireplace (*Vibra-tion* 3). But whereas Grosvenor lived to grow into a healthy, self-sufficient woman, her six-pound brother died at birth, having reputedly "stayed in the womb too long" (*Vibration* 3). Through this anecdote, Grosvenor vividly rewrites prevailing Black Arts and Black Power ideologies according to which the domineering black mother imprisons the male child in her womb. The death of her twin brother re-sults from his own fetal inertia. Morrison's better known presentation of the rea-soning behind Eva's decision to kill her son Plum in *Sula* follows a similar logic. She simply "had to keep him out" of her womb, Eva explains (72).

Grosvenor's efforts to reconfigure the masculinist biases of the nationalist aes-thetic also emerge through her formal experimentation with the (already femi-nized) genre of the cookbook. Perhaps most notably, while much of *Vibration Cooking* seems to be addressing black men as well as black women, by the end of the book Grosvenor takes as her actual reader a specific African American woman, her friend Stella. As would *Sula*, *Vibration Cooking* concludes by affirming the value of solidarity between African American women.[22] Whereas Morrison's Nel visits Eva in the nursing home only to hear herself pronounced interchangeable with Sula—"You. Sula. What's the difference?" (168)—the ending of the 1970 edition of *Vibration Cooking* finds Stella narrating her adventures via letters as she travels through South America and Africa while Grosvenor remains at home in New York. It is Stella, not Grosvenor, who broadens the book's horizons beyond the United States and Europe. It is Stella who sends Grosvenor the climactic message: "Child, after 350 years, I am home. Africa, the motherland. . . . It is not true that the Africans don't like or want us. Biggest lie the white man ever told. He told the Africans that we didn't like them either. Divide and conquer is his game but it is over" (175). Rather than expressing surprise that *Vibration Cooking*'s final trip "home" turns out to be taken by someone other than a traveling Geechee Girl, one might perhaps do well to take a page from Morrison's Eva and respond by inquiring, "Stella. Verta. What's the difference?" Either way, the truth of black solidarity is finally out.

It seems evident, though, that even if Stella is a fictive creation, she and Verta should not be read simply as "one and the same thing" (Morrison, *Sula* 119). On the one hand, Stella's voice and opinions do often sound decidedly similar to those of Grosvenor. After renting her "middle class" apartment, for example, Stella writes, bemoaning that her "neighbors complained about the strange smells coming out of my apt. I was so mad, I think I might cook some chitlins all day long just to really give them a good smell. They so used to eating smelless and tasteless food that they get uptight if you fry an onion" (164). But, on the other hand, it is important to recognize that Grosvenor had already attached the label "Home" to the first section of *Vibration Cooking*. It describes her relatives in South Carolina, her childhood in Philadelphia, and her successful but finally fraudulent "pass" as Princess Verta. Africa is clearly a part but not the whole of her identity and hence the likely purpose of her attribution of Afrocentric selfhood to Stella. The Geechee Girl cannot be so reductively defined.

Travel Notes

> What she does today she describes as Afro-Brazilian-Italian-Chinese-Geechee, a combination based on her heritage and what she has picked up in her travels or learned from cookbooks.
>
> Marian Burros, "Gullah Cooking:
> Improvising on Cultures Past," 1988

Of all the inconsistencies and ambiguities in Grosvenor's persona, of all the ways in which she worked to construct a place for African American women within the political and cultural scene of early 1970s black nationalism and white feminism, perhaps the most intriguing is her deployment of the self-description "Geechee Girl." Often used interchangeably with "Gullah," the term "Geechee" refers to the inhabitants of the Sea Islands, as well as to the creole language they speak (Major 194, 216). It is also a term of derision applied to dark-skinned blacks (Major 194). But in *Vertamae Cooks in the Americas' Family Kitchen*—a cookbook Grosvenor published in 1996 as an accompaniment to her PBS television program—she explains her continuing terminological preference by identifying Geechee as an "in-group" designation: "They call us Gullah, but 'we call weself Geechee'" (14). Whichever label one applies, the Sea Islands have long been of interest to stu-dents of black American culture. Not surprisingly, of course, the early studies tended to offer a derogatory representation of the Gullah peoples. In his 1930 book *A Social History of the Sea Islands*, Guion Griffis Johnson explained that the Sea Island Negroes "spoke a garbled English, imperfect words and expressions which they and their parents and grandparents had learned from the few whites with whom they came in contact" (127). But even as Johnson was rendering such judgments, other scholars were beginning to question the assumption that en-slaved Africans had carried with them to the New World no viable cultural tradi-tions. In particular, Melville Herskovits's study *The Myth of the Negro Past* (1941) contributed to the explosion of scholarly work on African retentions in the Amer-icas. Decades of often acrimonious debate over his thesis ensued, but by 1980 the *Journal of Black Studies* devoted an entire issue to the topic of "Sea Island Culture." Guest editors Mary Twining and Keith Baird carefully pronounced in their pref-ace: "As far as the Sea Islands are concerned it may perhaps be safely asserted that the issue now is not so much the debate over the existence of Africanisms but the continuation of research to determine just where and how much material exists" (385).[23]

In figuring herself as a Geechee, Grosvenor was thus participating in a much broader movement to reinterpret and revalue the African heritage of black Amer-icans. If the Sea Island peoples had previously been seen as pariahs, Grosvenor pa-raded her Geechee relatives as a badge of honor. Of course, the two difficulties in this scheme, as I have already mentioned, are her move to Philadelphia "when she was 9 or 10" (Burros C6) and, more intriguingly, her failure to have been born on the Sea Islands in the first place. In *Vibration Cooking*, Grosvenor does refer to a first cousin named Queen Esther who is "from out by Beaufort way" (42), but most of the relatives she describes are from the inland counties of Allendale and Hamp-ton—just like herself. In discussing her family background, Grosvenor neither takes time to distinguish island from inland Geechee culture, nor refers to herself as hailing from the coast. Once the book was reissued in 1986, though, the public construction of her origins began to undergo some shifts.

To wit: Marian Burros's *New York Times* profile of Grosvenor was accompanied by a photograph of a coastal scene—marshland lined with palm trees—which it-self contained inset photographs of Grosvenor and a plate of food. The pho-tographs' caption announces that "Vertamae Smart-Grosvenor, who is from the coastal region of South Carolina, makes her Frogmore stew with shrimp, sausage and corn" (C1). In the article's opening paragraph, Burros pursues this less-than-precise representation. Referring to Charleston as "not far from where [Grosvenor] was born," she fails to mention that this unnamed "where" lies over sixty miles west of Charleston, on the far side of what is now Interstate 95. Two other pho-tographs accompanying the article are of St. Helena Island, at whose famous Penn School Grosvenor was a writer-in-residence during the 1970s (C6). Burros invokes this information, along with Grosvenor's work in progress as a technical director for and actress in *Daughters of the Dust*, as a way of further associating her subject's background with Sea Island culture. Thus, she quotes Grosvenor using the first-person plural to explain the importance of Dash's film: "We have to preserve what remains of our African socioreligious beliefs and culture" (C1). Given that Burros also writes about how Grosvenor was forced to learn English from a "radio soap opera" after moving to Philadelphia (C6), readers lacking familiarity with *Vibration Cooking* (and South Carolina) would have every reason to infer from the article that Grosvenor was truly a child of the Sea Islands.

Ballantine soon joined in by illustrating the cover of the third edition of *Vibration Cooking* with a map of southeastern South Carolina. The map is positioned to include the coastal area stretching from Charleston to Beaufort. Grosvenor's birthplace is just barely visible on the far left edge of the book. Even so, the reader must be satisfied with locating "airfax" since, at least on my copy, the "F" did not quite survive the crop. The towns of Luray and Estill, home to Grosvenor's relatives the "Ritters and the Myerses and the Smarts" (*Vibration* 3), lie farther south but also farther west, and thus do not make an appearance on the cover at all. By the time *Vertamae Cooks in the Americas' Family Kitchen* appeared four years later, Grosvenor was reminiscing in detail about how, when she was a schoolchild in Philadelphia, she had informed a teacher: "E teif me pinders n e hand een ain onrabel e mout!" (14). Failing to understand that "a boy stole [her] peanuts and ran off without saying a word," the teacher demanded that Grosvenor "speak English!" (14). Oddly, though, memories of language barriers had not found their way into Grosvenor's recollections of her childhood in *Vibration Cooking*. There she uses southern black vernacular to represent the speech patterns of herself and her family.

My aim in raising these concerns is not to imply that Grosvenor has lied in "passing" herself off as a Geechee. As Sea Island historian Charles Joyner has explained, "On the coastal mainland adjacent to the Sea Islands are black people who share [the] folk culture and [the] creole language" of the Gullahs (Foreword x). Acknowledging that these mainland dwellers "are not—strictly speaking—Sea Islanders," Joyner further observes that the story of the Sea Islands is "in many ways . . . their story too" (x). Migration patterns from the islands to the mainland would readily account for Grosvenor's Gullah heritage. Rather, I aim to use this discussion of Grosvenor's ambiguous positioning in relation to the more typical island-oriented perception of Gullah peoples as a way of critiquing some problematic aspects of scholarly and now popular fascination with the Sea Islands. Whether or not Grosvenor recognized in 1970 that the emergent interest in Gullah culture would privilege as most "authentic" those people born and raised offshore, by the time Burros conducted her interview with Grosvenor, the standards for what it meant to be a Geechee Girl had clearly been raised.

The paradox in which Grosvenor has become implicated, it seems to me, is that Gullah culture is valorized for inscribing both motion and stasis. Scholars have looked to the Sea Islands as a site where remnants of the "originary" displacement of Africans to the Americas can be identified. In this sense, the Sea Island peoples are understood to code movement, but only a movement that is always already completed, always already in the past. As an almost inevitable result, much of our cultural romance with Gullah peoples has been structured by a desire for the Sea Islands to remain henceforth a site of cultural inertia. Having learned to recognize and value their encoding of the African diaspora, we necessarily bemoan continued creolization as a loss of authenticity.[24] And this is the issue, it seems to me, which is at the heart of the obfuscations over Grosvenor's place of origin. Grosvenor offered herself up as a traveling Geechee Girl to a world that has become increasingly fascinated with Gullah isolation.

Yet this is also the reason why I finally find Grosvenor's deployment of the trope of the "travel" book so compelling in its insistence on her right to ongoing cultural and personal hybridization. Despite having been born miles from the coast, despite having grown up in Philadelphia, despite having studied in France, despite having married a white sculptor and moved to Greenwich Village, despite having visited numerous countries and continents, Grosvenor has still claimed her identity as a Geechee. Far from weakening her sense of her heritage, her travels have expanded and fortified it. "I was a grown girl and across the ocean before I, as folklorist Zora Neale Hurston has described it, looked at home through the spyglass of anthropology and began my exploration into Afro-Atlantic foodways," she recalls in *Vertamae Cooks in the Americas' Family Kitchen* (17).

In this context, it is worth noting, moreover, that "travel" is actually a central concept of Sea Island religious experience, signifying the voyage undertaken by a seeker prior to conversion to the religious community:

> The most important indication of spiritual transformation was the vision or *travel* as interpreted by the spiritual parent. "This word *travel*," wrote one Methodist missionary, "is one of the most significant in their language, and comprehends all those exercises, spiritual, visionary and imaginative which make up an 'experience.'" (Creel 80)

Though Grosvenor herself does not suggest that her use of "travel" is influenced by the term's currency in Gullah culture, it still seems fitting that her cookbook deployed the concept by embracing its originary inscription of physical as well as spiritual, visionary, and imaginative motion.

As I explained at the outset of this chapter, because of her emphasis on the importance of travel and her often contradictory political orientation toward black internationalism as well as black nationalism, Grosvenor's writings on food resonate in a variety of ways with Paul Gilroy's influential theorization of the black diaspora. "The worth of the diaspora concept," he writes, "is in its attempt to specify differentiation and identity in a way which enables one to think about the issue of racial commonality outside of constricting binary frameworks—especially those that counterpose essentialism and pluralism" (*Black* 120). But whereas Gilroy tends to privilege music as the central cultural form through which the countermodernity of the black Atlantic has been articulated, I would suggest that Grosvenor's writings on black culinary history serve as a useful supplement to Gilroy's oppositional model. Most obviously, work on food provides scholars of the black Atlantic with a paradigm in which black women and questions of gender are not—or at least should not be—automatically marginalized. No less important, work on food encourages us to recognize barriers to, and even assumptions about the gender of, movement which discussions of black music can sometimes seem to skirt.

I have already offered some examples of how Grosvenor situates African American dietary practices in an international perspective. Early in *Vibration Cooking* Grosvenor reprints (or makes up?) a letter from her cousin Markana, who, having won the lottery, had moved to the West Indies (42–43). This letter provides a brief primer on yams. After delineating the differences among white, sweet, renta, yampy, and yellow yams, Markana parodies Gertrude Stein when she informs Grosvenor that "there is a yam called nigger yam. I won't even deal with that because after all a yam is a yam is a yam" (43). Other relatives and friends also send Grosvenor recipes for her cookbook. Stella, in particular, provides instructions for making South American and African dishes such as "Paltas Debray" (159), "Bamya" (173), and "Lumumba Gombo" (176). But the important thing to note here is that Grosvenor portrays herself as providing Stella, in turn, with recipes to cook for her newfound friends abroad, thus demonstrating that the direction of black Atlantic culinary influence has never been simply east to west. Grosvenor's letters are peppered with comments such as "Here's the beer beef dish you wanted" (160); "This is the short'nin bread recipe you asked for" (162); and "Here is a recipe for a dish that I made last night," which turns out to have been "Kidneys and Mushrooms" (168). In this fashion, Grosvenor—who implies that she herself was at the time homebound because of her responsibilities as the custodial parent of Kali and Chandra—demonstrates how African American women have become active participants in the creation of a black Atlantic culture, even when they themselves are not "free" to move.

Another strategy through which Grosvenor compensated for her temporarily stationary existence was to draw on textual research to interrogate how food itself is inscribed by the history of colonialism. For instance, she follows up her discussion of the American "cracker" who denied her right to wear African clothing with the following information:

> Potatoes are native to South America and were taken to Europe by the Spanish explorers "when they discovered South America." They discovered "Indians and potatoes and squash and peppers and turkeys and tomatoes and corn and chocolate." They took everything back to Europe except the Indians. The settlers who later came from Europe brought the descendants of these vegetables to North America. Now, if a squash and a potato and a . . . pepper can grow and look like their ancestors, I know damn well that I can walk around dressed like mine. (*Vibration* 118)

Here, too, her theorization challenges unidirectional models of culinary diaspora. Transported to Europe from South America, potatoes and squash and other foods incorporated these outside influences and later found their way back to their place of origin.[25]

While continuing in recent years to contribute to the development of diasporic black culture, Grosvenor acknowledges in *Vertamae Cooks in the Americas' Family Kitchen* that "[m]uch of our culinary past is lost history" (17), and to a certain extent she is right.[26] For example, despite the efforts of John Brown Childs to publicize the work of Arthur Schomburg, the latter's proposal for a book on Afro-Atlantic culinary history continues to be underutilized. Himself a Puerto Rican immigrant to the United States, by the 1920s Schomburg was construing "Negro" according to a transatlantic model of black identity, incorporating not just African Americans but also peoples of African descent from around the world—Spain, the Caribbean, South America, etc. Taking for granted the argument that would eventually establish Melville Herskovits's place in scholarly history, Schomburg proposed

> [t]o uncover if possible such traces of Africanism which still persist in American dishes. To compare, for instance, the delectable Fish Head Stew served to millionaire fishermen on Sea Islands with a slightly similar concoction prepared by the Djuka negroes among whom, I am told, the fish is eaten like corn on the cob and heads especially considered a delicacy, the bones being crunched audibly and with much gusto. In this connection, to mention that okra—and buckra—are words of African origin—and to write of the noble tradition of okra-gumboes, especially those served straight from the cooking pot. (9)

Providing further evidence for Gilroy's perception that historians of modernity have failed to recognize the role of black intellectuals in fomenting a transatlantic black counterculture, Schomburg's proposal clearly delineates his commitment to documenting the connections among black culinary practices throughout the diaspora.

At the same time, John Brown Childs's purpose in writing about Schomburg is to show how he, an utter bibliophile, had paradoxically maintained an awareness of the "people's culture" as a vibrant and living tradition in need of neither articulation nor preservation by an intellectual elite. Even though Schomburg wanted to include personality sketches of famous Negro cooks and their recipes, he was also adamant that he must "show that the well-known colored cooks are exceptional partly because their names are known whereas the true creative impulse in cooking as in all folk arts, is vested in anonymous thousands" (3). Similarly, in *The Black Atlantic*, Gilroy adheres to "C. L. R. James's idea that ordinary people do not need an intellectual vanguard to help them to speak or to tell them what to say," and he holds up musicians "as living symbols of the value of self-activity" (79). I am persuaded by Gilroy's argument that "the history and practice of black music" (77) warrant continued investigation for scholars interested in understanding black Atlantic cultural exchange outside the dominant strands of intellectual history. My only concern is that we not allow music's seeming evanescence to prevent us from recognizing the ways in which black women have been associated with the stationary "soul" harbor which enables black male diasporic movement.

"en la casa de verta"

> for on monday in 1969 on the streets
> was diamonds. downtown society bodegas one
> right after the other. avocado & tomato juice
> spaceships parked in front of vertas house/sparkling
> yellow metal with stickers from Venus Airlines
> Moon Shuttle Jupiter Car Service Mars heliport
> & all on monday by a bridge. 1969 year of the rooster

hot sauce/street beans. . . . . .
                caribbean rice on the fire
with african beans warming
        wow
                the centuries & centuries
of sea exploration & mixing.
                but here we all are
in vertas soul space kitchen
                taking off.

Victor Hernandez, Cruz "en la casa de verta," 1969

This concern is actually quite easy to explain. In his work on the relationship between black musical traditions and intellectuals, Andrew Ross observes that "soul
was something that *happened to the body as it was moving,* and therefore it was
nowhere more apparent than in the response to musical rhythms, whether carried
in the head, or heard through the air" (100). My earlier arguments about the ways
in which soul inscribed black maternity would lead me to respond that, at least during the Black Power era, soul was more accurately understood as something that
happened to black male bodies as they moved both toward and away from presumptively inert black female ones. Had this not been the case, Grosvenor might
not have chosen to deploy a jazz rather than a soul aesthetic in conceptualizing her
work on black culinary history. Herself a veteran of Sun Ra's Solar Myth Science
Arkestra, Grosvenor alludes frequently in *Vibration Cooking* to jazz musicians such
as Archie Shepp and jazz-influenced writers such as Amiri Baraka. In keeping with
this thematization of jazz, the original book ended with a section called "To Be
Continued." The 1986 and 1992 editions fulfilled this promise by altering the section's name to read "Continued" and adding several new vignettes. Her anticipa-
tion in the first edition of the book of a subsequent variation hearkens less to the
repetitive rhythms of soul than to the citational "spontaneity" of jazz. To the extent
that she affiliated herself primarily with the latter, more black male–dominated,
musical mode, Grosvenor disassociated her cookbook from the taint of "slave" maternity with which the majority of Black Arts practitioners were obsessed.

One of her anecdotes in *Vibration Cooking* seems intended to foreground precisely the difficulties she was facing in negotiating this tension between jazz and
soul. In a section called "Collards and Other Greens," Grosvenor reports:

> Collard greens almost caused me and Archie Shepp to break friendship. His play was
> being presented at the Chelsea Theatre and for the opening night party they were
> going to have a "soul food party." They asked me to cook the greens. Peggy and I cut
> up fifteen pounds of greens. We got calluses on our fingers. I called a friend of mine
> (an actor in the play) to ask him to drive me to the theater, and he said, "Didn't they
> tell you the show is not opening tonight? It's opening Thursday." (131–32)

Although she ends up including a recipe for "Collard Greens a la Shepp" (132),
Grosvenor makes clear her irritation at having her time-sensitive culinary labors
taken for granted by someone whose profession celebrated idiosyncratic usage of
time. In chapter 3 I pointed out that Bob Young and Al Stankus's *Jazz Cooks* pays

homage to black male cooking feats while acknowledging that actually these jazz "greats" often rely on the women in their families to "pinch hit." Since the musicians "travel so often," they obviously lack sufficient time to cook (Young and Stankus 6). When the men are out playing music or putting on plays, in other words, it is taken for granted that the women will "TCB" in the kitchen.

What concerns me, obviously, are the moments when discourses of black music revert to "constricting binary frameworks" in which black women's traditional association with the kitchen undermines the very possibility of figuring them in terms of movement. And this is a problem that seems to inhere in discourses of diasporic black identity as well. Gilroy again offers a perceptive reading of the sources of this tension. "The need to locate cultural or ethnic roots and then to use the idea of being in touch with them as a means to refigure the cartography of dispersal and exile is perhaps best understood," he argues, "as a simple and direct response to the varieties of racism which have denied the historical character of black experience and the integrity of black cultures" (*Black* 112). The question this raises, though, is whether black men and black women are positioned in comparable ways with respect to this compulsion to be "in touch with" black roots.

Consider, for example, one of the few spots in his book proposal where Arthur Schomburg specifically addresses the role of black women in the development of diasporic black culinary traditions. He planned

> [t]o maintain along with the traditional mammy cooks of the South that the exact formula for any but the most ordinary dishes, cannot be written down—that a pinch of this and a handful of that may be more ex[p]ressive than level tablespoonfuls in giving the feel of a dish. That no matter how ingredients are measured they must be combined with a sort of magic in order [to] achieve the perfect blend. That accurate oven thermometers and scientific renditions of certain inspired dishes are no more like the original than a photographic copy is like a Rembrandt. That it takes more— and less—than a knowledge of dietetics to make a cook. (6)

Because Schomburg otherwise fails to discuss the role of black women in his conception of Afro-Atlantic culinary history, one finishes reading this dynamic prospectus with the distinct impression that, for him, diasporic black culinary exchange is fundamentally anchored by ahistorical and immobile black mammies in the South.[27]

Given this context, the apt ambiguity of Victor Cruz's metaphor of "verta's soul space kitchen / taking off" is difficult to miss. Construing her kitchen as both a restful haven from "centuries & centuries / of sea exploration" and also a spaceship about to embark on a voyage of its own, his poem—which serves as the conclusion to all three editions of *Vibration Cooking*—recapitulates the complex undertaking through which Grosvenor balanced her traveling Geechee Girl persona with an homage to her forebears, who, lacking the wherewithal to "move," have divided their time between "miss ann's kitchen" and their own. In other words, if *Vibration Cooking* ends with Cruz's romantic invocation of an intergalactic black diaspora, elsewhere in her book Grosvenor still foregrounds the local interactions that have historically structured the day-to-day lives of many working-class African American women.

One of the more memorable occasions when Grosvenor's mother "came home to TCB" occurred when the budding thespian and "key" child Grosvenor managed to set the curtains afire while (prematurely) lighting the candles on her birthday cupcakes (*Vibration* 31). Seeing the flames, a neighbor called both the fire department and Grosvenor's mother, who rushed home from work. After the fire was extinguished and the young Verta Mae was found cowering under a bed, Mrs. Smart demanded of her daughter an explanation. As Grosvenor recollects the scene:

> I was a real bright reader and I had read that a doctor said that children had traumas. I thought a trauma was something that could happen to make you speechless and hysterical. So I tried that. I stuttered and stammered and got hysterical and cried and said that I couldn't remember because I had a traumatic experience. My mother gave me two minutes to recover my memory or else receive an emotional experience on my behind. (*Vibration* 33)

In the opening pages of *Black Boy*, Richard Wright had offered a parallel account of having set afire some "fluffy white curtains" out of feelings of boredom, anger, and neglect (6). When his (intentional) action resulted in a major fire, the young boy hid under the burning house until caught by his father. Though he acknowledges that his parents were relieved to have found him alive, the memory Wright stresses is that he "was lashed so hard and long that [he] lost consciousness" (8). In fact, his "mother had come close to killing" him (9). Grosvenor, by marked contrast, uses her anecdote to demonstrate her mother's unconditional love. Having "recovered in thirty seconds" from her traumatic experience in order to avoid a whipping, she observes that this was her "only fire. It is odd too, cause I used to cook all the time. Poor Mother never complained about all the food I messed up" (*Vibration* 33).

Gilroy rightly questions the tendency of critics to focus on Richard Wright's early, U.S.-oriented works (such as *Black Boy*) to the exclusion of his later, more "international" texts (*Black* 151–52). Yet it seems clear to me that the ongoing interrogation of African American women's writings does not allow for a complete, unquestioned reorientation of critical perception. In setting up Grosvenor's anecdote as a "rebuttal" of sorts to that of Wright, I may well be participating in what Gilroy has described as a "ritual public projection of the antagonistic relationship between black women and men" (*Black* 83) and therefore exacerbating conflicts over patriarchy within diasporic black culture which might be addressed in other ways. But if the alternative is to repress this portion of Grosvenor's text in favor of foregrounding segments that might be understood to engage with Wright's less misogynistic representations, the result can only be an impoverished understanding of Grosvenor's relationship to a theory of diasporic identity. After all, "public projections" of male dominance still reflect material imbalances of power stemming from gender difference.

Having said that, however, I can only end by acknowledging that my goal of using Grosvenor's writings on food as a way of seeking feminist "homes" for African American women within theories of the black diaspora sits at times uneasily with Grosvenor's own ambivalent investments in the perpetuation of black patriarchy. I stress "ambivalent" here because where Grosvenor is concerned, the terrain is always shifting. Most notably, the introduction to the 1992 edition of *Vibration Cooking* had explicitly reworked the Moynihan Report's attribution to black women of irresponsible reproductive practices. "The third coming of *Vibration Cooking or The Travel Notes of a Geechee Girl* took me by surprise," Grosvenor writes at the outset (xiii). "I feel like a woman who had a baby but didn't know she was pregnant" (xiii). Far from acting out the Moynihanian stereotype, Grosvenor depicts herself as giving birth not to a baby but a book. Yet, in keeping with her tendency to conjure the very specters that she has just denounced, she frames her introduction with a concluding meditation on African American mother-daughter connections, oriented around the moments when her own daughters gave birth. Grosvenor first reports: "On April 21, 1988, my grandson Oscar Brown IV was born to my youngest daughter Chandra and her husband Oscar Brown III, who also goes by the name of Bobo" (xxv). This information is followed by a narrative of the death of her own mother in April 1991. At her grandmother's funeral, "Kali was very sick. We thought it was grief and stress. She was pregnant. On the full moon of November 22, here comes Charlotte Rose Grosvenor-Jeffries, with big ruby red lips and long long fingers, just like mama . . ." (Grosvenor's ellipsis; xxvi).

The birth of Grosvenor's first grandchild—at which Grosvenor fainted—might be understood to represent the fortification of black patriarchy. The name "Oscar Brown IV" constructs the child as homunculus, a miniature reincarnation of its father. Chandra serves in this fiction as the vessel in which the genes of musicians Oscar Brown, Oscar Brown Jr., and Oscar Brown III are replicated. The second grandchild's birth, on the contrary, offers a critique of such patriarchal practices of naming. Not only is the child a daughter instead of the preferred son, but her surname is hyphenated. Charlotte Rose Grosvenor-Jeffries carries on the legacy of her maternal as well as paternal progenitor. She looks, moreover, like her mother, a Geechee-Girl femunculix, as it were. Yet, following family tradition, by the time *Vertamae Cooks in the Americas' Family Kitchen* appeared, the names of the "characters" had once again been changed. Grosvenor had ceased to use the "Smart-Grosvenor" which graced the 1986 and 1992 editions of *Vibration Cooking*, now signing herself simply "Vertamae Grosvenor." Charlotte Rose Grosvenor Jeffries had lost her hyphen as well. The cookbook itself is prefaced by a memorial to Grosvenor's son-in-law Oscar Brown III, who was killed in a car accident in Chicago in August 1996. Accompanied by a photograph of "The four O's"—Oscar Brown, Oscar Jr., Oscar III, and Oscar IV—the memorial provides an understandably mournful but, from a feminist perspective, still problematic representation of Grosvenor's late son-in-law (5). The impure traces of Chandra and her female predecessors in the perpetuation of the Oscar Brown dynasty have been rendered even more dramatically invisible.[28]

In an essay on *Daughters of the Dust*, Renée Curry has acknowledged that she feels "personally uncomfortable" as a white feminist with Julie Dash's well-known portrayal of the "Unborn Child" (347). Curry's anxiety is that such representations might lend themselves to appropriation by opponents of feminism who have already succeeded in undermining support for abortion rights by insinuating the fetus into mass consciousness as a legal person. I have chosen to conclude this chapter by dwelling on a moment in which I too feel discomfort in order to acknowledge my own complicity in the creation of the contradictory ideological forces that Grosvenor is trying to negotiate. Her celebration of the successful instantiation of black patriarchy may be intended as a counter to commonplace representations of African American men as operating outside family structures, but the photograph of the four "Oscar Browns" is also troubling for those who are working not only to establish maternity as a "legitimate" means of cultural inheritance but more fundamentally to question the imperative for heterosexual reproductivity itself.

Though Dash had initially created the Unborn Child in the wake of her own daughter's birth in 1984, early in the filming of *Daughters of the Dust* she chose to terminate an unplanned pregnancy rather than disrupt her work (R. Curry 348). "*Daughters* would become the child that I would bear that year," Dash explained in a book she published following the film's release (10). Discussing the ramifications of Dash's decision, Curry suggests that the Unborn Child is not "an emblem of the political right-to-life. . . . She is, rather, emblem of the spirit that cannot be touched, harmed, or forgotten; the spirit that cannot be removed ever from the past; the spirit that passes in and out of this world by choice" (352). Though I would wish to supplement this argument with more attention to the ways in which Dash is a product of, as well as a commentator on, her social context, Curry is surely right to remind us that the "same" discourses often operate differently in divergent cultural contexts.[29] In the next chapter, I will pursue this issue by considering how the connection between African American women and food has helped structure two interlocking discourses through which white feminist "body" politics have been articulated since the Black Power era: eating disorders and reproductive rights.

SEVEN

"How Mama Started to Get Large"

Eating Disorders, Fetal Rights, and Black Female Appetite

"Black women let themselves go," he said, even as he painted them as magnificent giants, breeding forth the warriors of the new universe. "They are so *fat*," he would say, even as he sculpted a "Big Bessie Smith" in solid marble, caressing her monstrous and lovely flanks with an admiring hand.

Alice Walker, Meridian, 1976

During the era when *Vibration Cooking* appeared, many African American women in addition to Vertamae Grosvenor were using discussions of culinary traditions to position themselves within an often hostile social, cultural, and political milieu. As we have seen, though, the discourse of soul was problematic not simply because white people were appropriating it and not simply because it was associated with the much maligned black middle class. The discourse was problematic because it also encoded American culture's ambivalent attitude toward black women, its desire for black female nurture and its concomitant fear of black female control. Grosvenor, as a result, has hardly been the only African American woman cookbook writer since the early 1970s to distance herself from the celebration of soul.

Perhaps most notably, by the time Grosvenor achieved fame, chef Edna Lewis had already been working to introduce younger generations to the "bountiful foods—vegetables, fruits, grains, beans"—she knew when growing up (quoted in Gee 128). Whereas Lewis's first cookbook, *The Edna Lewis Cookbook* (1972), advocates for fresh foods without specifying its author's racial identity, both *The Taste of Country Cooking* (1976) and *In Pursuit of Flavor* (1988) narrate her origins in a close-knit, all-black Virginia farming community and make clear that the "bountiful foods" she cherishes should emphatically not be confused with the chitterlings, cornbread, and greens popularized as authentically black fare during the Black Power era. Lewis, a *Southern Living* reporter has noted, "shudders at the idea of 'soul food'" (Gee 128), describing it as "hard-times food in Harlem—not true Southern food" (quoted in Gee 128).[1]

For many years now, Lewis has voiced concern that modern food production and distribution technologies have destroyed the "taste" of food. This aspect of her culinary career particularly interests me since most African American women cookbook writers with whose work I am familiar focus far more on the labor undertaken by black women in preparing food than on their practices of, and feelings about, consuming what they and others have created. Granted, such an omission makes perfect sense given the generic conventions of the cookbook. Yet the reader also intuits that these texts are somehow incomplete, that the whole point of the story is simply missing. It is for this reason, then, that Pearl Bailey's *Pearl's Kitchen* once again stands out. In the process of negotiating a viable subject position with respect to the contradictory ideology of soul, Bailey offers a truly remarkable reminiscence about how her own mother approached the emotionally charged activity of eating.

When Bailey was a child, her mother would rarely consume meals along with the family. Instead she would fill a small saucer with food and sit at the corner of the table. "Once in a while she would ask someone to put a little fat in the saucer for Mama and she would eat that" (6). Yet, despite her mother's apparently abstemious appetite, the young Pearl "noticed that Mama was getting larger and larger. Number one, she did a pretty good job with that little saucer at the corner of the table. Without our thinking of it, she really consumed as much as all the kids put together, bless her heart. But that was not the whole story about how Mama started to get large" (6). As it turns out, after breakfast each morning Bailey's mother would go out, ostensibly in order to play the numbers. One morning, however, she left one of her number slips behind. Having noticed her mother's oversight and hoping to perform a good deed, "little Pearlie Mae" set out with the slip in search of her (6). With evident amusement, Bailey recalls:

> Along the way I happened to pass a restaurant with a big plate-glass window. First I passed it by and then something struck me—I took a couple of skips backward and stuck my face up against the window. There sat my wonderful Mama, pancakes stacked as high as her head, sausage on a plate next to them, and there were home-fried potatoes and coffee. Mama had her head buried down eating away. (7)

Too young to understand the significance of her discovery, Bailey tapped on the window to attract her mother's attention. Displeased, to say the least, her mother informed her later, "It's a terrible thing when a Mother has to have her own children come spying on her" (7).

Though Bailey realizes in retrospect that she had embarrassed her mother, she never really attempts to come to terms with the import of this memory: "Going out to the restaurant and to place her policy slip each morning was about the only time Mama left the house. . . . Mama stayed in her house, which really was her castle, and she ran it efficiently and with great dedication" (7). True enough, but the story would surely also suggest that Bailey's mother was trying to satisfy other needs of which her family was not aware. Not unlike the pancake-craving Fannie

Hurst of *No Food with My Meals*, Bailey's mother inhabited a social structure that has cast many non-WASP women as unrelenting nurturers and consequently stigmatized their own expressions of hunger and desire. What this means is that we as readers never do get the "whole story" about how Bailey's mother "started to get large."

I do not presume to have access to that story myself. This chapter will, though, at least try to contextualize "Mama's" secret by asking how the widespread association of black women with food in U.S. culture has coexisted with a seeming paucity of discourses about what African American women eat. To pursue this question, I will examine how the construction of black female appetite in the post–World War II United States is inflected by, and in turn inflects, debates over the boundaries and ontological status of the "embodied" subject. More precisely, I will focus on the interlocking domains of eating disorders and fetal harm. Despite anecdotal evidence to the contrary such as this narrative from Pearl Bailey, African American women have, by and large, been perceived as absences in the discourses of eating disorders. At the same time, African American women have been very much a presence in the discourses of fetal harm—especially the purported epidemics of Fetal Alcohol Syndrome (FAS) and "crack babies" in the 1980s. Each of these topics has generated a tremendous amount of discussion in popular and academic circles but, for the most part, not in the same breath.[2]

My reasons for wishing to analyze these discourses together should not be surprising given the current articulation of eating, as well as drug-taking, via the rhetoric of "addiction." In an essay devoted to understanding the cultural logic that underwrites the emergence of this perception, Eve Sedgwick has observed:

> [I]f addiction can include ingestion, *or* refusal, *or* controlled intermittent ingestion of a given substance; and if the concept of "substance" has become too elastic to draw a boundary between the exoticism of the "foreign substance" and the domesticity of, say, "food"; then the locus of addictiveness cannot be the substance itself and can scarcely even be the body *itself*, but must be some overarching abstraction that governs the narrative relations between them. ("Epidemics" 131)

Whereas Sedgwick focuses on the "overarching abstraction" of "will" as that which "governs the narrative relations between" substance and body, I would like to posit black female appetite as a more culturally specific manifestation of this abstraction: it helps sustain the slippage of bodily pollution from the "foreign substance" of drugs and alcohol to the "domesticity" of food. The conjectural crossmapping of eating disorders and fetal harm that follows will explore how African American women have been caught up in, and how they have attempted to destabilize, the binary through which these discourses construct their appetites as either natural or pathological, as resistant to interrogation while subject to constant surveillance.

"Fat Is a Black Woman's Issue"

Dieting within a Black cultural context means being able to eat fried chicken, greens and cornbread and still lose weight.

Lloyd Gite and Jean Perry, "Diet: Losing Weight Soulfully," 1983

Anorexia nervosa refers to self-imposed starvation; bulimia is also called the binge-purge cycle. Since the early 1970s, both have been widely construed in popular and academic discourses as symptoms/syndromes displayed by young, presumptively heterosexual white women from middle- and upper-class nuclear families. In addition to the multitude of articles on dieting and body image in popular magazines aimed at young white women, I have in mind here mainly the work of white feminist scholars such as Kim Chernin and Joan Jacobs Brumberg, as well as the earlier essays of Susan Bordo. Less well known among humanists would be the clinical research of psychiatrists and other medical professionals who publish their findings in the *International Journal of Eating Disorders*, founded in 1981. Here, too, with very few exceptions, the object of their gaze has until recently been young, bourgeois, female, and white.[3] As readers who are familiar with this subject will realize, there are significant differences in the models proposed for interpreting eating disorders. Chernin and Bordo basically view disorderly eating as normative female behavior, Chernin from a feminist psychoanalytic perspective and Bordo from a feminist Foucauldian perspective. Brumberg sets forth an explanatory model in which biology, psychology, and culture interact, and she is somewhat more receptive than are Chernin and Bordo to biomedical analyses of eating disorders as a "pathology" that can be treated with a combination of drugs and therapy.

My initial question in approaching this topic (almost a decade ago) was: Why are African American women largely absent from these white-authored discourses of eating disorders? Diverse students, friends, and colleagues with whom I discussed the topic concluded that black women simply do not "get" them. Two of my African American women students reached this conclusion even in the context of offering unsolicited commentary about their experiences with Slim-Fast and Dexatrim. My early inquiries having thus led me to believe that this was a topic worth pursuing, I reframed the question. Rather than assuming that African American women were absent from discourses of eating disorders, I began asking: Where are African American women? How are they present? One answer was in the index and footnotes—literally, in Brumberg's otherwise meticulously researched 1988 history of anorexia, *Fasting Girls*. The sole entry in her index on African American women reads: "Blacks, as anorectics, 284n14" (361).

What intrigued me was why someone who interrogates the cultural construction of white female appetite with such brilliance would relegate African American women to a footnote. There Brumberg paraphrases the claim of medical researcher L. K. George Hsu that "the rarity among blacks of anorexia nervosa and bulimia is the result of cultural differences that protect young black women from the negative self-image and intense pressure for slimness that are part of the white middle-class experience" (284). Brumberg comments: "These data, if correct, are telling evidence of the separateness of black culture and white culture and their differential strengths" (284). The proviso "if correct" surely indicates that Brumberg recognized the inadequacy of such an analysis, particularly in its conflation of "negative self-image" with "intense pressure for slimness."[4] As sociologist Becky Thompson has pointed out, "ideology about black women's bodies has been invisibly inscribed onto what is professed about white women's bodies" (13). Black women are not just a footnote but a constitutive footnote; they are not just an absence in eating disorders but a constitutive absence, and this is an important distinction.

Whereas the creation of mammy/cook figures such as Aunt Jemima entailed a naturalization and/or biologization of black female cooking skills, these discourses of eating disorders have relied on a naturalization of black female appetite. This tendency is particularly apparent in the work of Kim Chernin. In her 1981 book *The Obsession*, Chernin argues that "women" have not been allowed to have a "natural" relationship to "our" appetites and bodies (1–3). Western culture fears fully developed womanhood, she writes, and thus the emergence of anorexia nervosa and bulimia in conjunction with the rise of second-wave feminism could be interpreted as a sign of younger women's conflicted feelings about their mothers and about inhabiting adult women's bodies. The anorectic attempts to resolve these conflicts by retaining the body of a child. In other words, "large size, maturity, voluptuousness, massiveness, strength, and power are not permitted if we wish to conform to our culture's ideal. Our bodies, which have knowledge of life, must undo this fullness of knowing and make themselves look like the body of a precocious child if we wish to win the approval of our culture" (94). For Chernin, "large size, maturity, voluptuousness, massiveness, strength, and power" are valorized terms, ideals to which "we" have not been "permitted" to aspire. But given that traits such as "strength" have long been attributed to African American women in the context of an indictment of black matriarchy, one can only wonder what relationship black women bear to Chernin's "we."

Viewed from this perspective, Chernin's complaint seems to be that the hegemonic subject positions available to bourgeois white women have not been constituted in the same way as the positions available to black women, particularly those of the lower classes. Yet she never explicitly addresses the fact that her model for the anorectic is an adolescent white female. Indeed, Chernin even includes a chapter in *The Obsession* called "The Matriarch" that invokes a mythic past of female power and has no direct reference to race. Intriguingly, however, near the outset of the book she quotes from "Free Flight" (c. 1980), by black feminist essayist and poet June Jordan (see *Obsession* 12). After acknowledging that "[n]othing fills me up at night," the poem's speaker proceeds to detail her sleep-interrupting desire for food ("cherry pie hot from the oven with Something Like Vermont / Cheddar Cheese," etc.) as a symptom of other emotional needs (Jordan 55). In a subsequent annotation of the poem, Chernin subsumes Jordan under the normatively white category "woman" and never questions her relationship to ideals such as "massiveness, strength, and power." To have acknowledged Jordan's race would have disrupted the models of female development Chernin was setting up. It would have forced her to confront the ways in which her conceptions of the "natural"—"natural bodies" and "natural appetites"—are already inscribed by differences of gender, race, class, and sexuality.

In the more recent essays collected in *Unbearable Weight* (1993), Susan Bordo has begun to assess the racial inscriptions of the consuming female body. Extrapolating from her subtle and innovative work on bourgeois white women and eating disorders, Bordo suggests that the hegemony of white popular culture and upward class mobility have resulted in increased pressure on African American women to become slender. In other words, notwithstanding the ongoing fissures between black and white culture, black women are internalizing expectations that they will emulate the controlled bodily boundaries once idealized mainly for middle-class white women. As Bordo explains:

> Arguably, a case could once be made for a contrast between (middle-class, heterosexual) white women's obsessive relations with food and a more accepting attitude toward women's appetites within African American communities. But in the nineties, features on diet, exercise, and body-image problems have grown increasingly prominent in magazines aimed at African American readers, reflecting the cultural reality that for most women today—whatever their racial or ethnic identity, and increasingly across class and sexual-orientation differences as well—free and easy relations with food are at best a relic of the past. (103)

Although my own work on food has been enormously enabled by Bordo's precedent, my interest in historicizing the cultural construction of eating disorders as an epistemological domain since the early 1970s leads me to believe that we cannot simply add women who are not middle-class, heterosexual, and white into the mix without fundamentally altering the discourses themselves. As Bordo herself points out, moreover, there have long been regulatory practices of black femininity—hair straightening, skin bleaching, etc.—and any discussion of black women's dietary habits needs ideally to be situated as part of a whole range of practices through which black women have historically "performed" their embodied identities.

In this respect, some of the most informative work on women of color and food is that by Becky Thompson, whose book *A Hunger So Wide and So Deep* (1994) interrogates what she redesignates as "eating problems" among African American, Latina, Jewish, and lesbian women.[5] "It is no surprise," Thompson points out, "that appetites and food take on metaphorical significance in a society in which women typically are responsible for food preparation and yet are taught to deny themselves ample appetites" (5). Working to disrupt the reductive privileging of gender in traditional discourses of eating disorders, Thompson argues that women across the spectrum of race, ethnicity, class, and sexual orientation display symptoms of a troubled relationship to their own bodies and consequently to food. Many eat to suppress emotions, particularly the post-traumatic stress of incest and sexual assault, as well as the ongoing frustrations of life in a white-supremacist, heterosexist, capitalist patriarchy. In this fashion, Thompson undermines the condescending presumption that women who suffer from eating problems are simply narcissists who are obsessed with their appearances. Her interviews with numerous women have led Thompson to conclude, quite to the contrary, that "discomfort with weight, bodies, and appetite are often the metaphors girls and women use to speak about atrocities. To hear only concerns about appearance or gender inequality is to miss the complex origins of eating problems" (12).

Clearly one might critique all this work, Thompson's included, for its tendency to naturalize the appetites and practices of bodily regulation enacted by men—though Bordo has since helped fill in this gap with typically pathbreaking work on masculinity ("Reading"). But my aim here is not primarily to intervene in the debate over whether eating disorders are normative or pathological, or to stake out the most purely constructivist position for myself. Rather, I want to stress several different points geared to my investigation into the status of black female appetite. Though for the purposes of this chapter I have found it useful to assimilate starving, bingeing, and purging under the rubric of "appetite," it is surely necessary to make distinctions among the discourses, practices, and spectacles of anorexia, bulimia, and obesity. If black women have functioned as foundational absences in the emergence of contemporary discourses of eating disorders, they most certainly have been highly visible in the specularization of corpulence in U.S. culture.

Donald Bogle recounts in *Toms, Coons, Mulattoes, Mammies, and Bucks*, for instance, the gastronomic lengths to which Louise Beavers was forced in order to replicate the stereotypical bodily boundaries of "mammy." Well known, as we have seen, for her portrayal of Delilah in John Stahl's film version of *Imitation of Life*, Beavers regularly went on "force-feed diets, compelling herself to eat beyond her normal appetite. Generally, she weighed close to two hundred pounds, but it was a steady battle for her to stay overweight. During filming, due to pressures, she often lost weight and then had to be padded to look more like a full-bosomed domestic who was capable of carrying the world on her shoulders" (63). *Imitation of Life*'s white female star, Claudette Colbert, remains intelligible as a sexual object—despite her entry into the public domain of business—in part by virtue of her visible physical difference from Beavers. The widespread conflation of African American female bodies and fat is, then, surely a function of the psychic needs of the dominant white society.

Responding to this harmful cultural legacy, in 1989 *Essence* magazine published an autobiographical essay entitled "Fat Is a Black Woman's Issue." Author Retha Powers, a college student, was herself appropriating the title of Susie Orbach's pathbreaking book *Fat Is a Feminist Issue* (1978). Orbach had helped pioneer second-wave feminism's exploration of dieting and food obsession as adaptive female behaviors, but hers was a polemic that also hedged in its treatment of women of color. Taking issue with such exclusions, Powers writes about her obsession with the "dirty, sinful act" of eating (78) and details her struggles to stop the self-destructive cycle of dieting, bingeing, purging, and laxative abuse. She questions the assumptions of various people who told her over the years not to worry about her dietary habits because, in their words, "fat is more acceptable in the Black community" (78). Whereas Kim Chernin sees pressure on middle-class white women to be thin as a form of cultural gynophobia, Powers implies that the *lack* of this pressure on her—as an African American woman—is a form of racism. Offering the logical corollary to Alice Walker's observation that "the black woman is herself a symbol of nourishment" ("Giving" 22–23), Powers asserts that she will "no longer accept the role of all-giving nurturer" (136).

Tania Modleski has explicated white investments in black female corpulence by analyzing contemporary American culture's "horror of the body" and "the special role played by the woman of color as receptacle of these fears" (*Feminism* 130). She argues, for example, that in the 1988 film *Crossing Delancey*, "The function of the fat, sexually voracious black woman . . . is to enable the white Jewish subculture, through its heterosexual love story, to represent itself in a highly sentimentalized, romanticized, and sublimated light, while disavowing the desires and discontents underlying the civilization it is promoting" (*Feminism* 130). It is imperative, Modleski continues, that we "consider the ways in which ethnic and racial groups are played off against—and play themselves off against—one another" (*Feminism* 130). In light of her comments, it is surely significant that both Orbach and Chernin explicitly refer to how their identities as Jewish women have shaped their attitudes toward food, eating, and body size. As Orbach recalls, "I was a Jewish beatnik and I would be *zaftig*" (xv).[6] Although Orbach and Chernin foreground their conflicted relationship to strictures of Anglo American rather than African American femininity, it seems clear that their self-perceptions are no less inflected by ideology about the bodies of black than of white women.

In her 1976 novel *Meridian*, Alice Walker might be said to prefigure the intertwined inscriptions of Jewish and African American femininity which were, at the time, emerging in discourses of eating disorders. Even though Truman Held complains that black women "let themselves go," it is evident that the "voluptuous black bodies" that he sculpts exert a strong hold on his imagination (168). Yet when his ex-wife, Jewish civil rights activist Lynne Rabinowitz, shows up on his doorstep to inform him of their daughter Camara's life-threatening injury at the hands of a white racist, Walker writes that Truman takes "her in from white parched face and cracked lips to the thick unstylish bulges she thought she was hiding under her coat" (170). In this fashion, *Meridian* reveals how scholarly discourses of eating disorders were inflected from the outset by conflicts between black and Jewish women. These conflicts were exacerbated by both the interracial sexual ethos of the "Freedom Summers" and the expulsion of Jewish activists from civil rights organizations in the wake of the rise of Black Power. Walker might even be understood to code a distinction between different types of female "fat." This distinction inheres, in part, in women's attitudes toward their own bodies, attitudes that reflect internalized cultural norms. Thus Walker attributes to Lynne feelings of shame about her size, as well as a desire once again to possess the body that Truman had formerly compared to "a straw in the wind" (168). Walker insinuates, moreover, that black men have been complicit in helping maintain such impossible-to-satisfy double standards.

Even while acknowledging that fat has functioned as a site of (and psychic resolution for) interracial and interethnic conflict, we should not overlook the fact that many African American women, like Walker, have redeployed the rhetoric and spectacle of the "large" black female body as a form of self-affirmation and political protest. Here one thinks of a tradition stretching from activists such as Sojourner Truth to contemporary rappers including Queen Latifah and Salt 'N' Pepa.

In her "Ladies First" video, for example, Queen Latifah flaunts her refusal to conform to U.S. culture's pervasive imagery of female slimness while also positioning
herself, according to Tricia Rose, "as part of a rich legacy of black women's activism, racial commitment, and cultural pride" (164). The members of Salt 'N'
Pepa, by contrast, often foreground "butts" in their videos. Rose claims that in so
doing they appropriate "a complex history of white scrutiny of black female bodies,
from the repulsion and fascination with and naked exhibition of Sara Bartmann as
'The Hottentot Venus' in the early 1800s to the perverse and exoticized pleasure
many Europeans received from Josephine Baker's aggressively behind-centered
dances" (167–68).[7]

   African American women have, then, always been "presences" in discourses
about food and U.S. identities, particularly in specular form as the naturalized fat
body. Consequently, it is important to recognize that what black women such as
Retha Powers, Alice Walker, June Jordan, and many others have been appropriating in recent years is not so much the practices of disorderly (or problematic) eating as the discourses themselves.[8] By writing themselves into an epistemological
domain according to which large numbers of white women have typically been
understood to enact an "unnatural" relationship to their appetites and bodies,
these African American women have been contesting normative black female
subject positions and insisting on their psychological complexity as human beings.
They are refusing to be the constitutive absence in one of the central binaries
through which the identities of white women in the United States have been constructed since the early 1970s.

   To talk about eating disorders as a discourse that can be appropriated as a tactic of resistance is obviously problematic, however, since it threatens to trivialize
the health hazards for African American women of symptoms such as excess
weight, bingeing and purging, and laxative abuse. Becky Thompson recounts the
story of one Puerto Rican woman, Vera, who has "reassessed the notion of bingeing as an addiction" (127) and led Thompson to question "whether there is something inherently wrong with using food as a comfort when something terrible occurs" (127). Yet even while pointing toward the necessity of questioning the
attribution of "addiction" to behaviors involving the consumption of food, indeed
even while pointing toward the necessity of questioning the heterosexist and
racist assumptions which underwrite the Western medical establishment as a
whole, Thompson still makes clear, as do the essays collected by Evelyn White in
The Black Women's Health Book (1990), that women of color, working-class women,
and lesbians have often lacked the opportunity to take advantage of beneficial aspects of institutionalized medicine.

   Because of their overdetermined positioning at the bottom of the U.S. socioeconomic ladder, women of color generally have less access to nutritional food and
health care than do typically more privileged whites; consequently, they are more
prone to preventable health problems such as hypertension and "sugar" diabetes.
Supporting their claims, the *New York Times* reported in January 1994: "Doctors
appear to be less likely to tell black women to quit smoking and drinking during
pregnancy than they are to tell white women" ("Study"). Given such racist inconsistencies in the medical care offered by U.S. physicians, one might well greet with

pleasure the news that the health of African American women is both under investigation and of interest to the newspaper of record. Yet, of course, I have an ulterior motive in referring to this particular story from the *Times*. I repeat: "Doctors appear to be less likely to tell black women to quit smoking and drinking *during pregnancy* than they are to tell white women."

As this news story makes clear, it would surely be inaccurate to imply that because black women have been situated as the "natural" in the domain of eating disorders, there have been no discourses emanating from white culture in recent years that expressly target (and construe as "unnatural") black female appetite. If the desires of middle-class white women have been constructed since the early 1970s in large part via anorexia and bulimia, so the desires of lower-class black women have been constructed in terms of motherhood and matriarchy. Young white women purportedly want nothing more than to be thin; young black women, nothing more than to have babies. The former are often understood to be engaged in a symbolic refusal of pregnancy; the latter, in an equally defiant embrace thereof. The discussions of crack babies and FAS that proliferated during the 1980s and early 1990s were, moreover, far more likely to result in the punishment of black (and, in the case of FAS, Native American) than white women.[9]

In other words, whereas doctors have been careful to warn pregnant white women to quit smoking and drinking, they have been far more likely to report analogous practices of black women to the police. In my work on soul food and black maternity, I have already interrogated the perception that the pregnant black body presents a "danger" to black manhood, and I have suggested that this incessant concern with black matriarchy has also enabled the expression of anxieties about the precarious status of white male dominance in the wake of the liberatory social movements of the 1960s and early 1970s. Here, then, I would like to resume this discussion by thinking further about the motivations underlying the displacement of discourses about black women's appetites onto the health of black fetuses. If Lauren Berlant is right to argue that the contemporary romance with the fetus marks a "crisis" in the (re)production of the "national body," a crisis which in turn reflects "major changes" in the "juridical and cultural logics of American personhood" ("America" 148), then my aim is to understand how the connection between black women and food is imbricated in this far-reaching national transformation.

"The Most Perilous Environment"

> Quite simply, the womb has become the most perilous environment in
> which humans have to live.
>
> Gerald Leach, *The Biocrats*, 1970

Midway through a 1990 article on the emergence of "fetal rights," *Nation* columnist Katha Pollitt pondered: "How have we come to see women as the major threat to the health of their newborns, and the womb as the most dangerous place a child will ever inhabit?" (410). Pollitt was responding to a trend that has been gaining force in conjunction with the opposing movements to legalize and (re)criminalize abortion, a trend epitomized by Gerald Leach's observation about the perils of life in the womb. Twenty-three years after *The Biocrats* was published, an evolutionary biologist at Harvard, David Haig, brought Leach's claim to fruition by using Darwinian theory to interpret human pregnancy. Because sexual reproduction results in a child's sharing "only half of its genes with the mother" (Lipsitch), Haig claims that many "difficulties in pregnancy probably come about because there are genetic conflicts between what is best for the mother's genes and what is best for fetal genes" (quoted in Lipsitch). But since under most circumstances the fetus cannot survive if the woman carrying it dies—although the proliferation of technologically sustained "post-mortem" pregnancies suggests how rapidly such circumstances are changing—Haig concludes that pregnancy is "a conflict of interest within a basically peaceful society" (quoted in Lipsitch).[10] Of course, such utero-phobia "is not a modern idea" (Corea 251). Yet the contemporary flowering of concerns about fetal endangerment is, many feminist scholars have contended, at least in part a backlash against second-wave white feminism and the Supreme Court's 1973 decision granting women a legal right to abortion.

Courtesy of modern technologies of vision such as sonograms, the fetus has indeed emerged as a "person" in its own right.[11] It is granted a status theoretically equal to, and in practice often above, that of the woman who carries it by doctors who now specialize in the field of Maternal-Fetal medicine rather than OB-GYN. The fetus is even the subject of advertisements by the General Motors corporation, whose researchers have been "developing the first 'pregnant' crash dummy" because, in their words, "Not all passengers can be seen. But they all need protection" (General). "Protection from whom?" one might well ask. In her provocative 1992 essay "The Abortion Question and the Death of Man," Mary Poovey explains how feminist use of both privacy and equality arguments in advocating reproductive freedom has inadvertently contributed to this sacralization of the fetus as a justification for curtailing women's rights. Certainly feminist arguments for the legalization of abortion have, she points out, been readily appropriated by those who oppose that right. Thus the slogan "Equal Rights for Women" becomes the bumper sticker "Equal Rights for Unborn Women." In the rhetoric of anti-abortionists, Poovey demonstrates, terms such as "'choice,' 'privacy,' and 'rights' invert effortlessly into their opposites, precisely because, regardless of who uses them, these terms belong to a single set of metaphysical assumptions" (249).

Such appropriations are enabled, in other words, by the fact that the "rights" discourses invoked by many feminists rely on the prior figuration of a body—what Poovey calls a "metaphysics of substance" (241)—which is normatively rational, bourgeois, white, heterosexual, and male. In this metaphysics, the mark of female difference is the womb, which means that, unlike the male body, the female body is always presumptively pregnable.[12] Poovey's response to this dilemma is to insist that advocates for women's reproductive rights not downplay differences among women such as class, race, sexuality, ethnicity, and nationality that determine any given woman's access to legal rights. She argues, moreover, that we need to develop a politics which foregrounds the contingency of the body and which recognizes that rights are only constituted in a matrix of relationships. The decision of an individual woman regarding whether to carry a pregnancy to term, for example, will inevitably have an impact on the larger social structure (economically, demographically, etc.), and it will often affect her immediate family and friends as well. In Poovey's view, acknowledging such complexities might work to secure, rather than undermine, the feminist goal of procuring reproductive self-determination by situating that goal in the context of a broader agenda for social justice.

My own thinking has been tremendously influenced by Poovey's incisive efforts to formulate an approach to reproductive practices which is less easily appropriated by opponents of feminism than current strategies have been, and which does not privilege heterosexual middle-class white women as the norm. Still, just as I have tried to reconceptualize the discourses of eating disorders from a perspective that begins with the subject positions typically made available to and frequently rescripted by African American women, so it might be useful to supplement Poovey's analysis by interpreting current debates over reproductive politics from an analogous point of view. After all, the discourses of fetal rights have not emerged solely as a backlash against contemporary white feminists, a backlash which is simply played out on the bodies of lower-class women of color because they are more vulnerable to social control than are wealthy whites. Rather, it seems to me that women of color have been a primary target of fetal rights activists because anxiety about black maternity has provided a primary template from which contemporary anxieties about white maternity have been derived.

Such fears often operate in fascistically friendly ways. Hence my initially optimistic response to the *New York Times* article about the failure of doctors to warn pregnant African American women about the dangers of smoking and drinking during pregnancy. Yet the punitive underpinnings of such concern for black women's health is amply illustrated by another article that the *New York Times* published the following day, coincidentally, under the heading "Hospital Is Accused of Illegal Drug Testing." The Medical University of South Carolina had instituted a drug-testing program "intended to force drug-addicted women who are pregnant to stop using drugs by threatening them with jail if they fail to cooperate with the hospital's regimen of prenatal visits and to attend a drug-treatment program" (Hilts A12). Virtually all the women targeted by this program were African Americans. Nationwide, as Dorothy Roberts has demonstrated, virtually all the women jailed for taking drugs while pregnant, forced to undergo unwanted caesareans, or otherwise subjected to forms of maternal "prior restraint" have been lower-class women of color.

Roberts insists that efforts to understand the motivating force behind this fixation on fetal contamination absolutely must begin with reference to the class, race, and sexuality of the women most likely to be punished for violating fetal endangerment laws. The discussions of crack babies that proliferated during the 1980s stemmed, she suggests, far more from a cultural imperative to control impoverished women of color than to ensure the health and safety of their children: "If prosecutors had instead chosen to prosecute affluent women addicted to alcohol or prescription medication, the policy of criminalizing prenatal conduct very likely would have suffered a hasty demise. Society is much more willing to condone the punishment of poor women of color who fail to meet the middle-class ideal of motherhood" ("Punishing" 1436). Roberts claims, moreover, that "[t]he government's choice of a punitive response" to prenatal drug use "perpetuates the historical devaluation of Black women as mothers" ("Punishing" 1423). Whereas Hortense Spillers explains the hegemony of American belief in the myth of black matriarchy as a legacy of slavery's erasure of the name of the black father, Roberts construes the more recent fixation on lower-class black maternity as, in part, a legacy of black women's abuse as "breeders" during slavery. Slaveholders would whip pregnant slaves by forcing them "to lie face down in a depression in the ground while they were whipped. This procedure allowed the masters to protect the fetus while abusing the mother" ("Punishing" 1438).[13] Such brutality "serves," Roberts says, "as a powerful metaphor for the evils of a fetal protection policy that denies the humanity of the mother" ("Punishing" 1438).[14]

As we have seen, Black Arts and Black Power discourses obsessively recycled this history but distorted it by construing the slave mother rather than a proslavery legal system as the threat to the autonomy of the black male child. Surely not coincidentally, in my opinion, it did so in the wake not just of the publication of the Moynihan Report but also of Lennart Nilsson's 1965 *Life* magazine photographs of the "Drama of Life before Birth," which pioneered the projection of the fetus into the pop cultural U.S. imagination. In chapter 3 I pointed out that one important subtext for the Moynihan Report's condemnation of black matriarchy was actually anxiety about declining birth rates and increasing workforce participation on the part of white women. Here I would add that, according to Mimi Abramovitz, what is often paraded as a "dramatic increase in the percentage of births to unmarried black women" since the 1960s "reflects a drop in the overall fertility and birth rates of *married* black women relative to *unmarried* black women, and not an increase in child bearing by the latter" (354). In fact, from 1970 to 1980 "the unmarried black birth rate . . . fell by 13 percent, while that of whites rose by 27 percent" (354). Younger white women have been bearing fewer children than their immediate predecessors of the baby-boom generation, but they have been more likely to do so outside of the patriarchally sanctioned auspices of marriage. Taken together, what these statistics can help explain is why, by the early 1970s, white men were beginning to identify with this newly "visible" fetus as a tactic for bemoaning their (perceived) loss of patriarchal authority. In so doing, I would stress, they were emulating a tactic already deployed with considerable success by black men.[15]

Granted, as Lisa Bower rightly insists, the "use of statistical data [often] summons forth an analytic framework . . . which is presumed to be neutral but actually sustains the erasure of difference except as a deviant outlier" (143). In her own work, Bower instead draws on Toni Morrison's *Playing in the Dark* to develop a tropological analysis of the spectral black presence in putatively objective social science discourses of reproduction. She suggests that "Africanism, understood as stereotypic views of blackness connected to substance-abusing women of color, functions 'metaphysically' to reaffirm white maternal identities that have been seriously eroded" (147). The punitive measures directed toward pregnant black women might thus be understood as one strategy through which the dominant white culture is negotiating changes wrought by the social movements of the 1960s and early 1970s, as well as the (not-unrelated) proliferation of assisted reproductive technologies. "A concern with fetal harm, like contemporary debates about family values, single mothers, and homosexualities, is a reaction to the unsettling of 'natural' categories of sexed, gendered identities," Bower contends (147). In a related vein, Valerie Hartouni has pointed out that the perception that there is an "infertility epidemic" among middle-class, professional white women has been fundamentally structured by assumptions about black female reproductive practices: "Both text and subtext are straightforward: white women want babies but cannot have them, and black and other 'minority' women, coded as 'breeders' (and welfare dependents) within American society, are having babies 'they' cannot take care of and whom 'we' do not want" (45).

Given the way the iconography of the pregnant black addict has been invoked as a strategy for displacing such anxieties about contemporary white female reproductive practices, it may well be a risky undertaking for African American women to foreground the individual body and appetite as a means of empowerment. As Poovey's analysis of the rhetoric of "rights" would suggest, such discourses can readily be redeployed to legitimate ideologies according to which the black female body has historically been construed as a source of pollution. I envision here a shift from *Fat Is a Feminist Issue* to "Fat Is a Black Woman's Issue" to "Fat Is a Black Fetal Issue"—and indeed studies of whether a "fatty" maternal diet causes childhood cancer have already been conducted.[16] Taking into account what we have already seen of how race and class structure the state's willingness to authorize the imprisonment of and invasive procedures on pregnant women, it hardly seems a stretch to suggest that the first person to be prosecuted for consuming too much fat while pregnant will not be a member of the white bourgeoisie.

Many of the contributors to *The Black Women's Health Book* acknowledge this double bind. To remain silent about black female health problems and appetites is to be complicit in a larger cultural erasure of the lives and needs of women of color. At the same time, it is problematic for African American women to appropriate discourses that originated via the inscription of their oppression. Can there exist an "anorexic" or "bulimic" black woman? Can there exist a Caucasian crack baby? Or is the former inevitably assimilated, analytically, into whiteness, and the latter, exiled to the domain of black Others? In his study of male sexuality and social dis-ease in late-nineteenth-century England, Ed Cohen has argued that we need to "imagine how we can historically problematize the ways the 'oppositional' terms of dominance come to be embedded within the categories of resistance" (213). Cohen is referring specifically to the widespread use of the term "queer" among activists for lesbian and gay rights, but his general point is surely applicable here as well. To develop an agenda for bettering black women's health, scholars and activists must work to formulate a vocabulary in which black women are not already inscribed as (1) natural, and therefore never in need of social benefits, such as health care, or (2) unnatural, and therefore always in need of social regulation.

In a 1987 address called "Sick and Tired of Being Sick and Tired," Angela Davis negotiated these contradictory obstacles by insisting on the "urgency of contextualizing Black women's health in relation to the prevailing political conditions. While our health is undeniably assaulted by natural forces frequently beyond our control, all too often the enemies of our physical and emotional well-being are social and political" (19). Davis proceeded to discuss Department of Defense spending, CIA operations in Angola, Reagan's nomination of Robert Bork to the Supreme Court, apartheid in South Africa, and continuing congressional support for the Nicaraguan Contras—all of which she construed as integral to the politics of black women's health. "We must," she concluded, "learn consistently to place our battle for universally accessible health care in its larger social and political context" (25). In her refusal to distinguish between bodily and social boundaries, in her affirmation of Audre Lorde's claim that "[b]attling racism and battling heterosexism and battling apartheid share the same urgency inside me as battling cancer," Davis offers a template for the sort of political praxis Mary Poovey seems to have in mind (Lorde, "Burst" 116; quoted in Davis 26). It is a template for a political praxis that at least attempts to be less than amenable to reappropriation by the reactionary right. The efficacy of such "politics unbound" is yet to be determined, but, in my perception, Davis's lead is a wise one to follow.

Accordingly, as a further attempt to contextualize my discussion of eating disorders and fetal rights in a broader sociopolitical framework, I need to complicate matters by drawing attention to a significant site of terminological, and therefore hermeneutic, slippage in the argument I have developed thus far. In her work on contemporary reproductive technologies, Hartouni observes that by portraying "a woman and the fetus she carries as two separate, adversarily related individuals— one a potential killer, the other innately *innocent*," members of the white male–dominated medical establishment "engender and promote the notion that, whereas women once nurtured their unborn, they now regularly abuse or neglect them and cannot be trusted not to. Where gestation was itself once the most *natural* of processes, it has now become treacherous" (emphasis added; 41).[17] What intrigues me are the implications of Hartouni's conterminous use of the adjectives "innocent" and "natural." I have foregrounded the natural/unnatural binary in this chapter because it has been central to the rhetoric of "soul" and attendant debates over black and counterculture culinary practices, as well as to the construction of eating disorders. Yet clearly Hartouni is correct to recognize that the language of "innocence" and "guilt" is fundamental to the fetal harm debate as it has developed since the Reagan era—particularly among the religious right.[18]

Retha Powers's perception of her appetite as "dirty" and "sinful" tends to suggest that she had internalized evangelical Christianity's abjection of black female bodies. If read in the context of the legal system's treatment of pregnant addicts, however, Powers's allusion to the language of guilt and innocence can also be readily translated into an explicitly juridical frame of reference, one more commonly perceived as pertaining to young urban black men than to black women. With this perspective in mind, I want to conclude with a gesture in the direction of my own future scholarly inquiries by suggesting that widespread fixation on racially unmarked, and therefore presumptively white, fetuses has been mirrored by contemporaneous fear of and fascination with young black male "criminality." The fetal harm debates are structured not just by assumptions that selfish white women are wantonly killing innocent white prisoners of their wombs, but that drug-addicted black women are brazenly breeding future black male inmates in theirs. As George Jackson had quite dramatically announced, birth, for black men, is simply a transfer from one type of prison to another.

"Convicted in the Womb"

> We can love each other, respect each other, care for each other, and yes indeed, embrace each other for the common purpose of saving our children. They too were convicted in the womb—the womb of social injustice, of economic inequity, of hypocritical churches, of death and destruction.
>
> Carl Upchurch, *Convicted in the Womb*, 1996

In keeping with my origins as a literary critic, for the time being I want to explore how these sociopolitical issues have been articulated in African American fiction published since the Black Power era. My focus will be on James Baldwin's *If Beale Street Could Talk* (1974), Gloria Naylor's *Linden Hills* (1985), and Brian Keith Jackson's *The View from Here* (1997). Spanning the past quarter of a century, these novels together reflect the shifting popular investments in the nexus among: black men, shit, and prison; black women, food, and wombs; and the fetus as a construct that mediates between the two. Whereas Baldwin's novel is narrated by a working-class pregnant black protagonist whose boyfriend is in jail, Naylor depicts the effects of imprisonment for reproductive transgressions on a middle-class black woman. Whereas Naylor offers up a young black man whose psychic investments are with the confined woman herself rather than with a fantasized inmate of her womb, Jackson attributes his novel's narrative voice to a woman's fetus. And, finally, whereas Baldwin and Jackson both reflect the social anxieties about the future of motherhood which underwrite not just their own but also the more widespread U.S. cultural investment in black female fat, Naylor pays homage to Alice Walker's *Meridian* by carnivalizing Truman Held's twinned accusation/vindication that black women "let themselves go."

Published the year after *Roe v. Wade* was decided, and easily Baldwin's most extended effort to represent the worldview of an African American woman in his fiction, *Beale Street* might be seen as an early meditation on the mutual constitution of contemporary discourses of white fetal innocence and black male criminality.[19] The novel is narrated by Clementine "Tish" Rivers, a pregnant black teenager who lives with her family in New York City. Her boyfriend Alonzo "Fonny" Hunt, a twenty-one-year-old black sculptor, has been wrongly accused of raping a Puerto Rican woman and locked away in New York's infamous prison, the Tombs. The novel follows the efforts of Tish, her family, and Fonny's family to find a way to raise bail and prove his innocence. It ends with Tish in labor and Fonny still locked away, the latter having embraced the experience of imprisonment as formative of his sense of himself as an "artisan" rather than an "artist" (208). Though *Beale Street* is most obviously responding to writings by Black Power activists that focused renewed attention on how the U.S. penal system functions as a tool of white supremacy, Baldwin's decision to create a pregnant narrator was surely no less overdetermined given the preponderance of debates over birth control, abortion rights, sterilization abuse, and racial genocide in the early 1970s.[20]

Baldwin does not explicitly ally himself in *Beale Street* with black men such as Elijah Muhammad and Dick Gregory who were, at the time, denouncing black women's use of birth control, but neither does he allow Tish to seriously consider obtaining an abortion. Shortly after disclosing her pregnancy to Fonny, who silently absorbs the news, she imposes an Aristotelian teleology onto her condition by thinking to herself that "the baby was the only real thing in the world, more real than the prison, more real than me" (5). As Poovey explains in her discussion of the contradictory logic of *Roe v. Wade*, the equation of a fetus with a baby "assumes that the fetus will be brought to term" and thus precludes "other possible outcomes" of a given pregnancy, including miscarriage as well as abortion (246). Tish's point of view also anticipates the current state of affairs whereby pregnant women have been rendered less "real" than the seemingly free-floating fetuses which prolife activists proudly fetishize.

It is actually Fonny who raises the possibility that Tish might choose to subvert this teleology when he inquires, "What you going to do, for real?" (6). After reassuring him of her commitment to carrying the pregnancy to term, Tish meditates, "I knew what he was thinking, but I can't let myself think about it—not now, watching him. I *must* be sure" (6). In this fashion, the book links its pronatalist stance for black women with a critique of the racist treatment of black men by the U.S. penal system. Baldwin has constructed a plot that effectively allows Tish no "choice" at all since she understands the pregnancy as her primary means of sustaining Fonny's will to fight. Tish marshals a circular narrative of liberation: Fonny must be freed because a baby is on the way, and because a baby is on the way, Fonny must be freed. At the same time, Baldwin also mimics a common trope of black men's prison writing when he represents Fonny's experience of solitary confinement as a period of gestation which enables a rebirth, a baptism which allows him to become a man. "Something hardens in him, something changes forever, his tears freeze in his belly," Baldwin writes (207). Fonny comes to realize that he is in prison not "for anything he has done" (207) but because of who he is. Precisely because he is not guilty of a crime, Fonny has lost his innocence.

Baldwin has Tish explain that Fonny has been "placed in solitary" in the first place "for refusing to be raped" (207). This passage alludes to the homosexual panic that often inflected black men's fear of sexual violence in prison, while also serving as a reminder of Baldwin's suppression in *Beale Street* of the homoerotic imaginings that are so central to the rest of his fiction. Given, however, Baldwin's undoubted familiarity with Eldridge Cleaver's attack on him in *Soul on Ice*, one could view his decision to ventriloquize a pregnant black woman as a rather wickedly parodic response. "It would have been a gas for me to sit on a pillow beneath the womb of Baldwin's typewriter and catch each newborn page as it entered this world of ours," Cleaver wrote of his former feelings of admiration for Baldwin's work (96), little suspecting that his target would respond with a novel's worth of revenge. At times, in fact, *Beale Street* might even be said to infantilize the homophobic black masculinity embraced by black nationalists such as Cleaver. Having explained that Fonny fought off the threatened sexual violence of other men, for example, Tish reports that her fiancé "will be here, he swears it, sitting in the shit, sweating and stinking, when the baby gets here" (207). Depicting Fonny as mired like a baby in his own excrement, Baldwin makes a mockery of Cleaver's homophobic attack.

Baldwin also uses Tish to call into question the rigid standards for masculinity which black nationalists generally advocated. She observes, for example, that "you can get very fucked up, here, once you take seriously the notion that a man who is not afraid to trust his imagination (which is all that men have ever trusted) is effeminate" (64). At the same time, Tish also refers dismissively to "faggots" elsewhere in the text (72), and Baldwin attributes typical Black Aesthetic ideologies about women to her. "All I could do was wait" (212), Tish thinks to herself more than once, thus literalizing the passive connotations of "expecting." Elsewhere she concludes that women "must watch and guide" but men "must lead" and that "dealing with the reality of men leaves a woman very little time, or need, for imagination" (64). As I explained in chapter 6, Toni Morrison had already reached precisely the opposite conclusion about black women in her New York Times Magazine essay on women's liberation, as well as in her second novel. Having had Sula unequivocally reject pregnancy and motherhood as the principal mode of black women's creative fulfillment—"I don't want to make somebody else. I want to make myself " (92)—Morrison also directly explicates Sula's unconventional personality as the result "of an idle imagination," one deprived of opportunities for creative gratification (121).[21]

As the decade progressed, other black women writers such as Alice Walker joined Morrison in challenging Black Power's relentless pronatalism and its own inability to imagine that black women might have aspirations that do not emanate from their wombs. For this reason, I was curious when I encountered promotional materials on the jacket cover of Brian Keith Jackson's The View from Here which explicitly situated the author, a black gay man, not in relation to a more obvious predecessor such as Baldwin, but rather "[i]n the tradition of Alice Walker and Toni Morrison." Certainly Jackson's focus is primarily on black female subjectivities, and in this he differs greatly from Baldwin. But given Morrison's and Walker's portrayals of Sula Peace and Meridian Hill, The View from Here strikes me as a decidedly ambiguous homage at best, considering Jackson's decision to render the story of a pregnant woman from the viewpoint of her fetus.

Set in rural Mississippi during the 1950s, The View from Here is the story of Anna Thomas, a patient but downtrodden black woman married to an abusive man. She is pregnant with her sixth child. Her husband, John Thomas, hopes that the fetus is a boy, like their other children, but still insists that it be given to his older sister Clariece to raise. The pompous wife of a kindly preacher, Clariece is presumed by the narrator to be responsible for her and her husband's failure to conceive a child of their own. This narrator, "Lisa," is the fetus to which Anna confides her hopes and fears, and which she desperately wishes to keep. In what does appear to be an homage to both Sula and The Color Purple, Jackson has Lisa include copies of letters written by Anna to her best friend, the bold and unorthodox Ida Mae Ramsey, who has fled the confines of the South for the excitement of Chicago and other northern cities. Although Ida Mae, like Sula Mae, dies before the novel is completed, Anna follows Celie in standing up for herself in the end: she refuses to surrender the expected child. As the novel closes, the narrative point of view shifts from the fetal to the adult Lisa, who explains that "Poppa" had learned the error of his ways and relented in time to be present at her birth.

Despite his conscious effort to pay tribute to Walker and Morrison, Jackson is clearly a product of a cultural moment marked by a fascination with "unborn children." Indeed, the novel's promotional material might just as easily have cited filmic influences such as Amy Heckerling's *Look Who's Talking* (1989) and certainly Dash's *Daughters of the Dust*. In keeping with the concerns about this development that I have already expressed, what particularly worries me about *The View from Here* are the ramifications of Jackson's desire to yoke the well-established tradition of African American women's novels of "coming to voice" together with these emergent discourses of fetal personhood. This is not to say that Jackson is oblivious to patriarchal structures of power. Lisa comments early in her (mother's) narrative, for example, that no one but Poppa ever "sat in his rocker. . . . It was his property to do with as he pleased—as was Momma and, for the time being, as was I" (5). Yet even here Lisa conveys some frustration with her inability to combat her father's authority because of her dependence on the actions of her "host-body." As long as Anna subordinates herself to John Thomas, "li'l Lisa" will also pay a price.

While gesturing in this fashion toward the perils of life in the womb, the novel also traces Lisa's growing autonomy. During much of the narrative, she highlights her dependence on her mother by presenting herself as lacking in physical as well as verbal autonomy. "I've been moving quite a bit today," Lisa announces at one point (140). "Every time I'd move, Momma would rub me, saying, 'You're goin' to be a fighter. I can tell that already,' and then I'd kick again. I couldn't help it" (140). But as the time of birth approaches, Lisa assumes responsibility for her actions. Thus, when Anna places the hand of her son Leo "over her stomach, waiting for me to kick," Lisa recollects, "I more than oblige, grasping for any extra room, room that doesn't seem to exist" (179). In deploying such imagery, Jackson reflects the contradictory logic by which the prolife movement has succeeded in representing the fetus as simultaneously deprived and possessed of human agency. The former claim lends credence to arguments that "unborn life" is deserving of special protection precisely because the fetus is utterly helpless; the latter, to arguments that fetuses are indistinguishable from other legal persons and, consequently, that abortion is synonymous with infanticide.

Lisa, moreover, certainly does not hesitate to let it be known when and how her mother's physical condition affects her. After John Thomas has lost his job at the mill and returns home drunk and angry, Anna faints. But while we are left to speculate about what is going on in Anna's mind, Lisa carefully delineates her own experience of the event:

I start feeling . . . feeling pressure, like the walls are closing in on me. I . . . I . . . there's noise. It's pounding, pounding real fast, and . . . and I can feel things rushing up past me, real fastlike. Momma starts breathing really heavylike and I hear Leo and Leon scream together, "Momma!" There is a release from around me, then nothing. Black. (Jackson's ellipses; 68)

Later, when "Poppa" mentions that Clariece will be coming to pay a visit to prepare for the adoption, Lisa observes, "There was no air getting to me. Momma had stopped breathing, but just for a few breaths" (91). Shortly thereafter, she recollects: "Since Poppa had been laid off, it was a constant struggle each day. I went hungry many times. Momma was so busy trying to find the peace in the struggle for peace that she'd sometimes forget to take care of herself" (94).

This last sentence marks yet another moment of narrative ambivalence. Lisa repeatedly alludes to the fact that her own survival depends on that of her mother. Yet Jackson has Lisa follow her acknowledged interest in self-preservation ("I went hungry many times") with a putatively altruistic observation about the obstacles that prevented Anna from taking "care of herself." He also has Lisa take frequent note of her mother's efforts to comfort and care for her. After Junior leaves "his plate of half-eaten biscuits" by the sink, for instance, Lisa reports that her mother "nibbles from his plate, more for my sake than for her own" (26). Perhaps Jackson is trying to undermine the prevailing conception of impoverished black women as threats to their fetuses. But such a representation also plays into the opposing conception of black women as "all-giving nurturers."

To fortify Anna's positioning as such a nurturer, Jackson triangulates the Anna/Ida dyad with Clariece. Rendered laughable by her malaprop-ridden speech—"if me and the Reverend James Caldwell was to have children, they wouldn't be *omitted* to stare at people like they was crazy" (117)—Clariece becomes truly vile by the end of the novel, when we learn that she has lied about the behavior of Anna's son Leon to encourage her husband to discipline the child physically (214). Lisa, moreover, blames Clariece for her uncle's behavior: "And of course, Uncle, trusting Auntie's judgment, would do as she said. Auntie never laid a hand on Leon, but to hurt him, she never had to. That was her way" (215). This needlessly harsh treatment of Clariece has precedent in Baldwin's similarly unflattering depiction of Fonny's mother and sisters. But whereas Mrs. Hunt, Adrienne, and Sheila are ridiculed primarily for their hostility toward Tish's pregnancy, Clariece, by contrast, is held up to contempt for her paired failure to bear a child and her desire to raise Anna's expected one. [22]

Jackson also attributes to Clariece his novel's most direct articulation of contemporary anxieties about the human condition of having once been vulnerable to the dietary practices of a woman. Invited to share a meal that Anna has prepared, Clariece condemns Anna's culinary choices by suggesting that her fetus will prove defective: "If this was the way I was being 'nourished,' she said, then she wasn't sure she wanted me" (150). Even more problematically, Jackson has already had Lisa describe how after finding out about the firings at the mill, "Momma runs over to Poppa and the smell of liquor makes me squirm" (66). One can only wonder if Jackson will welcome the eventual scientific affirmation of this phenomenon, which in the interim I will designate FASS, or Fetal Alcohol Smell Syndrome. It is in this truly disturbing image that the successes of opponents of women's reproductive rights over the past quarter of a century become most read-ily apparent. And it is for this reason, paradoxically, that the antifeminist *If Beale Street Could Talk* turns out to provide a template for a feminist critique of the maternal politics encoded in Jackson's putatively pro-womanist *The View from Here*.

As Baldwin's novel nears its conclusion, Fonny becomes "so skinny" that when Tish sees him, she frets about the need "to get some meat on [his] bones" (208); just after relating this encounter she thinks of herself as "heavy, heavy, heavy" (209). Here, then, *Beale Street* does insinuate a more treacherous connection between the growing "inmate" of Tish's womb and the shrinking prisoner of the Tombs. Yet, despite the obvious resonance between "womb" and "Tombs," for the most part *Beale Street* does not follow works such as *Soledad, Brother* or *The Biocrats* in presenting Tish as a threat to the fetus she carries. Indeed, just before she goes into labor at the end of the novel, her mother gives Tish some brandy to "settle [her] stomach" (211). She begins to feel herself "alone" as she sips (211). "Everything was still. Even the baby was still" (211). As I learned, to my chagrin, when teaching the novel for the first time in 1995, students who came of age during the Reagan era are likely to interpret this scene in a way that Baldwin, himself a heavy drinker, almost certainly did not intend.

Most memorably, one of my undergraduate students suggested to me privately that Tish's willingness to consume brandy might reflect her ambivalence about being pregnant in the first place. In this reading, the brandy constituted the return of her repressed desire to kill the "child." I admittedly failed in my efforts to contest this particular student's acceptance of FAS as an objective pathology rather than a historically overdetermined ideological construct. But I did at least prevail in the less radical goal of encouraging the class to ponder the changing social circumstances that led several of them, unlike Baldwin, to equate a few sips of brandy with a pint-a-day "habit." Though it is surely possible to read the scene as an expression of Tish's doubts about becoming a mother—she wants to be left "alone," after all—my students' ready recourse to a version of the racist ideology of the pregnant addict is even more bewildering given that Baldwin offers no suggestion in the novel that Tish poses a threat to the fetus. Despite my misgivings about *Beale Street*, then, in many ways I find the novel less troubling than *The View from Here*.

Needless to say, I have not gone out of my way to foreground aspects of Jackson's novel which lend themselves to feminist interpretations. Certainly it is not insignificant that the fetal narrator is a girl. Similarly, one might also dwell on Jackson's portrayal of the rebellious Ida Mae Ramsey. Just before her death, Ida Mae claims to have allowed a man to "tame" her (150), and on the way home for a visit she is murdered, presumably by a group of white men who have harassed her on the train (182). But if Jackson makes Ida Mae pay for her independence with her life, in fairness we need to note that Morrison's *Sula* so also had paid. Try as I might to situate *View* "in the tradition" of post-1960s African American women's writing, though, I cannot help but linger on a comment Lisa records about the fate of women under patriarchy: "But God had always made it so that women outlived men. That way women could have time to be by themselves—a time to be in the world without a reason bein' placed upon it" (138). The irony of Jackson's refusal to allow Anna to be alone is multiplied by our subsequent realization that the present-day Lisa is herself pregnant. As much as the novel attempts to sympathize with the plight of lower-class black women, Jackson fully affirms only those women characters who surrender their ability "to be by themselves": Gram, Anna, and now Lisa. In this respect, Gloria Naylor's decision to kill off the son of her female protagonist at the outset of Linden Hills can be understood as a symbolic assertion of black women's need—and right—to be left alone.

From Cleo to Creton

> The idle, overfed women among the black bourgeoisie are generally, to use their language, "dripping with diamonds." They are forever dieting and reducing only to put on more weight (which is usually the result of the food that they consume at their club meetings).
>
> E. Franklin Frazier, Black Bourgeoisie, 1957

Published at the height of the Reagan era, Linden Hills has been commonly read as both a retelling of Dante's Inferno and a novelistic affirmation of E. Franklin Frazier's dismissive belief that the black bourgeoisie has historically lacked an authentic connection to black cultural roots.[23] A discussion of Linden Hills offers a fitting conclusion to this chapter not because of its representation of fetuses—indeed, almost all of the novel's characters are childless—but rather because of the way Naylor carnivalizes the intersecting discourses of black maternity, black criminality, and black "domesticity" through her portrayal of a bulimic black woman. In effect, she offers up a narrative that is so intentionally contrived, so perfect in structure, that it demonstrates how late-capitalist attitudes about black women's appetites are underwritten by a fixation on their literally "grotesque" potentiality. In the process, Naylor fills in a few missing pieces of Pearl Bailey's story about "how Mama started to get large."

Situated precariously between allegory and realism, Linden Hills narrates the efforts of two young black men looking for odd jobs who spend the week before Christmas making the rounds, literally, of a wealthy black suburban neighborhood. Linden Hills was founded and maintained by a series of satanic patriarchs, Luther Nedeed and his literally clonelike progeny, and the more prestigious addresses are located at the bottom rather than the top of the hill. The inhabitants of the various levels of Linden Hills exhibit vices that correlate to those exhibited by the denizens of Dante's underworld, the upper levels being reserved for those whose sins are of the appetite and the lower levels for those whose sins are of reason (Ward 68). Embedded within this framing narrative of Willie ("White") Mason and Lester ("Shit") Tilson's descent through the "hell" (41) of Linden Hills is the story of Willa Prescott, wife of the current patriarch. Locked in the basement of their home by her husband for bearing a light-skinned son—a faulty copy of the child's dark-skinned male progenitor (Homans 376)—she passes her days recovering the buried history of her predecessors in the role of Mrs. Luther Nedeed. One of them, Evelyn Creton, has devoted her days to cooking, bingeing, and purging until, we are told, she literally "eat[s] herself to death" (190). The climax of the novel finds Willa making her way back up the steps from the basement, having chosen to reassume her identity as Luther's wife, just as her alter ego Willie, who, along with Lester, has been hired by Luther to decorate the family Christmas tree, inadvertently unlatches the basement door.

Margaret Homans has explained Luther's imprisonment of Willa, as well as her resulting excavation of the Bible, cookbooks, and photographs of the previous Nedeed wives, by arguing that Naylor is writing the story omitted by classical authors such as Plato, Virgil, and Dante—that of the "woman in the cave." The Nedeed men are guilty, she argues, of "the crime of making (or attempting to make) women into disposable machines for replicating men" (369). *Linden Hills* provides ample evidence to support such a reading. For example, the current Luther Needed justifies his decision to imprison Willa by invoking the absolute rights of patriarchy. "Woman," he thinks with contempt shortly before exiling Willa to the basement (19). "Somewhere inside of her must be a deep flaw or she wouldn't have been capable of such treachery. Everything she owned he had given her—even her name—and she had thanked him with this? . . . Obviously, he had allowed a whore into his home but he would turn her into a wife" (19).

As Henry Louis Gates Jr. subsequently pointed out, however, Homans's reading effectively evacuates Naylor's novel of its race, class, and historical specificity ("Significant" 621–23). Though *Linden Hills* is clearly critical of black women's subordination to patriarchy, we do need to proceed cautiously before reaching conclusions about Naylor's purpose in dwelling on the Nedeed men's imposition of the Law of the Father on black women, for she also seems quite interested in exploring the cultural logic which equates young black manhood with homophobic, misogynistic lawlessness. Gates himself helpfully demonstrates how *Linden Hills* problematizes Willie and Lester's feelings about their inscription within a system of presumptive heterosexuality (609–14). Both, for example, perceive that "most guys think you're a sissy if you like [poetry]" (*Linden* 27). Yet their relationship is obviously structured by homoeroticism. After spending the night in the same bed with Willie, Lester wakes up to find "himself bound in a respectable half nelson" by his sleeping friend (71). When Lester wakes Willie up, griping that "[y]ou hugging me worse than a woman," Willie's jocular response is: "And they said it wouldn't last" (72).

Not only more willing than Lester to acknowledge his homosexual desires, Willie is also presented by Naylor as sharing psychic identifications with the women of *Linden Hills*, particularly Luther's wife. He sympathizes with Mrs. Tilson and Roxanne despite Lester's criticism of their bourgeois tendencies (57–59); he is always attuned to Willa's cries of anguish (60); he tastes Willa's "absence" from the cake Luther has brought to Lycentia Parker's wake (147); moments before Willa is shown discovering the faceless photographs of Priscilla McGuire, he dreams that a store clerk refuses to sell him a camera because he has "no face" (211); he insists to Daniel Braithwaite that the name of Howard Dumont's wife "was Laurel" (252); he begins a poem about Willa with the line, "There is a man in a house at the bottom of a hill. And his wife has no name" (277).

Significantly, though, Naylor brings the connection between Willa and Willie to fruition in a scene that finds Willie and Lester confronted by the local police.

The two are discussing whether to continue pursuing employment farther down in Linden Hills when they hear the command "Freeze!" and find themselves looking down the barrels of drawn guns (195). Willie immediately recognizes that "[i]t wasn't a matter of innocence or guilt at that moment; it was a matter of trying to find a way to achieve the vital balance between moving too quickly, too slowly, and not at all, that would save his life until he could explain" (195). Naylor uses this incident to foreground the racist underpinnings of a penal system which takes up the question of innocence or guilt only after subjecting black men to "extra-judicial" punishment. Yet, in this instance, the two are saved when the "Cousin Tom" impersonation of their friend Norman staves off a potentially violent visit to jail (197). This means that Willa, not Lester and Willie, remains the only literal prisoner of *Linden Hills*. And though her son has been locked up too, it is impor-tant that Willa herself is the object of Willie's psychic investment.

Furthermore, albeit locked in a basement rather than a jail cell, Willa, like Baldwin's Fonny, experiences her solitary confinement as a moment of self-creation:

> She breathed in and out, her body a mere shelter for the mating of unfathomable will to unfathomable possibility. And in that union, the amber germ of truth she went to sleep with conceived and reconceived itself, splitting and multiplying to take over every atom attached to her being. That nucleus of self-determination held the tyran-nical blueprint for all divisions of labor assigned to its multiplying cells. Like other emerging life, her brain, heart, hands, and feet were being programmed to a purpose. (288–89)

This metamorphosis, which the narrator explicitly labels a "birth" (289), serves as an inventive appropriation of the pervasive womb-as-prison metaphor through which many black men have articulated their experience of racial oppression and their resulting psychological, spiritual, and/or ideological transformation. Granted, critics such as Homans have expressed reservations about Willa's ultimate decision to re-embrace her role as Luther's wife ("Woman" 397–99). Naylor herself has even said that she did not originally intend to have Willa make such a choice ("Conversation" 587). But since Willa does "accidently" kill Luther in the end, the book arguably follows through on its feminist critique of African American pa-triarchy, and in quite dramatic fashion at that.

At the same time, Naylor's exploration of the nexus between maternity and criminality needs to be situated in relation to her treatment of black female ap-petite. Becky Thompson mentions the novel's depiction of "multigenerational eat-ing problems among African-American women" (3) as evidence for her argument about the fraught relationship between women of color and food.[24] Certainly Willa's discovery of Evelyn Creton's bulimia does allow Naylor to make a direct commentary on the way that discourses of eating disorders were constructing black female appetite as "natural" in the mid-1980s. The narrator says of Willa as she ponders the record of Creton's dietary obsessions that "she never thought the word *unnatural*" (149). Yet it seems important to recognize that Naylor also goes out of her way to de-naturalize, as it were, the dietary practices of black men. Most mem-orably, especially given my earlier discussion of Dick Gregory, we are told that businessman Maxwell Smyth eats only "a careful selection of solids and liquids" so as to be able "to control not only the moment but the exact nature of the matter that had to bring him daily to" his lavishly appointed bathroom (105). As a result, "his entire life became a race against the natural—and he was winning" (104).

Maxwell might be understood as attempting to conform to the fiction of what Mikhail Bakhtin has described as the classical bourgeois body—a body whose boundaries are meticulously regulated, a body that appears finished and unchanging. If Maxwell achieves an almost perfect imitation of the classical norm, Lester's sister Roxanne more nearly anticipates the grotesque, that which representations of the classical body attempt to suppress. According to Bakhtin, grotesque realism foregrounds protuberances and orifices, as well as activities such as eating, drinking, defecating, copulating, and giving birth, all of which reveal the permeability of bodily boundaries (*Rabelais* 18–24). Thus we learn that Roxanne's "body gave the impression that it was just one good meal away from being labeled fat. And Roxanne was constantly on guard never to have that meal" (53).

The grotesque potential that Roxanne is determined to avert is most fully realized in Naylor's portrayal of Evelyn Creton in the belowground plot of the novel. Given her hyperbolized bingeing and purging, Creton emerges as the insatiable appetite of the book as a whole, the monstrous body whose insistent demands the aboveground characters attempt to deny. That the grotesque is most vividly inscribed in the bourgeois enclave of *Linden Hills* via a black woman should come as no surprise, since Bakhtin refers at one point to "negroes and moors" as "a grotesque deviation from the bodily norm" (*Rabelais* 230) and shortly thereafter observes that "woman is . . . the incarnation of this [lower bodily] stratum that degrades and regenerates simultaneously" (*Rabelais* 240). His remarks intimate that African American women are overdetermined to be perceived as the grotesque: they are excluded by, yet in many ways constitutive of, our conceptualization of the bourgeoisie.[25]

What, then, was Naylor's purpose in creating Evelyn Creton? In my opinion, most readings of the novel underestimate the sheer disruptive force of the novel's belowground plot; they underestimate the extent to which Creton, in particular, seems less a character than an anticharacter, perhaps the extent to which her representation is intended to alter our understanding of the novel as a whole.[26] The catalyst for my own interpretation is Bakhtin's claim that in carnivalesque iconography the descent into the underworld is often figured as a descent into the lower bodily stratum (*Rabelais* 368–436). This movement is replicated in *Linden Hills* by the placement of Creton's story in the center, or perhaps more accurately the bowels, of the novel. If, furthermore, we accept Bakhtin's understanding of the carnivalesque underworld as a "crossroads" between "official" and "popular" culture (*Rabelais* 395), then we can hypothesize that Evelyn Creton's story functions as a juncture where the book's academically sanctioned homage to Dante's *Inferno* is upended by its unofficial samplings of far more contemporary and popular texts. One could cite numerous examples, such as *Penthouse* (115) and *The Joy of Cooking* (140), but here I have in mind George Seaton's Christmas "classic" *Miracle on 34th Street*. In what I take to be yet another carnivalesque inversion, this admittedly speculative linkage does not become available to the reader until near the

end of *Linden Hills*, when we learn that Willie has been watching this film on television (271). [27]

Released in the summer of 1947, *Miracle* features Maureen O'Hara as Doris
Walker, a divorced white employee of Macy's department store. Early in the film,
Doris hires an elderly, rotund, white-bearded gentleman (Edmund Gwenn) to portray Santa Claus in the annual Thanksgiving Day parade. What quickly becomes
apparent, though, is that the man, who gives his name as Kris Kringle, thinks he
really is Santa Claus. When Kris advises customers to shop elsewhere for goods not
sold by Macy's, he is almost fired, until Mr. Macy realizes that restoring the true
"spirit of giving" to Christmas could be the best sales gimmick ever. Meanwhile,
Miracle follows the burgeoning romance between Doris and Fred Gailey (John
Payne), a lawyer who lives in the neighboring apartment. A self-described "real-
ist," Doris lacks faith—in men as well as in the existence of Santa Claus—and
Fred's goal is to restore her belief in both. Through a variety of plot machinations,
Kris ends up being committed to Bellevue, and Fred is left to prove, in court, that
the jolly old gentleman is indeed St. Nick. The movie ends with Doris, Fred, and
her daughter Susan (Natalie Wood) driving home from a Christmas party at the
rest home where Kris lives. They pass a house that looks just like one that Susan
has secretly wanted for Christmas. The child's wish is clearly to be fulfilled: rather
than being raised by a cynical single working mother in the city, a woman coded
in many ways as a lesbian, she will have a homemaker mom, a self-employed
lawyer dad, and a spacious suburban house with a yard.

Linden Hills reworks *Miracle* in numerous ways, only a few of which I will allude
to here. The plots of both are set in motion at Thanksgiving and climax with
Christmas. Whereas *Miracle* opens with the specter of a drunken Santa Claus (the
man whom Kris was hired to replace), a middle section of *Linden Hills* gives us
Michael Hollis, the alcoholic minister who portrays Santa Claus for poor children
visiting his affluent church. Just as the movie works to remake Doris Walker,
Macy's executive, into Mrs. Fred Gailey, suburban wife and mother, so we learn
that Willa Prescott has made a "choice" to give up both her surname and her career to become Mrs. Luther Nedeed (278). In *Miracle*, the goal is a house on a hill
in the suburbs—an image first introduced as a picture that Susan has cut out from
a magazine; in the novel the goal is a house at the bottom of a hill in the suburbs—in a neighborhood that, we are told, "had brought a photographer out from
Life magazine for pictures of the Japanese gardens and marble swimming pools"
(15). Both film and novel are thus centrally concerned with modern technologies
of representation, forcing us to question the nature of reality—or our access
thereto—under late capitalism. They operate at the intersection of (spiritual)
faith and (commodity) fetishism, with the movie suggesting cheerfully that the
two are interdependent and the novel insisting bleakly that they are opposed. Like
the novel, the movie rests precariously between allegory and realism, and it continually unsettles any interpretation which attempts to operate solely on one or
the other of these planes.

Beyond these parallels which lead me to claim *Miracle* as a more intriguing
proof text for *Linden Hills* than is the *Inferno*, there is one key scene in the movie
which I believe the novel as a whole is reworking. After hiring Kris as a substitute

Santa, Doris returns home to find that Susan is watching the parade from Fred's apartment. As Valentine Davies described the scene in a short novel written to exploit the film's success, Doris's African American servant Cleo "poke[s] her head out of the kitchen" to inform her employer of Susan's whereabouts (14). This brief but pivotal shot of Cleo in the kitchen doorway takes on significance when one juxtaposes it not just to the extended passages in Linden Hills describing Roxanne Tilson's binge eating and Evelyn Creton's monumental feats of cooking, but also to a later scene in which Naylor describes Willa's perception of her husband after she has emerged from the basement. Luther is trying to prevent her from entering the room where he is decorating the Christmas tree with Lester and Willie. But from Willa's perspective, Naylor writes, there was "[n]o meaning to his struggle except that it was pushing her back into the kitchen" (300). In this fashion, the novel insinuates the kitchen as a third term in its "prison" matrix of womb and basement.

When approached from the vantage point provided by the novel, Cleo's brief appearance in Miracle on 34th Street serves, of course, as a reminder of Hollywood's long-standing denial of the existence of the black middle class, the membership of which was expanding after World War II. It also reminds us that visual representations of bourgeois white women have historically entailed representations of black women's bodies and domestic labor as well. Simply put, Miracle needs Doris to have a Cleo in order to establish her identity as Doris. It is intriguing, therefore, that unlike many contemporaneous "movie maids," the actress who portrayed Cleo, Theresa Harris, was neither particularly dark-skinned nor at all overweight.[28] This casting decision was, in my opinion, not unmotivated since it further phallicizes Doris by enabling Cleo to function at the outset of the film as her subservient wife rather than her domineering mammy. The miracle needed on 34th Street, in other words, is a "real" man to disrupt their interracial butch/femme coupledom. But my mode of describing Harris also reveals that her appearance as Cleo is intelligible primarily as a function of the grotesque potentiality that the audience has been led, by portrayals of black women elsewhere in popular culture, to believe it contains. As Naylor has Maxwell say disparagingly of Roxanne Tilson (in an obvious allusion to Alice Walker's Meridian), "most black women have a tendency to let themselves go" (109). In this respect, Naylor's portrayal of Evelyn Creton might be said to incarnate Cleo's sublimated abjection. Her weight gain and weight loss parody the extreme vicissitudes in physical appearance demanded by Hollywood of black actresses in the role of the movie maid.

At the same time, when approached from the vantage point provided by the film, Creton's "regurgitating" function in Linden Hills can also be understood as a way for Naylor to foreground those analogous processes through which middle-class African Americans have constituted their identities by othering working-class black women—domestics in particular.[29] Yet, were we to construe the novel less as an allegory about the failings of wealthy black America than as an extended fantasy about the "what if's" of Miracle's surnameless Cleo—What if Cleo had been able to abandon Doris's kitchen and move to the suburbs herself?—then perhaps we could better appreciate it as an inquiry into the conditions of possibility for representing African American female embodiment in the first place. Whereas Miracle on 34th Street thematizes the mechanisms through which modern technologies of representation create (but never fulfill) in us a desire to transcend the realities of the grotesque body, Linden Hills exposes a double bind of black female existence: the representational practices that enable us to conceptualize the bour-geoisie are inextricable from the practices through which African American women have themselves historically been inscribed as the grotesque.

Lest this sound overly pessimistic, let me stress that Naylor's novel offers, to my way of thinking, a fascinating meditation on why debates over the substance and boundaries of U.S. identities so often revolve around the connection between African American women and food. Through her representation of Evelyn Cre-ton, Naylor demonstrates how seemingly disparate psychic, cultural, sociopolitical, and economic forces work together to render black female appetite a key site of national anxiety. Linden Hills does not attempt to "represent" contemporary U.S. life in all its multiethnic complexity; it does not offer solutions for women who have eating problems; and it does not enable us to halt the criminalization of preg-nant women who are perceived as threats to their fetuses. It does, though, demon-strate why any response we formulate to these and other social injustices needs to distinguish between ameliorating the symptoms and trying to alter the system which has given rise to those symptoms in the first place. Linden Hills uses allegory to show why life is so complex, and also to remind us that complexity is no excuse for political inaction.

Not surprisingly, Les Mayfield's 1994 remake of Miracle on 34th Street marked its distance from the original film by simply cutting the brief role of Cleo. But even less surprisingly, the 1994 version also could not resist conjuring up the sublimated specter of her former presence. At the Thanksgiving dinner shared by Dorey (Eliz-abeth Perkins), Susan (Mara Wilson), and Bryan (Dylan McDermott)—the film's updated versions of Doris, Susan, and Fred—Susan observes longingly of her atyp-ical participation in a traditional nuclear family scene that "this is kind of like TV." To make their "parody" complete, though, she insists that "we need either a kind of fat person who's our cook or a neighbor who's always at our house." Conve-niently spoken by an actor who was too young to understand the implications of what she was saying, this expression of desire for the absent Cleo—and the im-plicit acknowledgment that "Cleo" is always already a fantasy—succinctly encap-sulates the way that the connection between black women and food continues to anchor central aspects of late twentieth-century U.S. life. Although Linden Hills was published nine years prior to the release of the updated Miracle on 34th Street, Naylor perhaps anticipated that as long as we live in a world where Aunt Jemima products flourish, the carnivalizing Evelyn Creton will herself have a lengthy shelf-life.

Epilogue

In 1991 I concluded the first essay I published on African American culinary history with a poem by Katherine Tillman. Her "Cookery Jingles" appeared in the prefatory materials of *The Federation Cookbook* (1910), a collection of recipes "by the Colored Women of the State of California." The poem reads as follows:

She could draw a little, paint a little,
    Talk about a book.
She could row a boat, ride a horse,
    But alas she couldn't cook.
        She could gown, she could go,
            She could very pretty look
        But her best beau he was poor
            And he couldn't hire a cook.
When he learned the fatal truth
    His flight he quickly took
And his girl is single still,
    Because she couldn't cook!

        Believe not the love tales
            You find within a book
        Love's fate often turns on,
            The skill of a cook

Before a man marries
   'Tis the gown or the look,
But after the wedding
   He looks for a cook.
      'Tis said to a man's heart,
         The shortest route took
         Is reached through the region,
            Controlled by the cook!
Go forth then a blessing,
   You dear little book,
And happiness ever
   Attend the good cook. (n. pag.)

The same year my essay appeared, Claudia Tate edited a collection of Tillman's work, and the following year she discussed Tillman in a compelling study of African American women writers of the turn of the century. At the time I published "In Search of Our Mothers' Cookbooks," though, I had no idea who Tillman was. The irony of this situation was augmented by the fact that my essay described my work excavating the African American cookbook tradition—locating texts that have been "lost," in other words. Unaware of the extent of my own ignorance, I explained that I wished to conclude with Tillman's "Jingles" because they defied many of the era's common stereotypes of black womanhood and black cookery. The contributors to *The Federation Cookbook* were in California, not the South; they were—or represented themselves as—bourgeois, not poor. I concluded with Tillman's poem because as a feminist I was quite uncomfortable with her celebration of black female domesticity, and I was racked by competing desires either to suppress her poem or to offer an interpretation that recovered layers of ambiguity in its signification. But at the time I did neither. I simply reprinted the "Jingles" and advised readers to make of them what they would. What was most important, I decided, was that we know that Tillman's voice existed.

Several years down the road, and no longer so ignorant of Tillman's literary career, I still find this poem both fascinating and troubling. As scholars such as Tate and Ann duCille have shown, the frequent appearance of the "marriage plot" in writings by African American women during the late nineteenth and early twentieth centuries should not be automatically equated with political conservatism. While considering the detailed portrayal of "daily chores" in Tillman's 1893 domestic novella *Beryl Weston's Ambition* (see *Works* 207–46), for example, Tate points out: "It is precisely the realistic depiction of [Beryl's] household industry, combined with her dedicated desire to learn rigorous academic disciplines— geometry and Greek—that dramatizes not only what Tillman perceived as appropriate education for black women but also Tillman's refusal to polarize two distinct theories about Negro education" (182). (These theories are commonly associated with Booker T. Washington and W. E. B. Du Bois.) Extrapolating from Tate's analysis, we might note that even as Tillman is treating marriage in "Cookery Jingles" as a right/rite which symbolizes black bourgeois social and political equality, her advice to "Believe not the love tales / You find within a book" might well be taken as an effort to demystify heterosexual "romance" as an ideology that legitimates patriarchal domination of women.

Notwithstanding my (belated) recognition that Tillman's poem enacts several of the complicated strategies through which middle-class African American women have historically negotiated subject positions in a society that is hostile to their welfare, I was also quite tempted to launch this conclusion in a different fashion, with a brief discussion of the intersection of food and black female appetite in blues music. During an earlier incarnation, this book was slated to include a chapter focusing on the 1920s in which food and music would have been a central concern. In pursuing this work, I would have been taking a page from Hazel Carby's reading of women blues singers as a source of counterhegemonic discourse about black women's sexuality, as well as from her work on the efforts of middle-class black women to regulate the behavior of their working-class "sisters" who came North during the Great Migration ("It" and "Policing"). It does seem rather difficult to imagine the author of "Cookery Jingles" calling out "Gimme a pigfoot and a bottle of beer," as Bessie Smith most famously did.

In addition to using blues lyrics to explore how food enables the representation of black women as desiring subjects, I was also particularly interested in whether or how lesbian and bisexual singers such as Ma Rainey and Smith might have contested the myriad ways in which food is inscribed by, and in turn helps inscribe, the presumption of women's heterosexuality. Lil Johnson's rendition of "You'll Never Miss Your Jelly" offers a classic example of how this presumption often plays out in blues lyrics. Having explained, "My sweet man went away / didn't know the reason why," Johnson offers up to him the plaintive refrain, "If you don't like my sweet potato / what made you dig so deep / Dig my potato field / three, four times a week." My eventual decision to focus on the post–World War II period led me to abandon plans for this chapter. Given my extended treatment of homosocial bonds among men, however, and my insistent critique of the way the negotiation of these bonds entailed the configuration of black women as (presumptively heterosexual) mothers, I do wish to acknowledge before leaving off that the narrative I have pursued linking African American women to food would have been enriched by such an excursion.[1]

Part of my agenda in drawing attention to such roads not taken is simply to foreground the range of current academic debates to which work on food can offer a contribution. But I also wanted specifically to return once again to the early years of this century as a way of prefacing my final comments. The connections between African American women and food which I have been tracing emerged in conjunction with the far-reaching economic, technological, political, social, and cultural developments of the late nineteenth and early twentieth centuries. Lacking not just an economy through which commodified food products could circulate but also a mass-culture industry through which normative ideologies about sexuality, gender, race, ethnicity, class, and nation could be rendered widely available, the connection would not have manifested itself as it has. And though there has never really been an era when debates over the status of "American" identity have entirely subsided, the era upon which I finally chose to concentrate my inquiries clearly constituted another fraught moment in this recurrent national drama.

Former Black Panther Bobby Seale attempted to redeploy the iconography of his famous past in his 1988 cookbook *Barbeque'n with Bobby*. In his acknowledgments, Seale thanks Jerry Rubin for having encouraged him to write a cookbook while they "were both political prisoners in 1969 during the Great Chicago 8 Conspiracy Trial" (ix–x). Seale says that he "would go on and on, describing recipes detail by detail on how I would prepare my favorite dishes (jail food was horrendous . . . and with other prisoners we would rap many times about what I could cook or barbeque and what we would eat if we were out)" (Seale's ellipsis; x). These recollections eventually result in his offering of a "Declaration" called the "Barbeque Bill of Rights." It reads, in part, as follows:

> WHEN IN THE COURSE OF HUMAN DEVELOPMENT it becomes necessary for us, the citizens of the earth, to creatively improve the culinary art of barbe-que'n in our opposition to the overly commercialized bondage of "cue-be-rab" (barbecuing backwards); and to assume, within the realm of palatable biological reactions to which the laws of nature and nature's God entitle us, a decent respect for all the billions of human taste buds and savory barbeque desires; we the people declare a basic barbeque bill of rights which impels us to help halt, eradicate, and ultimately stamp out "cue-be-rab!" (27)

Over the years, I have often mentioned this "Declaration" while trying to explain to others my fascination with work on food, as well as my interest in the political and cultural legacy of the 1960s and early 1970s. My listeners typically disagree as to whether Seale's parodic reiteration of the "Declaration of Independence" is (1) proof of how far to the right the sociopolitical climate has shifted since the 1970s, (2) evidence that Black Power never harbored the revolutionary potential to which it aspired, (3) a result of the acceptance of the dictum that the personal is indeed political, or (4) a reminder that political resistance need not preclude personal and collective pleasure. My sense is that there is much truth to each of these interpretations.[2]

In keeping with my belief that cookbooks do indeed constitute a relatively democratic genre of writing, not least because they are populated by women's voices, I would like to end, however, not with Bobby Seale, but rather with another cookbook writer from the 1980s, someone who is not nationally known. In 1984 Aldeen Davis published her *Soul—Food for Thought* through the Pip Copy Center of Muscatine, Iowa. Like Seale and many other African American cookbook writers, Davis splices recipes with political commentary. A "Labor Day" section called "The Black Worker" (29), for example, offers the pithy observation: "To understand black is to understand work—and the denial of work" (30). After an astute excursus on how "white capital has used black labor to depress wages and divide the labor force" (30), Davis concludes this segment of her cookbook with these two paragraphs:

> Labor is the basis of all wealth, and wealth is an absolute necessity of civilized society. Emancipation failed to free the black worker and to provide for him an economic foundation.
> Often times, children are left out in planning picnics and outings. Why not make a batch of Sloppy Joes in your crockpot and supply plenty of buns, ketchup, mustard, etc. (30)

Soul—Food for Thought is full of disorienting juxtapositions such as this, when the only presumably generic "he" leaves me unsure whether Davis's "black worker" includes women, when the tone of her cooking tip leaves me wondering whether she conceptualizes cooking as a form of wealth-generating labor in itself. Later in the book, however, Davis affirms that "[p]assage of the ERA is essential for the economic equity deserved by all women, but especially the black woman" (129). A subsequent discussion of the "many black women who have achieved their goals in spite of the lack of ERA" (129) then leads to the following commentary: "Busy career women are always looking for good salads for two reasons—time and weight, but not necessarily in that order" (130). Hence Davis's inclusion of a recipe that nicely exemplifies Lloyd Gite and Jean Perry's concept of "losing weight soulfully": "Spinach Salad and Hot Bacon Dressing" (130).

Throughout this book I have argued that discourses about food have been mobilized in the United States (as elsewhere) for political ends. Nevertheless, because my research has compelled me to acknowledge the complex social reality that results in passages such as this by Davis, the process of writing has made me more aware of the limitations of totalizing narratives of domination and resistance. The connection between black women and food has resonated so deeply during this century in no small part because it enables the expression of nostalgic desire for a social order in which established hierarchies were not contested—a social order, in other words, that has never actually existed. But, as Davis's cookbook amply illustrates, this same connection has allowed others to assert both their individual idiosyncrasies and their communal desire to create a more equitable world.

Appendix

African American Cookbooks

Having completed this book, I now find myself possessed of file cabinets and shelves overflowing with source material, including about seven dozen cookbooks by African Americans or photocopies thereof. To help facilitate the work of other scholars interested in culinary history, I am here reprinting my current working bibliography of cookbooks by African Americans. As I mention in my acknowledgments, my research on this topic was made easier by former Colorado State University librarian David Lupton, who currently lives in Bayboro, North Carolina. After being put in contact by Barbara Haber, director of Radcliffe's Schlesinger Library, Mr. Lupton and I exchanged bibliographies in mid-1991. I certainly got the better end of that deal, as he was already aware of most of the titles I passed along to him, a couple of which eventually turned out to be false leads. Since that time, I have continued to update my list, with most of the new titles stemming from the 1990s. Approximately one-fourth of the titles on the following list first came to my attention courtesy of Mr. Lupton, and, if an opportunity presents itself, I understand that he hopes to publish an expanded bibliography of his own in another venue.

Over the years, I have managed to examine most of the books that our respective efforts turned up, but the list doubtless contains errors. I alone should be held responsible for them. Any attempt to formulate such a bibliography entails defining necessarily flexible rules of inclusion and exclusion. In addition to the common problems of determining the racial identification(s) of a long-dead author, the renewed attention to black diasporic culture in recent years has foregrounded for me the ideological biases inherent in my decision to use nationality as a way to delimit this list. Many of the books included are invested in transatlantic models of black identity, but the authors themselves are, as far as I know, all citizens of the United States. This issue is perhaps even more clearly epitomized by the status of the "creole" cookbook. I have included several such books on this list when the author displays some investment in African American culture, but I have not included cookbooks written by white authors that reflect a desire to rid the designation "creole" of its racial "impurities."

In pursuing this research, I have also run across numerous cookbooks which were written and/or published by white people but clearly derived from African Americans; many could easily be subsumed under the rubric of "plantation school" texts, for example: Emma and William McKinney's *Aunt Caroline's Dixieland Recipes* (1922), Katharin Bell's *Mammy's Cook Book* (1927), Natalie Scott's *'Mirations and Miracles of Mandy* (1929), and others. As recently as 1989, the *Washington Post* published an article by Caroline Mayer on *Viola's Favorite Recipes*, a short collection of recipes "by" Viola Lampkin, an African American woman from Berryville, Virginia. As it turns out, the cookbook originated when the daughter of Lampkin's former employer Micheline Clagett "set about trying to capture some of Lampkin's recipes in a cookbook" because Lampkin had retired and was no longer available to do the actual cooking (Mayer E16). Lampkin herself claims to have little use for written recipes. "I always have to add a little bit of something, or do something differently," she observes (quoted in Mayer E15). Several of these plantation texts are included in my main list of works cited. Since such cookbooks still reflect the labor of black cooks—indeed cookbooks, like novels, are surely what Bakhtin would term a "dialogized" genre (see "Discourse")—I am including a few others on this list but flagging with an asterisk any cookbooks that I know or suspect to have had substantial "non-black" input. In my own work, I have attempted to use such texts to examine power relations between cooks and employers, as well as how the insistence on improvisation has evolved, at least in part, as a strategy of resistance on the part of the cooks.

Thus far I know of only four cookery books by African Americans published prior to 1900. The earliest is Robert Roberts's *The House Servant's Directory* (1827). Twenty-one years later, Tunis Campbell followed suit with *Hotel Keepers, Head Waiters, and Housekeepers' Guide* (1848). Each stems from its author's employment in the public domain, and each is directed toward readers similarly situated. The other two early books with which I am familiar are Abby Fisher's *What Mrs. Fisher Knows about Old Southern Cooking* (1881) and E. T. Glover's *The Warm Springs Receipt-Book* (1897). Fisher was a former Alabama slave who became a cook for San Francisco society after the demise of Reconstruction. Though Glover, by contrast, never directly refers to his race, his preface would suggest that he was an African American. He writes, for instance, that "[t]he compilation of this book was suggested by a host of friends to whom I have catered for several years at the Warm Sulphur Springs, Virginia" (n. pag.), this being a standard locution used by early black writers to offset their "presumption" in taking up the pen. Like Roberts, Campbell, and Glover, furthermore, most of the black men who wrote cookery books in the first decades of the twentieth century—H. Franklyn Hall (1901), Rufus Estes (1911), and S. Thomas Bivins (1912)—were professional cooks.

Though African American women were still employed as cooks far more frequently in private homes than in the public realm in 1900, they also began publishing books on cookery at this time. In 1910 Bertha Turner compiled *The Federation Cookbook*, and, shortly thereafter, Mrs. W. T. Hayes published the *Kentucky
Cook Book* (1912). As we have seen, the former was clearly compiled by and intended for a readership of middle-class "club" women of color; Hayes refers to her
book, by contrast, as "the work of a colored cook of many years' experience . . . who
has had ample opportunity for experimenting and testing the recipes presented"
(Introduction n. pag.). Inasmuch as the period from 1880 to 1930 also witnessed
what historian Harvey Levenstein has described as a "revolution" in U.S. dietary
practices, the appearance of these African American cookery books makes this period seem germinal in the evolution of black culinary traditions. The texts I have
mentioned would all reward further scrutiny; it is telling, for example, that the
recipes offered by Bivins, the California women, and Hayes have more in common
with domestic science cookery than with what later emerged as "soul food." Many
of their recipes are comparable to those in *The Boston Cooking-School Cook Book*.

The middle decades of this century gave rise to a wide range of cookbooks by
African Americans. Some, such as Rebecca West's privately published *Rebecca's
Cookbook* (1942), foreground the traditional employment of black women as cooks
for whites. Others—for instance, Freda De Knight's *Ebony* magazine cookbook *A
Date with a Dish* (1948) and the National Council of Negro Women's *The Historical Cookbook of the American Negro* (1958)—construct a middle-class model of
black identity, the latter while deploying the language of racial uplift. The bulk of
my work has focused on recent history in large part because the post–World War II
era witnessed a proliferation of cookery books by African Americans. In their tendency to combine autobiography and creative writing with political and cultural
history—as exemplified by Aldeen Davis's commentary about black history in
Soul—Food for Thought (1984) and the short tales included in Alice McGill, Mary
Carter Smith, and Elmira Washington's *The Griots' Cookbook* (1985)—these post–
World War II books provide an important source of information about how both
famous and anonymous African Americans have created a sense of individual and
collective identity.

One of my personal favorites is Marva Joy Curry's *Everything You Always Wanted
to Know about Soul Food Cooking . . . and Were Afraid to Ask* (1983). The daughter
of Arkansas sharecroppers, Curry published her cookbook privately. It is written in
vernacular English and provides a telling contrast to many of the mass-marketed
"coffee-table" cookbooks now available. Most obviously, one might wish to com-
pare it with Liza Ashley's 1985 book *Thirty Years at the Mansion*, an "as told to"
volume that details Ashley's work as a cook in the Arkansas governor's mansion.
The book's introduction is by then-governor Bill Clinton and his wife Hillary, the
latter already in her post-Rodham phase. As I have indicated all along, I am hesitant to invoke the language of authenticity in distinguishing privately published
from regionally or nationally distributed cookbooks, but clearly it is important to
take into account the ramifications of publication venues for African American
culinary/cookbook history. The main problem with pursuing this undertaking, of
course, is that privately published cookbooks are difficult to locate in any system-

atic fashion. Mr. Lupton's continuing bibliographical work has focused particularly on these hard-to-find books.

Vertamae Grosvenor worries in *Vertamae Cooks in the Americas' Family Kitchen* that the emergence of "soul food" did as much harm as good in terms of the evolution of discourses about black dietary practices:

> In the 1960s and 1970s, when everyone was searching for his or her roots, one of the major cultural finds was Black American culinary heritage. I thought that finally we would have the flavor of Africa in the melting pot and that we would appreciate and celebrate it. "Soul food" got hot, but it was a passing thing. Folks went on believing that black cookery was a highly seasoned food group of bones and lard, created from "massa's leftovers," and people, including many soul food eaters, swallowed that tidbit of culinary history. (17)

I agree with Grosvenor that the soul food fad of the Black Power era was problematic for culinary as well as sociopolitical history. But I also think she is underestimating the heterogeneity and vibrancy of writing about black American culinary traditions, writing which preceded the emergence of soul food and especially which soul food helped generate in turn. The list that follows should provide some confirmation of this claim. Notwithstanding the "chitterling" and "improvisation" fixations which I have delineated, soul food has also worked to open up rather than foreclose debates over black culinary history, and that is surely not a bad thing. In her introduction to *Iron Pots and Wooden Spoons* (1989), Jessica Harris observes: "I hope that this book will fix the taste of cornbread, beans, collard greens, okra, chiles, molasses, and rum on our tongues for generations to come" (xxiv). My hope, in turn, is that this still-evolving cookbook bibliography will help fix the extensive history of African American writing about food in our memories for generations to come.

Chronological Bibliography of Cookbooks by African Americans

Compiled by
Doris Witt, with David Lupton

1800–1899

Roberts, Robert. *The House Servant's Directory, or a Monitor for Private Families: Comprising Hints on the Arrangement and Performance of Servants' Work . . . and Upwards of 100 Various and Useful Receipts, Chiefly Compiled for the Use of House Servants*. Boston: Munroe and Francis, 1827.

Campbell, Tunis G. *Hotel Keepers, Head Waiters, and Housekeepers' Guide*. Boston: n.p., 1848. Rpt. as *Never Let People Be Kept Waiting: A Textbook on Hotel Management*. Ed. Doris Elizabeth King. King Reprints in Hospitality History. Vol. 1. Raleigh, NC: Graphic, 1973.

Fisher, Abby. *What Mrs. Fisher Knows about Old Southern Cooking, Soups, Pickles, Preserves, Etc*. San Francisco: Women's Co-Operative, 1881. Rpt. with historical notes by Karen Hess. Bedford, MA: Applewood, 1995.

Glover, E. T. *The Warm Springs Receipt-Book*. Richmond, VA: Johnson, 1897.

1900–1919

Hall, H. Franklyn. *300 Ways to Cook and Serve Shell Fish: Terrapin, Green Turtle, Snapper, Oysters, Oyster Crabs, Lobsters, Clams, Crabs and Shrimps*. Philadelphia: Christian Banner, 1901.

Stoney, Mrs. Samuel G., comp. *The Carolina Rice Cook Book*. 1901. Rpt. as *The Carolina Rice Kitchen: The African Connection*. Ed. Karen Hess. Columbia, SC: U of South Carolina P, 1992.

Turner, Bertha, comp. *The Federation Cookbook: A Collection of Tested Recipes, Contributed by the Colored Women of the State of California*. Pasadena: n.p., 1910.

Estes, Rufus. *Good Things to Eat, As Suggested by Rufus: A Collection of Practical Recipes for Preparing Meats, Game, Fowl, Fish, Puddings, Pastries, Etc.* Chicago: Franklin, 1911.

Bivins, S. Thomas. *The Southern Cookbook: A Manual of Cooking and List of Menus, Including Recipes Used by Noted Colored Cooks and Prominent Caterers.* Hampton, VA: P of the Hampton Inst., 1912.

Hayes, Mrs. W. T. *Kentucky Cook Book: Easy and Simple for Any Cook, by a Colored Woman.* St. Louis: Tomkins, 1912.

1920–1939

Lyford, Carrie Alberta. *A Book of Recipes for the Cooking School.* Hampton, VA: Hampton Normal and Agricultural Inst., 1921.

Montana Federation of Negro Women's Clubs. *Cook Book.* Billings: Author, 1927.

Carver, George Washington. "105 Different Ways to Prepare the Peanut for the Table." Comp. and rpt. as appendix to *From Captivity to Fame, or the Life of George Washington Carver,* by Raleigh H. Merritt. 1929. 2nd ed. Boston: Meador, 1938. 133–230.

Schomburg, Arthur A. Untitled typescript. [Proposal for a history of African American cooking.] Arthur A. Schomburg Papers, Activities, and Writings. Folder 7, Box 12. SC Micro 2798, Reel 7. New York Public Library's Schomburg Center for Research in Black Culture, [c. 1920s?].

Negro Culinary Art Club of Los Angeles. *Eliza's Cook Book.* Los Angeles: Wetzel, 1936.

Mahammitt, Sarah Helen Tolliver. *Recipes and Domestic Service: The Mahammitt School of Cookery.* Omaha: n.p., 1939.

Richard, Lena. *Lena Richard's Cook Book.* New Orleans: Rogers, 1939. Rpt. as *New Orleans Cook Book.* Boston: Houghton, 1940.

1940–1959

West, Rebecca. *Rebecca's Cookbook.* Washington, DC: n.p., 1942.

Longrée, Karla. *Soybeans and Peanuts: Two Important Foods.* Hampton, VA: P of the Hampton Inst., 1945.

Gant, Bessie M. *Bess Gant's Cook Book.* 3rd ed. Culver City, CA: Murray and Gee, 1947.

De Knight, Freda. *A Date with a Dish: A Cook Book of American Negro Recipes.* New York: Hermitage, 1948. Rev. and rpt. as *The Ebony Cookbook: A Date with a Dish.* Chicago: Johnson, 1962, 1973.

Hart, Harry H., Sr. *Favorite Recipes of Williams College, with Training Table Records, Notes and Menus.* Williamstown, MA: Author, 1951.

*Watts, Edith Ballard. *Jesse's Book of Creole and Deep South Recipes.* With John Watts. New York: Weathervane, 1954.

What's Cookin' in Urban League Guild. Kansas City, MO: Bev-ron, 1955.

*Mignon, Frances, and Clementine Hunter. *Melrose Plantation Cookbook.* Natchitoches, LA: n.p., 1956.

National Council of Negro Women. *The Historical Cookbook of the American Negro.* Comp. and ed. Sue Bailey Thurman. Washington, DC: Corporate, 1958. Rpt. as *The National Council of Negro Women Presents the Historical Cookbook of the American Negro.* Memphis: Tradery-Wimmer, 1991. New York: Fireside-Simon, 1993.

Bowers, Lessie. *Plantation Recipes.* New York: Speller, 1959.

---

*Asterisk indicates substantial input by non-blacks.

1960–1969

Christian, Vance A. "Introduction to the Kitchen." School of Hotel Administration. Ithaca: Cornell U, c. 1963.

Rollins, Charlemae Hill. *Christmas Gif': An Anthology of Christmas Poems, Songs, and Stories.* Chicago: Follett, 1963. Rpt. as *Christmas Gif': An Anthology of Christmas Poems, Songs, and Stories, Written by and about African-Americans.* New York: Morrow Junior, 1993.

Bellamy, Frank. *His Finest Party Recipes Based on a Lifetime of Successful Catering.* Roswell, GA: n.p., 1965.

Morris, Flossie. *Flossie Morris Unusual Cookbook and Household Hints.* Nashville: Rich, 1967.

Muhammad, Elijah. *How to Eat to Live.* Chicago: Muhammad Mosque of Islam No. 2, 1967.

Gaskins, Ruth L. *A Good Heart and a Light Hand: Ruth L. Gaskins' Collection of Traditional Negro Recipes.* Annandale, VA: Turnpike, 1968. New York: Simon, 1969.

Hearon, Ethel Brown. *Cooking with Soul.* Milwaukee: Rufus King High School, 1968, 1971.

Kaiser, Inez Yeargan. *The Original Soul Food Cookery.* 1968. Rev. and rpt. as *Soul Food Cookery.* New York: Pitman, 1968.

Griffin, Hattie Rhinehart. *Soul-Food Cookbook.* New York: Hearthstone-Carlton, 1969.

Harwood, Jim, and Ed Callahan. *Soul Food Cookbook.* Concord, CA: Nitty Gritty, 1969.

Jeffries, Bob. *Soul Food Cookbook.* Indianapolis: Bobbs, 1969.

Kuffman, Dorothy, ed. *West Oakland Soul Food Cook Book.* Oakland, CA: Peter Maurin Neighborhood House, 1969.

Princess Pamela. *Soul Food Cookbook.* New York: Signet-NAL, 1969.

Roberts, Leonard E. *The Negro Chef Cookbook.* Falmouth, MA: Kendall, 1969. New York: Vantage, 1972.

The Tuesday Soul Food Cookbook. *Tuesday Magazine.* New York: Bantam, 1969.

1970–1979

Bowser, Pearl, and Joan Eckstein. *A Pinch of Soul.* New York: Avon, 1970.

Holdredge, Helen, comp. and ed. *Mammy Pleasant's Cookbook: A Treasury of Gourmet Recipes from Victorian America.* San Francisco: 101 Productions, 1970.

Jackson, Mahalia. *Mahalia Jackson Cooks Soul.* Nashville: Aurora, 1970.

Lee, Jimmy [J. Lee Anderson]. *Soul Food Cookbook.* New York: Award, 1970.

Soul Power Cook Book. Recipes from Students of Ravenswood High School, East Palo Alto, CA. Menlo Park, CA: Lane, 1970.

Verta Mae [Vertamae Smart Grosvenor; Vertamae Smart-Grosvenor]. *Vibration Cooking, or the Travel Notes of a Geechee Girl.* Garden City, NY: Doubleday, 1970. 2nd ed. New York: Ballantine, 1986. 3rd. ed. New York: One World-Ballantine, 1992.

Waddles, Charleszetta. *Mother Waddles Soulfood Cookbook.* Detroit: Mother Waddles Perpetual Mission. 2nd ed., 1970. 3rd ed., c. 1976.

Hill, Fannie. *Cooking with Fannie.* Washington, DC: Washington Gas, 1971.

Jackson, Mary, and Lelia Wishart. *The Integrated Cookbook, or the Soul of Good Cooking.* Chicago: Johnson, 1971.

*Lesberg, Sandy. *The Art of African Cooking.* New York: Dell, 1971.

Mendes, Helen. *The African Heritage Cookbook.* New York: Macmillan, 1971.

Lewis, Edna, and Evangeline Peterson. *The Edna Lewis Cookbook.* 1972. New York: Ecco, 1983.

Muhammad, Elijah. *How to Eat to Live.* Book No. 2. Chicago: Muhammad's Temple of Islam No. 2, 1972.

Bailey, Pearl. *Pearl's Kitchen: An Extraordinary Cookbook*. New York: Harcourt, 1973.
Gregory, Dick. *Dick Gregory's Natural Diet for Folks Who Eat: Cookin' with Mother Nature*. Ed. James R. McGraw, with Alvenia M. Fulton. 1973. New York: Perennial-Harper, 1974.
Millsap, Delma Winfield. *The Way I Do Things*. Columbus, OH: Author, 1974.
Pilgrim Soul: A Cook Book. Kansas City, MO: Young Women's Guild, 1975.
Burgess, Mary Keyes. *Soul to Soul: A Soul Food Vegetarian Cookbook*. Santa Barbara, CA: Woodbridge, 1976.
Hendricks, Bobby. *Barbeque with Mr. Bobby Que*. Memphis: Wimmer, 1976.
Lewis, Edna. *The Taste of Country Cooking*. 1976. New York: Borzoi-Knopf, 1977.
Mitchell, Willa. *Black American Cookbook: A Book of Favorite Recipes*. Shawnee Mission, KS: Circulation Service, 1976.
Moten, Bea. *200 Years of Black Cookery*. Vol. 1. Indianapolis: Leonbea, 1976.
Delicious Afro-American Meals for Pregnant Women and Their Families. New York: Maternity Infant Care–Family Planning Project, 1977.
Mitchell, Willa. *Black American Cookbook*. Vol. 2. Pleasanton, KS: Fundcraft, 1977.
Tillman, Mrs. Walter. *My Mother Cooked My Way through Harvard with These Creole Recipes*. Hattiesburg: U and College P of Mississippi, 1977.
Burton, Nathaniel, and Rudy Lombard. *Creole Feast: 15 Master Chefs from New Orleans Reveal Their Secrets*. New York: Random, 1978.
Darden, Norma Jean, and Carole Darden. *Spoonbread and Strawberry Wine: Recipes and Reminiscences of a Family*. 1978. New York: Fawcett Crest, 1982.
Jackson, Ruth. *Ruth Jackson's Soulfood Cookbook*. Memphis: Wimmer, 1978.
Mitchell, Willa. *Black American Cookbook: Black Heritage Recipes to Treasure*. Vol. 3. Shawnee Mission, KS: Circulation Service, c. 1978.
Munson, Bessie. *Bless the Cook*. 1978. 2nd ed. Arlington, TX: Arlington Century, 1980.
Hunter, Flora M. *Born in the Kitchen: Plain and Fancy Plantation Fixin's*. 3rd ed. Tallahassee, FL: Pine Cone, 1979.
Owens, Mildred V., comp. *Cook Book: Favorite Recipes from Our Best Cooks*. Souls Outreach Baptist Church. Shawnee Mission, KS: Circulation Service, c. 1979.
Shabazz, Lana. *Cooking for the Champ: Muhammad Ali's Favorite Recipes*. New York: Jones-McMillon, 1979.

1980–1989

Carter, Georgia H. *The Best of Granny*. New York: Vantage, 1980.
Crawford, Fred D. *A Christmas Cookbook from Williamsburg*. Williamsburg, VA: Williamsburg, 1980.
Four Great Southern Cooks. Atlanta: DuBose, 1980.
Holmes, Buster. *The Buster Holmes Restaurant Cookbook*. 1980. Gretna, LA: Pelican, 1983.
Rooks, Nancy, and Vester Presley. *The Presley Family Cookbook*. Memphis: Wimmer, 1980.
Edwards, Gary. *Onj E Fun Ori Sa (Food for the Gods)*. New York: Yoruba Theological Archministry, 1981.
Nelson, Esther B. *Cotton Patch Cooking*. Sacramento, CA: Folks, 1981.
Vaughn, David L. *How to Feed Up to Ten People for under 10 Dollars*. 1981. New York: Author, 1982.
Williams, Milton, and Robert Windeler. *The Party Book: Everything You Need to Know for Imaginative and Never-Fail Entertaining at Home*. Garden City, NY: Doubleday, 1981.
*Guckelsberger, Marianne. *Soul Food: Die Ernährung von Schwarzen in den USA als Ausdruck ihrer Kultur*. Hohenschaftlarn bei München: K. Renner, 1982.

McQueen, Adele B. *West African Cooking for Black American Families*. New York: Vantage, 1982.

Ritzberg, Charles. *A Book of Favorite Recipes: The Americanization of African Cooking*. Shawnee Mission, KS: Circulation Service, 1982.

Beckford, Ruth. *A Little of This . . . and Some of That . . .; Cooking with Style*. 2 vols. Oakland, CA: Author, 1983.

Curry, Marva Joy. *Everything You Always Wanted to Know about Soul Food Cooking . . . and Were Afraid to Ask*. N.p.: n.p., 1983.

May, Mark. *Mark May's Hog Cookbook*. Silver Spring, MD: Rosedale, 1983.

Moore-Johnson, Eunice. *From My Mama's Kitchen*. Tacoma, WA: Lakewood, 1983.

300 Years of Black Cooking in St. Mary's County, Maryland. St. Mary's County Community Affairs Committee. 1983. Rev. ed. Leonardtown, MD: n.p., 1983.

Ashley, Alice. *A Hundred Years of Delights: An Epicurean's Cookbook*. New York: Hearthstone-Carlton, 1984.

Davis, Aldeen. *Soul—Food for Thought*. Muscatine, IA: Pip Copy Center, 1984.

Dupuy, Chachie. *Chachie's New Orleans Cooking*. Indianapolis: Bobbs-Merrill, 1984. Rev. and rpt. as *Chachie Dupuy's New Orleans Home Cooking*. New York: Macmillan, 1985.

Hassell, Frances M., ed. *Reflections of an African American Kitchen*. A Collection of Recipes Submitted by Employees of the Universal Life Insurance Company. Memphis: Hassell House, 1984.

Leslie, Austin. *Chez Helene: House of Good Food*. New Orleans: De Simonin, 1984.

*Parker, Euradel. *"Old Virginia" Favorite Southern Recipes*. San Francisco: Author, 1984.

Rogers, Charles M. *Everybody's Cook Book: Uptown-Downtown Cuisine*. With Henry Willis, Jacquelyn Ifill, and William Allen. Decatur, AL: Rogers, 1984.

Stafford, Joseph. *The Black Gourmet: Favorite Afro-American and Creole Recipes from Coast to Coast*. 1984. Rev. ed. Detroit: Harlo, 1988.

Ali, Shahrazad. *How Not to Eat Pork (or Life without the Pig)*. Atlanta: Civilized, 1985.

Ashley, Liza. *Thirty Years at the Mansion: Recipes and Recollections*. As told to Carolyn Huber. Little Rock, AR: August House, 1985.

*Burn, Billie, comp. *Stirrin' the Pots on Daufuskie*. Hilton Head, SC: Impressions, 1985.

Butler, Cleora. *Cleora's Kitchens: The Memoir of a Cook and Eight Decades of Great American Food*. Tulsa, OK: Council Oak, 1985.

Chance, Jeanne Louise Duzant. *Ma Chance's French Caribbean Creole Cooking*. Ed. and comp. June Kelly. New York: Putnam, 1985.

Harris, Jessica B. *Hot Stuff: A Cookbook in Praise of the Piquant*. New York: Atheneum, 1985.

McGill, Alice, Mary Carter Smith, and Elmira M. Washington. *The Griots' Cookbook: Rare and Well-Done*. Columbia, MD: Fairfax, 1985.

Carter, Georgia H. *The Second Best of Granny: Family Recipes*. New York: Vantage, 1986.

*Grant, Cissy Finley, comp. and ed. *"I Just Quit Stirrin' When the Tastin's Good": The Chalfonte Hotel Recipe Collection*. With [Chef] Helen Dickerson. Cape May, NJ: Chalfonte, 1986.

The Black Gourmet Cookbook: A Unique Collection of Easy-to-Prepare, Appetizing, Black American, Creole, Caribbean, and African Cuisine. Westland, MI: Mademoiselles Noires, 1987.

Burns, LaMont. *Down Home Southern Cooking*. Garden City, NY: Doubleday, 1987.

Dixon, Ethel. *Big Mama's Old Black Pot Recipes*. Alexandria, LA: Stoke Gabriel, 1987.

Hovis, Gene. *Gene Hovis's Uptown Down Home Cookbook*. With Sylvia Rosenthal. Boston: Little, 1987.

Paige, Howard. *Aspects of Afro-American Cookery*. Southfield, MI: Aspects, 1987.

*Peevy, Evelyn Sears. *Cooking with Tidewater's Own*. Norfolk, VA: Guide, 1987.

Soul Food with Music Magazine. Bethesda, MD: Wedet, 1987–[?].

Amen I, Ra Un Nefer. *Optimizing Health through Nutrition*. Bronx: Khamit, 1988.

Jackson, Linda, and Malik Jackson. *The Sweet Jassmine Natural Food Cookbook*. Takoma Park, MD: n.p., 1988.

Lampkin, Viola. *Viola's Favorite Recipes*. Olathe, KS: Cookbook Publishers, 1988.

Lewis, Edna. *In Pursuit of Flavor*. New York: Borzoi-Knopf, 1988.

Nabwire, Constance, and Bertha Vining Montgomery. *Cooking the African Way*. Minneapolis: Lerner, 1988.

Seale, Bobby. *Barbeque'n with Bobby: Righteous, Down-Home Barbeque Recipes by Bobby Seale*. Berkeley: Ten Speed, 1988.

Tate, Bibby, and Ethel Dixon. *Colorful Louisiana Cuisine in Black and White*. 1988. Gretna, LA: Pelican, 1990.

Ferguson, Sheila. *Soul Food: Classic Cuisine from the Deep South*. New York: Weidenfeld, 1989.

Harris, Jessica. *Iron Pots and Wooden Spoons: Africa's Gifts to New World Cooking*. 1989. New York: Ballantine-Random, 1991.

Kondo, Nia, and Zak Kondo. *Vegetarianism Made Simple and Easy: A Primer for Black People*. Washington, DC: Nubia, 1989.

Marsh, Carole. *The Kitchen House: How Yesterday's Black Women Created Today's American Foods*. Our Black Heritage Series. N.p.: Gallopede, 1989.

Starr, Kathy. *The Soul of Southern Cooking*. Jackson: UP of Mississippi, 1989.

Wright, Keith T. *A Healthy Foods and Spiritual Nutrition Handbook*. 1989. 2nd ed. Philadelphia: Author [Health Masters], 1990.

Peters, Pat. *Soul Food for Body and Soul*. 2 vols. St. Louis: Open Door, c. 1980s.

1990–1998

Chase, Leah. *The Dooky Chase Cookbook*. Gretna, LA: Pelican, 1990.

Guillory, Queen Ida. *Cookin' with Queen Ida: "Bon Temps" Creole Recipes (and Stories) from the Queen of Zydeco Music*. With Naomi Wise. Rocklin, CA: Prima, 1990.

Pinderhughes, John. *Family of the Spirit Cookbook: Recipes and Remembrances from African-American Kitchens*. New York: Simon, 1990.

Copage, Eric V. *Kwanzaa: An African-American Celebration of Culture and Cooking*. New York: Quill-William Morrow, 1991.

Evans, Louis. *Louis Evans' Creole Cookbook*. Gretna, LA: Pelican, 1991.

Harris, Jessica B. *Sky Juice and Flying Fish: Traditional Caribbean Cooking*. New York: Fireside-Simon, 1991.

National Council of Negro Women. *The Black Family Reunion Cookbook: Recipes and Food Memories*. Memphis: Tradery, 1991. New York: Fireside-Simon, 1993.

Soul Vegetarian Cookbook. Soul Vegetarian Cafe and Exodus Carryout. Washington, DC: Communicators, 1992.

Williams, Susan, ed. *The McClellanville Coast Cookbook*. McClellanville, SC: McClellanville Arts Council, 1992.

Woods, Sylvia, and Christopher Styler. *Sylvia's Soul Food: Recipes from Harlem's World-Famous Restaurant*. New York: Hearst-Morrow, 1992.

Young, Bob, and Al Stankus. *Jazz Cooks: Portraits and Recipes of the Greats*. New York: Stewart, Tabori, and Chang, 1992.

Abdulassamad, Kariem. *Cooking with Rhythm*. Pennsauken, NJ: F-J Associates, 1993.

Chambers, Melvett G. *Soul Cookin' Southern Style*. Denver, CO: Author, 1993.

Cotton, Ida. *Mother Cotton's Goodies: HomeStyle Recipes.* N.p.: Literacy Council of Northern Virginia, 1993.

Jenkins, Yvonne M. *A Traveler's Collection of Black Cooking.* New York: Carlton, 1993.

Mitchell, Patricia B. *Soul on Rice: African Influences on American Cooking.* N.p.: n.p., 1993.

National Council of Negro Women. *The Black Family Dinner Quilt Cookbook: Health Conscious Recipes and Food Memories.* With Dorothy I. Height. Memphis: Tradery-Wimmer, 1993. New York: Fireside-Simon, 1994.

Sanchez, Tani D., comp. *Meals and Memoirs: Recipes and Recollections of African Americans in Tucson, Arizona.* Tucson: African American Historical and Genealogical Society, Tucson Chapter, 1993.

Williams, Thelma, comp. *Our Family Table: Recipes and Food Memories from African-American Life Models.* Memphis: Wimmer, 1993.

Bernstein, Rebecca Sample, Jodi Evert, Susan Mahal, and Mark Salisbury. *Addy's Cookbook: A Peek at Dining in the Past with Meals You Can Cook Today.* Middleton, WI: Pleasant, 1994.

Chase, Leah, and Johnny Rivers. *Down Home Healthy: Family Recipes of Black American Chefs.* Bethesda, MD: National Institutes of Health, National Cancer Inst., 1994.

The Joy of Not Cooking. Washington, DC: Delights of the Garden, 1994.

La Tham, Aris. *Sunfired Foods: Cookless Recipes by Aris La Tham.* Bethesda, MD: Sun, 1994.

Medearis, Angela Shelf. *The African-American Kitchen: Cooking from Our Heritage.* New York: Dutton, 1994.

Nash, Jonell. *Essence Brings You Great Cooking.* New York: Amistad-Penguin, 1994.

National Council of Negro Women. *Celebrating Our Mothers' Kitchens: Treasured Memories and Tested Recipes.* Memphis: Tradery-Wimmer, 1994.

Parham, Vanessa Roberts. *The African-American Child's Heritage Cookbook.* South Pasadena, CA: Sandcastle, 1994.

Brady, April A. *Kwanzaa Karamu: Cooking and Crafts for a Kwanzaa Feast.* Minneapolis: Carolrhoda, 1995.

Burke, Cathryn Boyd, and Susan P. Raia. *Soul and Traditional Southern Food Practices, Customs, and Holidays.* Chicago: American Dietetic Assoc., 1995.

Cusick, Heidi Haughy. *Soul and Spice: African Cooking in the Americas.* San Francisco: Chronicle, 1995.

Harris, Jessica B. *A Kwanzaa Keepsake: Celebrating the Holiday with New Traditions and Feasts.* New York: Simon, 1995.

———. *The Welcome Table: African-American Heritage Cooking.* New York: Simon, 1995.

MacK-Williams, Kibibi. *African American Life: Food and Our History.* Vero Beach, FL: Rourke, 1995.

Medearis, Angela Shelf. *A Kwanzaa Celebration: Festive Recipes and Homemade Gifts from an African-American Kitchen.* New York: Dutton-Penguin, 1995.

Sanders, Dori. *Dori Sanders' Country Cooking: Recipes and Stories from the Family Farm Stand.* Chapel Hill: Algonquin-Workman, 1995.

Smith, Barbara. *B. Smith's Entertaining and Cooking for Friends.* With Kathleen Cromwell. New York: Artisan, 1995.

Banks-Payne, Ruby. *Ruby's Low-Fat Soul Food Cookbook.* Chicago: Contemporary, 1996.

Carter, Danella. *Down-Home Wholesome: 300 Low-Fat Recipes from a New Soul Kitchen.* New York: Dutton, 1996.

Foreman, George, and Cherie Calbom. *George Foreman's Knock-Out-the-Fat Barbeque and Grilling Cookbook.* New York: Villard-Random, 1996.

Grosvenor, Vertamae [Vertamae Smart-Grosvenor]. *Vertamae Cooks in the Americas' Family Kitchen.* San Francisco: KQED Books, 1996.

Jones, Wilbert. *The New Soul-Food Cookbook: Healthier Recipes for Traditional Favorites.* Secaucus, NJ: Carol, 1996. Rev. and rpt. as *The Healthy Soul Food Cookbook: How to Cut the Fat but Keep the Flavor.* Secaucus, NJ: Citadel, 1997.

Nash, Jonell. *Low-Fat Soul.* New York: Ballantine, 1996.

Tillery, Carolyn Quick. *The African-American Heritage Cookbook: Traditional Recipes and Fond Remembrances from Alabama's Renowned Tuskegee Institute.* New York: Carol, 1996.

Medearis, Angela Shelf. *Entertaining Ideas from the African-American Kitchen.* New York: Dutton, 1997.

Medearis, Angela Shelf, and Michael R. Medearis. *African American Arts: Cooking.* New York: Twenty-First Century, 1997.

Pinkney, Andrea Davis, and J. Brian Pinkney. *I Smell Honey.* San Diego: Harcourt, 1997.

Smalls, Alexander. *Grace the Table: Stories and Recipes from My Southern Revival.* With Hettie Jones. New York: HarperCollins, 1997.

Jones, Wilbert. *Mama's Tea Cakes: 101 Delicious Soul Food Desserts.* Secaucus, NJ: Carol-Birch Lane, 1998.

Randall, Joe, Toni Tipton-Martin, and Joseph G. Randall. 1998. *A Taste of Heritage: New African-American Cuisine.* New York: Macmillan.

Shange, Ntozake. *If I Can Cook / You Know God Can.* Boston: Beacon, 1998.

White, Joyce. *Soul Food: Recipes and Reflections from African-American Churches.* New York: HarperCollins, 1998.

Forthcoming

National Council of Negro Women. *Mother Africa's Table: A Chronicle of Celebration through West African and African American Recipes and Cultural Traditions.* Ed. Cassandra Hughes Webster. New York: Main Street-Doubleday.

Weber, Valerie, and Jeraldine Jackson. *Food in Grandma's Day.* Minneapolis: Carolrhoda.

Notes

Prologue

1. My use of the term "articulation" derives loosely from Ernesto Laclau and Chantal Mouffe. In their work on hegemony, they define articulation as "any practice establishing a relation among elements such that their identity is modified as a result of the articulatory practice" (105).

2. For a memorable example of the racial progress theme, see Gary Smith's *Sports Illustrated* profile of Woods (52); for a memorable example of the white racial anxieties that linger at the edges of such narratives, see Tim Rosaforte's biography of Woods (12).

3. Consider, for instance, Alex Tresniowski's celebration in a June 1997 *People* cover story of Earl Woods's successful instantiation of patriarchy in his second marriage (98).

4. For articles from the popular press which attempted to negotiate these concerns about the future of racial categorization, see John Leland and Gregory Beals's "In Living Colors," Alex Tresniowski's "Rising Son," and an uncredited *Ebony* cover story titled "Black America and Tiger's Dilemma."

5. For instance, both Kobena Mercer and Lauren Berlant have published insightful essays that use "1968" in the title.

6. Works by the following authors have served me as useful guides to twentieth-century U.S. history: Howard Zinn, Paula Giddings, Jacqueline Jones, John D'Emilio and Estelle Freedman, Sara Evans (*Born*), Ronald Takaki, and John Hope Franklin. For my work on the post–World War II era, I have also turned for information especially to William Van Deburg, as well as to Sara Evans (*Personal*), Alan Crawford, John D'Emilio, Manning Marable, Todd Gitlin, Hugh Davis Graham, Alice Echols, and James Patterson. Though I by no means agree with the ideological slant of all of these authors, I have found it enlightening to seek out differing perspectives. The many other historical studies on which I have drawn for more focused assistance are listed elsewhere.

7. See the articles by Lena Williams on Sylvia Woods, by Rick Bragg on the chitlin drive-through chain, and by Carole Sugarman on the vegetarian soul food restaurants. Let me stress, though, that soul food has never gone out of style since the demise of Black Power in the mid-1970s, and health has long been a concern. The following series of arti-

cles from *Essence* illustrates my point: "Soul Food: Vegetarian Style" (1979); "Food with New Soul" (1982); Lloyd Gite and Jean Perry's "Diet: Losing Weight Soulfully" (1983); and Jonell Nash's "Today's New Black Cookstyle" (1985).

8. Psyche Williams's essay "Interpreting History through African American Foodways" has complicated my thinking about food, gender, and class dynamics in Hopkins's *Contending Forces*.

9. My interpretation of the gendered underpinnings of the materiality/abstraction binary might be located in the context of a well-known debate between Jonathan Culler and Tania Modleski over the masculinist implications of hypothesizing a readership position. See Culler 43–64 and Modleski, "Feminism" 131–35. In their own subsequent debate over *Linden Hills*, Margaret Homans and Henry Louis Gates Jr. return to and reconfigure the Culler-Modleski exchange. See Homans, "Woman" 370–71, and Gates, "Significant" 615–16, as well as Homans's more recent essay "Racial Composition," which historicizes her contestation with Gates.

10. My understanding of domestic labor is informed not just by Davis's essay, but also by the long and vibrant history of feminist engagement with Marxism, in which she has figured prominently. The paradigmatic Marxist statement on women's oppression is, of course, Frederick Engels's 1884 study *The Origin of the Family, Private Property, and the State*, which interpreted the subordination of women as a function of the development of private property. For now-classic work on the relationship between Marxism and feminism and/or explorations of domestic labor from a socialist-feminist perspective, see Lise Vogel 73–92 and 151–75, Christine Delphy, Jean Gardiner, Gloria Joseph, Gayle Rubin, and Heidi Hartmann. More recently, Gayatri Spivak has brought together poststructuralist theory and Marxist political economy, while Chandra Mohanty, Faye Harrison, Angela Gilliam, and Nellie Wong have contributed essays to *Third World Women and the Politics of Feminism* which argue for "international coalitions among third world women in contemporary capitalist societies, particularly on the basis of a socialist-feminist vision" (Mohanty, "Cartographies" 5). Finally, Cynthia Enloe has explored the role of food and domestic service in the global industrial-imperial economy. See especially 124–50 and 177–94.

I refer to other scholarly studies specifically devoted to black women and domestic service in chapters 1 and 2. Here, though, I would also point out that Alice Childress's 1956 book *Like One of the Family*, a compilation of columns about a fictive African American domestic servant, still offers a brilliant introduction to the race, gender, and class politics of housework. Trudier Harris's innovative examination of complicity and resistance among black women domestics in African American literature, *From Mammies to Militants*, helped me understand the significance of Childress's accomplishment, as well as of materialist-feminist approaches to African American women's writing.

11. Linda Nochlin had earlier raised these and related issues in her 1971 essay "Why Have There Been No Great Women Artists?"

12. I first offered this critique of Leonardi in a 1991 article, "In Search of Our Mothers' Cookbooks" (23–24). Working independently, Anne Goldman made the same point the following year in a wonderful essay that focused largely on Chicana cookbooks (170–72).

13. My first attempt to discuss Grosvenor's experimentation with the genre of the cookbook appeared in my 1991 article which critiqued Leonardi's essay. Around this same time, Jennifer Brody, Nicole King, Quandra Prettyman (131–33), Sandi Russell (169–70), and Rafia Zafar ("Cooking") were also undertaking valuable work on Grosvenor.

14. See the appendix for an overview of the development of the African American cookbook "tradition," at least as it appears to me at this stage of my work.

15. All the same, Graeme Turner's *British Cultural Studies* offers a useful introduction. See also the essays collected in *Cultural Studies*, edited by Lawrence Grossberg, Cary Nel-

son, and Paula Treichler; and in *Black British Cultural Studies*, edited by Houston Baker Jr., Manthia Diawara, and Ruth Lindeborg.

16. Here I have in mind, for example, the work of Raymond Williams, Stuart Hall, Paul Gilroy, Hazel Carby, Vron Ware, and Kobena Mercer.

17. See Derrida's *Of Grammatology* 1–93.

18. I should, though, mention Linda Keller Brown and Kay Mussell's wonderful coedited volume *Ethnic and Regional Foodways in the United States*, which consists primarily of work by anthropologists. See especially the essays by Roger Abrahams and C. Paige Gutierrez.

19. Though *Purity and Danger* ostensibly focused on "primitive" societies, it is surely not a coincidence that the book appeared just four years after Rachel Carson had helped spearhead the environmental and natural foods movements in the United States with the publication in 1962 of *Silent Spring*.

20. See Stallybrass and White 200–1; Butler, *Gender* 79–93 and 133–34; Butler, *Bodies* 1–23 and 243, n. 2; Young 141–48; and McClintock 71–74 and 270–73.

21. Here I am paraphrasing McClintock's claims.

22. I have also been challenged by Spillers's "The Permanent Obliquity of an In(pha)llibly Straight" and her more recent "All the Things You Could Be by Now If Sigmund Freud's Wife Was Your Mother."

23. John Singleton's *Boyz N the Hood* (1991) garnered perhaps the most attention among the films of the early 1990s, but one might also mention Mario Van Peebles's *New Jack City* (1991), Matty Rich's *Straight out of Brooklyn* (1991), Joseph P. Vasquez's *Hangin' with the Homeboys* (1991), Ernest R. Dickerson's *Juice* (1992), Allen Hughes and Albert Hughes's *Menace II Society* (1993), Boaz Yakin's *Fresh* (1994), and Spike Lee's *Clockers* (1995). With the release of Larry Cohen's *Original Gangstas* in 1996, however, the trend had largely abated and black film history was repeating itself as farce.

24. I have in mind books by Robyn Wiegman, Darrell Dawsey, and Phillip Brian Harper, as well as books coedited by Herb Boyd/Robert Allen and Marcellus Blount/George Cunningham. Wiegman's book appeared in 1995; the rest, in 1996.

25. It would be pointless at this time to try to offer a thorough listing of titles. For now, let me simply mention a few authors whose work I have found stimulating. Eve Sedgwick's writings (*Between* and *Epistemology*) have been pivotal for work on masculinity and homosociality and continue to help define the field. The essays collected by Michael Warner in *Fear of a Queer Planet* and by Henry Abelove, Michèle Aina Barale, and David Halperin in *The Lesbian and Gay Studies Reader* offer a useful introduction to lesbian/bisexual/gay and queer theory. My thinking has been complicated as well by studies of whiteness by Walter Benn Michaels, Richard Dyer, David Roediger, Vron Ware, Eric Lott, Ruth Frankenberg, and others.

26. Excellent work on this topic can be found in the essays collected by Gina Dent and Michele Wallace in *Black Popular Culture*, as well as in the essays collected by Marcellus Blount and George Cunningham in *Representing Black Men*. In the former collection, see especially the contributions of Gilroy, Wallace, and Davis; in the latter, of Awkward, Thomas, and Alexander.

Chapter One

1. And, as Judith Williamson's *Decoding Advertisements* has helped me understand, "good taste" would also be the attribute of the consumer who chooses to buy Aunt Jemima products.

2. Agnew's description is slightly inaccurate. The kerchief was replaced with a headband during a late-1960s makeover.

3. See Joshua Gamson 100 on the *TV Guide* scandal.

4. Elizabeth Alexander also used the Jemima/Oprah connection as a point of departure in a 1991 conference paper on black women, food, and popular iconography ("Imitation").

5. Louis Althusser uses the term "interpellation" to describe the material practices (i.e., ideologies) through which individuals are constituted as subjects in capitalism.

6. See Gamson 170 for one fan's explanation of her interest in Winfrey's wealth.

7. Unlike "quota queen" Lani Guinier (whose nomination to a leading post in the U.S. Justice Department was withdrawn by Bill Clinton) and "condom queen" Joycelyn Elders (who was forced to resign as Clinton's Surgeon General), Ronald Reagan's Cadillac-driving "welfare queen" was never linked to an individual African American woman.

8. See, for example, discussions of the ideology and/or portrayal of black womanhood in Sharon Harley and Rosalyn Terborg-Penn; Angela Davis, "Legacy"; Barbara Christian; Ann Allen Shockley, "Black"; bell hooks, *Ain't*; Patricia Bell Scott; Jewelle Gomez; Deborah Gray White; Janet Sims-Wood; Patricia Hill Collins 67–90; Patricia Morton; and K. Sue Jewell, *From*. Much of the post-1950s scholarship on black stereotypes emerged initially in response to Stanley Elkins's controversial book *Slavery* (1959). Elkins focused primarily on what he called the "Sambo" stereotype, which Deborah Gray White subsequently criticized as normatively male (17–21).

9. The additions to the field just since the trademark's 1989 update include works by Lauren Berlant, "National"; Patricia Morton; Megan Granda; K. Sue Jewell, *From*; Audrey Edwards; Phil Patton; Marilyn Kern-Foxworth; Patricia Turner; Kenneth Goings; and Diane Roberts. In this context, I should also mention M. M. Manring's *Slave in a Box: The Strange Career of Aunt Jemima*, which is scheduled for publication in 1998 and which will clearly be a valuable resource. For other, mostly pre-1989 discussions of Aunt Jemima, see Harrison John Thornton 242–43; I. E. Lambert 57–58; Hannah Campbell 40–42; Arthur Marquette 137–58; Stan Pantovic; K. Sue Jewell, "Analysis" 110 ff.; James Anderson 99; Stanley Sacharow 63–65; Jim Hall 76–77; Hal Morgan 55; Joseph Boskin 139–41; Dawn Reno, "Familiar" and *Collecting* (see index listing on 147); Jackie Young 7–27; Jacquie Greenwood; Cathy Campbell; Fred Brown Jr.; Douglas Congdon-Martin 61, 72, and 139; and Thomas Hine 90–92.

10. The company did clearly open its archives to Harrison John Thornton, who published his scholarly study *The History of the Quaker Oats Company* in 1933. Thornton offers only minimal information about the Aunt Jemima trademark (233 and 242–43), but this omission is at least suggestive of the degree of importance Thornton perceived the brand to have had in 1933. Archives from the advertising agencies responsible for the Aunt Jemima account are, by contrast, generally accessible. The J. Walter Thompson agency held the account from 1909 until June 1935, and again from 1953 until the present. The agency's archives are located at Duke University's Hartman Center for Sales, Advertising and Marketing History, and they include some information about former advertising campaigns conducted by the company for Aunt Jemima products. According to Elizabeth Dunn at the center, nothing is available about current campaigns. The account was also held for a time by the firm of Lord and Thomas. The archives for this agency are located at the State Historical Society of Wisconsin. A staff member there reports, however, that only copies of advertisements are on file.

11. I have included all Aunt Jemima advertisements referred to in this chapter in the list of works cited under the general heading "Aunt Jemima products." The listings are alphabetized according to the main caption for each advertisement. Parenthetical references to these advertisements are to the first word from the caption.

12. Compared to some of the advertisements from earlier in the century, the "legend" series did seem muted in its racism. See, for example, an October 1910 issue of the *Ladies'*

Home Journal, in which readers were offered a simianized Aunt Jemima dangling from a rope attached to a box of the pancake flour ("Your").

13. Listed under the subheading "Crushed to Death," the brief story reads as follows: "Mrs. Nancy Green, colored, 89 years old, 4543 Prairie avenue, was fatally injured when struck by an automobile driven by H. S. Seymour, colored, 4730 Prairie avenue" ("3").

14. See, for example, the sections on the Agricultural Building in William Cameron 66–73, Hubert Howe Bancroft 341–98, and *The Graphic History of the Fair* 70–85. Among more recent works covering the 1893 fair—including scholarly studies by David Burg, Jeanne Madeline Weimann, Robert Rydell, and John Findling—none mention the Aunt Jemima exhibit, though Rydell does refer to the appearance of "Aunt Jemimah" at the 1898 Omaha exposition (119).

15. Entertainment preview listings from November 1889 include (by title, date, and page number): *Gazette*, 14th, 4; *Gazette*, 17th, 4; *Herald*, 14th, 4; *Herald*, 16th, 4; *Herald*, 17th, 2; and *News*, 15th, 2. Advertisements from November 1889 include: *News*, 15th, 2; *Gazette*, 16th, 3; *Gazette*, 17th, 6; and *Herald*, 17th, 2. Reviews from November 1889 include: *Herald*, 18th, 4; *News*, 18th, 2; and *Gazette*, 18th, 5.

16. Demonstrating how the narrative line of the performance was subordinated to its set pieces, the *Herald* reviewer further observed: "The plot of 'The Emigrant' is sufficiently well laid to form an interesting feature of the comedy, and the scenes have been so judiciously arranged that the interest is maintained from the rising of the curtain to the final tableaux. Like many other modern comedies, it is so written as to give the star the most liberal opportunity to display his powers" (18 Nov. 1889: 4).

17. Discussing the December 1886 offerings at the Novelty Theatre in Williamsburgh, NY, Odell refers in passing to "P. F. Baker, formerly of Baker and Farron" (XIII: 387). After the St. Joseph performance, the *Gazette*, too, had referred to Baker's former partnership with Farron (18 Nov. 1889: 5).

18. For discussions of the racialization of the Irish in the nineteenth-century United States, see Lemons 106, Roediger 133–63, and Ignatiev.

19. According to Willie Lyle, another common version of "Old Aunt Jemima," composed by James Grace and "[s]ung with rapturous applause by Billy Kersands," ran in part as follows: "My old missus promise me, / Old Aunt Jemima, oh, oh, oh, [repeat after each line] / When she died she[']d set me free, / She lived so long her head got bald, / She swore she would not die at all" (also quoted in Toll 260). Toll believes that the song probably originated with white rather than black minstrels because of its "overt protest message and its lack of even a face-saving comic 'victory' for the black character" (260). Yet he also concludes that this version "had real meaning for blacks, who could endorse its protest against whites' broken promises while they laughed at the idea of a bald white woman (perhaps also a jibe at the idea of whites having 'good hair')" (260). Thomas Talley offers yet another version, called simply "Aunt Jemima," in his *Negro Folk Rhymes* (1922): "Ole Aunt Jemima grow so tall, / Dat she couldn' see de groun'. / She stumped her toe, an' down she fell / From de Blackwoods clean to town. / W'en Aunt Jemima git in town, / An' see dem 'tony' ways, / She natchully faint an' back she fell / To de Backwoods whar she stays" (Talley edition 107; Wolfe edition 92–93). It is unclear whether Talley, a chemistry professor at Fisk University, considered this version to have originated among African Americans, but obviously he decided it warranted inclusion in his collection. In Lott's opinion, "the minstrel show's humor, songs, and dances were so culturally mixed as, in effect, to make their 'racial' origins quite undecidable" (*Love* 94). See also Toll 268, n. 41, for references to other versions of "Old Aunt Jemima."

20. See Paula Giddings 17–131 for an illuminating discussion of racial uplift, the "woman question," and antilynching campaigns.

21. *The Reason Why* is reprinted, along with Wells's antilynching tracts *Southern Horrors* and *A Red Record*, in the *Selected Works of Ida. B. Wells-Barnett*.

22. See also Robert Snyder's description of the performances of Jewish vaudevillian Belle Baker (112).

23. In "National Brands/National Body," Berlant examines Hurst's novel and the two subsequent film versions (John Stahl's 1934 film having been followed by Douglas Sirk's better known remake in 1959) to consider "how they collectively imagine the American body politic from the points of view of the overembodied women who serve it" (115). Berlant's attention to the relationships among female embodiment, national identity, and racial difference has provided a valuable model for my thinking.

24. Kenneth Goings notes that the image of black women—as exemplified in black collectibles—was "slimmed down" from the 1930s to the 1950s (63), but Robinson's portrayal of Aunt Jemima seems to have been an exception to this general trend.

25. Rydell writes: "With Aunt Jemimah serving pancakes from a griddle in the Home Kitchen of the Manufacturing Building, the [1898] Omaha exposition promoters successfully consigned blacks to a class apart and introduced midwesterners to the paradigm of race relations advocated by the designers of the New South" (119). See also Ayers 132–59 for an informative discussion of race relations in the post-Reconstruction South.

26. Between the Civil War and World War I, the "servant problem" dominated the pages of magazines aimed at white women. In the North, the stereotypical domestic was usually an inept Irish immigrant, often "Bridget" or "Erin"; in the South, the servant was almost always an African American woman, typically "Aunt Chloe" or "Dinah." As David Katzman explains, by the second half of the nineteenth century, the growth of the middle class combined with the abolition of slavery and the increasing availability of factory jobs to make the demand for servants outpace their supply (223–65).

27. See Mimi Abramovitz 181–213 for a useful account of how women's labor was constructed during the decades following Aunt Jemima's inception.

28. Kern-Foxworth reprints Dunnavant's poem in *Aunt Jemima, Uncle Ben, and Rastus*. Given my concern in this chapter with scholarly accuracy in work on Aunt Jemima, I should acknowledge here that I have been unable to locate a copy of her source to confirm the citation.

29. George Washington Cable's 1880 novel *The Grandissimes*, which Ladd discusses briefly, exemplifies this concern.

30. At the very least, the fairly long-standing association of pancakes with Mardi Gras festivities could have rendered Aunt Jemima products suspect in some conservative Protestant quarters. Indeed, "Shrove Tuesday" had been redubbed "Pancake Tuesday" as early as 1825 (*Compact* 2063). As William Pierson has demonstrated, moreover, the racially hybrid foundations of Mardi Gras were well established in the public mind during the nineteenth century (121–36). Waverley Root and Richard de Rochemont claim that both waffles and pancakes are of Dutch origin (302), but this would be in keeping with Pierson's acknowledgment of the Pennsylvania Dutch influences on New Orleans carnival culture (122–24).

31. Marilyn Kern-Foxworth offers the most comprehensive discussion of the women who have enacted the trademark in *Aunt Jemima* 66–70. She also focuses specifically on Texas native and Aunt Jemima impersonator Rosie Lee Moore Hall in a two-part series called "Aunt Jemima" published in 1989.

32. I have never seen the phrase "flapjacks to the queen's taste" incorporated in Aunt Jemima advertisements. The phrase "to the queen's taste," however, was used in contemporaneous campaigns for Cream of Wheat.

33. The *Defender* was actually far more grudging in its coverage of the 1933 Century of Progress Exposition, noting in an August headline that "'Negro Day' at Fair Flops: Parade Is

Worst in History of City." Anna Robinson's appearance at the fair, which Marquette claims to have been such a success, received no coverage from the *Defender* at all.

34. This coverage was reversed by the time another Aunt Jemima impersonator, Chicago resident Edith Wilson, died in 1981. A noted blues singer as well as one of the regular black performers on the *Amos 'n' Andy* radio series, Wilson portrayed Aunt Jemima from 1948 until 1966, at least according to one obituary ("'Aunt Jemima' of "). The *Tribune* published a brief article taking note of her demise and informing its readers that she "was Quaker Oats' 'Aunt Jemima' for 18 years" ("Edith"), but the *Defender*, by contrast, carried no notice of her death that I could find. Derrick Stewart-Baxter writes that Wilson was "criticised by members of her race" for her "shameful" behavior in portraying Aunt Jemima (31). Wilson's response, as Stewart-Baxter records it, was to claim that "Jemima is a well-loved character—almost a folk figure who gives out love and kindness, so how can that be bad?" (31).

35. This advertisement appeared, among other places, in the March 1928 issue of *Good Housekeeping*.

36. Curiously, in 1945 Hughes invited Edith Wilson to be the guest of honor at one of his famous "Yard Dog" parties. Rampersad reports that Wilson was at the time already doing radio advertisements for Aunt Jemima products (*I Dream* 245).

37. See Cleaver 151. The text of Malcolm X's attack on the Quaker Oats trademark has only recently come to light. For a discussion and reprinting of it, see Phil Patton 82.

38. Donaldson's work is reproduced and (briefly) discussed in *Tradition and Conflict* 64. Overstreet's work is reproduced and discussed in *Tradition* 52, Elsa Honig Fine 260–62, and Lucy Lippard 235–36. DePillars's work is reproduced and discussed in Lippard 235–36.

39. A contributor to the *Village Voice* has described the alleged "model for the current Aunt Jemima," Ethel Ernestine Harper, as having "Afro-Asiatic almond-shaped eyes" and a "Nubian face" (C. Campbell 45). Meanwhile, Kern-Foxworth attributes the "savvy Creole cooking instructor" comment to a writer for *Black Ethnic Collectibles* (Kern-Foxworth, "Aunt Jemima Is" 58). Unfortunately, I have yet to locate the original source of this latter quotation, since the article by Jacquie Greenwood ("Black Promotional Products") to which the usually reliable Kern-Foxworth appears to be referring does not contain it. Regardless, given such characterizations, it hardly seems an exaggeration to describe the trademark as an ideal test case for Homi Bhabha's theorization of hybridity, a point of rupture where the "'denied' knowledges" of U.S. racial/ethnic multiplicity "enter upon the dominant discourse [of black/white racial difference] and estrange the basis of its authority—its rules of recognition" ("Signs" 114).

40. Saar's work is reproduced and discussed in Whitney Chadwick 318–19, Samella Lewis 200–2, Lucy Lippard 234–36, and *Gumbo* 239–47.

41. Tesfagiorgis's work is reproduced and discussed in Robert Henkes 113–20 and discussed in *Gumbo* 289–92. Ringgold's work is reproduced on the front cover of and discussed in *Faith Ringgold* 21; it is also discussed in *Gumbo* 225–28. Because Tesfagiorgis feels strongly that her work should be viewed in color, I am not reproducing it here in black and white. In the background of her painting are "African textiles and patchwork quilts creating a rhythmic pattern of color and textures" (Henkes 114). Represented as a traditional mammy, Aunt Jemima "is somewhat fused into" these textiles (Henkes 114), her gaze directed toward an African sculpture of mother and child. In the foreground, superimposed over Aunt Jemima, is a dancing Zulu doll.

42. Cathy Campbell points out that, like Nancy Green, Ethel Ernestine Harper died in a car accident (45).

43. Intriguingly, when discussing the Aunt Jemima rag doll promotion, Dawn Reno refers to Jemima's "husband, Uncle Mose; daughter, Diana; and son, Wade Davis" ("Famil-

iar" 69). Presumably the "Davis" refers to one of the early manufacturers of Aunt Jemima products, R. T. Davis, which either denies Uncle Mose the patriarchal prerogative of naming his children or else suggests that Davis (but not, notably, Colonel Higbee) had fathered Diana and Wade.

44. I should note that there are many other Aunt Jemima "appropriators" among African American visual artists, whose work I do not discuss in this chapter, including Robert Colescott, Joyce Scott, and Mary Le Ravin. For information on Colescott, see Lippard 238; for information on Scott, see Lippard 236, Arlene Raven, and *Gumbo* 252–53; for information on Ravin, see *Gumbo* 143.

45. For discussion of this dozens chant, see K. Sue Jewell's *From Mammy to Miss America* 62.

Chapter Two

1. Constance Penley has succinctly summarized the primal scene as "the name Freud gave to the fantasy of overhearing or observing parental intercourse, of being on the scene, so to speak, of one's own conception" (68). For Freud's explication of this concept, see "From" 498–519.

2. This is not to say that signs of such mounting tensions were not present earlier. For example, Gillian Brown has discussed how Harriet Beecher Stowe sets up competing models of northern and southern domesticity to critique the moral foundations of antebellum southern society in *Uncle Tom's Cabin*.

3. According to Katzman, Villard's comments appeared in "The Negro and the Domestic Problem," *Alexander's Magazine* I (15 Nov. 1905): 6. I have not yet seen the original.

4. Partly as a result of the demographic shift of African Americans from the rural South to the urban North during the early decades of this century, the 1920s and early 1930s witnessed a resurgence of such plantation school discourses, including plantation school cookbooks. See, for example, the texts by Emma and William McKinney, Katharin Bell, Natalie Scott, Betty Benton Patterson, and Emma Speed Sampson. John Egerton (16) and Alan Grubb (172–73) offer discussion of this historically mutating portrayal of black cooks.

5. Katzman's *Seven Days a Week* offers a comprehensive overview of domestic service in the period from 1870 to 1920. See especially 184–265. For other useful works on black women and domestic service in the twentieth century, see Judith Rollins, Susan Tucker, and Elizabeth Clark-Lewis. For other helpful studies of domestic service and/or domesticity in the United States, see Faye Dudden, Glenna Matthews, and Phyllis Palmer.

6. See Harvey Levenstein's *Revolution at the Table* for astute analyses of the causes and ramifications of these changes—such as fluctuating gender roles, (im)migration, and industrialization—during the period from 1880 until 1930.

7. Susan Tucker's otherwise interesting *Telling Memories among Southern Women: Domestics and Their Employers in the Segregated South* is typical of what I have in mind here. "Employers" refers only to white women, which reinforces the assumption that men bear no responsibility for domestic labor.

8. This is a central claim of Sedgwick's *Epistemology of the Closet*.

9. I have gathered these dates from Claiborne's autobiography, *A Feast Made for Laughter* (Acknowledgments, n. pag., and 127–29), as well as from Bryan Miller's *New York Times* article on Claiborne's retirement party.

10. The reference to "notoriety" stems primarily from a $4,000 dinner he and longtime collaborator Pierre Franey consumed at a restaurant in France in 1975. Claiborne had bid $300 at a TV auction for a dinner for two anywhere in the world. After he published an article celebrating the sumptuous repast on the front page of the *New York Times* ("Just"),

many incensed readers wrote to condemn what they considered unethical and immoral extravagance in the face of world hunger. Claiborne relates his version of the events in *Feast* 219–29. For other versions of the incident, see John Hess and Karen Hess 157–59 and Chris Chase 68–72.

11. See Claiborne's articles "Cooking with Soul" and "They Want $100 a Plate for Soul Food—and an All-Star Show."

12. See Florence Fabricant for an overview of the exclusionary practices of haute cuisine.

13. The "daughters" of Virginia, she claims, were "not to be outdone either in services or patriotism" and so "set about at once the inauguration of a plan of rigid retrenchment and reform in the domestic economy, while at the same time exhibiting to their sisters a noble example of devotion and self-sacrifice" (vii). Other postbellum cookbook writers refer euphemistically to the same problem: e.g., Mary Stuart Smith (v).

14. Tyree's allusion to a theory/practice binary is surely also evocative of what Valerie Smith and Deborah McDowell ("*Changing*" 156–75), among others, have critiqued as a tendency among contemporary white feminist academics to view women of color as the experiential grounds for proving (or disproving) their theoretical claims. In this academic scenario, black practice is said to give rise to white theory.

The following authors exemplify the historical evolution of white usage of the theory/practice cooking distinction during the first half of this century: Antoinette B. Hervey 368; Harriet Ross Colquitt xv–xvi; Eleanore Ott 88; and Duncan Hines 105. Grubb offers a more extended discussion of nineteenth-century southern cookbooks as a source of "a wealth of information concerning the society they were designed to serve" (155).

15. See Glenn 5 and 11; Dupree xiv.

16. Katzman cites several sources to bolster his claim that "[i]n the former slave states, black servants were equally common in households headed by wage earners as in those headed by white-collar workers" (185).

17. Žižek develops his theory of the "symptom" in *The Sublime Object of Ideology* 11–84. Though I am drawing on this aspect of his work here, Judith Butler's critique of his fixation on "The Rock of the Real" strikes me as compelling (*Bodies* 198 and 202–3).

18. Grubb also quotes from and discusses this passage, without mentioning the implicit racial issues at stake (174).

19. By 1900, according to Egerton, several types of biscuit-making machines were available: "One especially popular model, called a beaten biscuit break, was manufactured by J. A. DeMuth of St. Joseph, Missouri. It consisted of two nickel-plated rollers mounted one above the other on a marble slab, which in turn was attached to a cast-iron base similar to that of a sewing machine" (219).

20. I take the phrase "happy eaters" from the subtitle of Calvin Trillin's *American Fried: Adventures of a Happy Eater*. Popular women's magazines of the turn of the century both mourned the loss of "mammy" and celebrated the emergence of factory-made bread. See, for example, H. R. Clissold's 1911 *Good Housekeeping* article "A Revolution in Bread-Making."

21. In other words, whereas in *Capital*, Marx had condemned commodity fetishism as a process of mystification whereby "the definite social relation between men" takes on "the fantastic form of a relation between things" (165), these southerners clearly invoked and wanted to maintain the "definite social relation" between mistress or master and slave.

22. Or, at least, representations of the white southern male psyche in literature tend to reinforce such stereotypes. Here I am thinking particularly of a tradition epitomized, in this century, by William Faulkner's Quentin Compson in *The Sound and the Fury* and *Absalom, Absalom!*

23. Jeffrey Masson has most famously contested what he calls Freud's "suppression of the

seduction theory." By reading Claiborne's recollection as truthful, however, I do not intend my work as a contribution to this ongoing debate.

24. Steven Marcus pioneered the use of Freud's work to open up space for exploring fla-gellatory literature—in his case, that of Victorian England—as "a kind of last-ditch com-promise with and defense against homosexuality" (260). See his essay "A Child Is Being Beaten" from *The Other Victorians* 252–65. Since then, many scholars have appropriated Freud's essay for cultural criticism. See, for example, my citation of Tania Modleski in the next paragraph, as well as David Leverenz's work on Melville (279–306).

25. The double entendre with "shadow" is intended. According to Clarence Major, the term was deployed from the 1880s through the 1930s to refer to African Americans. It had been "picked up from derogatory white use" and rescripted (407).

26. Claiborne's passive phrasing in the opening sentence hearkens to his syntactically slippery description of the process by which beaten biscuits were made. The expectation that boys be athletic does not, in his perception, stem from a specified source: he is the ob-ject of agentless authority.

27. Here I am extrapolating from one of Claiborne's passing remarks. Shortly before re-counting the beginnings of his physical relationship with his father, Claiborne writes: "Until I was thirteen years old, my father . . . did not make a great mark on my life" (*Feast* 18).

28. In this reading, I am implicitly working from Sedgwick's theorization of male ho-mosocial desire as part of a continuum stretching from homophobia to male bonding to male homosexuality (*Between* 1–2).

29. See Foucault's *The Order of Things*.

30. It is perhaps relevant in this context that Claiborne's private encounter with Hugh in the early 1930s would have been roughly contemporaneous with widely publicized white demands for vigilant "justice" in the trial of the Scottsboro boys in Alabama.

31. One should also be aware of Janet Halley's argument that, at least in legal discourse, the "difference *between* the categories homosexual and heterosexual is systematically related to differences *within* the category heterosexual" (83). In other words, heterosexuality is "a highly unstable, default characterization for people who have not marked themselves or been marked by others as homosexual" (83). Halley's work is useful in challenging reductive representations of heterosexuality as a monolithic phenomenon.

32. Robyn Wiegman reads Baraka's claim as an example of Black Power's reversal of the lynching paradigm (85).

Chapter Three

1. To the extent that I have been able to draw on the work of Hall, Mercer, and British cultural studies in general, I am indebted to the example of Eric Lott. In his own study of early blackface minstrelsy, Lott uses Hall's model to argue that "audiences involved in early minstrelsy were not universally derisive of African-Americans or their culture" ("Seeming" 224), and it is Lott, not Hall, who refers to this interracial dynamic as "a complex play of re-pulsion and attraction" ("Seeming" 227).

2. See, for example, William Van Deburg's impressively researched and, for my work, immensely helpful history of Black Power, *New Day in Babylon*. Van Deburg subdivides his lengthy chapter on "Black Power in Afro-American Culture: Folk Expressions" (192–247) into "Soul Style," "Soul Music," "Soulful Talk," "Soulful Tales," and "Soul Theology." Not even granted its own section, soul food is subsumed under "Soul Style" and given a cursory treatment in less than three pages. Gender is a fundamental category of neither soul food nor of Van Deburg's Black Power analysis. My interest in this issue was stimulated in part by

Andrew Ross's incisive chapter on white patronage of black culture in *No Respect* (65–101).

3. My use of the term "practices" stems from Michel de Certeau's *The Practice of Everyday Life*. See xi.

4. Some of the more obvious examples of the groups I have in mind here would include the Urban League (UL), Southern Christian Leadership Conference (SCLC), Student Nonviolent Coordinating Committee (SNCC), Congress of Racial Equality (CORE), National Council of Negro Women (NCNW), National Welfare Rights Organization (NWRO), Republic of New Afrika (RNA), US Organization, Nation of Islam (NOI), Black Panthers, and Black Arts movement. Though divergent in membership, structure, and purpose—some separatist, others assimilationist; some oriented primarily toward conventional political issues, others toward artistic and cultural expression—these organizations shared a fundamental concern with how to be black, with how to counter the continued denial of political rights and cultural recognition to blacks, in white America.

One could cite any number of works to discuss poststructuralist criticism of the Western humanistic subject. But as my reference to the "juridical" subject would suggest, my own thinking has been particularly influenced by feminist legal theory, including work by Catherine MacKinnon, Zillah Eisenstein, Dorothy Roberts, Deborah Rhode, Joan Hoff, Drucilla Cornell, Patricia Williams, Janet Halley, Ruth Colker, and Martha Albertson Fineman. The essays collected by Adrien Katherine Wing in *Critical Race Feminism* offer a particularly helpful introduction to work in critical legal/race theory from perspectives attuned to the intersections of gender, sexuality, race, and class.

5. Abrahams further observes: "Thinking of someone as a pig-eater is hardly to banish him [or her] from your table . . .; but thinking of someone as being a pig *does* affect whether or not we want to sit down with him [or her] at a table. Thus does eating enter the system by which we 'type' people" (21).

6. Throughout 1969 and the early part of 1970, articles on soul food appeared in organs of the white press such as *Good Housekeeping* ("Soul Food!"); *McCalls* (Grosvenor, "Soul"); *Time* ("Eating"); the *New York Times* (Claiborne, "They"; Cook); and the *New York Times Magazine* (Claiborne, "Cooking"). Though many African Americans were publishing soul food cookbooks during this era (see the appendix), *Ebony* magazine seemed somewhat reluctant to embrace the fad (*Essence* was not founded until May 1970), perhaps because of the magazine's historical role as a vehicle for representing black bourgeois lifestyles in U.S. popular culture. Thus, for example, in February and August 1971 *Ebony*'s long-standing "A Date with a Dish" column offered up titles such as "Classic Meals of the South" and "Historic Recipes from Mammy Pleasant." But it took until 1975 before *Ebony* really began to jump on board with "200 Years of 'Makin' Do,'" and even then the rubric of "soul" was noticeably absent.

7. John Egerton offers a terrific introduction to these issues, while Tony Larry Whitehead provides a more scholarly, but still accessible, ethnographic approach.

8. I conflate gay male sexuality with anal sexuality advisedly. As D. A. Miller has pointed out, in the Western social order, the anus is "the popularly privileged site of gay male sex, the orifice whose sexual use general opinion considers (whatever happens to be the state of sexual practices among gay men and however it may vary according to time and place) the least dispensable element in defining the true homosexual" (127).

9. Signorile was a founding editor of *OutWeek*, a short-lived gay and lesbian weekly in New York City. The contemporary practice of "outing" is intricately associated not with anti-Communism but with HIV and AIDS. For useful discussions of Signorile and/or outing, see Douglas Crimp 6–7 and Larry Gross. In addition, Cindy Patton's "Tremble, Hetero

Swine!" offers a terrific and metaphorically memorable (for me, at least) analysis of "New Right" discourses about queerness and the pitfalls of "identity politics."

10. In this context, it is also perhaps worth noting that Baraka's former wife Hettie Cohen Jones has written that at some point during their relationship, which spanned the period when Baraka wrote his "Soul Food" essay, he had "confessed to me some homosexual feelings, though never any specific experiences" (86). And lest my meaning be misconstrued, I should also note that though I intend "fetish" to be understood here primarily in its Freudian sense, my inclination is toward Linda Williams's comment that "a Marxian, political analysis of the prior *social* fact of the devaluation of women must always be factored into a discussion of the Freudian fetish" (106).

11. If anything, I think Ellison is drawing on the charged metaphor of the "closet" to articulate the damage inflicted on the psyches of those targeted by racism. By contrast, in a discussion of Nella Larsen's *Passing*, Deborah McDowell argues convincingly that the reader is encouraged "to place race at the center of any critical interpretation" of *Passing* when, in fact, a more subversive reading might focus on sexual passing, on the closeting of lesbian desire (Introduction xxiii).

12. Stanley Edgar Hyman also refers to the yam scene near the end of his essay "The Folk Tradition," which gave rise to Ellison's famous rejoinder "Change the Joke and Slip the Yoke." (They were published together as "The Negro Writer: An Exchange" in *Partisan Review* in 1958.)

13. On this topic, see also John D'Emilio's "Capitalism and Gay Identity," which argues that lesbian and gay identity was made possible by capitalism's development of a wage economy.

14. Oliver's "Nourishing the Speaking Subject" provided me with an immensely helpful introduction to Kristeva's theorization of abjection. I have also benefited from her *Reading Kristeva*, which offers a sympathetic but still critical explication of the Kristevan oeuvre.

15. See, for example, Jack Kerouac's *On the Road* (1956) and Norman Mailer's "The White Negro" (1957). As Barbara Ehrenreich has argued (52–67), the Beat ideal was indeed a "world of men" (Kerouac 202) of the sort that Kerouac celebrates in his book. It was a world structured by homoeroticism and sexism, as well as by class and racial disavowal.

16. Here I should point out that in the course of critiquing Kristeva's theory of the Semiotic in *Gender Trouble*, Judith Butler has also argued that Kristeva fails to interrogate the social construction of the inside/outside binary.

17. In her work on pornography, Laura Kipnis has argued—following Bakhtin, Stallybrass, and White—that working-class (white) male fascination with the grotesque (i.e., bodily protuberances, orifices, and excretions, etc.) should be interpreted, at least in part, as an expression of resistance to ideologies of bourgeois propriety. Although Kipnis sometimes seems to imply that the working class actually is a site of the grotesque, her argument has complicated my own thinking about the uses of scatological humor in African American culture, such as this scene from *Invisible Man*.

18. Similarly, Norma Jean Darden and Carole Darden point out in *Spoonbread and Strawberry Wine* (1978) that "it is the onion that reduces the odor" of chitterlings as they cook (265).

19. These tendencies are discussed by Paula Giddings 325–35, Madhu Dubey 14–32, and Phillip Brian Harper 39–53.

20. Nor was such language restricted to black men. Nikki Giovanni famously inquired "Can you stab-a-jew" in "The True Import of the Present Dialogue" (318), and in "Poem for Black Boys," she referred to "the big bad sheriff on his faggoty white horse" (325). Harper

discusses briefly the ramifications of the use of such rhetoric by black women participants in the Black Arts movement (51–52).

21. The phrase "structure of feeling" stems from Raymond Williams. In *Marxism and Literature*, he explains it as "a structured formation which, because it is at the very edge of semantic availability, has many of the characteristics of a pre-formation, until specific articulations—new semantic figures—are discovered in material practice" (134).

22. For examples of the general thematization of excrement, see Malcolm X 152 and George Jackson 168. Though H. Rap Brown was not in prison at the time he wrote *Die Nigger Die!*, he uses "shit" in mounting his frequent attacks on the black bourgeoisie (see 7 and 62).

23. Similarly, George Jackson alludes several times to unease with homosexual practices in Soledad prison and conveys to his family particular concern over the emergent sexuality of his younger brother, Jon (94 and 108–9).

24. See Michele Wallace's *Black Macho and the Myth of the Superwoman* 67–68 and Shelton Waldrep's "Being Bridges" 168–75 for related discussions of Cleaver's attack on Baldwin. In an essay dating from 1974 and reprinted in *The Isis (Yssis) Papers*, Frances Cress Welsing offers one of the more notoriously homophobic interpretations of black male homosexuality as an aberrational response to white dominance.

25. Neal makes this argument in his famous 1972 chart "Some Reflections on the Black Aesthetic." See 13.

26. "I pushed out of the womb against my mother's strength," Jackson had actually continued (10).

27. Emily Martin offers a wonderful discussion of the medicalization of female reproductive practices in *The Woman in the Body* 54–67. I discuss other feminist work on pregnancy, abortion, and childbirth in chapter 7.

28. See, for example, the essays collected in Toni Cade Bambara's anthology *The Black Woman*, as well as Joyce Ladner's study *Tomorrow's Tomorrow*.

29. Gaskins's comment is also quite revelatory of the extent to which the obligation to cook has functioned as a tactic of maintaining gender role conformity and, consequently, of male dominance. Her insistence that "[n]o woman ever enters the church empty-handed" is no less prescriptive than descriptive in import.

30. In "Mass Culture as Woman," Andreas Huyssen famously argued that modernism equated mass culture with femininity. The same dynamic was, I think, operative in the Black Aesthetic.

31. African American women whose cookbooks incorporate some discussion of grandmother-mother-daughter and/or other female-bonding relationships include (and here I mention just a scattering published since the late 1960s): Princess Pamela, Pearl Bowser and Joan Eckstein, Vertamae Grosvenor, Mary Keyes Burgess, Edna Lewis, Ruth Jackson, Bessie Munson, Norma Jean Darden and Carole Darden, Marva Joy Curry, Ethel Dixon, Sheila Ferguson, Kathy Starr, and Queen Ida Guíllory.

32. As explained by Freud, the "cloacal" theory is the common childhood belief that "babies are born through the bowel like a discharge of faeces" (*Three* 62).

Chapter Four

1. Mattias Gardell's *In the Name of Elijah Muhammad* offers a detailed exploration of Farrakhan's tenure at the helm of the NOI, including a brief discussion of the possible implications of the Million Man March. I cite other essays on the march in note 27 of this chapter.

2. Lee had claimed that only a black film director could adequately adapt *The Autobiography of Malcolm X* to the screen; other African Americans had intimated that Lee's take on the story would be too bourgeois. For discussions of this debate, see the articles and review essays by Hilton Als, Rita Kempley, and Greg Tate, as well as an uncredited *New York Times* reproduction of a conversation between Lee and Henry Louis Gates Jr. titled "Just Whose 'Malcolm' Is It, Anyway?"

3. In this second example, I am working from the actual filmed version. The screenplay dialogue differs slightly. See Lee and Wiley 230-31.

4. In the *Autobiography*, the character Bembry is named Bimbi. It is, moreover, Malcolm X's brother Reginald who (in a letter) instructs Malcolm X as follows: "Malcolm, don't eat any more pork, and don't smoke any more cigarettes. I'll show you how to get out of prison" (155). The references to white women are not in Malcolm X's version of the exchange.

5. My discussion of the NOI has drawn mainly on works by Claude Clegg III, Sonsyrea Tate, Mattias Gardell, Cynthia S'thembile West, Martha Lee, E. U. Essien-Udom, C. Eric Lincoln, Louis Lomax, and Malcolm X. These works supplemented primary sources that included Elijah Muhammad's *Message to the Blackman in America, How to Eat to Live,* and *How to Eat to Live, Book No. 2.* I also read extensively in the Nation's early newspaper, *Muhammad Speaks,* from its inception in 1961 until the early 1970s. Studies of women in the Nation have, until recently, been less readily available. One can only hope that West's Ph.D. dissertation and Tate's personal memoir presage the emergence into public discourse of the viewpoints of Muslim women. Though I am less willing than is West to downplay the ramifications of the Nation's patriarchal teachings, including its pronatalist mandate, her careful attention to the manifold ways in which Muhammad's women followers created their own spaces for activism within a restrictive structure offers a tremendous contribution to the scholarly literature on the NOI.

6. Gardell offers a useful overview of the various theories about Farad Muhammad's identity (50-54).

7. Essien-Udom points out that, in addition to the actual members of the Nation, by 1960 Elijah Muhammad could claim fifty thousand supporters and untold sympathizers (84).

8. Some of this money was also used to underwrite Muhammad's palatial living quarters, expensive automobiles, and overseas travel (Clegg 113-14); he was also long rumored to have had financial support from other sources as well, such as white-supremacist groups who were likewise promoting, albeit for diametrically opposed reasons, racial segregation (Clegg 152-56).

9. Writing in 1962, Essien-Udom argued that "the movement has an attraction for Negro men, because their male ego has been subordinated to the female's in Negro society. Muslim women appear to accept their men as 'first among equals,' and in theory, at least, regard the man as the breadwinner and the head of the family. . . . The reversal of customary roles between husband and wife has compensations for both parties" (102). Numerous scholars who have studied the Nation, such as C. Eric Lincoln, have also perpetuated this fiction, counting male dominance as among the most significant accomplishments of Elijah Muhammad (Lincoln 23 and 30-31). Paula Giddings (among others) critiques the patriarchal ideology of the Nation (317-18).

10. Again, middle- and upper-class black women have, by and large, been better situated to emulate this restrictive role than were the predominantly lower-class black women who constituted the majority of Muhammad's female followers.

11. In addition to proselytizing in person about the necessity to avoid foods such as pork, cornbread, and collard greens, by at least the early 1960s members of the Nation had

been distributing to each convert an eighteen-page mimeographed pamphlet containing dietary advice called "Some of the Foods We Eat and Do Not Eat" (Essien-Udom 226–27). And when Malcolm X began publishing the Nation's newspaper, *Muhammad Speaks*, in 1961, Muhammad used it as yet another vehicle for spreading his dietary gospel. He usually called the articles and columns on food he published therein "How to Eat to Live," and his main target was pork. In addition, the newspaper's advertisers also criticized pork, often in a quite graphic fashion (see, e.g., Your).

12. The audience for Muhammad's books and columns would have been relatively small, but by the late 1960s his dietary strictures also filtered out in other ways, for example via the widely read writings of Cleaver, Malcolm X, George Jackson, and many others who had been exposed to his teachings, including scholars and reporters.

13. See chapter 3.

14. But whereas Kristeva often seems to be arguing that abjection of the maternal body precedes and enables the establishment of the Symbolic order, Judith Butler would surely insist that patriarchy deploys discourses of maternal abjection in order to legitimate, and perpetuate, its existence (*Gender* 79–83).

15. The following discussion draws on both volumes of *How to Eat to Live* and on articles published in *Muhammad Speaks*. Except in instances where I am quoting directly at some length, I will not attempt to specify a page reference since these volumes are exceedingly repetitive.

16. Douglas's predecessors had tended to view the biblical rules as an illogical assortment of prohibitions unrelated to the larger social order, prohibitions with little discernable internal coherence. Her highly influential move was to argue instead that "the only way in which pollution ideas make sense is in reference to a total structure of thought whose keystone, boundaries, margins and internal lines are held in relation by rituals of separation" (*Purity* 41).

17. On an organizational level, Muhammad is known to have met with Ku Klux Klan and American Nazi Party leaders to negotiate agreements for peaceful coexistence since their otherwise opposing movements were united by ideological hostility toward integration. In addition to being perceived as an economic threat, Jews—especially "liberal" Jews—were therefore also stigmatized because of their support for the integrationist agenda of the Civil Rights movement (Clegg 149–89). Mattias Gardell offers an informative assessment of the history of black/Jewish interaction in his book on Farrakhan (245–54).

18. On this issue, I would privilege an analysis that insists on fighting anti-Jewish ideologies such as those spread by the NOI while also understanding the creation of Israel from the perspective provided by postcolonial theory. See, for example, Edward Said's essay "An Ideology of Difference."

19. While pointing out in passing that Muhammad's dietary strictures were linked to his sociopolitical vision, Lee uses the passage to intimate that Muhammad's "venomous warnings" against pork functioned primarily to link hogs to white people (30). She lists as her source for the quotation an 18 February 1966 issue of *Muhammad Speaks*, p. 11. A "How to Eat to Live Column" by Muhammad does appear on this page of this issue, but the specific quotation that Lee cites does not appear. Unfortunately, I have been unable to locate her original source to confirm Muhammad's locution.

20. Of course, the chapter-opening epigraph from New York–based soul food restaurant owner Princess Pamela (a small-scale capitalist entrepreneur) should serve as a reminder that this conflation of women and pork was by no means allowed to pass unresisted by African American women. Albeit engaging in what Adrienne Rich might term "compulsory culinary heterosexuality," Princess Pamela was at least formulating a model of selfhood in which black women were the desiring subjects instead of solely the desired objects. Lisa

Jones, daughter of Amiri Baraka and Hettie Jones, has created a performance piece called *Combination Skin* that bases one of its characters on Princess Pamela (see Raven 23 and 36–41).

21. In an earlier, unpublished version of this chapter, I discussed how women within the Nation of Islam had reconfigured Muhammad's teachings in newspaper columns published in *Muhammad Speaks*, as well as in cookbooks. In her *Cooking for the Champ* (1979), for example, boxer Muhammad Ali's personal cook Lana Shabazz offers a recipe for "Miss Becky's Pickled Calf's Feet" (22) that might easily have found a home in a soul food cookbook.

22. Moynihan himself drew for support on Frazier's *The Negro Family in the United States*, which was first published in 1939 and subsequently abridged and reprinted in 1948 and (not coincidentally) 1966. Daryl Scott has argued that the tendency of scholars to link Moynihan with Frazier obscures important historical, methodological, and political differences in their works. Unlike Moynihan, Scott insists, Frazier construed black "matriarchal" families as adaptive and did not consider them to result in "pathological" personality structures (41–55 and 150–56). Though I am persuaded by Scott's analysis of why Frazier did not participate in the "tangle of pathology" representation of black culture, it is clear that Frazier was still an important precursor for Moynihan's advocacy of patriarchal family structures since, as Scott himself admits, Frazier believed that urbanization would allow the black man to take up "his rightful and desirable place as head of the household" (Scott 50).

23. Angela Davis's "Racism, Birth Control and Reproductive Rights" offers an excellent socialist-feminist take on the sometimes "blatantly racist premises" of the campaign for "voluntary motherhood" as epitomized by many middle-class white activists for birth control (202). For more on this topic, see Linda Gordon and Robert Weisbord.

24. However, he would actually permit it under the narrowly circumscribed conditions of rape, incest, and risk to the pregnant woman's health.

25. See Said's *Orientalism* 201–25 and 285–328. Also relevant to my reading of Elijah Muhammad would be Phillip Brian Harper's argument that the biracial male exposes contradictions in the social construction of black masculinity (103–8).

26. Michael Eric Dyson refers to Perry's "plausible" but, in his opinion, uninformative claim in a 1992 *New York Times Book Review* essay covering numerous works on Malcolm X (33).

27. Herb Boyd offers an overview, as a sympathetic journalist/participant, of the controversy surrounding the march in "The Million Man March." More detailed (albeit one-sidedly positive) assessments are provided by David Dent, Houston Baker Jr. ("America's"), and Clyde Taylor in a special "March" section of the inaugural issue of *Black Renaissance/Renaissance Noire*. Robert Reid-Pharr offers a much more compelling critique of the march in "It's Raining Men."

28. Lee has Evan Sr. tell his son Evan Jr. that Angelou is a "great woman." Despite labeling herself a "womanist" in a 1987 interview (Elliot 184), Angelou has been known to maintain a distance from feminist politics. Presumably she warranted Lee's approval, therefore, because she, unlike Angela Davis, was willing to subordinate any latent womanist impulses for the greater good of affirming black male leadership. Davis, after all, had critiqued the masculinist underpinnings of the march at a widely discussed news conference (see Marriott).

29. Wahneema Lubiano offers an incisive discussion of the problematic implications of Lee's patriarchal pro-work ideology as it plays out in some of his pre-*Bus* films in her essay "But Compared to What?"

30. See West's *New York Times* editorial.

31. None of the film reviews I have located even includes this character in the cast

index. Jamal is also a Muslim, but because his institutional affiliation is left unspecified, he is not clearly coded as a member of the NOI.

32. Kobena Mercer's insightful and challenging essays on Mapplethorpe's photography—an initial indictment followed by a rethinking of Mercer's own erotic investments in representations of nude black male bodies—are printed together as "Reading Racial Fetishism" in *Welcome to the Jungle*.

33. Discussions of the crisis of fatherhood emerged in Frazier's work, were picked up by Moynihan, and have been perpetuated in recent years by William Julius Wilson in *The Truly Disadvantaged*.

34. My awareness of the ways in which the film's inclusion of women and its references to wives and girlfriends function to "fix" the sexuality of the men has been heightened by Phillip Brian Harper's discussion of the responses of black male NBA stars and affiliates to 'Magic" Johnson's announcement of his HIV status (22–38).

35. Witness here Louis Farrakhan's much-commented-upon facility with the violin.

Chapter Five

1. See Patricia Turner for a discussion of how racist memorabilia associate African American children with watermelon (15).

2. Dustin Hoffman reenacts this scene as the star of Bob Fosse's film *Lenny* (1974).

3. This is a central claim of Eric Lott's *Love and Theft*.

4. See Hefner 18 on this issue as well.

5. Watkins discusses Gregory at length in *On the Real Side* 495–503.

6. Signed to a three-year contract at the Playboy Club in 1961, Gregory had started at what was for the time a by no means meager $250/week, but his salary rapidly escalated (*Nigger* 145).

7. Not surprisingly, from the very outset his humor anticipated the central role food would come to play in his sociopolitical agenda. One of the jokes he included in *From the Back of the Bus*, for example, used food to satirize Jim Crow: "So much of this segregation bit is in the mind. People aren't just segregating us. They're segregating themselves too. Like, how many of you have ever tasted hominy grits? Black-eyed peas? Chitlins? No law against it. . . . You try it tomorrow, and I guarantee you won't turn one shade darker. . . . It doesn't make sense—prejudice against foods. I mean, I've been eating gefilte fish for years—even before I knew Sammy Davis, Jr. . . ." (Gregory's ellipses; 107).

8. Warren Belasco points out that it was not until after the takeover of People's Park in 1969 that "the trickle of hip visitors to the health food underground swelled into a steady stream" (17).

9. Haki Madhubuti also notes the Muhammad/Fulton/Gregory connection in his chapter "What's Food Got to Do with It?" from *Black Men*. See 199.

10. In keeping with my commentary in the last chapter about the sexuality of both Elijah Muhammad and Malcolm X, it is worth noting that Gregory's remarks could also be interpreted as having called into question the status of Muhammad's sexuality. This speculation is supported by Malcolm X's subsequent observation: "My Muslim instincts said to attack Dick—but, instead, I felt weak and hollow. I think Dick sensed how upset I was and he let me get him off the subject. I knew Dick, a Chicagoan, was wise in the ways of the streets, and blunt-spoken. I wanted to plead with him not to say to anyone else what he had said to me—but I couldn't; it would have been my own admission" (296).

11. There is, though, one brief comparison of Elijah Muhammad to Abraham Lincoln in *No More Lies* 235.

12. See, for example, Fulton's advertisement for her Pioneer Natural Health Restaurant in the December 1961 issue of *Muhammad Speaks* (Pioneer).

13. Colonic irrigations and enemas are, he points out, different procedures, the former being the more thorough and therefore preferable of the two (*Natural* 49–50).

14. The phrase "purifying the system" is from the dedication to *Dick Gregory's Political Primer*: "To Dr. Alvenia Fulton, Dr. Roland Sidney, America's health-food stores, chiropractors, and naturopaths, and all others concerned with purifying the system" (vii).

15. Other primarily black counterculture groups were also valorizing a natural foods diet during this era. Perhaps most notable given subsequent events, Philadelphia's MOVE organization was advocating a raw-fruits-and-vegetables philosophy by the early 1970s. John Anderson and Hilary Hevenor point out that the wife of future MOVE founder Vincent Leaphart (a.k.a. John Africa) had in 1965 "joined the Kingdom of Yahweh, a religious sect whose members were required to maintain a vegetarian diet" (2).

16. See Gregory's *The Shadow That Scares Me* 69 and Adams 45. Readers interested in an astute analysis of the evolution of the cattle industry might also wish to consult Jeremy Rifkin's *Beyond Beef*.

17. Readers familiar with contemporary U.S. popular culture will be aware that similar anxieties structure Ivan Reitman's 1994 film *Junior*, the plot of which enables Arnold Schwarzenegger's character to become both the biological father and the gestational mother of his child.

18. Chisholm was the first African American woman to serve in Congress (from 1969 to 1983) and the first African American woman to mount a campaign for the U.S. presidency (in 1972). Paula Giddings discusses the combination of racism and sexism Chisholm encountered from white feminists and black male activists after she announced her presidential candidacy (337–40).

19. For other contemporaneous black feminist arguments for birth control, see Toni Cade Bambara's "The Pill" and Joanna Clark's "Motherhood." Of course, as Joyce Ladner pointed out in her landmark study *Tomorrow's Tomorrow*, large numbers of African Americans, including women, were opposed to abortion in the early 1970s unless the pregnant woman's health was endangered. But Ladner also explains that the opposition of many was not uninflected by their realistic perception of abortion as a "back-alley" procedure that could endanger the woman's life (262–69).

20. Sara Evans discusses the divisions among women activists of this era in *Born for Liberty* 93–143.

21. Even as he disavowed the conservative focus on changing the values and behaviors of the poor, William Julius Wilson proposed this solution to (black) poverty in *The Truly Disadvantaged*. The entire book is obsessed with the problem of "female-headed households," but see especially 150–51, where Wilson acknowledges that he is more concerned to create jobs for black men than for black women. Wilson's remedy for the black "underclass" is clearly to encourage black women to marry and become financially dependent on a black male provider. For a politically leftist critique of Wilson's position, see Adolph Reed's "The Liberal Technocrat."

22. The essays collected by Robert Staples in *The Black Family*—which has gone through four editions since 1971—offer an excellent introduction to the range of this sociological discourse on black families and to its largely conservative impulses. The 1991 edition does include essays on "alternative" family structures such as lesbians and gays, but as Staples's own essays (e.g., "The Political Economy of Black Family Life") amply demonstrate, much of the volume presumes that the heterosexual, patriarchal family structure should be normative. By contrast, several of the essays in the *Nation's* special issue on "Scapegoating the Black Family" (1989), edited by Jewell Handy Gre-

sham and Margaret Wilkerson, offer politically progressive perspectives on these same topics.

23. Here one need only consider the disapprobation with which a 1986 Domestic Policy Council report on the family referred to a woman who characterized the Aid to Families with Dependent Children (AFDC) program as "the invisible husband [who] gives you food, housing, medical protection, pays your bills and lets you stay home and take care of children" (quoted in Abramovitz 352). One should be aware, though, of Mimi Abramovitz's contention that "AFDC ultimately *challenged* rather than reinforced the family ethic" in that it "increasingly legitimized the female-headed family by providing it with the economic resources to establish independent households" (353).

24. Legal theorist Martha Albertson Fineman has, however, offered an antiheterosexist argument for why the judicial system should consider caregiving rather than sexuality the central purpose of families.

25. Similarly, Carole Horn wrote in a review of *Natural Diet*: "It may not be a permanent solution, but at least it will give you time to ponder the other possibilities" (7).

26. For samples of Murphy's sexism and homophobia, see his live stand-up performance recorded in *Eddie Murphy Raw* (1987).

27. Here one might note, too, that Mama Klump refers to "colon cleansing" in one of the dinner scenes, which explicitly links her to anal-eroticism.

28. Freud posits this connection in his short essay "Character and Anal Eroticism."

29. In *Contested Closets*, Larry Gross argues that the "outing" of entertainment mogul Barry Diller was justified since he had promoted Murphy's career (71, 203, and 247), but he mentions no questioning of Murphy's own professed sexual orientation.

30. Gregory was clearly the best known African American popularizer of either vegetarian or fruitarian fare during an era when the majority of African American cookbooks were devoted to celebrating soul food. Three years after he published his dietary manual, a California woman, Mary Keyes Burgess, attempted to combine the two trends in *Soul to Soul*. By the late 1980s, African American cookbooks devoted to vegetarianism and/or health food were beginning to flourish again, as evidenced by the writings of Nia and Zak Kondo, Keith Wright, and Leah Chase and Johnny Rivers. In addition, two of the restaurants and one of the men profiled in Sugarman's article have published vegetarian cookbooks or pamphlets: the Soul Vegetarian Cafe, Delights of the Garden, and Aris La Tham.

31. Presumably Sugarman and/or the *Washington Post* found it appropriate to subsume the Panamanian immigrant La Tham into a narrative of African American culture to market the article to Washington's substantial black middle class. The next chapter attempts to think further about the relationship of African American dietary practices to the construction of diasporic black identities.

Chapter Six

Unless otherwise specified, all page references to *Vibration Cooking* are to the original 1970 edition.

1. For competing views on the question of whether the film's portrayal of Ibo Landing is nostalgic, see Jacqueline Bobo 179 and Toni Cade Bambara, "Reading" 122. Even though I make this claim about the presentation of food rituals, I concur with Bambara that the film as a whole questions both the viewer's and its own investments in nostalgia.

2. See the appendix for a (doubtless partial) listing of cookbooks published during this era.

3. For wonderful discussions of Grosvenor's manipulation of "masking" as a strategy for

subverting stereotypes about African American women, see Prettyman 131–33 and Zafar, "Cooking" 75–78. I mention other early scholarly work on Grosvenor in note 13 to the prologue of this book.

4. Prior to embarking on the interracial relationship, Robert Grosvenor had moved in privileged social circles. His sister, for example, had been a debutante alongside the future Jacqueline Kennedy Onassis (Garland 88). Grosvenor says that her husband was not only put "out of the social register" after their wedding, but that "he was cut off from about 12 million dollars" (quoted in Garland 88).

5. I have decided to refer to her as "Vertamae Grosvenor" in this chapter because her most recent cookbook, *Vertamae Cooks in the Americas' Family Kitchen* (1996), was published under that name.

6. In a 1970 *New York Times* article that appeared a month after the publication of *Poems by Kali*, Barbara Campbell profiled the child poet. A typical example of Kali's work is "Lady Bird": "Lady Bird / Lady Bird / Fly away. Home / Your house is on fire / And Rap's on the phone" (K. Grosvenor 35).

7. Rafia Zafar offers a persuasive counterexplanation of Grosvenor's motive. She speculates that Grosvenor's "mainstream readers would likely" connect her to "the more 'famous' white authors; she would thus have us know that it is from black women cooks and writers that she draws her courage and inspiration" ("Cooking" 78).

8. Barnard was the white South African surgeon who made "White" men the beneficiaries of the first attempted heart transplants, using "Coloured" donors.

9. See also *Vibration* 14.

10. In 1992 she substituted "universal" for "nonracial" and "African-American" for "Afro-American" in this paragraph (xvi).

11. Though, of course, mass-marketed fruits and vegetables are hardly free of chemical additives and preservatives.

12. Lacking an opportunity to research the claim firsthand in England, I have tried but thus far failed to verify the citation from my position stateside in Iowa. Many thanks to the British Library Newspaper Library for helping me in this undertaking.

13. Zafar points out that Grosvenor's refusal to locate herself in relation to a husband should also be interpreted as a feminist gesture ("Cooking" 78).

14. For another typical manifestation of this concern, see Jessica Harris's ode to "the cleanliness evidenced by cooks in the direst of conditions" in *Iron Pots and Wooden Spoons* (xxii).

15. This is not to say that white women should not be critiqued for their (willing) role in the subordination of black women, but rather that we should not lose sight of the myriad benefits that white men have derived from a system that absolves them of responsibility for, and therefore disassociates them from, domestic labor.

16. Her dietary preferences called into question, Renay allows: "Some of *us* don't like them either!" (87).

17. In the chapter called "The Jet Set and Beautiful People" from the original edition, Grosvenor observed of the costume parties of the rich and famous that she "wouldn't pay no faggot six hundred dollars to dress me up like a fool" (150). The 1986 edition deleted the homophobic language, and Grosvenor offered a grudging apology in the introduction to the effect that she "should have said 'homosexual.' I apologize for that and for 'Roy Wilkins Sauce' on page 100, but the rest stands. The book is honest. It's what it is, what it was, and I live with it" (xix). By 1992, though, when Ballantine evidently wanted to market the book to a socially progressive audience, the original slur and the only marginally less offensive apology were both gone.

18. Dubey further claims, however: "The extremely stylized narrative voice of *The Fla-*

gellants prohibits a smooth reading and, compulsively drawing attention to the construct-edness of its fictional language, succeeds in derealizing the seeming transparency of ideo-logical discourse" (152).

19. As evidence for her interpretation, McDowell cites passages such as the well-known description of Sula as lacking an "ego" and therefore under "no compulsion to verify her-self—be consistent with herself" (Morrison, *Sula* 119). While paying more attention than McDowell to Morrison's failure to follow through on *Sula's* feminist gestures, Dubey also in-sists that the book challenges what she has identified as the central principles of Black Aes-thetic ideology.

20. Grosvenor describes her as a "beautiful" woman with "Indian blood" who "had high cheekbones and long black hair," as well as "a wonderful house" (15).

21. I sent a letter to Morrison in 1997 inquiring whether she had been familiar with *Vi-bration Cooking* at the time she wrote *Sula*, my assumption being that her work as an editor would have made it difficult for her not to know about Grosvenor's widely publicized cook-book. Morrison's assistant René Shepperd sent a fax informing me that Morrison was not aware of Grosvenor's cookbook at the time she wrote *Song of Solomon* [sic].

22. Deborah McDowell has discussed some of the implications of the construction of audience by black women novelists in her essay "The Changing Same."

23. In their preface, Twining and Baird also offer a brief overview of the debate over the retention of Africanisms as it played out between two "main antagonists," Herskovits and E. Franklin Frazier (383). Readers wishing to learn more about the Sea Islands might do well to begin with Charles Joyner's *Down by the Riverside* and Patricia Jones-Jackson's *When Roots Die*.

24. Here let me say that I, too, consider the exploitation of both Gullah peoples and the coastal environs by wealthy developers as a cause for concern. But a good many Sea Is-land dwellers have willingly sold their land rights for a substantial amount of money, which they have used to pursue a variety of personal goals, and any narrative formulated to discuss Sea Island development needs to take these complexities of agency and individual desire into account.

25. Jessica Harris also discusses this "reciprocal flow of foodstuffs from the New World to Africa and back" in *Iron Pots and Wooden Spoons* (xii).

26. By 1986, when her daughters were adults, Grosvenor had been back on the road and was able to add new vignettes to *Vibration Cooking* describing her visits to New Mexico, the White House, Cuba, Mississippi, and Brazil. Each of these visits is memorialized by a recipe, including an uncharacteristically fawning portrayal of Jimmy and Rosalind Carter.

27. One should note, in addition, that Schomburg's lyrical celebration of "the tradi-tional mammy cooks of the South" obviously tends, in its evocation of contemporaneous Aunt Jemima advertisements, to undermine any simplistic understandings of ethnographic authenticity. In this way, the boundaries between progressive and reactionary culinary ide-ologies become hopelessly confused.

28. Whereas Grosvenor's introduction to the 1992 edition of *Vibration Cooking* seems to pay homage to the woman-centered "Geechee" birthing scene that concludes Ntozake Shange's *Sassafrass, Cypress & Indigo*, *Vertamae Cooks in the Americas' Family Kitchen* might be more accurately placed in the lineage of Gloria Naylor's novel *Linden Hills*, in which the succession of Luther Nedeeds is maintained through the denial of black women's roles in human reproduction. Like Luwanna Packerville, Evelyn Creton, Priscilla McGuire, and Willa Prescott—good Nedeed wives one and all—Chandra Grosvenor's identity is erased by the memorial to Oscar Brown III. I discuss the novel at greater length in chapter 7.

29. In an essay on Dash and Tracey Moffatt, Patricia Mellencamp discusses several is-sues related to the ones Curry raises (149–59).

Chapter Seven

1. Similarly, in *Spoonbread and Strawberry Wine* (1978), Norma Jean and Carole Darden were willing to deploy some of soul's ideological underpinnings (e.g., the emphasis on improvisation). But they, too, refrain from using the rubric of soul food, and they experiment with the genre of the cookbook so as to contest the Moynihanian representation of black family life as a "tangle of pathology." Whether the Dardens succeeded in contesting it is open to question, however: *New York Times* food writer Mimi Sheraton still described *Spoonbread and Strawberry Wine* as "a warm and loving memoir of life in an exceptional black family" (98). See Rafia Zafar ("Cooking") for an illuminating comparison of Grosvenor and the Dardens.

2. One important exception is Susan Bordo. Her brilliant and innovative book *Unbearable Weight* includes essays that attend to both body size/weight and maternity.

3. Two fairly early exceptions include James Gray, Kathryn Ford, and Lily Kelly's "The Prevalence of Bulimia in a Black College Population" (1987); and L. K. George Hsu's "Are the Eating Disorders Becoming More Common in Blacks" (1987).

4. A 1990 *Essence* story by Bebe Moore Campbell titled "Body Love" categorizes the "hated" body parts of black women as hair, nose, teeth, butt, skin color, lips, breasts, and legs.

5. Thompson points out that the phrase "eating disorders" implies "that some psychological frailty or inadequacy is the agent of the illness. In short, those suffering from eating problems are thought to be decadent, self-absorbed, and heavily implicated in their own troubles" (1). Hence her own preference for the designation "eating problems." Since my aim here is primarily one of historicization, I am continuing to use the standard medical rubric even though I find Thompson's argument for a shift in terminology convincing.

6. Brumberg points out that she is neither "a recovered anorectic nor . . . the mother of an anorexic daughter" (1), and she describes the evolution of her scholarly interest in the subject, but otherwise she does not dwell on possible personal investments she might have in her subject matter.

7. Roxanne Brown's 1990 *Ebony* article "Full-Figured Women Fight Back" offers a less explicitly politicized example of how other African American women have appropriated the large female body as a mode of cultural affirmation.

8. To cite two more examples, several contributors to *The Black Women's Health Book* (1990), edited by Evelyn White, incorporate discussion of dietary practices into a comprehensive agenda to improve the mental and physical health of black women, as does bell hooks in *Sisters of the Yam* (1993). In these works, food is treated in conjunction with drugs and alcohol as a "substance" which African American women can and do abuse. See especially 67–77 of hooks, as well as Georgiana Arnold's "Coming Home" in White.

9. Discourses about Fetal Alcohol Syndrome began to revolve around Native American women primarily because of the publication of *The Broken Chord* in 1989, in which Michael Dorris describes his experiences raising an adopted Native American child said to be suffering from the syndrome. Margit Stange has offered an incisive analysis of the ramifications of this development for Native American women accused of drinking while pregnant.

10. Valerie Hartouni has looked briefly at efforts to bring to term the pregnancies of dead women in *Cultural Conceptions* 26–32.

11. Rosalind Petchesky discusses the significance of technologies enabling fetal visualization in *Abortion and Woman's Choice* (335–45). See also Robyn Rowland's discussion of fetal personhood (118–55) and Hartouni's work on the social construction of vision in relation to fetal politics (51–67). In addition, Emily Martin and Ruth Hubbard have been important influences on my thinking about how scientific discourse legitimates the use of often unnecessary medical technologies.

12. For feminist legal approaches to this topic, see Zillah Eisenstein's *The Female Body and the Law* and Ruth Colker's *Pregnant Men*.

13. In the context of her work on fetal identification, Berlant has also drawn on the precedent of slavery ("America" 147).

14. Roberts has more recently developed her arguments in the realm of bioethics in "Reconstructing the Patient." Other excellent work in feminist bioethics is collected, along with Roberts's essay, by Susan Wolf in *Feminism and Bioethics*.

15. For an excellent discussion of how discourses of white and black maternity were interarticulated during the 1950s and 1960s, see Rickie Solinger's *Wake Up Little Susie*. Her chapter on "The Making of the 'Matriarchy'" is particularly compelling in its discussion of "how black illegitimacy was used to support both arguments about the biological bases of black inferiority and antiblack public policies" (41). By contrast, in her chapter on "White Men and Pregnancy" from *Unmarked*, Peggy Phelan has interpreted New Right antiabortion politics in terms of white male "psychic fear about *paternity*" (132), namely its changing relationship to the visibility/invisibility binary.

16. See Janet Raloff's 1990 article "Mom's Fatty Diet May Induce Child's Cancer." More recently, scientists have suggested that the diets of pregnant women may be to blame for heart disease in their adult children. See Jane Brody's 1996 article "Life in the Womb May Affect Adult Heart Disease Risk."

17. My discussion has already suggested that African American women have never been "trusted not to" harm or kill their fetuses. Most obviously, as Eugene Genovese acknowledges in *Roll, Jordan, Roll*, slaveholders feared that slave women used abortifacients or engaged in infanticide (496–97).

18. In a widely read *New York Times* editorial on the prolife movement, Harold Bloom famously labeled as "post-Christian" gnosticism the contempt for the body evinced among diverse U.S. religious fundamentalists. In the process, however, he elided the sexual, gender, race, and class inscriptions of both the fetuses being sacralized and the abjected maternal bodies. For a fuller elaboration of his views, see Bloom's book *The American Religion*.

19. For useful studies of women and/or issues of gender in *Beale Street*, see Hortense Spillers's "The Politics of Intimacy" and Trudier Harris's chapter on the novel in *Black Women in the Fiction of James Baldwin* (128–63). Spillers's essay, in particular, anticipates many of my concerns. In addition, although not about *Beale Street*, Cora Kaplan's "A Cavern Opened in My Mind" has stimulated my thinking about Baldwin, gender, and abjection.

20. See Jerome Miller for an informative analysis of the racist treatment of African American men by the U.S. criminal justice system.

21. Spillers also draws on this passage from *Sula* to conclude her critique of Baldwin's portrayal of Tish and the other women in *Beale Street* ("Politics" 105).

22. The only extended representation of Fonny's family occurs on the evening when Tish informs them of her pregnancy (66–81). Laden with misogynistic dialogue and behavior, the scene eventually devolves into an ugly verbal fight among the women.

23. Naylor authorized the interpretation of *Linden Hills* as a revisioning of Dante in "A Conversation" with Toni Morrison (582). For other readings of *Linden Hills* as a Dantean allegory, see the reviews by Angela Carter, Robert Jones, Michiko Kakutani, Mel Watkins ("Circular"), and Sherley Anne Williams, as well as the article by Catherine Ward. Most of these reviews presume that Naylor's goal is to critique the black middle class.

24. Charles Toombs has also offered a helpful discussion of food and the construction of racial/class identity in *Linden Hills*, though one might wish that he had also interrogated how food inflects, and is inflected by, the novel's gender dynamics.

25. My thinking on these issues has been influenced by Mary Russo's work in *The Fe-*

male Grotesque. She draws an important distinction between the "carnival" grotesque (stemming from Bakhtin) and the "uncanny" grotesque (stemming from Freud and Wolfgang Kayser) which space limitations prevent me from pursuing here (7).

26. I should mention, however, that K. A. Sandiford has used Bakhtin's theories of "dialogism" and "heteroglossia" to develop an excellent study of the novel's representation of, among other things, the Nedeed wives.

27. The section for December 24 begins as follows: "The final credits for *Miracle on 34th Street* rolled onto the screen of Willie's secondhand black-and-white set. He reached for his *TV Guide* and sighed. That was it for the night" (271). One of the frustrations of reading *Linden Hills* is that we never find out what happens to the characters we meet on a given day. I am intrigued, therefore, by the way the reference to *TV Guide* opens up the possibility that our normative, linear practices of novel reading might need to give way to a nonlinear alternative according to which we realize that *Linden Hills* is itself structured by days of the week as a mock *TV Guide*. With its vision of a world turned upside down and inside out, the novel may seem to be intended as a parody of black efforts to imitate white bourgeois life. But what I have concluded is that *Linden Hills* is better understood as a parody of commodified representations of all bourgeois life—a parody of parodies, as it were.

28. Harris is not credited in the available videotapes of the film, and most of the numerous film reviews did not bother to include her name in the cast index. One exception is Bosley Crowther's *New York Times* review.

29. In keeping with my earlier efforts to complicate our understanding of how this process played out in the popularization of soul food, however, I would not wish to be understood as affirming any simplistic indictments of the black bourgeoisie. For discussions of why such indictments can be problematic, see Henry Louis Gates Jr., "Significant" 618, and Deborah McDowell, "*Changing*" xvii.

Epilogue

1. Here I was also informed in my thinking by Eric Garber's important work on lesbian/gay subcultures in the Harlem of the 1920s.

2. Seale had also written an early memoir about his participation in the Black Panther Party, *Seize the Time* (1970), but for alternate perspectives on both him and the Panthers, one might wish to consult Elaine Brown's *A Taste of Power* (1992) and Hugh Pearson's *The Shadow of the Panther* (1994).

Works Cited

Abelove, Henry, Michèle Aina Barale, and David M. Halperin, eds. *The Lesbian and Gay Studies Reader*. New York: Routledge, 1993.

Abrahams, Roger. "Equal Opportunity Eating: A Structural Excursus on Things of the Mouth." *Ethnic and Regional Foodways in the United States: The Performance of Group Identity*. Ed. Linda Keller Brown and Kay Mussell. Knoxville: U of Tennessee P, 1984. 19–36.

Abramovitz, Mimi. *Regulating the Lives of Women: Social Welfare Policy from Colonial Times to the Present*. Boston: South End, 1988.

Adams, Carol J. *The Sexual Politics of Meat: A Feminist-Vegetarian Critical Theory*. New York: Continuum, 1990.

"Aged Woman Killed When Autos Crash." *Chicago Defender* 8 Sept. 1923, natl. ed., sec. 1: 1.

Agnew, Jean-Christophe. "Shop Till You Drop: How the West Was Sold." Rev. of *Satisfaction Guaranteed*, by Susan Strasser. *Village Voice Literary Supplement* Dec. 1989: 29–30.

Alexander, Elizabeth. "'Imitation of Life'? Black Women and Food in Popular Iconography, from Jemima to Oprah." Black Women's Texts and the Culture of Food Panel. MLA Convention. Hilton, San Francisco. 29 Dec. 1991.

———. "Ladders." *The Venus Hottentot*. Charlottesville: UP of Virginia, 1990. 13.

———. "'We're Gonna Deconstruct Your Life': The Making and Un-Making of the Black Bourgeois Patriarch in *Ricochet*." *Representing Black Men*. Ed. Marcellus Blount and George P. Cunningham. New York: Routledge, 1996. 157–71.

Als, Hilton. "Picture This: On the Set, the Street, and at Dinner with X Director Spike Lee." *Village Voice* 10 Nov. 1992: 39–40+.

Althusser, Louis. "Ideology and Ideological State Apparatuses (Notes towards an Investigation)." 1969, 1970. *Lenin and Philosophy and Other Essays*. Trans. Ben Brewster. London: New Left, 1971. 121–73.

Anderson, Dave. "Champ Diet: Sandwiches or Seaweed?" *New York Times* 13 Nov. 1992, final late ed.: B7.

Anderson, James D. "Aunt Jemima in Dialectics: Genovese on Slave Culture." Rev. of *Roll*,

Jordan, Roll, by Eugene D. Genovese. *Journal of Negro History* 61.1 (Jan. 1976): 99–114.

Anderson, John, and Hilary Hevenor. *Burning Down the House: MOVE and the Tragedy of Philadelphia.* New York: Norton, 1987.

Andrews, Benny. "Jemimas, Mysticism, and Mojos: The Art of Betye Saar." *Encore American and Worldwide News* 17 Mar. 1975: 30.

Appadurai, Arjun. "How to Make a National Cuisine: Cookbooks in Contemporary India." *Comparative Studies in Society and History: An International Quarterly* 30.1 (Jan. 1988): 3–24.

Arnold, Georgiana. "Coming Home: One Black Woman's Journey to Health and Fitness." *The Black Women's Health Book: Speaking for Ourselves.* Ed. Evelyn C. White. Seattle: Seal, 1990. 269–79.

"'Aunt Jemima' of Pancake Box Fame, Dies at 76." *Knoxville News-Sentinel* 2 Apr. 1981: 9.

Aunt Jemima products. "At the World's Fair in '93 Aunt Jemima Was a Sensation." Advertisement. *Saturday Evening Post* 12 Feb. 1921: 45.

———. "Aunt Jemima Bids Goodbye to the Old Plantation." Advertisement. *Saturday Evening Post* 15 Jan. 1921: 66.

———. "Buckwheats with the 'Tang' Men Hanker For." Advertisement. *Ladies' Home Journal* Jan. 1927: 91.

———. "The Cook Whose Cabin Became More Famous Than Uncle Tom's." Advertisement. *Saturday Evening Post* 8 May 1920: 125.

———. "How Aunt Jemima Saved the Colonel's Mustache and His Reputation as a Host." Advertisement. *Saturday Evening Post* 25 Sept. 1920: 75.

———. "I'se in Town, Honey." Advertisement. *Ladies' Home Journal* Dec. 1896: 46.

———. "She Mixed Four Different Flours in a Special Way." Advertisement. *Good Housekeeping* Mar. 1928: 142.

———. "A Surprise from the Good Old Days . . . Buckwheats with the Taste Men Hanker For." Advertisement. *Ladies' Home Journal* Jan. 1929: 58.

———. "Your Grocer Has a Fresh Supply." Advertisement. *Ladies' Home Journal* Oct. 1910: 53.

"Aunt Jemima Trademark Design to Be Updated." News Release. Chicago: Quaker Oats, 27 Apr. 1989.

"Awards at the Fair: More Exhibits Catalogued for the Bronze Medals." *Chicago Daily Tribune* 18 Oct. 1893, last ed.: 10.

Awkward, Michael. "A Black Man's Place(s) in Black Feminist Criticism." *Representing Black Men.* Ed. Marcellus Blount and George P. Cunningham. New York: Routledge, 1996. 3–26.

Ayers, Edward L. *The Promise of the New South: Life after Reconstruction.* New York: Oxford UP, 1992.

Bailey, Pearl. *Pearl's Kitchen: An Extraordinary Cookbook.* New York: Harcourt, 1973.

Baker, Houston A., Jr. "America's War on Decency and a Call to the Mall: Black Men, Symbolic Politics, and the Million Man March." *Black Renaissance/Renaissance Noire* 1.1 (Fall 1996): 70–81.

———. *Blues, Ideology, and Afro-American Literature: A Vernacular Theory.* Chicago: U of Chicago P, 1984.

———. *Workings of the Spirit: The Poetics of Afro-American Women's Writing.* Chicago: U of Chicago P, 1991.

Baker, Houston A., Jr., Manthia Diawara, and Ruth H. Lindeborg, eds. *Black British Cultural Studies: A Reader.* Chicago: U of Chicago P, 1996.

Bakhtin, Mikhail. "Discourse in the Novel." 1934–35. *The Dialogic Imagination: Four Essays by* M. M. *Bakhtin*. Ed. Michael Holquist. Trans. Caryl Emerson and Michael Holquist. Austin: U of Texas P, 1981. 259–422.

———. *Rabelais and His World.* Trans. Helene Iswolsky. 1965. Bloomington: Indiana UP, 1984.

Baldwin, Chuck. "What's Wrong with a Joke among Friends?" Editorial. *Iowa City Press-Citizen* 29 Apr. 1997: 11A.

Baldwin, James. *The Fire Next Time.* 1963. New York: Vintage-Random, 1993.

———. *If Beale Street Could Talk.* 1974. New York: Laurel-Dell, 1988.

———. "Many Thousands Gone." 1951. *Notes of a Native Son.* Boston: Beacon, 1955. 24–45.

Bambara, Toni Cade. "The Pill: Genocide or Liberation?" 1969. *The Black Woman: An Anthology.* Ed. Toni Cade Bambara. New York: Mentor-Penguin, 1970. 162–69.

———. "Reading the Signs, Empowering the Eye: *Daughters of the Dust* and the Black Independent Cinema Movement." *Black American Cinema.* Ed. Manthia Diawara. New York: Routledge, 1993. 118–44.

———, ed. *The Black Woman: An Anthology.* New York: Mentor-Penguin, 1970.

Bancroft, Hubert Howe. *The Book of the Fair; an Historical and Descriptive Presentation of the World's Science, Art and Industry, as Viewed through the Columbian Exposition at Chicago in 1893, Designed to Set Forth the Display Made by the Congress of the Nations, of Human Achievements in Material Form, So As the More Effectually to Illustrate the Progress of Mankind in All the Departments of Civilized Life.* Vol. 2. Chicago: Bancroft, 1893.

Baraka, Amiri [LeRoi Jones]. "American Sexual Reference: Black Male." 1965. *Home: Social Essays.* New York: Morrow, 1966. 216–33.

———. "Black Art." 1969. *The Black Poets.* Ed. Dudley Randall. New York: Bantam, 1971. 223–24.

———. *Black Music.* New York: Morrow, 1967.

———. *Blues People: Negro Music in White America.* New York: Morrow, 1963.

———. "Soul Food." 1962. *Home: Social Essays.* New York: Morrow, 1966. 101–4.

Baro, Gene. "Soul Food." *Vogue* Mar. 1970: 80+.

Baruch, Elaine Hoffman, and Lucienne J. Serrano, eds. *Women Analyze Women: In France, England, and the United States.* New York: New York UP, 1988.

Baudrillard, Jean. "Simulacra and Simulations." 1981. Trans. Paul Foss, Paul Patton, and Philip Beitchman. *Jean Baudrillard: Selected Writings.* Ed. Mark Poster. Stanford: Stanford UP, 1988.

Beecher, Catharine E., and Harriet Beecher Stowe. *The American Woman's Home: or, Principles of Domestic Science; Being a Guide to the Formation and Maintenance of Economical, Healthful, Beautiful, and Christian Homes.* New York: Ford, 1869.

Belasco, Warren J. *Appetite for Change: How the Counterculture Took On the Food Industry, 1966–1988.* New York: Pantheon, 1989.

Bell, Katharin. *Mammy's Cook Book.* 1927. New York: Holt, 1928.

Bennett, Lerone, Jr. *The Negro Mood and Other Essays.* 1964. New York: Ballantine, 1965.

Berlant, Lauren. "America, 'Fat,' the Fetus." *Boundary 2: A Journal of Postmodern Literature* 21.3 (Fall 1994): 145–95.

———. "National Brands/National Body: *Imitation of Life.*" *Comparative American Identities: Race, Sex, and Nationality in the Modern Text.* Ed. Hortense J. Spillers. New York: Routledge, 1991. 110–40.

———. "'68, or Something." *Critical Inquiry* 21.1 (Autumn 1994): 124–55.

Berry, Riley M. Fletcher. "The Black Mammy Memorial Institute: How a Southern School Is Training Colored Women in the Household Arts. Here Is Real Progress." *Good Housekeeping* 53 (July–Dec. 1911): 562–63.

Bhabha, Homi K. "The Other Question: Stereotype, Discrimination and the Discourse of Colonialism." 1992. *The Location of Culture*. London: Routledge, 1994. 66–84.

———. "Signs Taken for Wonders: Questions of Ambivalence and Authority under a Tree outside Delhi, May 1817." 1985. *"Race," Writing, and Difference*. Ed. Henry Louis Gates Jr. Chicago: U of Chicago P, 1986. 163–84.

"Black America and Tiger's Dilemma." *Ebony* July 1997: 28–34+.

Black Women's Liberation Group. "Statement on Birth Control." *Sisterhood Is Powerful: An Anthology of Writings from the Women's Liberation Movement*. Ed. Robin Morgan. New York: Vintage-Random, 1970. 404–6.

Bloom, Harold. *The American Religion: The Emergence of the Post-Christian Nation*. New York: Simon, 1992.

———. "New Heyday of Gnostic Heresies: Bush, Abortion and the American Religion." Editorial. *New York Times* 26 Apr. 1992, late ed., sec. 4: 19.

Blount, Marcellus, and George P. Cunningham, eds. *Representing Black Men*. New York: Routledge, 1996.

Bobo, Jacqueline. *Black Women as Cultural Readers*. New York: Columbia UP, 1995.

Bogle, Donald. *Toms, Coons, Mulattoes, Mammies, and Bucks: An Interpretive History of Blacks in American Films*. 1973. Exp. ed. 1989. New York: Continuum, 1991.

Bordo, Susan. "Reading the Male Body." 1993. *Building Bodies*. Ed. Pamela L. Moore. New Brunswick: Rutgers UP, 1997. 31–73.

———. *Unbearable Weight: Feminism, Western Culture, and the Body*. Berkeley: U of California P, 1993.

Boskin, Joseph. *Sambo: The Rise and Demise of an American Jester*. New York: Oxford UP, 1986.

Bourdieu, Pierre. *Distinction: A Social Critique of the Judgment of Taste*. 1979. Trans. Richard Nice. Cambridge: Harvard UP, 1984.

Bower, Lisa C. "The Trope of the Dark Continent in the Fetal Harm Debates: 'Africanism' and the Right to Choice." *Expecting Trouble: Surrogacy, Fetal Abuse and New Reproductive Technologies*. Ed. Patricia Boling. Boulder: Westview, 1995. 142–55.

Bowser, Pearl, and Joan Eckstein. *A Pinch of Soul*. New York: Avon, 1970.

Boyd, Herb. "The Million Man March." *Brotherman: The Odyssey of Black Men in America—An Anthology*. Ed. Herb Boyd and Robert L. Allen. New York: One World-Ballantine, 1996. 875–80.

Boyd, Herb, and Robert L. Allen, eds. *Brotherman: The Odyssey of Black Men in America—An Anthology*. New York: One World-Ballantine, 1996.

Boyz N the Hood. Dir. and writ. John Singleton. Perf. Larry Fishburne, Ice Cube, Cuba Gooding Jr., Nia Long, Morris Chestnut, Tyra Ferrell, and Angela Bassett. Columbia, 1991. Videocassette. Burbank, CA: Columbia Tristar, 1992.

Bragg, Rick. "A Delicacy of the Past Is a Winner at Drive-In." *New York Times* 10 Nov. 1996, natl. ed., sec. 1: 10.

Brillat-Savarin, Jean Anthelme. *The Physiology of Taste*. 1825. Trans. M. F. K. Fisher. San Francisco: North Point, 1986.

Brody, Jane E. "Life in Womb May Affect Adult Heart Disease Risk." *New York Times* 1 Oct. 1996, final late ed.: C1+.

Brody, Jennifer D. "'Recipes for Life': The Metaphysics of Food in *Sassafrass, Cypress, and Indigo* and *Vibration Cooking*." Black Women's Texts and the Culture of Food Panel. MLA Convention. Hilton, San Francisco. 29 Dec. 1991.

Brown, Elaine. *A Taste of Power: A Black Woman's Story*. New York: Pantheon, 1992.

Brown, Fred, Jr. "Collecting African-American Images." *Washington Post* 6 Feb. 1990, final ed.: C5.

Brown, Gillian. "Getting in the Kitchen with Dinah: Domestic Politics in *Uncle Tom's Cabin*." *American Quarterly* 36.4 (Fall 1984): 503–23.

Brown, H. Rap. *Die Nigger Die!* New York: Dial, 1969.

Brown, James. "Say It Loud (I'm Black and I'm Proud)." Pt. 1. *James Brown: 20 All Time Greatest Hits!* New York: PolyGram, 1991.

Brown, Linda Keller, and Kay Mussell, eds. *Ethnic and Regional Foodways in the United States: The Performance of Group Identity.* Knoxville: U of Tennessee P, 1984.

Brown, Roxanne. "Full-Figured Women Fight Back: Resistance Grows to Society's Demand for Slim Bodies." *Ebony* Mar. 1990: 27–31.

Brown, Sterling A. "*Imitation of Life*: Once a Pancake." Rev. of *Imitation of Life*, by Fannie Hurst. *Opportunity: Journal of Negro Life* 13.3 (Mar. 1935): 87–88.

Brumberg, Joan Jacobs. *Fasting Girls: The History of Anorexia Nervosa.* 1988. New York: Plume-Penguin, 1989.

Burg, David F. *Chicago's White City of 1893.* Lexington: UP of Kentucky, 1976.

Burgess, Mary Keyes. *Soul to Soul: A Soul Food Vegetarian Cookbook.* Santa Barbara, CA: Woodbridge, 1976.

Burros, Marian. "Gullah Cooking: Improvising on Cultures Past." *New York Times* 4 May 1988, late ed.: C1+.

Burton, Annie Louise. *Memories of Childhood's Slavery Days.* 1909. Abr. in *Black Women in Nineteenth-Century American Life: Their Words, Their Thoughts, Their Feelings.* Ed. Bert James Loewenberg and Ruth Bogin. University Park: Pennsylvania State UP, 1976. 95–103.

Butler, Judith. *Bodies That Matter: On the Discursive Limits of "Sex".* New York: Routledge, 1993.

———. *Gender Trouble: Feminism and the Subversion of Identity.* New York: Routledge, 1990.

Bynum, Caroline Walker. *Holy Feast and Holy Fast: The Religious Significance of Food to Medieval Women.* Berkeley: U of California P, 1987.

Cable, George Washington. *The Grandissimes.* New York: Scribner's, 1880.

Cameron, William E., ed. *History of the World's Columbian Exposition.* Chicago: Columbian History, 1893.

Campbell, Barbara. "'Poems by Kali': A Little Black Girl Speaks Her Mind." *New York Times* 7 July 1970, late city ed.: 42.

Campbell, Bebe Moore. "Body Love: Have You Ever Hated the Way You Look? Meet Eight Women Who Each Learned to Love Every Part of Her Beautiful Body." *Essence* Jan. 1990: 44–49.

Campbell, Cathy. "A Battered Woman Rises: Aunt Jemima's Corporate Makeover." *Village Voice* 7 Nov. 1989: 45–46.

Campbell, Hannah. *Why Did They Name It . . .?* New York: Fleet, 1964.

Caputi, Jane. "'Specifying' Fannie Hurst: Langston Hughes's 'Limitations of Life,' Zora Neale Hurston's *Their Eyes Were Watching God*, and Toni Morrison's *The Bluest Eye* as 'Answers' to Hurst's *Imitation of Life*." *Black American Literature Forum* 24.4 (Winter 1990): 697–716.

Carby, Hazel. "It Jus Be's Dat Way Sometime: The Sexual Politics of Women's Blues." *Radical America* 20.4 (June/July 1986): 9–22.

———. "Policing the Black Woman's Body in an Urban Context." *Critical Inquiry* 18.4 (Summer 1992): 738–55.

———. *Reconstructing Womanhood: The Emergence of the Afro-American Woman Novelist.* New York: Oxford UP, 1987.

Carson, Rachel. *Silent Spring.* 1962. Boston: Houghton, 1987.

Carter, Angela. "Hell in the Suburbs." Rev. of *Linden Hills*, by Gloria Naylor. *Washington Post Book World* 24 Mar. 1985: 7.

Chadwick, Whitney. *Women, Art, and Society*. London: Thames and Hudson, 1990.

Chase, Chris. *The Great American Waistline: Putting It On and Taking It Off*. New York: Coward, 1981.

Chase, Leah, and Johnny Rivers. *Down Home Healthy: Family Recipes of Black American Chefs*. Bethesda, MD: National Institutes of Health, National Cancer Inst., 1994.

Chernin, Kim. *The Hungry Self: Women, Eating, and Identity*. 1985. New York: Perennial-Harper, 1986

———. *The Obsession: Reflections on the Tyranny of Slenderness*. 1981. New York: Perennial-Harper, 1982.

Chesnutt, Charles W. "The Goophered Grapevine." 1887. *The Conjure Woman*. 1899. Ann Arbor: U of Michigan P, 1969. 1–35.

Childress, Alice. *Like One of the Family: Conversations from a Domestic's Life*. 1956. Boston: Beacon, 1986.

Childs, John Brown. "Afro-American Intellectuals and the People's Culture." *Journal of Theory and Society* 13 (1984): 69–90.

Chisholm, Shirley. "Facing the Abortion Question." 1970. *Black Women in White America: A Documentary History*. Ed. Gerda Lerner. 1972. Vintage-Random, 1973. 602–7.

Christian, Barbara. "Images of Black Women in Afro-American Literature: From Stereotype to Character." 1975. *Black Feminist Criticism: Perspectives on Black Women Writers*. New York: Pergamon, 1985. 1–30.

Claiborne, Craig. "Cooking with Soul." *New York Times Magazine* 3 Nov. 1968: 102–9.

———. *Craig Claiborne's Southern Cooking*. New York: Times-Random, 1987.

———. *A Feast Made for Laughter: A Memoir with Recipes*. Garden City, NY: Doubleday, 1982.

———. "Just a Quiet Dinner for Two in Paris: 31 Dishes, Nine Wines, a $4,000 Check." *New York Times* 14 Nov. 1975, late city ed.: 1+.

———. "They Want $100 a Plate for Soul Food—and an All-Star Show." *New York Times* 24 Apr. 1969, late city ed.: 52.

Clark, Joanna. "Motherhood." *The Black Woman: An Anthology*. Ed. Toni Cade Bambara. New York: Mentor-Penguin, 1970. 63–72.

Clark-Lewis, Elizabeth. *Living In, Living Out: African American Domestics and the Great Migration*. New York: Kodansha, 1996. Rpt. of *Living In, Living Out: African American Domestics in Washington, D.C., 1910–1940*. Washington, DC: Smithsonian, 1994.

"Classic Meals of the South." *Ebony* Aug. 1971: 174–78.

Cleaver, Eldridge. *Soul on Ice*. 1968. New York: Laurel-Dell, 1992.

Clegg, Claude Andrew, III. *An Original Man: The Life and Times of Elijah Muhammad*. New York: St. Martin's, 1997.

Clissold, H. R. "A Revolution in Bread-Making." *Good Housekeeping* 53 (July–Dec. 1911): 485–87.

Clockers. Dir. Spike Lee. Writ. Richard Price and Spike Lee. Perf. Mekhi Phifer, Harvey Keitel, John Turturro, Isaiah Washington, and Delroy Lindo. Universal-40 Acres, 1995. Videocassette. Universal City, CA: MCA, 1996.

Cohen, Ed. *Talk on the Wilde Side: Toward a Genealogy of a Discourse on Male Sexualities*. New York: Routledge, 1993.

Cole, Catherine M. "Reading Blackface in West Africa: Wonders Taken for Signs." *Critical Inquiry* 23.1 (Autumn 1996): 183–215.

Colker, Ruth. *Hybrid: Bisexuals, Multiracials, and Other Misfits under American Law.* New York: New York UP, 1996.

———. *Pregnant Men: Practice, Theory, and the Law.* Bloomington: Indiana UP, 1994.

Collins, Patricia Hill. *Black Feminist Thought: Knowledge, Consciousness, and the Politics of Empowerment.* 1990. New York: Routledge, 1991.

Colquitt, Harriet Ross. *The Savannah Cook Book: A Collection of Old Fashioned Receipts from Colonial Kitchens.* Charleston, SC: Walker, Evans, and Cogswell, 1933.

Combahee River Collective. "A Black Feminist Statement." 1977. *But Some of Us Are Brave.* Ed. Gloria T. Hull, Patricia Bell Scott, and Barbara Smith. New York: Feminist, 1982. 13–22.

The Compact Edition of the Oxford English Dictionary. Vol. 2. 1971 ed.

Congdon-Martin, Douglas. *Images in Black: 150 Years of Black Collectibles.* West Chester, PA: Schiffer, 1990.

Cook, Joan. "An Author's Party with Soul." *New York Times* 11 Dec. 1968, late city ed.: 40.

Cooper-Lewter, Nicholas C., and Henry H. Mitchell. *Soul Theology: The Heart of Black American Culture.* San Francisco: Harper, 1986.

Corea, Gena. *The Mother Machine: Reproductive Technologies from Artificial Insemination to Artificial Wombs.* 1985. New York: Perennial-Harper, 1986.

Cornell, Drucilla. *Beyond Accommodation: Ethical Feminism, Deconstruction, and the Law.* New York: Routledge, 1991.

———. *The Imaginary Domain: Abortion, Pornography and Sexual Harassment.* New York: Routledge, 1995.

Crawford, Alan. *Thunder on the Right: The "New Right" and the Politics of Resentment.* New York: Pantheon, 1980.

Creel, Margaret Washington. "Gullah Attitudes toward Life and Death." *Africanisms in American Culture.* Ed. Joseph E. Holloway. 1990. Bloomington: Midland-Indiana UP, 1991. 69–97.

Crimp, Douglas. "Right On, Girlfriend!" *Social Text* 33 (1992): 2–18.

Crossing Delancey. Dir. Joan Micklin Silver. Writ. Susan Sandler. Perf. Amy Irving, Reizl Bozyk, Peter Riegert, and Jeroen Krabbe. Warner, 1988. Videocassette. Burbank, CA: Warner, 1989.

Crowther, Bosley. Rev. of *Miracle on 34th Street,* dir. George Seaton. *New York Times* 5 June 1947, late city ed.: 32.

Culler, Jonathan. *On Deconstruction: Theory and Criticism after Structuralism.* Ithaca: Cornell UP, 1982.

Curry, Marva Joy. *Everything You Always Wanted to Know about Soul Food Cooking . . . and Were Afraid to Ask.* N.p.: n.p., 1983.

Curry, Renée R. "*Daughters of the Dust,* the White Woman Viewer, and the Unborn Child." *Teaching What You're Not: Identity Politics in Higher Education.* Ed. Katherine J. Mayberry. New York: New York UP, 1996. 335–56.

Darden, Norma Jean, and Carole Darden. *Spoonbread and Strawberry Wine: Recipes and Reminiscences of a Family.* 1978. New York: Fawcett Crest, 1982.

Dash, Julie. *Daughters of the Dust: The Making of an African American Woman's Film.* With Toni Cade Bambara and bell hooks. New York: New, 1992.

Daughters of the Dust. Dir., writ., and prod. Julie Dash. Perf. Cora Lee Day, Alva Rodgers, Adisa Anderson, Kaycee Moore, Barbara O, Eartha D. Robinson, Bahni Turpin, Cheryl Lynn Bruce, and Vertamae Smart-Grosvenor. 1991. Videocassette. New York: Kino on Video, 1992.

Davies, Valentine. *Miracle on 34th Street.* New York: Harcourt, 1947.

Davis, Aldeen. *Soul—Food for Thought*. Muscatine, IA: Pip Copy Center, 1984.

Davis, Angela Y. "The Approaching Obsolescence of Housework: A Working-Class Perspective." *Women, Race and Class*. 1981. New York: Vintage-Random, 1983. 222–44.

———. "Black Nationalism: The Sixties and the Nineties." *Black Popular Culture*. Ed. Gina Dent. A Michele Wallace project. Seattle: Bay, 1992. 317–24.

———. "The Legacy of Slavery: Standards for a New Womanhood." *Women, Race and Class*. 1981. New York: Vintage-Random, 1983. 3–29.

———. "Racism, Birth Control and Reproductive Rights." *Women, Race and Class*. 1981. New York: Vintage-Random, 1983. 202–21.

———. "Sick and Tired of Being Sick and Tired: The Politics of Black Women's Health." *The Black Women's Health Book: Speaking for Ourselves*. Ed. Evelyn C. White. Seattle: Seal, 1990. 18–26.

Davis, Ossie. "On Malcolm X." Eulogy. *The Autobiography of Malcolm X*. By Malcolm X, with Alex Haley. 1965. New York: Ballantine, 1973. 457–60.

Dawsey, Darrell. *Living to Tell about It: Young Black Men in America Speak Their Piece*. New York: Anchor-Doubleday, 1996.

de Certeau, Michel. *The Practice of Everyday Life*. Trans. Steven Rendall. Berkeley: U of California P, 1984.

Deleuze, Gilles. *Coldness and Cruelty*. 1967. Rpt. in *Masochism: Coldness and Cruelty/Venus in Furs*. Trans. Jean McNeil. New York: Zone, 1989.

Delphy, Christine. "Patriarchy, Domestic Mode of Production, Gender, and Class." 1970. Trans. Diana Leonard. *Marxism and the Interpretation of Culture*. Ed. Cary Nelson and Lawrence Grossberg. Urbana: U of Illinois P, 1988. 259–67.

D'Emilio, John. "Capitalism and Gay Identity." *Powers of Desire: The Politics of Sexuality*. Ed. Ann Snitow, Christine Stansell, and Sharon Thompson. New York: Monthly Review, 1983. 100–13.

———. *Sexual Politics, Sexual Communities: The Making of a Homosexual Minority in the United States, 1940–1970*. Chicago: U of Chicago P, 1983.

D'Emilio, John, and Estelle B. Freedman. *Intimate Matters: A History of Sexuality in America*. New York: Harper, 1988.

Dent, David J. "Million Man March: Whose Reality?" *Black Renaissance/Renaissance Noire* 1.1 (Fall 1996): 58–68.

Dent, Gina, ed. *Black Popular Culture*. A Michele Wallace project. Seattle: Bay, 1992.

Derrida, Jacques. *Of Grammatology*. 1967. Trans. Gayatri Chakravorty Spivak. Baltimore: Johns Hopkins UP, 1976.

Rev. of *Dick Gregory's Natural Diet for Folks Who Eat: Cookin' with Mother Nature*, by Dick Gregory. *New York Times Book Review* 13 May 1973: 40.

Dixon, Ethel. *Big Mama's Old Black Pot Recipes*. Alexandria, LA: Stoke Gabriel, 1987.

Dorris, Michael. *The Broken Chord*. New York: Harper, 1989.

Do the Right Thing. Dir. and writ. Spike Lee. Perf. Spike Lee, Danny Aiello, Richard Edson, Ruby Dee, Ossie Davis, Giancarlo Esposito, Bill Nunn, and John Turturro. Universal, 1989. Videocassette. Universal City, CA: MCA, 1989.

Dotson, Mary L. "The Story of a Teacher of Cooking." *Tuskegee and Its People: Their Ideals and Achievements*. Ed. Booker T. Washington. New York: Appleton, 1905. 200–10.

Douglas, Mary. *Natural Symbols: Explorations in Cosmology*. 1973. New York: Pantheon-Random, 1982.

———. *Purity and Danger: An Analysis of the Concepts of Pollution and Taboo*. 1966. London: Ark-Routledge, 1984.

Douglass, Frederick. *Narrative of the Life of Frederick Douglass, an African Slave*. 1845. The

Classic Slave Narratives. Ed. Henry Louis Gates Jr. New York: Mentor-NAL, 1987. 243–331.

Dove, Rita. "Motherhood." 1986. *Selected Poems.* New York: Vintage-Random, 1993. 185.

———. "Why I Turned Vegetarian." 1983. *Selected Poems.* New York: Vintage-Random, 1993. 125.

Dubey, Madhu. *Black Women Novelists and the Nationalist Aesthetic.* Bloomington: Indiana UP, 1994.

Du Bois, W. E. B. *The Souls of Black Folk.* 1903. New York: Vintage–Library of America, 1990.

duCille, Ann. *The Coupling Convention: Sex, Text, and Tradition in Black Women's Fiction.* New York: Oxford UP, 1993.

Dudden, Faye E. *Serving Women: Household Service in Nineteenth-Century America.* Middletown, CT: Wesleyan UP, 1983.

Dunbar, Paul Laurence. "When De Co'n Pone's Hot." *Lyrics of Lowly Life.* 1896. New York: Dodd, 1908. 132–34.

Dunnavant, Sylvia. "Aunt Jemima." *An Affair of the Heart.* Madison, WI: National Minority Campus Chronicle, 1983. Rpt. in *Aunt Jemima, Uncle Ben, and Rastus: Blacks in Advertising, Yesterday, Today, and Tomorrow.* By Marilyn Kern-Foxworth. Westport, CT: Greenwood, 1994. 103.

Dupree, Nathalie. *New Southern Cooking.* New York: Borzoi-Knopf, 1986.

Dyer, Richard. "White." *Screen* 29.4 (1988): 44–64.

Dyson, Michael Eric. "Who Speaks for Malcolm X? The Writings of Just About Everybody." *New York Times Book Review* 29 Nov. 1992: 3+.

"Eating Like Soul Brothers." *Time* 24 Jan. 1969: 57.

Echols, Alice. *Daring to Be Bad: Radical Feminism in America, 1967–1975.* Minneapolis: U of Minnesota P, 1989.

Eckels, Jon. "Hell, Mary." *A Broadside Treasury, 1965–1970.* Ed. Gwendolyn Brooks. Detroit: Broadside, 1971. 43.

Eddie Murphy Raw. Dir. Robert Townsend. Writ. and perf. Eddie Murphy. Videocassette. Paramount, 1987.

"Edith Wilson, Actress, Is Dead." *Chicago Tribune* 31 Mar. 1981, natl. ed., sec. 2: 6.

Edwards, Audrey. "From Aunt Jemima to Anita Hill: Media's Split Image of Black Women." *Media Studies Journal* 7.1–2 (Winter–Spring 1993): 215–22.

Edwards, Paul K. *The Southern Urban Negro as a Consumer.* 1932. New York: Negro Universities-Greenwood, 1969.

Egerton, John. *Southern Food: At Home, on the Road, in History.* 1987. Chapel Hill: U of North Carolina P, 1993.

Ehrenreich, Barbara. *The Hearts of Men: American Dreams and the Flight from Commitment.* Garden City, NY: AnchorDoubleday, 1983.

Eichenwald, Kurt. "The Two Faces of Texaco: The Right Policies Are on the Books, but Not Always on the Job." *New York Times* 10 Nov. 1996, natl. ed, sec. 3: 1+.

Eisenstein, Zillah R. *The Color of Gender: Reimaging Democracy.* Berkeley: U of California P, 1994.

———. *The Female Body and the Law.* Berkeley: U of California P, 1988.

Elkins, Stanley M. *Slavery: A Problem in American Institutional and Intellectual Life.* 1959. New York: Universal Library-Grosset, 1963.

Elliot, Jeffrey M., ed. *Conversations with Maya Angelou.* Jackson: UP of Mississippi, 1989.

Ellison, Ralph. "Change the Joke and Slip the Yoke." *Partisan Review* 25.2 (Spring 1958): 212–22. Part II of "The Negro Writer in America: An Exchange."

———. *Invisible Man.* 1952. New York: Vintage-Random, 1995.

Engels, Frederick. *The Origin of the Family, Private Property, and the State.* 1884. New York: Pathfinder, 1972.

Enloe, Cynthia. *Bananas, Beaches, and Bases: Making Feminist Sense of International Politics.* 1989. Berkeley: U of California P, 1990.

Essien-Udom, E. U. *Black Nationalism: A Search for an Identity in America.* 1962. New York: Dell, 1964.

Evans, Sara M. *Born for Liberty: A History of Women in America.* New York: Free, 1989.

———. *Personal Politics: The Roots of Women's Liberation in the Civil Rights Movement and the New Left.* 1979. New York: Vintage-Random, 1980.

Ewen, Elizabeth. *Immigrant Women in the Land of Dollars: Life and Culture on the Lower East Side, 1890–1925.* New York: Monthly Review, 1985.

Fabricant, Florence. "For Blacks, Chef Jobs Finally Call." *New York Times* 20 Oct. 1993, final late ed: C1+.

Faith Ringgold: Twenty Years of Painting, Sculpture and Performance (1963–1983). New York: Studio Museum of Harlem, 1984.

Farmer, Fannie Merritt. *The Original Boston Cooking-School Cook Book.* New York: Weathervane, n.d. Rpt. of *The Boston Cooking-School Cook Book.* Boston: Little, 1896.

Farrakhan, Louis. "Exercise to Stay Alive! The War against Obesity (Fat), Part Three." *Final Call* 19 Aug. 1991: 20–21+.

———. "How to Give Birth to a God." 1987. *Back Where We Belong: Selected Speeches by Minister Louis Farrakhan.* Ed. Joseph D. Eure and Richard M. Jerome. Philadelphia: PC International, 1989. 83–113.

———. "The Re-Unification of the Black Family." Temple Theater, Tacoma, WA. 26 Jan. 1990. Cited in *In the Name of Elijah Muhammad: Louis Farrakhan and the Nation of Islam.* By Mattias Gardell. Durham: Duke UP, 1996. 336 and 434.

Faulkner, William. *Absalom, Absalom!* New York: Random, 1936.

———. *The Sound and the Fury.* New York: Random, 1929.

Feinberg, Andrew. "The Richest Woman on TV? Oprah: How She Amassed Her 250-Million Fortune." *TV Guide* 26 Aug.–1 Sept. 1989: 2–7.

Ferguson, Sheila. *Soul Food: Classic Cuisine from the Deep South.* New York: Weidenfeld, 1989.

Ferrell, Carolyn. "Eating Confessions." *Callaloo* 12.3 (Summer 1989): 453–64.

Findling, John E. *Chicago's Great World's Fairs.* Manchester, UK: Manchester UP, 1994.

Fine, Elsa Honig. *The Afro-American Artist: A Search for Identity.* New York: Holt, 1973.

Fineman, Martha Albertson. *The Neutered Mother, the Sexual Family, and Other Twentieth Century Tragedies.* New York: Routledge, 1995.

Flournoy, David. "Testament." *Black Voices from Prison.* Etheridge Knight and Other Inmates of Indiana State Prison. 1968. New York: Merit-Pathfinder, 1970. 29–32.

"Food with New Soul." *Essence* Oct. 1982: 94–96+.

Foucault, Michel. *The History of Sexuality: An Introduction.* 1976. Trans. Robert Hurley. 1978. New York: Vintage-Random, 1990. Vol. 1 of *The History of Sexuality.*

———. *The Order of Things: An Archaeology of the Human Sciences.* 1966. New York: Vintage-Random, 1973.

Frankenberg, Ruth. *White Women, Race Matters: The Social Construction of Whiteness.* Minneapolis: U of Minnesota P, 1993.

Franklin, John Hope, and Alfred A. Moss Jr. *From Slavery to Freedom: A History of African Americans.* 7th ed. New York: Knopf, 1994.

Frazier, E. Franklin. *Black Bourgeoisie.* 1957. New York: Free-Simon, 1997.

———. *The Negro Family in the United States.* Chicago: U of Chicago P, 1939.

Fresh. Dir. and writ. Boaz Yakin. Perf. Samuel L. Jackson, Giancarlo Esposito, Sean Nelson, and N'Bushe Wright. Miramax, 1994. Videocassette. Burbank, CA: Buena Vista, 1994.

Freud, Sigmund. "Character and Anal Eroticism." 1908. *The Freud Reader*. Ed. Peter Gay. New York: Norton, 1989. 293–97.

———. "A Child Is Being Beaten: A Contribution to the Study of the Origin of Sexual Perversions." 1919. *The Standard Edition of the Complete Psychological Works of Sigmund Freud*. Ed. and trans. James Strachey. London: Hogarth, 1958. Vol 17. 177–204.

———. "From the History of an Infantile Neurosis." 1918. *Collected Papers*. Trans. Alix Strachey and James Strachey. New York: Basic, 1959. Vol. 3. 471–605.

———. *Jokes and Their Relation to the Unconscious*. 1905. Ed. and trans. James Strachey. 1960. New York: Norton, 1989.

———. *Three Essays on the Theory of Sexuality*. 1905. Trans. and ed. James Strachey. New York: Basic, 1962, 1975.

Friday, Nancy. "These Ugly Ducks Swim in a Shallow Pond." *New York Times* 18 Aug. 1996, final late ed., sec. 2: 9.

Fussell, Betty Harper. "He Likes to Write and Likes to Cook." Rev. of *A Feast Made for Laughter*, by Craig Claiborne. *New York Times Book Review* 10 Oct. 1982: 12+.

Gallop, Jane. *The Daughter's Seduction: Feminism and Psychoanalysis*. Ithaca: Cornell UP, 1982.

Gamson, Joshua. *Claims to Fame: Celebrity in Contemporary America*. Berkeley: U of California P, 1994.

Garber, Eric. "A Spectacle in Color: The Lesbian and Gay Subculture of Jazz Age Harlem." *Hidden from History: Reclaiming the Gay and Lesbian Past*. Ed. Martin Bauml Duberman, Martha Vicinus, and George Chauncey Jr. New York: NAL-Penguin, 1991. 318–331+.

Gardell, Mattias. *In the Name of Elijah Muhammad: Louis Farrakhan and the Nation of Islam*. Durham: Duke UP, 1996.

Gardiner, Jean. "Women's Domestic Labor." 1975. *Capitalist Patriarchy and the Case for Socialist Feminism*. Ed. Zillah R. Eisenstein. New York: Monthly Review, 1979. 173–89.

Garland, Phyl. "Vibes from Verta Mae: 'Double-O Soul' Chef Authors Fascinating Guide to 'Vibration' Cooking." *Ebony* Mar. 1971: 86–94.

Gaskins, Ruth L. *A Good Heart and a Light Hand: Ruth L. Gaskins' Collection of Traditional Negro Recipes*. Annandale, VA: Turnpike, 1968.

Gates, Henry Louis, Jr. "Significant Others." *Contemporary Literature* 29.4 (Winter 1988): 606–23.

———. *The Signifying Monkey: A Theory of African-American Literary Criticism*. New York: Oxford UP, 1988.

Gee, Denise. "The Gospel of Great Southern Food." *Southern Living* June 1996: 126–28.

General Motors products. "Not All Passengers Can Be Seen. But They All Need Protection." Advertisement. *Washington Post* 16 May 1994, final ed.: A16.

Genovese, Eugene D. *Roll, Jordan, Roll: The World the Slaves Made*. 1974. New York: Vintage-Random, 1976.

Get on the Bus. Dir. Spike Lee. Writ. Reggie Rock Bythewood. Perf. Ossie Davis, Charles S. Dutton, Andre Braugher, Thomas Jefferson Byrd, Gabriel Casseus, Harry Lennix, Hill Harper, Wendell Pierce, Roger Guenveur Smith, Isaiah Washington, DeAundre Bonds, and Richard Belzer. Columbia—40 Acres, 1996. Videocassette. Culver City, CA: Columbia Tristar, 1997.

Giddings, Paula. *When and Where I Enter: The Impact of Black Women on Race and Sex in America*. New York: Bantam, 1984.

Gilbert, Douglas. *American Vaudeville: Its Life and Times.* New York: Whittlesey-McGraw, 1940.

Gilliam, Angela. "Women's Equality and National Liberation." *Third World Women and the Politics of Feminism.* Ed. Chandra Talpade Mohanty, Ann Russo, and Lourdes Torres. Bloomington: Indiana UP, 1991. 215–36.

Gilroy, Paul. *The Black Atlantic: Modernity and Double Consciousness.* Cambridge: Harvard UP, 1993.

———. "It's a Family Affair." *Black Popular Culture.* Ed. Gina Dent. A Michele Wallace project. Seattle: Bay, 1992. 303–16.

Giovanni, Nikki. "Poem for Black Boys." 1968. *The Black Poets.* Ed. Dudley Randall. New York: Bantam, 1971. 325–26.

———. "The True Import of the Present Dialogue: Black vs. Negro." 1970. *The Black Poets.* Ed. Dudley Randall. New York: Bantam, 1971. 318–19.

Gite, Lloyd, and Jean Perry. "Diet: Losing Weight Soulfully." *Essence* Aug. 1983: 117–18.

Gitlin, Todd. *The Sixties: Years of Hope, Days of Rage.* New York: Bantam, 1987.

Glenn, Camille. *The Heritage of Southern Cooking.* New York: Workman, 1986.

Goings, Kenneth W. *Mammy and Uncle Mose: Black Collectibles and American Stereotyping.* Bloomington: Indiana UP, 1994.

Goldman, Anne. "'I Yam What I Yam': Cooking, Culture, and Colonialism." *De/Colonizing the Subject: The Politics of Gender in Women's Autobiography.* Ed. Sidonie Smith and Julia Watson. Minneapolis: U of Minnesota P, 1992. 169–95.

Gomez, Jewelle L. "A Cultural Legacy Denied and Discovered: Black Lesbians in Fiction by Women." *Home Girls: A Black Feminist Anthology.* Ed. Barbara Smith. New York: Kitchen Table, 1983. 110–23.

Gordon, Linda. *Woman's Body, Woman's Right: A Social History of Birth Control in America.* 1976. New York: Penguin, 1977.

Graham, Hugh Davis. *The Civil Rights Era: Origins and Development of National Policy, 1960–1972.* New York: Oxford UP, 1990.

Granda, Megan Ruth. "Aunt Jemima in Black and White: America Advertises in Color." Thesis. U of Texas at Austin, 1992.

The Graphic History of the Fair, Containing a Sketch of International Expositions, a Review of the Events Leading to the Discovery of America, and a History of the World's Columbian Exposition Held in the City of Chicago, State of Illinois, May 1 to October 31, 1893. Chicago: Graphic, 1894.

Gray, James J., Kathryn Ford, and Lily M. Kelly. "The Prevalence of Bulimia in a Black College Population." *International Journal of Eating Disorders* 6.6 (1987): 733–40.

"Green." Obituary. *Chicago Daily Tribune* 31 Aug. 1923, final ed.: 10.

Greenwood, Jacquie. "Black Promotional Products." *Black Ethnic Collectibles* July/Aug. 1988: 12–13.

Gregory, Dick. *Dick Gregory in Living Black and White.* CP 417. N.p.: Colpix, c. 1961.

———. *Dick Gregory's Natural Diet for Folks Who Eat: Cookin' with Mother Nature.* Ed. James R. McGraw, with Alvenia M. Fulton. 1973. New York: Perennial-Harper, 1974.

———. *Dick Gregory's Political Primer.* Ed. James R. McGraw. New York: Perennial-Harper, 1972.

———. *From the Back of the Bus.* Ed. Bob Orben. Phot. Jerry Yulsman. New York: Dutton, 1962.

———. "My Answer to Genocide." *Ebony* Oct. 1971: 66–72.

———. *Nigger: An Autobiography.* With Robert Lipsyte. 1964. New York: Pocket-Simon, 1965.

———. *No More Lies: The Myth and the Reality of American History.* Ed. James R. McGraw. 1971. New York: Perennial-Harper, 1972.

———. *The Shadow That Scares Me.* Ed. James R. McGraw. Garden City, NY: Doubleday, 1968.

———. *Up from Nigger.* With James R. McGraw. New York: Stein, 1976.

———. *What's Happening?* Contrib. Bob Orben and Jim Sanders. Phot. Jerry Yulsman. New York: Dutton, 1965.

———. *Write Me In!* Ed. James R. McGraw. New York: Bantam, 1968.

"Gregory in 8th Month of Protest Fast." *Los Angeles Times* 1 Jan. 1972, morn. ed., sec. 1: 17.

Gresham, Jewell Handy, and Margaret B. Wilkerson, eds. "Scapegoating the Black Family: Black Women Speak." Special Issue. *Nation* 24–31 July 1989: 115–48.

Gross, Larry. *Contested Closets: The Politics and Ethics of Outing.* Minneapolis: U of Minnesota P, 1993.

Grossberg, Lawrence, Cary Nelson, and Paula Treichler, eds. *Cultural Studies.* New York: Routledge, 1992.

Grosvenor, Kali. *Poems by Kali.* Garden City, NY: Doubleday, 1970.

Grosvenor, Vertamae Smart [Verta Mae; Vertamae Smart-Grosvenor]. "The Kitchen Crisis: A Rap." *Amistad I: Writings on Black History and Culture.* Ed. John A. Williams and Charles F. Harris. New York: Vintage-Random, 1970. 293–300.

———. "Soul Food." *McCalls* Sept. 1970: 72–75.

———. *Thursdays and Every Other Sunday Off: A Domestic Rap by Verta Mae.* Garden City, NY: Doubleday, 1972.

———. *Vertamae Cooks in the Americas' Family Kitchen.* San Francisco: KQED Books, 1996.

———. *Vibration Cooking, or the Travel Notes of a Geechee Girl.* Garden City, NY: Doubleday, 1970. 2nd ed. New York: Ballantine, 1986. 3rd. ed. New York: One World-Ballantine, 1992.

Grubb, Alan. "House and Home in the Victorian South: The Cookbook as Guide." *In Joy and in Sorrow: Women, Family, and Marriage in the Victorian South, 1830–1900.* New York: Oxford UP, 1991. 154–75+.

Guillory, Queen Ida. *Cookin' with Queen Ida: "Bon Temps" Creole Recipes (and Stories) from the Queen of Zydeco Music.* With Naomi Wise. Rocklin, CA: Prima, 1990.

Gumbo Ya Ya: Anthology of Contemporary African-American Women Artists. Ed. Sylvia Moore. New York: Midmarch, 1995.

Gutierrez, C. Paige. "The Social and Symbolic Uses of Ethnic/Regional Foodways: Cajuns and Crawfish in South Louisiana." *Ethnic and Regional Foodways in the United States: The Performance of Group Identity.* Ed. Linda Keller Brown and Kay Mussell. Knoxville: U of Tennessee P, 1984. 169–82.

Hall, Jim. *Mighty Minutes: An Illustrated History of Television's Best Commercials.* New York: Harmony, 1984.

Hall, Stuart. "New Ethnicities." *Black Film/British Cinema.* Ed. Kobena Mercer. London: ICA, 1988. 27–31.

———. "What Is This 'Black' in Black Popular Culture?" *Black Popular Culture.* Ed. Gina Dent. A Michele Wallace project. Seattle: Bay, 1992. 21–33.

Halley, Janet E. "The Construction of Heterosexuality." *Fear of a Queer Planet.* Ed. Michael Warner. Minneapolis: U of Minnesota P, 1993. 82–102.

Hangin' with the Homeboys. Dir. and writ. Joseph P. Vasquez. Perf. Mario Joyner, Doug E. Doug, John Leguizamo, Nestor Serrano, Kimberly Russell, and Mary B. Ward. New Line, 1991. Videocassette. Burbank, CA: SVS-Triumph, 1991.

Harley, Sharon, and Rosalyn Terborg-Penn, eds. *The Afro-American Woman: Struggles and Images.* Port Washington, NY: Kennikat, 1978.

Harper, Phillip Brian. *Are We Not Men? Masculine Anxiety and the Problem of African-American Identity.* New York: Oxford UP, 1996.

Harris, Jessica. *Iron Pots and Wooden Spoons: Africa's Gifts to New World Cooking.* 1989. New York: Ballantine-Random, 1991.

Harris, Middleton. *The Black Book.* With Morris Levitt, Roger Furman, and Ernest Smith. New York: Random, 1974.

Harris, Trudier. *Black Women in the Fiction of James Baldwin.* Knoxville: U of Tennessee P, 1985.

———. *From Mammies to Militants: Domestics in Black American Literature.* Philadelphia: Temple UP, 1982.

Harrison, Faye V. "Women in Jamaica's Urban Informal Economy: Insights from a Kingston Slum." *Third World Women and the Politics of Feminism.* Ed. Chandra Talpade Mohanty, Ann Russo, and Lourdes Torres. Bloomington: Indiana UP, 1991. 173–96.

Hartmann, Heidi I. "Capitalism, Patriarchy, and Job Segregation by Sex." 1976. *Women, Class, and the Feminist Imagination: A Socialist-Feminist Reader.* Ed. Karen V. Hansen and Ilene J. Philipson. Philadelphia: Temple UP, 1990. 146–81.

Hartouni, Valerie. *Cultural Conceptions: On Reproductive Technologies and the Remaking of Life.* Minneapolis: U of Minnesota P, 1997.

The Hate That Hate Produced. News Beat. WNTA-TV Channel 13, New York. July 1959. Videocassette. Syracuse: Syracuse U, c. 1980s.

Haverly, J. H. "Old Aunt Jemima." *Haverly's Genuine Colored Minstrels' Songster.* New York: New York Popular, c. 1879. 13.

Hayden, Robert. "Aunt Jemima of the Ocean Waves." *Words in the Mourning Time.* New York: October House, 1970. 18–21.

Heath, G. Louis, ed. *Off the Pigs! The History and Literature of the Black Panther Party.* Metuchen, NJ: Scarecrow, 1976.

Hefner, Hugh M. Introduction. *From the Back of the Bus.* By Dick Gregory. New York: Dutton, 1962. 11–18.

Henkes, Robert. *The Art of Black American Women: Works of Twenty-Four Artists of the Twentieth Century.* Jefferson, NC: McFarland, 1993.

Herskovits, Melville J. *The Myth of the Negro Past.* New York: Harper, 1941.

Hervey, Antoinette B. "The Saints in My Kitchen." *Outlook* 100 (17 Feb. 1912): 367–71.

Hess, John L., and Karen Hess. *The Taste of America.* New York: Grossman-Viking, 1977.

Hilts, Philip J. "Hospital Is Accused of Illegal Drug Testing." *New York Times* 21 Jan. 1994, late ed.: A12.

Hine, Thomas. *The Total Package: The Evolution and Secret Meanings of Boxes, Bottles, Cans, and Tubes.* Boston: Little, 1995.

Hines, Duncan. *Duncan Hines' Food Odyssey.* New York: Crowell, 1955.

"Historic Recipes from Mammy Pleasant." *Ebony* Feb. 1971: 108–12.

Hoff, Joan. *Law, Gender, and Injustice: A Legal History of U.S. Women.* New York: New York UP, 1991.

Homans, Margaret. "'Racial Composition': Metaphor and the Body in the Writing of Race." *Female Subjects in Black and White: Race, Psychoanalysis, Feminism.* Ed. Elizabeth Abel, Barbara Christian, and Helene Moglen. Berkeley: U of California P, 1997. 77–101.

———. "The Woman in the Cave: Recent Feminist Fictions and the Classical Underworld." *Contemporary Literature* 29.3 (Fall 1988): 369–402.

hooks, bell. *Ain't I a Woman: Black Women and Feminism.* Boston: South End, 1981.

———. "The Chitlin Circuit: On Black Community." *Yearning: Race, Gender, and Cultural Politics*. Boston: South End, 1990. 33–40.

———. *Sisters of the Yam: Black Women and Self-Recovery*. Boston: South End, 1993.

Hopkins, Pauline E. *Contending Forces: A Romance Illustrative of Negro Life North and South*. 1900. New York: Oxford UP, 1988.

Horn, Carole. "What Comes Naturally." Rev. of *The Wild Flavor*, by Marilyn Kluger; *How to Enjoy Your Weeds*, by Audrey Wynne Hatfield; *Flower Cookery*, by Mary MacNicol Fleet; *The Forgotten Art of Flower Cookery*, by Leona Woodring Smith; *Rainbow Farm Cookbook*, by Lynne Andersen; *The Potato Book*, by Myrna Davis; and *Dick Gregory's Natural Diet for Folks Who Eat*, by Dick Gregory. *Washington Post Book World* 23 Sept. 1973: 6–7.

Hsu, L. K. George. "Are the Eating Disorders Becoming More Common in Blacks." *International Journal of Eating Disorders* 6.1 (1987): 113–24.

Hubbard, Ruth. *The Politics of Women's Biology*. New Brunswick: Rutgers UP, 1990.

Hughes, Langston. "Limitations of Life." 1938. *Black Theater U.S.A.: Forty-Five Plays by Black Americans, 1847–1974*. Ed. James V. Hatch, with Ted Shine. New York: Free, 1974. 656–57.

———. "Soul Food." 1965. *The Return of Simple*. Ed. Akiba Sullivan Harper. New York: Hill and Wang, 1994. 127–33.

Hurst, Fannie. *Imitation of Life*. 1933. New York: Pyramid, 1974.

———. *No Food with My Meals*. New York: Harper, 1935.

Hurston, Zora Neale. "Glossary of Harlem Slang." *Spunk: The Selected Stories of Zora Neale Hurston*. Berkeley: Turtle Island, 1985. 91–96.

———. *Their Eyes Were Watching God*. 1937. Urbana: U of Illinois P, 1978.

Huyssen, Andreas. "Mass Culture as Woman: Modernism's Other." *Studies in Entertainment: Critical Approaches to Mass Culture*. Ed. Tania Modleski. Bloomington: Indiana UP, 1986. 188–207.

Hyman, Stanley Edgar. "The Folk Tradition." *Partisan Review* 25.2 (Spring 1958): 197–211. Part I of "The Negro Writer: An Exchange."

Ibee [Jack Pulaski]. "Aunt Jemima." *Variety* 20 Oct. 1922: 18. Rpt. in *Selected Vaudeville Criticism*. Ed. Anthony Slide. Metuchen, NJ: Scarecrow, 1988. 2–3.

Ignatiev, Noel. *How the Irish Became White*. New York: Routledge, 1995.

Imitation of Life. Dir. John M. Stahl. Perf. Claudette Colbert, Louise Beavers, Rochelle Hudson, Fredi Washington, and Ned Sparks. Universal, 1934.

Imitation of Life. Dir. Douglas Sirk. Perf. Lana Turner, Juanita Moore, Sandra Dee, Susan Kohner, and John Gavin. Universal, 1959. Videocassette. Universal City, CA: MCA, 1985.

Jackson, Brian Keith. *The View from Here*. New York: Pocket-Simon, 1997.

Jackson, George. *Soledad Brother: The Prison Letters of George Jackson*. New York: Bantam, 1970.

Jackson, Ruth. *Ruth Jackson's Soulfood Cookbook*. Memphis: Wimmer, 1978.

Jarrett, Vernon. "Dick Gregory's Health Advocacy." *Chicago Tribune* 23 May 1973, final ed., sec. 1: 18.

———. "One Man's Debt to Dick Gregory." *Chicago Tribune* 28 Nov. 1973, final ed., sec. 1: 26.

Jeffries, Bob. *Soul Food Cookbook*. Indianapolis: Bobbs, 1969.

Jewell, K[aren] Sue [Warren]. "An Analysis of the Visual Development of a Stereotype: The Media's Portrayal of Mammy and Aunt Jemima as Symbols of Black Womanhood." Diss. Ohio State U, 1976.

———. *From Mammy to Miss America and Beyond: Cultural Images and the Shaping of US Social Policy*. New York: Routledge, 1993.

Johnson, Guion Griffis. *A Social History of the Sea Islands.* Chapel Hill: U of North Carolina P, 1930.

Johnson, Lil. "You'll Never Miss Your Jelly." *The Blues Line: A Collection of Blues Lyrics from Leadbelly to Muddy Waters.* Comp. Eric Sackheim. 1969. Hopewell, NJ: Ecco, 1993. 44.

Jones, Hettie. *How I Became Hettie Jones.* New York: Grove, 1990.

Jones, Jacqueline. *Labor of Love, Labor of Sorrow: Black Women, Work and the Family, from Slavery to the Present.* 1985. New York: Vintage-Random, 1986.

Jones, LeRoi. See Baraka, Amiri.

Jones, Robert. "A Place in the Suburbs." Rev. of *Linden Hills,* by Gloria Naylor. *Commonweal* 112 (3 May 1985): 283–85.

Jones-Jackson, Patricia. *When Roots Die: Endangered Traditions on the Sea Islands.* Athens: U of Georgia P, 1987.

Jordan, June. "Free Flight." *Passion: New Poems, 1977–1980.* Boston: Beacon, 1980. 55–59.

Joseph, Gloria. "The Incompatible Menage à Trois: Marxism, Feminism, and Racism." *Women and Revolution: A Discussion of the Unhappy Marriage of Marxism and Feminism.* Ed. Lydia Sargent. Boston: South End, 1981. 91–107.

Joyner, Charles. *Down by the Riverside: A South Carolina Slave Community.* Urbana: U of Illinois P, 1984.

———. Forward. *When Roots Die.* By Patricia Jones-Jackson. Athens: U of Georgia P, 1987. ix–xvii.

The Joy of Not Cooking. Washington, DC: Delights of the Garden, 1994.

Juice. Dir. Ernest R. Dickerson. Writ. Gerard Brown and Ernest R. Dickerson. Perf. Omar Epps, Jermaine Hopkins, Tupac Shakur, Khalil Kain, Cindy Herron, Vincent Laresca, and Samuel L. Jackson. Paramount-Island World, 1991. Videocassette. Hollywood, CA: Paramount, 1992.

Junior. Dir. Ivan Reitman. Writ. Kevin Wade. Perf. Arnold Schwarzenegger, Danny DeVito, Emma Thompson, Frank Langella, and Pamela Reed. Universal-Northern Lights, 1994. Videocassette. Universal City, CA: MCA Universal, 1995.

"Just Whose 'Malcolm' Is It, Anyway?" *New York Times* 31 May 1992, final late ed., sec. 2: 13+.

Kakutani, Michiko. "Dante in Suburbia." Rev. of *Linden Hills,* by Gloria Naylor. *New York Times* 9 Feb. 1985, late ed.: 14.

Kaplan, Cora. "'A Cavern Opened in My Mind': The Poetics of Homosexuality and the Politics of Masculinity in James Baldwin." *Representing Black Men.* Ed. Marcellus Blount and George P. Cunningham. New York: Routledge, 1996. 27–54.

Katzman, David M. *Seven Days a Week: Women and Domestic Service in Industrializing America.* 1978. Urbana: U of Illinois P, 1981.

Kelley, Robin D. G. "Looking B(l)ackward: African-American Studies in the Age of Identity Politics." Introduction. *Race Consciousness: African-American Studies for the New Century.* Ed. Judith Jackson Fossett and Jeffrey A. Tucker. New York: New York UP, 1997. 1–16.

Kempley, Rita. "Spike Lee's Epic on a Human Scale." Rev. of *Malcolm X,* dir. Spike Lee. *Washington Post* 18 Nov. 1992, final ed.: C1+.

Kern-Foxworth, Marilyn. "Aunt Jemima Is 100, but Looking Good." *Media History Digest* 9.2 (Fall–Winter 1989): 54–58.

———. "Aunt Jemima: Part I." *Black Ethnic Collectibles* Jan.–Feb. 1989: 18–19.

———. "Aunt Jemima: Part II." *Black Ethnic Collectibles* Mar.–Apr. 1989: 18–19+.

———. *Aunt Jemima, Uncle Ben, and Rastus: Blacks in Advertising, Yesterday, Today, and Tomorrow.* Westport, CT: Greenwood, 1994.

———. "Plantation Kitchen to American Icon: Aunt Jemima." *Public Relations Review* 16.3 (Fall 1990): 55–67.

Kerouac, Jack. *On the Road.* New York: Signet-NAL, 1957.

Key, Janet. "At Age 100, a New Aunt Jemima." *Chicago Tribune* 28 Apr. 1989, north ed., sec. 3: 1+.

King, Nicole R. "Cook/Book: A Bibliographic Study of African American Women Recipe Writers." Black Women's Texts and the Culture of Food Panel. MLA Convention. Hilton, San Francisco. 29 Dec. 1991.

Kipnis, Laura. "(Male) Desire and (Female) Disgust: Reading *Hustler.*" *Cultural Studies.* Ed. Lawrence Grossberg, Cary Nelson, and Paula Treichler. New York: Routledge, 1992. 373–91.

Kondo, Nia, and Zak Kondo. *Vegetarianism Made Simple and Easy: A Primer for Black People.* Washington, DC: Nubia, 1989.

Kristeva, Julia. *Powers of Horror: An Essay on Abjection.* 1980. Trans. Leon S. Roudiez. New York: Columbia UP, 1982.

Laclau, Ernesto, and Chantal Mouffe. *Hegemony and Socialist Strategy: Towards a Radical Democratic Politics.* London: Verso, 1985.

Ladd, Barbara. "'The Direction of the Howling': Nationalism and the Color Line in *Absalom, Absalom!*" *American Literature* 66.3 (Sept. 1994): 525–51.

Ladner, Joyce A. *Tomorrow's Tomorrow: The Black Woman.* 1971. Lincoln: U of Nebraska P, 1995.

Lambert, I. E. *The Public Accepts: Stories behind Famous Trade-Marks, Names and Slogans.* Albuquerque: U of New Mexico P, 1941.

Langhorne, Orra. "Domestic Service in the South." *Journal of Social Science* 39 (Nov. 1901): 169–75. Rpt. in *Southern Sketches from Virginia, 1881–1901.* Ed. Charles E. Wynes. Charlottesville: UP of Virginia, 1964. 108–12.

La Tham, Aris. *Sunfired Foods: Cookless Recipes by Aris La Tham.* Bethesda, MD: Sun, 1994.

Leach, Gerald. *The Biocrats.* New York: McGraw, 1970.

Lee, Don L. See Madhubuti, Haki R.

Lee, Jimmy [J. Lee Anderson]. *Soul Food Cookbook.* New York: Award, 1970.

Lee, Martha F. *The Nation of Islam: An American Millenarian Movement.* 1988. Syracuse: Syracuse UP, 1996.

Lee, Spike, and Ralph Wiley. *By Any Means Necessary: The Trials and Tribulations of the Making of Malcolm X . . . Including the Screenplay.* New York: Hyperion, 1992.

Leland, John, and Gregory Beals. "In Living Colors: Tiger Woods Is the Exception That Rules. For His Multiracial Generation, Hip Isn't Just Black and White." *Newsweek* 5 May 1997: 58–60.

Lemons, J. Stanley. "Black Stereotypes as Reflected in Popular Culture, 1880–1920." *American Quarterly* 29.1 (Spring 1977): 102–16.

Lenny. Dir. Bob Fosse. Writ. Julian Barry. Perf. Dustin Hoffman, Valerie Perrine, Jan Miner, and Stanley Beck. Marvin Worth, 1974. Videocassette. Culver City, CA: MGM/UA, 1989.

Leonardi, Susan J. "Recipes for Reading: Summer Pasta, Lobster à la Riseholme, and Key Lime Pie." *PMLA* 104.3 (May 1989): 340–47.

Levenstein, Harvey. *Revolution at the Table: The Transformation of the American Diet.* New York: Oxford UP, 1988.

Leverenz, David. *Manhood and the American Renaissance.* Ithaca: Cornell UP, 1989.

Levinson, Arlene. "Teach-Ins Mark Final Hours: Churches Hum in Prayer as Deadline Nears." *Richmond (Virginia) News Leader* 15 Jan. 1991: A2.

Lévi-Strauss, Claude. "The Culinary Triangle." Trans. Peter Brooks. *Partisan Review* 4 (Fall 1966): 586–95.

———. *The Raw and the Cooked: Introduction to a Science of Mythology.* 1964. Trans. John

Weightman and Doreen Weightman. Chicago: U of Chicago P, 1983. Vol. 1 of *Mythologiques*.

Lewis, Edna. *In Pursuit of Flavor.* New York: Borzoi-Knopf, 1988.

———. *The Taste of Country Cooking.* 1976. New York: Borzoi-Knopf, 1977.

Lewis, Edna, and Evangeline Peterson. *The Edna Lewis Cookbook.* 1972. New York: Ecco, 1983.

Lewis, Samella. *Art: African American.* Los Angeles: Hancraft, 1990.

Lincoln, C. Eric. *The Black Muslims in America.* 1961, 1973. 3rd ed. Grand Rapids, MI: William B. Eerdmans, 1994.

Lippard, Lucy R. *Mixed Blessings: New Art in a Multicultural America.* New York: Pantheon, 1990.

Lipsitch, Marc. "Genetic Tug-of-War May Explain Many of the Troubles of Pregnancy: Study Depicts Conflict between Fetus and the Pregnant Woman." *New York Times* 20 July 1993, final late ed.: C3.

Lomax, Louis E. *The Negro Revolt.* New York: Harper, 1962.

———. *When the Word Is Given . . . A Report on Elijah Muhammad, Malcolm X, and the Black Muslim World.* Cleveland: World, 1963.

Look Who's Talking. Dir. and writ. Amy Heckerling. Perf. John Travolta, Kirstie Alley, Olympia Dukakis, George Segal, and Abe Vigoda. Tri-Star, 1989. Videocassette: Burbank, CA: RCA/Columbia, 1990.

Lorde, Audre. *A Burst of Light.* Ithaca: Firebrand, 1988.

———. *Zami: A New Spelling of My Name.* Freedom, CA: Crossing, 1982.

Lott, Eric. *Love and Theft: Blackface Minstrelsy and the American Working Class.* New York: Oxford UP, 1993.

———. "'The Seeming Counterfeit': Racial Politics and Early Blackface Minstrelsy." *American Quarterly* 43.2 (June 1991): 223–54.

———. "White Like Me: Racial Cross-Dressing and the Construction of American Whiteness." *Cultures of United States Imperialism.* Ed. Amy Kaplan and Donald E. Pease. Durham: Duke UP, 1993. 474–95.

Lubiano, Wahneema. "'But Compared to What?': Reading Realism, Representation, and Essentialism in *Do the Right Thing, School Daze,* and the Spike Lee Discourse." *Black American Literature Forum* 25.2 (Summer 1991): 253–82.

Lyle, Willie E. "Old Aunt Jemima." *Willie E. Lyle's Great Georgia Minstrels Song Book.* De Witt's Song and Joke Book Series; no. 204. New York: De Witt, c. 1875. 20.

MacKinnon, Catherine A. *Feminism Unmodified: Discourses on Life and Law.* Cambridge: Harvard UP, 1987.

———. *Toward a Feminist Theory of the State.* Cambridge: Harvard UP, 1989.

Madgett, Naomi Long. "In Search of Aunt Jemima (Alias Big Mama)." *Exits and Entrances.* Detroit: Lotus, 1978. 35.

Madhubuti, Haki R. [Don L. Lee]. *Black Men: Obsolete, Single, Dangerous? The Afrikan American Family in Transition: Essays in Discovery, Solution and Hope.* Chicago: Third World, 1990.

———. "Re-Act for Action." 1969. *The Black Poets.* Ed. Dudley Randall. New York: Bantam, 1971. 296.

Mailer, Norman. "The White Negro." *Dissent* 4.3 (Summer 1957): 276–93.

Major, Clarence, ed. *Juba to Jive: A Dictionary of African-American Slang.* 1970. Rev. New York: Penguin, 1994.

Malcolm X. Dir. Spike Lee. Writ. Spike Lee, Arnold Perl, and James Baldwin. Perf. Denzel Washington, Angela Bassett, Albert Hall, Al Freeman Jr., and Delroy Lindo. Warner/40 Acres, 1992. Videocassette. Burbank, CA: Warner, 1993.

Manring, M. M. *Slave in a Box: The Strange Career of Aunt Jemima*. Charlottesville: UP of Virginia, 1998.

Marable, Manning. *Race, Reform, and Rebellion: The Second Reconstruction in Black America, 1945–1990*. Rev. ed. Jackson: UP of Mississippi, 1991.

Marcus, Steven. *The Other Victorians: A Study of Sexuality and Pornography in Mid-Nineteenth-Century England*. New York: Basic, 1966.

Marquette, Arthur F. *Brands, Trademarks and Good Will: The Story of the Quaker Oats Company*. New York: McGraw, 1967.

Marriott, Michel. "Black Women Are Split over All-Male March on Washington." *New York Times* 14 Oct. 1995, final late ed., sec. 1: 8.

Martin, Emily. *The Woman in the Body: A Cultural Analysis of Reproduction*. Boston: Beacon, 1987.

Marx, Karl. *Capital: A Critique of Political Economy*. Vol. 1. 1867. Trans. Ben Fowkes. 1976. New York: Vintage-Random, 1977.

Maslin, Janet. "An Anniversary Tribute to the Million Man March." Rev. of *Get on the Bus*, dir. Spike Lee. *New York Times* 16 Oct. 1996, final late ed.: C11.

Masson, Jeffrey Moussaieff. *The Assault on Truth: Freud's Suppression of the Seduction Theory*. New York: Farrar, 1984.

Matthews, Glenna. *"Just a Housewife": The Rise and Fall of Domesticity in America*. New York: Oxford UP, 1987.

Mayer, Caroline E. "'A Real Gift for Cooking': Viola Lampkin's Thanksgiving Traditions." *Washington Post* 15 Nov. 1989, final ed: E1+.

Mayfield, Julian. "You Touch My Black Aesthetic and I'll Touch Yours." 1971. *The Black Aesthetic*. Ed. Addison Gayle Jr. Garden City, NY: Anchor-Doubleday, 1972. 23–30.

McClintock, Anne. *Imperial Leather: Race, Gender and Sexuality in the Colonial Contest*. New York: Routledge, 1995.

McDowell, Deborah E. "Boundaries: Or Distant Relations and Close Kin—*Sula*." 1988. Exp. and rpt. in *"The Changing Same": Black Women's Literature, Criticism, and Theory*. Bloomington: Indiana UP, 1995. 101–17.

———. *"The Changing Same": Black Women's Literature, Criticism, and Theory*. Bloomington: Indiana UP, 1995.

———. "'The Changing Same': Generational Connections and Black Women Novelists—*Iola Leroy* and *The Color Purple*." 1984. Exp. and rpt. in *"The Changing Same": Black Women's Literature, Criticism, and Theory*. Bloomington: Indiana UP, 1995. 34–57.

———. Introduction. *Quicksand and Passing*. By Nella Larsen. New Brunswick: Rutgers UP, 1986. ix–xxxv.

———. "Reading Family Matters." *Changing Our Own Words: Essays on Criticism, Theory, and Writing by Black Women*. Ed. Cheryl A. Wall. New Brunswick: Rutgers UP, 1989. 75–97+.

McKinney, Emma and William. *Aunt Caroline's Dixieland Recipes*. Chicago: Laird, 1922.

Mellencamp, Patricia. "Haunted History: Tracey Moffatt and Julie Dash." *Discourse: Theoretical Studies in Media and Culture* 16.2 (Winter 1993–94): 127–63.

Menace II Society. Dir. Allen Hughes and Albert Hughes. Writ. Tyger Williams. Perf. Tyrin Turner, Larenz Tate, Samuel L. Jackson, Glenn Plummer, and Julian Roy Doster. New Line, 1993. Videocassette. New York: New Line, 1993.

Mercer, Kobena. "'1968': Periodizing Postmodern Politics and Identity." *Cultural Studies*. Ed. Lawrence Grossberg, Cary Nelson, and Paula Treichler. New York: Routledge, 1992. 424–49.

———. "Reading Racial Fetishism: The Photographs of Robert Mapplethorpe." 1986, 1989. *Welcome to the Jungle*. New York: Routledge, 1994. 171–219.

Michaels, Walter Benn. "The Souls of White Folk." *Literature and the Body: Essays on Populations and Persons.* Ed. Elaine Scarry. Baltimore: Johns Hopkins UP, 1988. 185–209.

Miller, Bryan. "12-Chef Farewell Meal for Claiborne." *New York Times* 20 May 1988, late ed.: C20.

Miller, D. A. "Anal Rope." *Representations* 32 (Fall 1990): 114–33.

Miller, Jerome G. *Search and Destroy: African-American Males in the Criminal Justice System.* Cambridge: Cambridge UP, 1996.

Miracle on 34th Street. Dir. and writ. George Seaton. Perf. Edmund Gwenn, Maureen O'Hara, John Payne, and Natalie Wood. Fox, 1947. Videocassette. Livonia, MI: Playhouse, 1987.

Miracle on 34th Street. Dir. Les Mayfield. Writ. John Hughes and George Seaton. Perf. Richard Attenborough, Elizabeth Perkins, Dylan McDermott, and Mara Wilson. Fox, 1994. Videocassette. Los Angeles: Fox, 1994.

Modleski, Tania. "Feminism and the Power of Interpretation: Some Critical Readings." *Feminist Studies/Critical Studies.* Ed. Teresa de Lauretis. Bloomington: Indiana UP, 1986. 121–38.

———. *Feminism without Women: Culture and Criticism in a "Postfeminist" Age.* New York: Routledge, 1991.

Mohanty, Chandra Talpade. "Cartographies of Struggle: Third World Women and the Politics of Feminism." Introduction. *Third World Women and the Politics of Feminism.* Ed. Chandra Talpade Mohanty, Ann Russo, and Lourdes Torres. Bloomington: Indiana UP, 1991. 1–47.

———. "Under Western Eyes: Feminist Scholarship and Colonial Discourses." *Third World Women and the Politics of Feminism.* Ed. Chandra Talpade Mohanty, Ann Russo, and Lourdes Torres. Bloomington: Indiana UP, 1991. 51–80.

Morgan, Hal. *Symbols of America.* New York: Steam-Viking, 1986.

Morrison, Toni. *Beloved.* 1987. New York: Plume-Penguin, 1988.

———. *The Bluest Eye.* 1970. New York: Plume-Penguin, 1994.

———. *Playing in the Dark: Whiteness and the Literary Imagination.* Cambridge: Harvard UP, 1992.

———. *Song of Solomon.* 1977. New York: Signet-NAL, 1978.

———. *Sula.* 1973. New York: Plume-Penguin, 1982.

———. *Tar Baby.* New York: Signet-NAL, 1981.

———. "What the Black Woman Thinks about Women's Lib." *New York Times Magazine* 22 Aug. 1971: 14–15+.

Morton, Patricia. *Disfigured Images: The Historical Assault on African-American Women.* New York: Praeger, 1991.

"Movie Maids: Eight New Hollywood Films Backtrack to Hack Racial Stereotypes in Casting Negro Actors as Usual Maids and Menials." *Ebony* Aug. 1948: 56–59.

Moynihan, Daniel P. *The Negro Family: The Case for National Action* ["The Moynihan Report"]. 1965. *Black Matriarchy: Myth or Reality?* Ed. John H. Bracey Jr., August Meier, and Elliott Rudwick. Belmont, CA: Wadsworth, 1971. 126–59.

Muhammad, Elijah. *How to Eat to Live.* Chicago: Muhammad Mosque of Islam No. 2, 1967.

———. *How to Eat to Live.* Book No. 2. Chicago: Muhammad's Temple of Islam No. 2, 1972.

———. *Message to the Blackman in America.* Chicago: Muhammad Mosque of Islam No. 2, 1965.

———. "The Truth about Pork (The Pig)." *Muhammad Speaks* Oct./Nov. 1961: 5.

Munson, Bessie. *Bless the Cook.* 1978. 2nd ed. Arlington, TX: Arlington Century, 1980.

Nash, Jonell. "Today's New Black Cookstyle: Our Cookery Keeps Up with Today's Health Movement." *Essence* May 1985: 166–67.

National Council of Negro Women. *The Black Family Reunion Cookbook: Recipes and Food Memories.* 1991. New York: Fireside-Simon, 1993.

Naylor, Gloria. *Bailey's Cafe.* 1992. New York: Vintage-Random, 1993.

———. *Linden Hills.* 1985. Viking-Penguin, 1986.

Naylor, Gloria, and Toni Morrison. "A Conversation." *Southern Review* 21.3 (July 1985): 567–93.

Neal, Larry. "Some Reflections on the Black Aesthetic." 1970. *The Black Aesthetic.* Ed. Addison Gayle Jr. 1971. New York: Anchor-Doubleday, 1972. 12–15.

"'Negro Day' at Fair Flops: Parade Is Worst in History of City." *Chicago Defender* 19 Aug. 1933, natl. ed., sec. 1: 2.

New Jack City. Dir. Mario Van Peebles. Writ. Keith Critchlow and Barry Michael Cooper. Perf. Wesley Snipes, Ice-T, Mario Van Peebles, Chris Rock, and Judd Nelson. Warner, 1991. Videocassette. Burback, CA: Warner, 1991.

Nilsson, Lennart, and A. Rosenfeld. "Drama of Life before Birth." *Life* 30 Apr. 1965: 54–72A.

Nochlin, Linda. "Why Have There Been No Great Women Artists?" 1971. *Women, Art, and Power and Other Essays.* New York: Harper, 1988. 145–78.

The Nutty Professor. Dir. Jerry Lewis. Writ. Jerry Lewis and Bill Richmond. Perf. Jerry Lewis, Stella Stevens, Howard Morris, and Kathleen Freeman. Paramount, 1963. Videocassette. Hollywood, CA: Paramount, 1996.

The Nutty Professor. Dir. Tom Shadyac. Perf. Eddie Murphy, Jada Pinkett, John Ales, and James Coburn. Universal, 1996. Videocassette. Universal City, CA: MCA, 1996.

Odell, George C. D. *Annals of the New York Stage.* 15 vols. New York: Columbia UP, 1927–49. Vol. 11 (1879–1882), 1939. Vol. 13 (1885–1888), 1942.

Oliver, Kelly. "Nourishing the Speaking Subject: A Psychoanalytic Approach to Abominable Food and Women." *Cooking, Eating, Thinking: Transformative Philosophies of Food.* Ed. Deane W. Curtin and Lisa M. Heldke. Bloomington: Indiana UP, 1992. 68–84.

———. *Reading Kristeva: Unraveling the Double-Bind.* Bloomington: Indiana UP, 1993.

One Million Strong: The Album. Prod. John Atterberry, Jimmy Thomas, and Jalal Farrakhan. Hollywood, CA: Mergela, 1995.

Orbach, Susie. *Fat Is a Feminist Issue: The Anti-Diet Guide to Permanent Weight Loss.* 1978. New York: Berkley-Paddington, 1979.

Original Gangstas. Dir. Larry Cohen. Writ. Audrey Rattan. Perf. Fred Williamson, Jim Brown, Pam Grier, Paul Winfield, Isabel Sanford, and Richard Roundtree. Orion, 1996. Videocassette. Los Angeles: Orion, 1996.

Ortner, Sherry B. "Is Female to Male as Nature Is to Culture?" *Woman, Culture, and Society.* Ed. Michelle Zimbalist Rosaldo and Louise Lamphere. Stanford: Stanford UP, 1974. 67–87.

Ott, Eleanore. *Plantation Cookery of Old Louisiana.* New Orleans: Harmanson, 1938.

Palmer, Phyllis. *Domesticity and Dirt: Housewives and Domestic Servants in the United States, 1920–1945.* Philadelphia: Temple UP, 1989.

Pantovic, Stan. "Black Antiques Reveal History of Stereotypes." *Sepia* 23.7 (July 1974): 44–48.

Patterson, Betty Benton. *Mammy Lou's Cook Book.* New York: McBride, 1931.

Patterson, James T. *Grand Expectations: The United States, 1945–1974.* New York: Oxford UP, 1996.

Patton, Cindy. "Tremble, Hetero Swine!" *Fear of a Queer Planet: Queer Politics and Social Theory.* Ed. Michael Warner. Minneapolis: U of Minnesota P, 1993. 143–77.

Patton, Phil. "Mammy: Her Life and Times." *American Heritage* Sept. 1993: 78–87.

Pearson, Hugh. *The Shadow of the Panther: Huey Newton and the Price of Black Power in America*. Reading, MA: Addison, 1994.

Pener, Degen. "Egos and Ids: Dick Gregory Is Back." *New York Times* 6 June 1993, late ed., sec. 9: 4.

Penley, Constance. "Time Travel, Primal Scene, Critical Dystopia." 1986. *Close Encounters: Film, Feminism, and Science Fiction*. Ed. Constance Penley, Elisabeth Lyon, Lynn Spigel, and Janet Bergstrom. Minneapolis: U of Minnesota P, 1991. 63–80.

Perry, Bruce. *Malcolm: The Life of a Man Who Changed Black America*. Barrytown, NY: Station Hill, 1991.

Petchesky, Rosalind Pollack. *Abortion and Woman's Choice: The State, Sexuality, and Reproductive Freedom*. 1984. Rev. ed. Boston: Northeastern UP, 1990.

Petersen, Clarence. "Gregory: No Lightweight He." *Chicago Tribune* 5 May 1972, final ed., sec. 2: 1.

Phelan, Peggy. *Unmarked: The Politics of Performance*. New York: Routledge, 1993.

"Philanthropic Food Factories: Cheery and Sanitary Conditions Surrounding the Production of Our Food Supply. A Notable Phase of Progress." *Good Housekeeping* 53 (July–Dec. 1911): 553–60.

Pierce, Charles P. "The Man. Amen." *Gentleman's Quarterly* Apr. 1997: 196–203+.

Pierson, William D. *Black Legacy: America's Hidden Heritage*. Amherst: U of Massachusetts P, 1993.

Pioneer Natural Health Restaurant. "Pioneer Natural Health Restaurant." Advertisement. *Muhammad Speaks* Dec. 1961: 31.

Polite, Carlene Hatcher. *The Flagellants*. 1966. Trans. Pierre Alien. New York: Farrar, 1967.

Pollitt, Katha. "'Fetal Rights': A New Assault on Feminism." *Nation* 26 Mar. 1990: 409–18.

Poovey, Mary. "The Abortion Question and the Death of Man." *Feminists Theorize the Political*. Ed. Judith Butler and Joan Scott. New York: Routledge, 1992. 239–56.

Powers, Retha. "Fat Is a Black Woman's Issue." *Essence* Oct. 1989: 75+.

Prettyman, Quandra. "Come Eat at My Table: Lives with Recipes." *Southern Quarterly* 30.2–3 (Winter–Spring 1992): 131–40.

Princess Pamela. *Soul Food Cookbook*. New York: Signet-NAL, 1969.

Public Enemy. *Fear of a Black Planet*. Prod. Hank Shocklee, Carl Ryder, Eric (Vietnam) Sadler, and Keith Shocklee. New York: CBS Records-Columbia, 1990.

Raloff, Janet. "Mom's Fatty Diet May Induce Child's Cancer." *Science News* 6 Jan. 1990: 5.

Rampersad, Arnold. *I Dream a World, 1941–1967*. New York: Oxford UP, 1988. Vol. 2 of *The Life of Langston Hughes*.

———. *I, Too, Sing America, 1902–1941*. New York: Oxford UP, 1986. Vol. 1 of *The Life of Langston Hughes*.

Raven, Arlene. "Feminist Rituals of Re-Membered History: Lisa Jones, Kaylynn Sullivan, Joyce Scott." *Women and Performance: A Journal of Feminist Theory* 4.1 (1988–89): 23–42.

Reed, Adolph. "The Liberal Technocrat." Rev. of *The Truly Disadvantaged*, by William Julius Wilson. *Nation* 6 Feb. 1988: 167–70.

Reed, Ishmael. *Mumbo Jumbo*. 1972. New York: Scribner-Simon, 1996.

Reid-Pharr, Robert "It's Raining Men: Notes on the Million Man March." *Transition* 6.1 (Spring 1996): 36–49.

Reno, Dawn E. *Collecting Black Americana*. New York: Crown, 1986.

———. "Familiar Faces in Advertising: Aunt Jemima and Rastus, the Cream of Wheat Man." *The Antique Trader Weekly* 22 July 1992: 68–69.

Rhode, Deborah L. *Justice and Gender: Sex Discrimination and the Law*. Cambridge: Harvard UP, 1989.

Rich, Adrienne. "Compulsory Heterosexuality and Lesbian Existence." *Signs: Journal of Women in Culture and Society* 5.4 (Summer 1980): 631–60.

Rifkin, Jeremy. *Beyond Beef: The Rise and Fall of the Cattle Culture*. New York: Dutton-Penguin, 1992.

Roberts, Diane. *The Myth of Aunt Jemima: Representations of Race and Region*. New York: Routledge, 1994.

Roberts, Dorothy E. "Punishing Drug Addicts Who Have Babies: Women of Color, Equality, and the Right of Privacy." *Harvard Law Review* 104.7 (May 1991): 1419–82.

———. "Reconstructing the Patient: Starting with Women of Color." *Feminism and Bioethics: Beyond Reproduction*. Ed. Susan M. Wolf. New York: Oxford UP, 1996. 116–43.

Robinson, Amy. "It Takes One to Know One: Passing and Communities of Common Interest." *Critical Inquiry* 20.4 (Summer 1994): 715–36.

Robinson, Dorothy. "What I'm Talkin' 'bout Is Roots." Rev. of *The Black Book*, by Middleton Harris, et al. *Ms.* (June 1974): 40–41.

Roediger, David. *The Wages of Whiteness: Race and the Making of the American Working Class*. London: Verso, 1991.

Rogin, Michael. *Blackface, White Noise: Jewish Immigrants in the Hollywood Melting Pot*. Berkeley: U of California P, 1996.

Rollins, Judith. *Between Women: Domestics and Their Employers*. Philadelphia: Temple UP, 1985.

Root, Waverley, and Richard de Rochemont. *Eating in America: A History*. 1976. New York: Ecco, 1981.

Rosaforte, Tim. *Tiger Woods: The Makings of a Champion*. New York: St. Martin's, 1997.

Rose, Tricia. *Black Noise: Rap Music and Black Culture in Contemporary America*. Hanover, NH: UP of New England, 1994.

Ross, Andrew. *No Respect: Intellectuals and Popular Culture*. New York: Routledge, 1989.

Roudiez, Leon S. Translator's Note. *Powers of Horror*. By Julia Kristeva. 1980. New York: Columbia UP, 1982. vii–x.

Rowland, Robyn. *Living Laboratories: Women and Reproductive Technologies*. Bloomington: Indiana UP, 1992.

Rubin, Gayle. "The Traffic in Women: Notes on the 'Political Economy' of Sex." 1976. *Women, Class, and the Feminist Imagination: A Socialist-Feminist Reader*. Ed. Karen V. Hansen and Ilene J. Philipson. Philadelphia: Temple UP, 1990. 74–113.

Rushin, Donna Kate. "The Black Back-Ups." *Home Girls: A Black Feminist Anthology*. Ed. Barbara Smith. New York: Kitchen Table, 1983. 60–63.

Russell, Sandi. *Render Me My Song: African-American Women Writers from Slavery to the Present*. New York: St. Martin's, 1990.

Russo, Mary. *The Female Grotesque: Risk, Excess and Modernity*. New York: Routledge, 1994.

Rydell, Robert W. *All the World's a Fair: Visions of Empire at American International Expositions, 1876–1916*. Chicago: U of Chicago P, 1984.

Sabbah, Fatna A. *Woman in the Muslim Unconscious*. 1982. Trans. Mary Jo Lakeland. New York: Pergamon, 1984.

Sacharow, Stanley. *Symbols of Trade: Your Favorite Trademarks and the Companies They Represent*. New York: Art Direction, 1982.

Said, Edward W. "An Ideology of Difference." 1985. *"Race," Writing, and Difference*. Ed. Henry Louis Gates Jr. Chicago: U of Chicago P, 1986. 38–58.

———. *Orientalism*. 1978. New York: Vintage-Random, 1979.

Sales, Grover. "Dagos and Niggers and Kikes Oh My." Reply to Richard Lingeman's rev. of

The Official Politically Correct Dictionary and Handbook, by Henry Beard and Christopher Cerf. *Nation* 7 Dec. 1992: 686.

Sampson, Emma Speed. *Miss Minerva's Cook Book: De Way to a Man's Heart.* Chicago: Reilly, 1931.

Sanders, Dori. *Clover.* Chapel Hill: Algonquin, 1990.

Sandiford, K. A. "Gothic and Intertextual Constructions in *Linden Hills.*" *Arizona Quarterly* 47.3 (Autumn 1991): 117–39.

Schomburg, Arthur A. Untitled typescript. [Proposal for a history of African American cooking.] Arthur A. Schomburg Papers, Activities, and Writings. Folder 7, Box 12. SC Micro 2798, Reel 7. New York Public Library's Schomburg Center for Research in Black Culture, [c. 1920s?].

Schwartz, Hillel. *Never Satisfied: A Cultural History of Diets, Fantasies and Fat.* New York: Anchor-Doubleday, 1986.

Scott, Daryl Michael. *Contempt and Pity: Social Policy and the Image of the Damaged Black Psyche, 1880–1996.* Chapel Hill: U of North Carolina P, 1997.

Scott, Natalie V. *'Mirations and Miracles of Mandy: Some Favorite Louisiana Recipes.* New Orleans: True, 1929.

Scott, Patricia Bell. "Debunking Sapphire: Toward a Non-Racist and Non-Sexist Social Science." *But Some of Us Are Brave: Black Women's Studies.* Ed. Gloria T. Hull, Patricia Bell Scott, and Barbara Smith. New York: Feminist, 1982. 85–98.

Seale, Bobby. *Barbeque'n with Bobby: Righteous, Down-Home Barbeque Recipes by Bobby Seale.* Berkeley: Ten Speed, 1988.

———. *Seize the Time: The Story of the Black Panther Party and Huey P. Newton.* New York: Random, 1970.

Sedgwick, Eve. *Between Men: English Literature and Male Homosocial Desire.* New York: Columbia UP, 1985.

———. "Epidemics of the Will." 1992. *Tendencies.* Durham: Duke UP, 1993. 130–42.

———. *Epistemology of the Closet.* Berkeley: U of California P, 1990.

Shabazz, Lana. *Cooking for the Champ: Muhammad Ali's Favorite Recipes.* New York: Jones-McMillon, 1979.

Shange, Ntozake. *From Okra to Greens.* St. Paul, MN: Coffee House, 1984.

———. *Sassafrass, Cypress & Indigo.* New York: St. Martin's, 1982.

Shapiro, Laura. *Perfection Salad: Women and Cooking at the Turn of the Century.* New York: Farrar, 1986.

Sheraton, Mimi. "Cookbooks." Rev. of *English Bread and Yeast Cookery,* by Elizabeth David; *The Breads of France,* by Bernard Clayton Jr.; *More Classic Italian Cooking,* by Marcella Hazan; *Julia Child and Company,* by Julia Child; *Recipes from the Regional Cooks of Mexico,* by Diana Kennedy; *Spoonbread and Strawberry Wine,* by Norma Jean Darden and Carole Darden; and *Entertaining,* by Robert Carrier. *New York Times Book Review* 3 Dec. 1978: 14+.

Shockley, Ann Allen. "The Black Lesbian in American Literature: An Overview." 1979. *Home Girls: A Black Feminist Anthology.* Ed. Barbara Smith. New York: Kitchen Table, 1983. 83–93.

———. *Loving Her.* 1974. Tallahassee: Naiad, 1987.

Silberman, Charles E. *Crisis in Black and White.* New York: Random, 1964.

Sims-Wood, Janet. "The Black Female: Mammy, Jemima, Sapphire, and Other Images." *Images of Blacks in American Culture: A Reference Guide to Information Sources.* Ed. Jesse Carney Smith. Westport, CT: Greenwood, 1988. 235–56.

Sitkoff, Harvard. *The Struggle for Black Equality, 1954–1992.* 1981. Rev. ed. New York: Hill and Wang, 1993.

Slide, Anthony. *The Encyclopedia of Vaudeville.* Westport, CT: Greenwood, 1994.

———. *The Vaudevillians: A Dictionary of Vaudeville Performers.* Westport, CT: Arlington, 1981.

Smart-Grosvenor, Vertamae. See Grosvenor, Vertamae Smart.

Smith, Bessie. "Gimme a Pigfoot." *Bessie Smith: The Collection.* New York: CBS/Columbia, 1989.

Smith, Gary. "The Chosen One." *Sports Illustrated* 23 Dec. 1996: 28–53.

Smith, Kyle. "Double Trouble: A Pickup Turns into a Drag for Eddie Murphy." *People Weekly* 19 May 1997: 93–96.

Smith, Mary Stuart. *Virginia Cookery-Book.* New York: Harper, 1885.

Smith, Valerie. "Black Feminist Theory and the Representation of the 'Other.'" *Changing Our Own Words: Essays on Criticism, Theory, and Writing by Black Women.* Ed. Cheryl A. Wall. New Brunswick: Rutgers UP, 1989. 38–57+.

Smith, Welton. "The Nigga Section." 1968. *The Black Poets.* Ed. Dudley Randall. New York: Bantam, 1971. 282–83.

Snyder, Robert W. *The Voice of the City: Vaudeville and Popular Culture in New York.* New York: Oxford UP, 1989.

Sobel, Bernard. *A Pictorial History of Vaudeville.* New York: Citadel, 1961.

Solinger, Rickie. *Wake Up Little Susie: Single Pregnancy and Race before Roe v. Wade.* New York: Routledge, 1992.

"Soul Food!" *Good Housekeeping* July 1970: 110–16.

"Soul Food: Vegetarian Style." *Essence* Aug. 1979: 112–13.

Soul Vegetarian Cookbook. Soul Vegetarian Cafe and Exodus Carryout. Washington, DC: Communicators, 1992.

Spillers, Hortense J. "'All the Things You Could Be by Now If Sigmund Freud's Wife Was Your Mother': Psychoanalysis and Race." *Critical Inquiry* 22.4 (Summer 1996): 710–34.

———. "Mama's Baby, Papa's Maybe: An American Grammar Book." *Diacritics* 17.2 (Summer 1987): 65–81.

———. "'The Permanent Obliquity of an In(pha)llibly Straight': In the Time of the Daughters and the Fathers." *Changing Our Own Words: Essays on Criticism, Theory, and Writing by Black Women.* Ed. Cheryl A. Wall. New Brunswick: Rutgers UP, 1989. 127–49+.

———. "The Politics of Intimacy: A Discussion." *Sturdy Black Bridges: Visions of Black Women in Literature.* Ed. Roseann P. Bell, Bettye J. Parker, and Beverly Guy-Sheftall. Garden City, NY: Anchor-Doubleday, 1979. 87–106.

Spivak, Gayatri Chakravorty. "Can the Subaltern Speak?" *Marxism and the Interpretation of Culture.* Ed. Cary Nelson and Lawrence Grossberg. Urbana: U of Illinois P, 1988. 271–313.

Stafford, Joseph. *The Black Gourmet: Favorite Afro-American and Creole Recipes from Coast to Coast.* 1984. Rev. ed. Detroit: Harlo, 1988.

Stallybrass, Peter, and Allon White. *The Politics and Poetics of Transgression.* Ithaca: Cornell UP, 1986.

Stange, Margit. "The Broken Self: Fetal Alcohol Syndrome and Native American Selfhood." *Body Politics: Disease, Desire, and the Family.* Ed. Michael Ryan and Avery Gordon. Boulder, CO: Westview, 1994. 126–36.

Staples, Robert. "The Political Economy of Black Family Life." 1986. *The Black Family: Essays and Studies.* Ed. Robert Staples. 4th ed. Belmont, CA: Wadsworth, 1991. 248–56.

———, ed. *The Black Family: Essays and Studies.* 1971. 4th ed. Belmont, CA: Wadsworth, 1991.

Starr, Kathy. *The Soul of Southern Cooking.* Jackson: UP of Mississippi, 1989.

Stewart-Baxter, Derrick. *Ma Rainey and the Classic Blues Singers*. New York: Stein, 1970.

Stoddard, Lothrop. *The Rising Tide of Color against White World-Supremacy*. New York: Scribner's, 1920.

Stowe, Harriet Beecher. *Uncle Tom's Cabin, or, Life among the Lowly*. Boston: Jewett, 1852.

Straight out of Brooklyn. Dir. and writ. Matty Rich. Perf. George T. Odis, Ann D. Sanders, Lawrence Gilliard, Mark Malone Jr., Reana E. Drummond, and Barbara Sanon. Samuel Goldwyn-American Playhouse, 1991. Videocassette. New York: HBO, 1991.

Strasser, Susan. *Satisfaction Guaranteed: The Making of the American Mass Market*. New York: Pantheon, 1989.

"Study Finds Racial Disparity in Warnings to the Pregnant." *New York Times* 20 Jan. 1994, final late ed.: A16.

Sugarman, Carole. "Fruitful and Multiplying: African-American Vegetarians Serve Up Good-for-the-Soul Food." *Washington Post* 18 May 1994, final ed.: E1+.

Sundquist, Eric J., ed. *Cultural Contexts for Ralph Ellison's* Invisible Man. Boston: Bedford-St. Martin's, 1995.

Sweet Sweetback's Baadasssss Song. Dir., writ., and prod. Melvin Van Peebles. Perf. Melvin Van Peebles, Rhetta Hughes, Simon Chuckster, and John Amos. 1971. Videocassette. Demarest, NJ: Sun, n.d.

Takaki, Ronald. *A Different Mirror: A History of Multicultural America*. Boston: Little, 1993.

Talley, Thomas W. *Negro Folk Rhymes: Wise and Otherwise*. New York: Macmillan, 1922. Exp. and rpt. as *Thomas W. Talley's Negro Folk Rhymes*. Ed. Charles K. Wolfe. Knoxville: U of Tennessee P, 1991.

Tate, Claudia. *Domestic Allegories of Political Desire: The Black Heroine's Text at the Turn of the Century*. New York: Oxford UP, 1992.

Tate, Greg. "Can This Be the End for Cyclops and Professor X?" *Village Voice* 10 Nov. 1992: 41–43.

Tate, Sonsyrea. *Little X: Growing Up in the Nation of Islam*. New York: HarperSanFrancisco, 1997.

Taylor, Clyde. "One in a Million." *Black Renaissance/Renaissance Noire* 1.1 (Fall 1996): 83–101.

Thomas, Kendall. "'Ain't Nothin' Like the Real Thing': Black Masculinity, Gay Sexuality, and the Jargon of Authenticity." *Representing Black Men*. Ed. Marcellus Blount and George P. Cunningham. New York: Routledge, 1996. 55–69.

Thompson, Becky W. *A Hunger So Wide and So Deep: American Women Speak Out on Eating Problems*. Minneapolis: U of Minnesota P, 1994.

Thornton, Harrison John. *The History of the Quaker Oats Company*. Chicago: U of Chicago P, 1933.

"3 Intoxicated Drivers Given Bridewell Term." *Chicago Daily Tribune* 31 Aug. 1923, final ed.: 10.

Tillman, Katherine [Davis Chapman]. "Cookery Jingles." *The Federation Cookbook: A Collection of Tested Recipes, Contributed by the Colored Women of the State of California*. Comp. Bertha Turner. Pasadena, CA: n.p., 1910. N. pag.

———. *The Works of Katherine Davis Chapman Tillman*. Ed. Claudia Tate. New York: Oxford UP, 1991.

Toklas, Alice B. *The Alice B. Toklas Cook Book*. New York: Harper, 1954.

Toll, Robert. *Blacking Up: The Minstrel Show in Nineteenth-Century America*. New York: Oxford UP, 1974.

Toombs, Charles P. "The Confluence of Food and Identity in Gloria Naylor's *Linden Hills*: 'What We Eat Is Who We Is.'" *College Language Association Journal* 37.1 (Sept. 1993): 1–18.

Torgovnick, Marianna. *Gone Primitive: Savage Intellects, Modern Lives*. Chicago: U of Chicago P, 1990.

Tradition and Conflict: Images of a Turbulent Decade, 1963–1973. New York: Studio Museum in Harlem, 1985.

Tresniowski, Alex. "Rising Son." *People Weekly* 16 June 1997: 96–102.

Trillin, Calvin. *American Fried: Adventures of a Happy Eater*. Garden City, NY: Doubleday, 1974.

Tucker, Susan. *Telling Memories among Southern Women: Domestic Workers and Their Employers in the Segregated South*. New York: Schocken, 1988.

Turner, Bertha, comp. *The Federation Cookbook: A Collection of Tested Recipes, Contributed by the Colored Women of the State of California*. Pasadena: n.p., 1910.

Turner, Graeme. *British Cultural Studies: An Introduction*. 1990. New York: Routledge, 1992.

Turner, Patricia A. *Ceramic Uncles and Celluloid Mammies: Black Images and Their Influence on Culture*. New York: Anchor-Doubleday, 1994.

Twining, Mary A., and Keith E. Baird. "The Significance of Sea Island Culture." Preface. *Journal of Black Studies* 10.4 (June 1980): 379–86.

———, eds. "Sea Island Culture." Special Issue. *Journal of Black Studies* 10.4 (June 1980): 379–492.

"200 Years of 'Makin' Do.'" *Ebony* Aug. 1975: 152–56.

Tyree, Marion Cabell. *Housekeeping in Old Virginia*. Louisville: Morton, 1879. Rpt. Louisville, KY: Favorite Recipes, 1965.

Upchurch, Carl. *Convicted in the Womb: One Man's Journey from Prisoner to Peacemaker*. New York: Bantam, 1996.

Van Deburg, William L. *New Day in Babylon: The Black Power Movement and American Culture, 1965–1975*. Chicago: U of Chicago P, 1992.

Verzemnieks, Inara. "No Belly Laughs from a Big Audience." *Washington Post* 20 July 1996, final ed.: B1.

Vogel, Lise. *Marxism and the Oppression of Women: Toward a Unitary Theory*. New Brunswick: Rutgers UP, 1983.

Waddles, Charleszetta. *Mother Waddles Soulfood Cookbook*. 3rd ed. Detroit: Mother Waddles Perpetual Mission, 1976.

Waldrep, Shelton. "'Being Bridges': Cleaver/Baldwin/Lorde and African-American Sexism and Sexuality." *Critical Essays: Gay and Lesbian Writers of Color*. Ed. Emmanuel S. Nelson. New York: Harrington Park, 1993. 167–80.

Waldron, Clarence. "Gladys Knight Records New Album and Tells Why She Doesn't Try to Compete with Today's Young Singers." *Jet* 7 Nov. 1994: 56–59.

Walker, Alice. *The Color Purple*. NY: Pocket-Simon, 1982.

———. "Giving the Party: Aunt Jemima, Mammy, and the Goddess Within." *Ms*. May–June 1994: 22–25.

———. "In Search of Our Mothers' Gardens." 1974. *In Search of Our Mothers' Gardens: Womanist Prose*. New York: Harcourt, 1983. 231–43.

———. *Meridian*. 1976. New York: Pocket-Simon, 1986.

———. "Olive Oil." *Ms*. Aug. 1985: 35–36+.

Wallace, Michele. *Black Macho and the Myth of the Superwoman*. 1979. London: Verso, 1990.

———. "*Boyz N the Hood* and *Jungle Fever*." *Black Popular Culture*. Ed. Gina Dent. A Michele Wallace project. Seattle: Bay, 1992. 123–31.

Ward, Catherine C. "Gloria Naylor's *Linden Hills*: A Modern *Inferno*." *Contemporary Literature* 28.1 (Spring 1987): 67–81.

Ware, Vron. *Beyond the Pale: White Women, Racism and History*. London: Verso, 1992.

Warner, Michael, ed. *Fear of a Queer Planet: Queer Politics and Social Theory*. Minneapolis: U of Minnesota P, 1993.

Watermelon Man. Dir. Melvin Van Peebles. Perf. Godfrey Cambridge, Estelle Parsons, Erin Moran, and Howard Caine. Columbia, 1970. Videocassette. Chicago: Facets, n.d.

Watkins, Mel. "The Circular Driveways of Hell." Rev. of *Linden Hills*, by Gloria Naylor. *New York Times Book Review* 3 Mar. 1985: 11.

———. "The Lyrics of James Brown: Ain't It Funky Now, or Money Won't Change Your Licking Stick." *Amistad 2*. Ed. John A. Williams and Charles F. Harris. New York: Random, 1971. 21–42.

———. *On the Real Side: Laughing, Lying, and Signifying—The Underground Tradition of African–American Humor That Transformed American Culture, from Slavery to Richard Pryor*. 1994. New York: Touchstone-Simon, 1995.

Weeden, Howard [Miss]. "Beaten Biscuit." *Bandanna Ballads*. New York: Doubleday, 1899. 70.

———. "The Old Biscuit Block." *Old Voices*. New York: Doubleday, 1904. N. pag.

Weimann, Jeanne Madeline. *The Fair Women*. Chicago: Academy Chicago, 1981.

Weisbord, Robert G. *Genocide? Birth Control and the Black American*. Westport, CT: Greenwood, 1975.

Wells, Ida B. *Selected Works of Ida B. Wells-Barnett*. Comp. Trudier Harris. New York: Oxford UP, 1991.

Welsing, Frances Cress. "The Politics behind Black Male Passivity, Effeminization, Bisexuality, and Homosexuality." 1974. *The Isis (Yssis) Papers*. Chicago: Third World, 1991. 81–92.

West, Cornel. "Why I'm Marching in Washington." Editorial. *New York Times* 14 Oct. 1995, final late ed., sec. 1: 19.

West, Cynthia S'thembile. "Nation Builders: Female Activism in the Nation of Islam, 1960–1970." Diss. Temple U, 1994.

White, Deborah Gray. *Ar'n't I a Woman? Female Slaves in the Plantation South*. New York: Norton, 1985.

White, Evelyn C., ed. *The Black Women's Health Book: Speaking for Ourselves*. Seattle: Seal, 1990.

Whitehead, Tony Larry. "Sociocultural Dynamics and Food Habits in a Southern Community." *Food in the Social Order: Studies of Food and Festivities in Three American Communities*. Ed. Mary Douglas. New York: Russell Sage, 1984. 97–142.

Wideman, John Edgar. *Sent For You Yesterday*. 1983. Rpt. in *The Homewood Trilogy*. New York: Avon, 1985. 345–531.

Wiegman, Robyn. *American Anatomies: Theorizing Race and Gender*. Durham: Duke UP, 1995.

Williams, Lena. "Preparing Soul Food Can Now Be as Easy as Opening a Can." *New York Times* 26 May 1993, final late ed.: C3.

Williams, Linda. *Hard Core: Power, Pleasure, and the "Frenzy of the Visible."* Berkeley: U of California P, 1989.

Williams, Patricia J. *The Alchemy of Race and Rights: Diary of a Law Professor*. Cambridge: Harvard UP, 1991.

———. *The Rooster's Egg: On the Persistence of Prejudice*. Cambridge: Harvard UP, 1995.

Williams, Psyche A. "Interpreting History through African American Foodways." Race, Material Culture and American Studies Panel. ASA Convention. Hyatt Regency, Washington, DC. 1 Nov. 1997.

Williams, Raymond. *Marxism and Literature*. New York: Oxford UP, 1977.

Williams, Sherley Anne. "Roots of Privilege: New Black Fiction." Rev. of *Linden Hills*, by

Gloria Naylor; *Sarah Phillips*, by Andrea Lee; and *Betsey Brown*, by Ntozake Shange. *Ms*. June 1985: 69–72.

Williamson, Judith. *Decoding Advertisements: Ideology and Meaning in Advertising*. London: Marion Boyars, 1978.

Wilson, William Julius. *The Truly Disadvantaged: The Inner City, the Underclass, and Public Policy*. Chicago: U of Chicago P, 1987.

Wing, Adrien Katherine, ed. *Critical Race Feminism: A Reader*. New York: New York UP, 1997.

Witt, Doris. "In Search of Our Mothers' Cookbooks: Gathering African-American Culinary Traditions." *Iris: A Journal about Women* 26 (Fall–Winter 1991): 22–27.

Wolf, Susan M., ed. *Feminism and Bioethics: Beyond Reproduction*. New York: Oxford UP, 1996.

Wolfe, Tom. *Radical Chic and Mau-Mauing the Flak Catchers*. New York: Farrar, 1970.

Wong, Nellie. "Socialist Feminism: Our Bridge to Freedom." *Third World Women and the Politics of Feminism*. Ed. Chandra Talpade Mohanty, Ann Russo, and Lourdes Torres. Bloomington: Indiana UP, 1991. 288–96.

Wright, Keith T. *A Healthy Foods and Spiritual Nutrition Handbook*. 1989. 2nd ed. Philadelphia: Author [Health Masters], 1990.

Wright, Richard. *Later Works: Black Boy (American Hunger)/The Outsider*. Ed. Arnold Rampersad. New York: Library of America, 1991.

X, Malcolm. *The Autobiography of Malcolm X*. As told to Alex Haley. 1965. New York: Ballantine, 1973.

X-Niggaz. "Wake Up." Rec. Fonki Flex Studio, Indianapolis. *One Million Strong: The Album*. Prod. John Atterberry, Jimmy Thomas, and Jalal Farrakhan. Hollywood, CA: Mergela, 1995.

Young, Bob, and Al Stankus. *Jazz Cooks: Portraits and Recipes of the Greats*. New York: Stewart, Tabori, and Chang, 1992.

Young, Iris Marion. *Justice and the Politics of Difference*. Princeton: Princeton UP, 1990.

Young, Jackie. *Black Collectables [sic]: Mammy and Her Friends*. West Chester, PA: Schiffer, 1988.

Your Super Market. "Pork Kills!" Advertisement. *Muhammad Speaks* 5 Jan. 1973: 24.

Zafar, Rafia. "Cooking Up a Past: Two Black Culinary Narratives." *GRAAT* 14 (1996): 73–84.

———. "The Proof of the Pudding: Of Haggis, Hasty Pudding, and Transatlantic Influence." *Early American Literature* 31.2 (1996): 133–49.

Zinn, Howard. *A People's History of the United States*. 1980. Rev. ed. New York: Harper-Perennial, 1990.

Žižek, Slavoj. *The Sublime Object of Ideology*. London: Verso-New Left, 1989.

Index

abjection, 16, 67, 69, 71, 81, 85–86, 89, 108, 111, 117, 151, 197, 243n.14, 251n.19: and black maternity, 92–93, 108, 117; defined, 16, 85, 118; displaced, 87, 89, 90, 91–92

abortion, 116, 128, 182, 193–94: black attitudes toward, 116, 128, 138, 246n.19; and "post-Christian" gnosticism, 251n.18; and prolife movement, 193, 201; rights, 181; *Roe v. Wade*, 6–7, 193, 198, 199. *See also* birth control; fetal harm; genocide

Abrahams, Roger, 81, 239n.5

Abramovitz, Mimi, 247n.23

Adams, Carol, 135

addiction, 185, 194, 198, 203

African American feminist theory, 11, 16–17, 18

African American literature, 7–11, 198, 201, 212

African American men: and affection, 119; construed as "criminals," 15, 197–98, 206; as "endangered," 17; gender identity of, 92; homoerotic investments in, 86, 121; objectified, 121–22; and patriarchy, 4–5; prison writings of, 87, 92; and response to oppression, 206; as sexists, 124–25; subjectivity of, 76, 191; unity of, 119

African American middle class. *See* black bourgeoisie

African American women: abjection of, 197; as assertive, 5; and black Atlantic culture, 176; as consumers, 22, 188; cookbook authors, 11, 99–100, 184; and domesticity, 212; erasure of, 5, 24, 36, 150; health care of, 192, 196; as kitchen "dominatrixes," 14; relationship to food of, 4, 5, 6, 7–8, 53, 125, 151, 156, 185, 210, 213, 215; and reproductive autonomy, 138; self-representations of, 17; subjectivity of, 76, 80, 200; unity of, 171; U.S. attitude toward, 183; as welfare/quota/condom queens, 24, 232n.7; writers, 7–8. *See also* maternity, black; matriarchy, black

Afrocentrism, 10–11, 50, 51, 172

Agnew, Jean-Christophe, 23

Aid to Families with Dependent Children (AFDC). *See* welfare

Alexander, Elizabeth, 17, 21, 44, 52–53

Ali, Yokemi, 150

Allah, Bilal, 124–25

Allen, Barbara, 22

Angelou, Maya, 120, 244n.28

anthropology, 13, 15

apartheid (South African), 197

Apollo Theatre, 133

Appadurai, Arjun, 12–13

appetite, 196: of black women, 23, 185, 187, 188, 192, 197, 204, 210; blues music as paradigm for, 213; and criminality, 15, 206; and desire, 35; and masculinity, 189; and maternity, 206; and obesity, 146; as pathological, 15; and racial identity, 4; suppression of, 36; of white women, 186

articulation, 4, 229n.1

Asian women: as exploited laborers, 5; as "submissive," 5

Aunt Jemima, 5, 14, 187, 210: advertising campaigns, 26–27, 37, 40, 42–43, 45, 50, 55, 231n.1, 232n.10, 232n.12, 234n.32; and African Americans, 6, 40–41, 42, 43, 44, 52–53; black appropriations of, 44–48, 49–53; and blackface minstrelsy, 28–31, 33, 45; and Col. Higbee, 26, 41; as a commodity, 24, 30, 36–37, 39; and creole/Creole identity, 41–42, 46, 50–51, 235n.39; and Disneyland restaurant, 27; "family" of, 235n.43; and homoeroticism, 31–33; and immigrant labor (*see* immigrants); impersonators of, 26–27, 31, 234n.33, 235n.34; and nostalgia, 37; and Quaker Oats (*see* Quaker Oats); and R. T. Davis (Milling Company), 26, 27, 28, 33, 55; scholarship on, 25–26, 232n.10; and slave iconography, 22, 30, 36, 44; and slogans, 26,

Doris Witt is associate professor of English at the University of Iowa. She has published in the fields of food studies, African American studies, and technoculture and is a member of the advisory board for *Food, Culture, and Society*.